FIGHTING WITH
POPSKI'S PRIVATE ARMY

PARK YUNNIE
of Popski's Private Army

With new material by
Ben Owen of P.P.A.
&
Don Yunnie

Greenhill Books, London
Stackpole Books, Pennsylvania

This book is dedicated to
'Popski'
in memoriam

Greenhill Books

This edition of
Fighting With Popski's Private Army
first published 2002 by
Greenhill Books, Lionel Leventhal Limited,
Park House, 1 Russell Gardens, London NW11 9NN
www.geenhillbooks.com
and
Stackpole Books, 5067 Ritter Road,
Mechanicsburg, PA 17055, USA

British Library Cataloguing in Publication data:
Yunnie, Park
Fighting With Popski's private army. – New ed. –
(Greenhill military paperbacks)
1. Yunnie, Park   2. World War, 1939–1945 – Secret
service – Mediterranean Region   3. World War, 1939–1945 –
Personal narratives
I. Title
940.5'486'41'092

ISBN 1-85367-500-8

Library of Congress Cataloging in Publication Data:
A catalog record is available.

Publishing History:
Fighting With Popski's Private Army was first published in 1959
by Hutchinson & Co, London, as *Warriors on Wheels.*
This edition is a reproduction of the first, with the addition
of new text by Ben Owen and Don Yunnie; plus fifteen
original photographs, which appear courtesy of Ben Owen.

Typeset in Great Britain by DP Photosetting, Aylesbury, Bucks.
Printed and bound in Great Britain by CPD (Wales), Ebbw Vale

An Appreciation
of Captain Bob Yunnie of 'B' Patrol, P.P.A.

Although I am not particularly enamoured of the expression 'a one-off' in anything other than engineering terms, I must admit that it is an apt description of Bob Yunnie. I first met him when I joined P.P.A. during the War. There was talk in the Unit that he was a 'mad Scotchman' who hogged all the jobs going. I decided that these were qualities I wished to be associated with, and on my request I was allowed to join 'B' Patrol. And never regretted it.

Popski, in his speech to us on the disbandment of P.P.A., said that he considered his greatest achievement was in making such a cosmopolitan crowd as we were into a band of brothers. I would say that we were a big family—and 'B' Patrol was a smaller family within that big family. My own family at home had broken up with the death of my mother when I was twelve years old, and the death of my father not long afterwards. Now, here in 'B' Patrol, I was again to live day and night, night and day, with twelve or so men who became as close to me as anyone else has ever come in my life.

We did not have the usual army discipline in P.P.A. to keep us striving in the mountains, snows and rivers of Italy. It was our mutual respect for each other—the determination to pull just as strongly as the others in a bid to make us a team to be proud of. I was always irked by newcomers to the Unit who immediately began addressing the officers by their surnames, so we patrolmen in 'B' Patrol got together and decided that from then on we would address Bob Yunnie as 'Skipper'.

The Skipper was a brilliant navigator, but what always amazed me was the way he would consult his map just once and then lead us for hours over mountains and valleys, and through rivers, just as if he were native to the area. He was a very impatient man, and always reminded me of a budgerigar in a cage, going backward and forward. We would stop for perhaps a meal or a drink of tea—which he would drink, scalding hot, in almost one gulp—and then there he would be, hopping about, impatient to get going, while the rest of us were trying to drink, not managing to and often having to pour it away. One day I reminded him that it was a crime in the army to waste tea. He took the tip, but still imitated a budgerigar each time we paused for a break.

We must have confused the Germans no end with our dashes up and down the mountains, travelling as like as not along a 'carripath'—a goat track. Our nippy, very mobile jeeps, in the hands of experienced drivers, darted here and there, barely concealing more than four feet of the vehicle above the ground. We must have been very difficult to spot and to engage, although we experienced spandaus and mortars, and occasionally 88mm guns.

One day, after we had forded a deep, fast-flowing river—and had removed the fan-belt to prevent the water being washed over the engine—we had paused to allow the engines to cool off, when suddenly the Skipper made a sudden dart towards a deep fissure in a mountainside. It must have been worn through the ages by water rushing down. It was a V shape, and anything from twenty to thirty feet deep. We engaged four-wheel and booster drive in our jeep, and the vehicle almost stood on its rear in its bid to climb the mountain. Ali Stewart turned to me and said, 'Nobody in the wide world but this mad Scotchman Bob Yunnie would even think about driving up a place like this.'

When we arrived at the top of this mountain it was to find a vast flat tableland—miles and miles of lovely green turf such as we had never seen since leaving Britain years before. With the jeep engines cooling off again, Ali and I ran around like schoolboys pretending to pass a football. We drove further through this wonderland to find flocks of sheep, with their shepherds living in small stone huts. Some of them didn't even know—or didn't care—about the War. On other journeys we had to bolster the roadside with stones and trees, working against the mountain with the picks and shovels we were carrying, and with hundreds of feet below us waiting to devour us if we made one false step.

Looking back, I think that the world was far from big enough for Bob Yunnie. He should have been born years ago, at the time of the first explorers of the planet. Perhaps, if we conquer the Universe in the future, he will come back among us as a spaceman.

BEN OWEN
'B' Patrol, P.P.A., 2002

Author's Note

This is the true story of a small group of men who enjoyed World War II. The war was not of their seeking, few of them knew anything about war or wanted it, but when it came they volunteered as a matter of course.

One by one, led by a love of adventure, they gravitated to a special service unit called 'Popski's Private Army'. I was second-in-command of Popski's Private Army. I was the first recruit. I trained the men and knew them intimately. I fought with them and joked with them. I shared their triumphs, their failures and their fears. I saw some of them die. I loved these men and was honoured by their friendship and their faith.

This story should have been written long ago, when the war ended. It was, but in a different form, and never published; now I have found time to rewrite it, just as it happened during the years of the war.

PARK YUNNIE
Captain Bob Yunnie, M.C.

Prologue

'But, Popski,' I asked, 'how on earth did you get away with it?'

Major Vladimir Peniakoff, M.C., Russian-born, ex-sugar manu-facturer of Cairo (code-name 'Popski'), regarded me with pene-trating, green-flecked eyes—commanding eyes accustomed to searching sun-baked desert horizons; aged about forty-five or six, thick-set, deeply tanned, bald, dynamic, minus a finger taken by a German machine-gun bullet in the recent Barce raid, Popski was a man to be reckoned with: an individualist, a forceful personality to whom people gave way, a man who, having once decided upon a course of action, never deviated. Cultured, well-read, a man of the world and the master of five languages, Popski had volunteered the minute war broke out and had been commissioned to the General List in Cairo; unorthodox, adventurous, with a genuine flair for intelligence work, fluent in Arabic and familiar with the Libyan Desert, he had quickly established a reputation and was going from strength to strength. He had come from G.H.Q. Middle East where the proposal to form a sabotage unit of his own had just been sanctioned; he was telling me about it.

'It was Shan Hackett's idea,' he smiled reminiscently. 'When the brigadier asked what I wanted to call the unit I hesitated and he suggested "Popski's Private Army". I said I'd take it. Shan promised to fix it with the War Office.'

'Popski's Private Army . . . Popski's Private Army.' I repeated the words slowly, lovingly, turning them round my tongue, savouring their richness as one savours the bouquet of a good wine. What a perfect name for a sabotage unit to work behind the enemy lines! I regarded Popski with admiration.

'You'd get away with murder, Popski,' I laughed. 'When do we move?'

Popski's desert-tanned face grew serious.

'As soon as possible, Bob. Looks like Monty's going to break

9

through at Alamein and it'll be another race for Benghazi. We want to be in on it. I'll give you a fortnight to get ready.'

Fourteen days wasn't a very long time in which to raise and equip a new unit.

'A fortnight!' I exclaimed. 'Hell, Popski, that's a tall order.'

Popski turned on his devastating charm.

'You can do it, Bob,' he flattered, 'here's your G1098. Get cracking,' and he handed me my authority to draw vehicles, guns and equipment.

I glanced through the military document placed in my hands. M.E./W.E./866/1 officially designated us No. 1 Demolition Squadron, Middle East. How prosaic! Popski's Private Army was a far better name.

'What do we wear, Popski?'

'Ordinary desert dress with black Tank Corps berets and P.P.A. shoulder flashes. Our unit badge is the astrolabe. I'm having cap badges and shoulder flashes made.'

'What about men?'

'I'll do the recruiting. You get cracking on the stores and equipment.'

'Is Jan coming?'

Jan Caneri, a Free French officer, was a friend from earlier days of the war, when he, Popski and I were company commanders in the Libyan Arab Force. A friendship had sprung up between the three of us which we had maintained after leaving the force.

'He's on ops at the moment. He'll join us later.'

'Good.'

It was nearly six o'clock on a sultry October afternoon in 1942. We were sitting in Popski's Cairo flat in sharia Malika Farida. The rumble of traffic in the streets below, the sing-song intonations of the news vendors and flower-sellers drifted through the open balcony windows, mingling with the heavy scent of jasmine. I rose and stood on the balcony, looking down upon the crowded scene, the press of military vehicles and horse-drawn gharries, the saluting, jostling, jabbering khaki-clad figures making for the clubs and bars, the white-gowned, tarbushed Egyptians being roughly elbowed out of the way. I was happy. Cut off west of Benghazi in the last retreat, I had walked 400 miles across the desert to Tobruk, gone to hospital for a while, and then for the past three months had been kicking my heels at base depot waiting to join

Popski. Now the days of boredom were over; I had a worthwhile job at last.

And excitement was in the air; retreat was a thing of the past, the big push was coming. A new star of unexpected brilliance shone in the Middle East military firmament; Lieutenant-General Bernard A. Montgomery had infused new life into a weary Eighth Army; and tanks, guns, reinforcements and supplies of all kinds were pouring into the delta. A new cycle of events was taking shape.

An apt slogan suddenly came to mind, as if wafted to me from the lively Cairo scene; I smiled and re-entered the room. Popski was relaxed on a couch, smoking a cigarette, thinking, planning.

'You'll need a recruiting slogan, Popski. What about "Join Popski's Private Army and Enjoy the War"?'

Popski looked up at me and laughed.

'I'll take it,' he said.

I

A LINE of military vehicles wound its way across the Libyan Desert, bound for the Oasis of Kufra. Popski sat at the wheel of the leading jeep, his eyes on the moving shadow of the sun-compass clamped to the instrument panel in front. In the seat beside him Bell, his gunner-driver, sat with pencil and note-pad, logging their route. Ahead of them, dancing in the heat-haze, fantastic shapes of sand and rock marked the ragged escarpment of the Gilf Kebir.

Popski glanced at the speedometer and shook his head.

'Give me the map-board, Bell.'

Bell lifted the map-board from his knees and apprehensively handed it to Popski. Navigation wasn't Bell's strong point; he felt ill at ease.

Popski looked at the grubby log on the map-board and from the grubby log to Bell.

'Do you know what you're doing, Bell?'

Driver Bell went red in the face.

'N-not really, sir,' he stammered.

'Then why the hell didn't you tell me?' Popski exploded. 'You're here to learn. If you don't understand a thing, ask.'

Bell looked sheepish.

'Yes, sir,' he said meekly.

Popski held up a sunburned hand and the line of vehicles halted. He wheeled his jeep and drove to the end of the column, braking level with the last jeep. I looked at him expectantly.

'Yes, Popski?'

'We're wrong somewhere, Bob. According to the speedometer reading we should be in the gap by now. There's no sign of it. Either the bearing's wrong or I've made a mistake somewhere. Stay here till I make a reconnaissance.'

13

'O.K., Popski.'

Popski revved away in a rising cloud of dust. I called to Sergeant Waterson in the next jeep.

'Brew up, Sarge. We're waiting.'

Sergeant Waterson cocked a blue eye in the direction of the nearest 3-tonner and swung from his jeep.

'*Shay, Mohammed*,' he bawled to the Senussi guide perched on top of the load.

Mohammed Mustapha grinned, showing perfect white teeth.

'*Aywah*,' he answered, and slid off the truck.

Driver Davies jumped down and from the back of the 3-tonner lifted a perforated petrol tin which he scooped half full with sand, poured petrol over it and threw in a lighted match. The contents took fire with a swoosh and Davies shielded his face from the flame.

Driver Weldon jumped from the driving-seat of the other 3-tonner, poured water into a blackened tea-can and stuck it on top of the fire; Sergeant Waterson reached over the tailboard and drew out a tin of condensed milk. 'Catch!' he shouted to the group by the fire and tossed it through the air. Weldon cupped his hands and caught it neatly, like a cricketer catching a ball.

When the water boiled, Sergeant Waterson threw in a handful of tea, stirred the contents with a stick, lifted the can off the fire and tapped it with the stick to make the tea-leaves sink to the bottom; the tinny sound echoed strangely in the still desert air. Driver Weldon jabbed two holes in the top of the condensed milk-tin with the spike of his jack-knife and poured a thick spout of milk into the tea.

'Come and get it,' Waterson yelled.

We all grabbed our enamel mugs and gathered round the tea-can.

'What's the form, sir?' Waterson asked.

'Bearing's wrong. We're too far north,' I replied between gulps of tea. 'Popski's gone to look for tracks.'

We stood in a group in the blistering sun, drinking tea. The desert was all about us, a silent, heat-filled waste of sand shimmering under a cloudless sky. Nothing moved but the dancing mirage; apart from ourselves there wasn't a living thing for hundreds of empty miles. We were five days out from Cairo, halted on a wrong bearing, 400 miles from Kufra; lost.

14

In the absence of its commander, I surveyed Popski's Private Army. It wasn't much to look at—three small jeeps and two big 3-tonners, one officer (myself), a dozen men, three Senussi Arabs; a hastily recruited, raw, untrained and untried unit. Popski only had any real desert experience. The rest of us were just tyros; keenness, willingness to learn, our only assets.

I looked at the low-slung, racy jeeps with their welded array of water- and petrol-can brackets, their twin-mounted Vickers machine-guns, the grooved yellow sand-channels clamped to the sides. I looked at the overloaded 3-ton Chevrolet trucks with their sawn-off driving-cabins and the single machine-gun mounted in front. I looked at the men, at Sergeant Waterson from the King's Dragoon Guards with his piercing blue eye staring from under the brim of the peaked New Zealander's hat shading his face from the sun; at Corporal Locke with the piratical black patch over one eye; at Driver Davies with the baggy shorts a size too big for his waist; at Driver Weldon with the scrubby beginnings of a beard on his chin; at little Jock Welsh, the fitter from R.E.M.E.; at Petrie, our navigator, a thoughtful young man who lived with the stars; at Bill Wilson, my driver, desperately keen to make good; at Mohammed Mustapha, at Abdel Salem Othman, at Yunes Yusef Abdallah, our three Senussi guides crouched over a fire some distance apart, brewing their sweet Arab tea. A motley crew.

'Why did you join?' I asked Driver Davies, who was helping himself to more tea.

'Browned-off with base, sir. I wanted something to do.'

'And you, Jock?' I asked Fitter Welsh.

'Same mucking reason, sir. Browned-off with base.'

A black speck appeared on the horizon. It grew bigger and bigger. . . .

'Popski,' somebody said.

I shaded my eyes from the glare and watched Popski's jeep come sailing through the mirage; his wheels appeared to revolve without touching the sand.

When he drew up beside me I handed him a mug of hot tea.

He pushed the motoring goggles away from his eyes.

'I've found the track. We're miles out.'

'I knew the bearing was wrong. That signal was corrupt.'

Popski gulped a mouthful of tea.

15

'It's that clot Waddington's fault. He promised me the wire-less in Cairo. It's waiting for us in Kufra. We shouldn't have left without one.'

'Too late to worry about it now,' I said philosophically.

Popski gulped the last of his tea and handed me the mug.

'Thanks, Bob. That was good. Follow me.'

Popski drove to the head of the column. Sergeant Waterson bawled:

'All aboard!'

Driver Davies poured the tea-leaves into a russet heap on the sand and hung the empty tea-can on its hook under the tail-board of his 3-tonner; Driver Weldon emptied the perforated fire-can and pitched it in the back; the three Senussi ran to the trucks, clutching their tea-pot and glasses, trailing their *jerds* in the sand.

Self-starters rasped, engines revved, and the column moved on. . . .

Following the sand-blown wheel-tracks of a Long Range Desert Group patrol we twisted and turned through the maze of basalt teeth which filled the gap between the towering black cliffs of the silent Gilf Kebir. Hades itself could be no more terrifying than this dead valley of petrified rock, bleached camel bones, sifting sand, heat, mirage and diabolical stillness; the note of our exhausts death-rattled against the lifeless mushroom rocks and our voices, echoing hollowly in the riven gullies, cackled like the souls of the damned. 'Fly, fly from this forgotten vale,' they seemed to cry, 'the living have no place here, this is a haunt of the dead.'

The sand was soft. Popski, an experienced desert driver, changed into lowest booster gear and chugged jerkily through it. Petrie, behind him, stuck and had to use sand-channels. Weldon, following close behind in his overloaded 3-tonner, felt his rear wheels sink in. He changed down, accelerated madly and sank his truck to the tailboard. He got down and stood looking at the buried wheels, scratching his head.

'How the mucking hell did I do that?'

Davies, churning along behind him, bogged down also, but not quite so deeply; seeing Weldon dig in, he learned from his mistake, and stopped in time. Waterson and I drove alongside in

16

our lighter jeeps; we felt our rear wheels sink in as soon as we applied the brakes.

Waterson regarded Weldon's bellied 3-tonner with a jaundiced eye.

'We'll have to unload that bastard,' he groaned.

Popski, chugging on ahead like a motor-boat in a choppy sea, looked back to see how we fared, saw the mess we were in, wheeled about and came back. He gear-braked his jeep to a stop on a patch of hard sand without sinking the wheels. I marvelled and walked across to him, feeling the burning heat of the sand through my desert boots.

'We'll have to unload Weldon's 3-tonner, Popski.'

He nodded and lit a cigarette; the operation would take time.

We jumped from our vehicles and set about unloading Weldon's truck. The temperature was 100°F. and there wasn't any shade.

Off came the heavy petrol- and water-cans, the boxes of hand-grenades, the road mines, the rolls of plastic 808 high explosive, the pans of Vickers ammunition, the boxes of compo rations. . . .

Weldon and Davies took spades and dug the sand from the buried wheels.

'Deeper,' said Waterson, 'deeper yet . . . now put in your sand-channels.'

They put the perforated, grooved steel channels under the rear wheels.

'Right, Weldon,' said Waterson, 'lowest gear and let in your clutch gently.'

Weldon climbed to the driver's seat, started his engine, grated into first gear and let in the clutch. . . .

The rear wheels spun, throwing out sand, gripped on the channels and the truck moved forward a few inches. We all rushed behind and shoved.

'Keep going, keep going,' we yelled.

The 3-tonner jerked forward a few feet, rode over the sand-channels and sank in again.

'Stop!' we yelled frantically. 'Stop!'

Weldon declutched. We picked up the sand-channels, ran forward and pushed them under the wheels.

'Take 'er away.'

Weldon revved and his truck moved forward again, rode over the channels and kept moving.

'Keep going,' we encouraged him, 'keep going, keep going,' and picked up the sand-channels and ran alongside, throwing them under the moving wheels. . . .

Popski watched our antics from the comfort of his crawling jeep; he'd done the same thing himself, hundreds of times; now it was our turn to learn.

Three hundred yards further on Weldon drove on to a patch of hard sand and drew up his truck; we muttered 'Thank God', wiped our dripping brows and walked back to ferry the load. . . .

'What a bloody life,' groaned Fitter Welsh, staggering through the churned-up sand with a box of grenades on his shoulder.

'Shouldn'ta joined, chum,' jeered Davies, easing the compo box on his back.

'Get your knees browned,' laughed Corporal Locke, coming back for another load.

'Stop ticking, Welsh,' admonished Sergeant Waterson, striding past with his arms full of high explosive.

'Watch ye dinna blaw up, Sarge,' tittered Bill Wilson.

'I'll blaw you up, Wilson. Get a jerk on.'

When Weldon's load was ferried and re-stowed on his 3-tonner we went back and helped Davies through the soft patch; then we formed up and drove on again. . . .

The fantastically shaped basalt pillars shrunk in size, the sand became harder and we left the silent, eerie Gilf behind; the soaring black cliffs became a dark line against the sky and gradually disappeared. The empty desert stretched in front of us, a vast solitude of undulating, yellow-ochre sand in which nothing moved but the dancing, shimmering heat-waves. Sand, sand, sand; not a bush, nor a blade of grass, no living thing; no water; not even a rock nor a stone, no landmark of any kind; nothing but sand, hot, burning sand, with the *khamseen*, the searing desert wind, blowing in our faces, cracking our lips, drying our throats, filling eyes and ears and nostrils with a fine, sandy dust. . . .

Day after day we rode over the blistering surface of the great inner desert, navigating its uncharted wastes like a convoy of ships at sea, steering our course by the shadow of the sun on a needle, checking our position at night by the stars. Popski led, followed by Petrie, logging his route; then Weldon's lumbering 3-tonner, followed by Davies in his; Waterson followed Davies in his jeep, with Yunes beside him; Bill Wilson and I brought up the rear.

One day was very like another. It began at crack of dawn with Waterson's parade-ground voice bellowing 'Wakey, wakeeey' as he went from truck to truck rousing the sleeping crews. . . . We cursed him inaudibly, wriggled out of our warm sleeping-bags, pulled on sweaters against the morning chill—for the desert is cold at night—and physical-jerked the sleep from our eyes. . . . The cooks for the day made breakfast—burgoo-porridge, two rashers of bacon, biscuits and jam, two or three cups of sweet tea. . . . Self-starters rasping . . . engines revving and left running to warm up, with the exhaust note burbling clearly in the crisp desert air. . . . Then Popski would beckon and we would take up our map-boards and gather round him for details of the day's route . . . stow sleeping-bags . . . and wait for the sun to cast a shadow on the sun-compass. . . .

We drove until noon and halted for a rest. We had to, because for an hour the sun was directly overhead and cast no shadow, so that we couldn't navigate. . . . We gathered round the tailboard of Davies' 3-tonner and Waterson rationed out the midday meal—biscuits and cheese, pickles, tinned fruit, lime-juice powder and water. When it was consumed we thrust our heads under the trucks for the only shade there was and dozed a while, feeling the sun burning our trunks and legs. . . . At one o'clock we drove on again, guided by the shadow cast by the westering sun . . . and pulled into leaguer an hour before dusk . . . vehicle maintenance first—fill up with petrol from Weldon's 3-tonner, lightening his over-load; check water and oil levels, tyre pressures, chassis nuts and bolts; clean guns . . . then rum issue—a mouthful of water, rum and lime-juice powder which miraculously removed bodily fatigue . . . followed by the evening meal—bully-beef stew . . . and the enchanting hour of dusk when the rapidly falling sun, dropping over the desert's rim in a last flurry of blazing gold, filled the dunes with mystic light and transformed the glaring waste into a haunting fairyland of marching rainbow hues, phalanxes of burnished gold, brave companies of purple and mauve, charging squadrons of violet . . . and the wind, the desert sculptor, blowing spume

19

from the crests of the dunes in fluttering pennants of indigo . . . twinkling stars strewn richly in the velvet cupola of night.

Petrie's work began when ours finished; as soon as the stars shone forth he set up his theodolite and became engrossed. We lay close to the vehicle wheels snug in our sleeping-bags, talking in undertones, cracking jokes or lying quietly, thinking, and looking up at the distant stars, seeing the earth revolve. One by one we'd feel drowsy and drop off to sleep while Petrie continued to flip the pages of his astronomical charts in the light of a shaded torch, muttering to himself, calculating and re-calculating the divisions of his astro-fix; behind him, some distance apart, our faithful Senussi crouched round their flickering fire, keeping watch. . . .

It came upon us one morning, a raging furnace of howling, swirling, screaming sand which darkened the midday sky and blotted out the sun. The desert rose from its bed like a storm at sea and lashed us unmercifully with mountainous waves of sting-ing, biting grit which scratched the glass of our goggles, cut the skin of our cheeks and scraped the paint from our vehicles.

'Sand-storm coming!' Popski yelled. 'Turn round—backs to the wind!'

The column swung round and halted, tailboards to the storm, like cattle in a field, backs to the rain; we sat hunched in our seats, shielding our ears, waiting for the smother to envelop us. . . .

It hit us like a whip-lash, taking our breath, leaving us cowed and defenceless, whimpering with pain. We couldn't breathe. Hot, smarting dust clogged our nostrils, seared the backs of our throats, coated our tongue and gritted in our teeth; drifts of fine-blown sand formed in the folds of our clothing, blew into our pockets and found its way through to our skins; sand piled up in the trucks, forming miniature dunes, stuck to the oily and greasy parts of the chassis, blew under the bonnet and sifted into the carburettor, the magneto, the unsealed working parts; grating sand filtered into the Vickers guns, jamming the ammunition pans; sand found its way into everything, everywhere. Each truck was isolated in its own drift, cut off from the others by an impene-trable wall of frenzied, shrieking grit; we couldn't see, we daren't open our mouths to speak; we could only crouch half-suffocated, cut, whipped and savaged by the pitiless, rasping sand. . . .

Hours passed and the storm howled unabated. It seemed that

all the sands of Libya and of the vaster Sahara beyond were in open revolt; the sun had gone from the world, never to return; something had happened in outer space. God had gone berserk, worlds were in collision, a tidal wave of sand was sweeping the universe and carrying all before it; it was the end of the world, we would never see the sun again, we would all be buried alive; or so it seemed to us huddled blindly in our sand-swept trucks, hidden in a cloud of angry dust, a hundred miles from Kufra. . . .

The maelstrom swept over and raced towards Cairo, leaving us weak, battered and breathless, half-buried in sand. For a time a blood-red hunter's moon hung overhead like a curse and became a blazing sun when the final turmoil subsided and we saw blue sky again.

A great peace lay over the cleansed and chastened desert, but its face had changed; old dunes had been levelled, new ones formed, and our wheel-tracks were wholly obliterated, wiped out like chalk from a slate. The desert had been born anew.

'Christ,' said Sergeant Waterson, rising from his drift and shaking the sand from his clothes, 'have you seen this?'

'This' was the side of the truck, polished like a mirror, every vestige of paint sanded off.

I stood back from the column and surveyed the aftermath. Sand-drifts hid the wheels, up to the polished mudguards; a sculptured sand-dune curved from every tailboard. Closing my eyes I visualized snow instead of sand; that's what it was like, a Christmas party of motorists caught and marooned in a snow-storm. Least affected were our three Senussi; high up on the back of the 3-tonners they had wrapped themselves in their blanket *jerds* and weathered the storm like cocoons.

Bill Wilson pressed the self-starter. I put my hands to my ears. Rasp . . . rasp . . . rasp. The sound resembled a rusty file scraping rusty metal. . . . Rasp . . . rasp . . . rasp. Every truck was the same, like old crocks found in a car cemetery. . . .

'Clean guns,' Waterson shouted.

'Brew up,' somebody cried.

'Have to clean out the mucking carburettor,' Davies cursed when his grinding engine died on him for the third time. . . .

'Now you can see why navigation is so important,' Popski explained to Bell. 'Where would you be if you'd been following tracks without logging your route?'

'I'd be lost, sir,' said Bell, brightly.

'Exactly, Bell. That's where dead-reckoning comes in.'

Popski reached for his map-board, shook it and blew off the sand. Bell panicked, knowing what was coming.

'Where are we, Bell?'

Bell stared at the buff-coloured paper, like a child at castor-oil, and felt his neck getting hot.

'There,' he said desperately, prodding the map with a grimy forefinger.

His finger landed very close to the right place; it was a lucky guess. Popski was surprised and looked at him.

'How did you know, Bell?'

Realizing he'd guessed correctly, Bell smiled superiorly.

'Dead-reckoning, sir.'

'Tell me, Bell——' Popski started to say.

'*Come and get it!*'

Waterson's clarion call saved him.

We stood by our halted vehicles and stared at a horizon of rootless palm-trees dancing in blue water above a long line of yellow sand-dunes.

'Mirage,' I muttered.

'Kufra,' said Popski.

'Ouch!' cried Waterson, withdrawing his hand from a jeep bonnet upon which eggs would have rapidly fried. 'Mucking hot, that. . . .'

'Kufra,' said Popski again, 'there's no mistaking those yellow dunes.'

Hours later we straggled into the Oasis of Kufra, religious shrine of the Senussi sect, operational headquarters of the Long Range Desert Group, past the shelled Italian fort on the hill, past a huddle of dilapidated mud huts clustered round a battered mosque, past clumps of motionless palm-trees, past lagoons of blue water, more palm-trees with trucks under them draped in camouflage nets and buff, bearded soldiers sitting about. . . .

We parked in the shade of the palms beside a pool of clear water, and Popski walked through the oasis to report to O.C. L.R.D.G. I sat by the pool of clear water, touching it to make sure it wasn't mirage. Water, I thought, what glorious, heavenly stuff, and touched again, just to make sure. . . . I was still there, lost in a watery contemplation, when Popski returned, looking a trifle upset.

'What's the matter, Popski?' I asked tactlessly.

He scowled at me.

'We hold the record from Cairo. Eleven days. We should have done it in five.'

2

KUFRA! The mythical oasis hidden away in the heart of the Libyan Desert, the isolated, jealously guarded shrine of the fanatical Senussi, the oasis in which no white man had set foot until after the First World War. Kufra, the outlandish, the unattainable, brought within a few hours' journey of Cairo by the modern aeroplane.

I wandered round the oasis with Mohammed Mustapha, soothed by the song of the rustling date-palms. We visited the Italian fort on the hill, captured by the Long Range Desert Group; we walked through the fly-ridden alleys of the mud village near the ruined mosque which Mohammed, but not I, an infidel, was permitted to enter; we sat in the shade of the date-palms by the blue lagoon. It was here, Mohammed told me, in a vibrant voice, that the Senussi fought their last battle with the colonizing Italians; it was from here, he told me bitterly, that 'Butcher' Graziani took the hostage sheiks to Benghazi under guise of friendship and hung them, living, in the public square, suspended by the chin from iron hooks. 'The Italians came and seized our land and murdered our sheiks,' he hissed with flashing eyes. 'We hate them.'

In 1942 Kufra was the desert nerve centre, the controlling brain from which the Long Range Desert Group patrols drove forth to harry the German and Italian divisions strung out along the Mediterranean coast. Six hundred miles, more or less, separated Kufra from the coast, 600 miles of empty sand and sand-dunes upon which no rain ever fell. The outer desert was no man's land—the strip along the coast; it changed hands frequently with the ebb and flow of retreat and advance; but the inner desert was sacrosanct, the acknowledged preserve of the

Long Range Desert Group, and no enemy patrols dared venture into its guarded fastness.

But events on the coast were moving fast. Eighth Army had reached Benghazi and was driving on to Tripoli; Kufra would soon be obsolete for the first time since the desert war began, for no British general had previously driven the enemy round the Gulf of Syrte.

'We're moving to Zella, Bob,' Popski informed me, 'Kufra's too far south. The whole of L.R.D.G.'s moving up.'

This was cheering news for, having been at such pains to get into the desert war, I was beginning to fear it would be over before we'd had an opportunity to do anything. But I needn't have worried; there were adventures aplenty in store for me.

I drew the promised wireless set—an ill-fated one as later events will reveal—replenished the 3-tonners with petrol, water and rations and we set course for the Oasis of Zella in the Fezzan— 500 miles north-west as the crow flies.

The journey was sheer delight. Rough edges rubbed off by the buffeting we had received on the 700-mile drive from Cairo, the unit had settled down and come to its second wind. Friendships had been formed and capabilities assessed; we worked as a team. We no longer bogged our vehicles every few hundred yards, but skilfully avoided the soft patches, recognizing them from afar. Desert driving became a pleasure instead of a pain and, happy in a new-found confidence, we raced one another across flat stretches of hard sand at sixty miles an hour, plunged through crested sand-dunes like ships through foaming waves, and gear-braked our vehicles to a stop without sinking-in the wheels.

'Jings, sirr, isna this grrand!' enthused Bill Wilson, happy as a child, as we zoomed over a gamboge stretch of sand, wind-swept smooth as a billiard-table, with the speedometer needle flickering about the sixty mark. 'Better than Brooklands, sirr.'

'Better than base depot, eh, Bill?' I shouted at him into the wind.

'Gosh, sirr,' his voice whipped back, 'I dinna wint tae ging back therre.'

We were in the war, but out of it, enjoying the fun of the chase, thrilling to the joy of high blue skies, pure, sunlit air, speed, and the freedom of the unfenced, open desert; and at nights, with our wireless set, we were no longer isolated from the rest of the world, but could tune-in to the latest news of Eighth Army's triumphant advance, and lie in our cosy sleeping-bags under the stars, listening to dance music from Cairo or London, feeling we belonged!

Our compass-course took us through the Oasis of Tazerbo, a smelly cluster of mud huts in a grove of wind-bitten date-palms with a few scrawny hens scratching about and glaucoma-eyed bedouin staring at us suspiciously, a miserable sand-swept water-hole guarded by the dunes of the Kalansho Sand Sea, a place of loneliness and soughing wind, of heat and flies and listlessness surrounded by silence, a place forgotten by God.

Beyond Tazerbo's flanking dunes the face of the desert changed. We came to wadis and scrub, gnarled acacia bushes, gravel and outcrops of rock; gazelle rose at our approach, bounded in front of our wheels, leaping and bucking, and swerved out of our path. Rifles were raised and levelled, but no shots fired; something in the grace and beauty of those lovely wild creatures darting terrified side-glances out of soft, brown eyes stayed our hands. . . .

Over a rocky plateau of sharp, flinty stones which tore at our burning tyres—down a steep wadi with the chassis rattling and banging on the rough, uneven surface . . . across a corrugated agony of ribbed, hard-blown sand, yellow and glaring in the fierce sunlight . . . twisting and turning through a never-ending morass of high, crested dunes with the *khamseen* blowing spume from their tops in feathery tails and scorching our aching throats, we came to the Oasis of Zella—and blew up a truck on a mine.

An Italian garrison had recently evacuated the oasis, leaving mines in its sandy approaches. We expected mines and were on the look-out for them and the annoying thing about this one was that it didn't explode when the leading jeep rode over it. Popski drove over it first, then Petrie; neither of them set it off. Weldon came third in his lumbering 3-tonner, naturally thought the way was clear and followed. His much heavier front wheel exploded the deeply buried mine. There was a sudden flash, a loud explosion and Weldon felt himself being tossed about like a cork on an angry wave as the front of his truck violently plunged and reared.

Popski and Petrie looked round when they heard the explosion behind them . . . and looked at each other; the rest of us stopped behind Weldon's halted 3-tonner. Jock Welsh, the fitter, jumped from Davies' truck and ran to Weldon's to inspect the damage; one wheel was buckled, the front axle twisted and rusty water dripped ominously from the radiator.

'That shook you, Weldon,' Welsh laughed heartlessly.

'That shook 'im,' chorused Davies and Robinson.

But Weldon just sat with his fingers to his ears, shaking his head and opening and closing his mouth, too literally shaken to appreciate the joke; nor was he ever the same again.

'They've discovered a dump of Italian mines, Bob,' Popski informed me the following day when we were comfortably leaguered in the oasis, 'L.R.D.G. want you to blow it up. See that you make a good job of it.'

'You leave it to me, Popski.'

I went in search of Waterson.

'Get some eight-o-eight, Sarge. We've got to blow a mine dump.'

The mines were in a cavern in the sand-dunes on the outskirts of the oasis. I stooped at the mouth and peered inside. When my eyes grew accustomed to the inner gloom, I distinguished tier upon tier of long, blue-black Italian road-mines. 'This should go up with a nice bang, Sarge,' I smiled. 'How much eight-o-eight do you think?'

Sergeant Waterson bent and surveyed the dump with his piercing blue eye.

'A pound, sir?' he suggested.

'Let's make it two,' I said, 'just to be sure. Popski wants us to make a good job of it.' (A quarter of a pound would have been ample!)

Plastic 808 high explosive comes in quarter-pound rolls, wrapped in greaseproof paper. Dark brown in colour, pliable, it could easily be mistaken for toffee. We tied eight rolls together, stuck in a couple of detonators and connected up a long fuse. I laid the lethal charge inside the mouth of the cave, against the first tier of mines.

'Ready?'

I touched off the fuse and we walked quickly away. . . .

The dunes suddenly erupted in a great mushroom of billowing sand and smoke, just like the pictures of the first atom bomb on Bikini, and a thunderous explosion reverberated through the oasis

—breaking every window in the L.R.D.G. quartermaster stores (the one-time Italian barracks) a quarter of a mile away!

Popski dropped a bombshell in my lap early the following morning.

'L.R.D.G. are sending patrols into the Jebel Nefusa,' he told me. 'I'm sending Corporal Locke and two jeeps with Hunter's patrol. Waterson and I in the other two jeeps will go with Lazarus. You'll stay here and have the 3-tonner repaired.'

I jibbed. I remonstrated. I cajoled. I pleaded. I begged. Finally, I cursed and I swore.

Popski was adamant.

'The second-in-command's job,' he informed me disarmingly, 'is to be second-in-command. We can't both go, Bob. One of us must stay behind. Who will command P.P.A. if we both get bumped off?'

I glowered at him rebelliously.

'It's only a reconnaissance, Bob,' he soothed. 'You'll be in on it when we start raiding. In the meantime get the 3-tonner fixed up and everything ready to move.'

Reluctantly, I gave up my jeep and watched Popski, Waterson, Locke and Petrie get ready to move out. Heart-broken, I watched the spare-wheel bracket of the last jeep disappear amongst the sand-dunes; and turned and called for Fitter Welsh.

'Come on, Jock,' I said miserably, 'let's get this mucking 3-tonner fixed up.'

3

Popski and the others had been gone five days. The damaged 3-tonner was repaired and, with its twin, loaded and ready to move at a moment's notice. I was sitting disconsolately in the shade of a date-palm doodling in the sand with a sliver of stick when I heard a shout.

I looked up . . . and my depression lifted.

Jan Caneri was striding towards me, swinging a bulging army haversack, a broad grin on his bespectacled, desert-tanned face.

I jumped up and ran to meet him. I hadn't seen him for months.

'Jan!' I exclaimed delightedly, slapping him on the back. 'Where did you spring from?'

'I was in El Agheila, Bob,' he explained in his slightly French-accented English. 'I saw an L.R.D.G. convoy come in. One of the drivers told me Popski was in Zella so I cadged a lift and 'ere I am. Where's Popski?'

I told him, and we sat down under the palm-tree.

When World War II broke out, Monsieur Jean Caneri, a French citizen with a law degree from the Sorbonne, was serving his term of conscription as a sergeant in the French Army in Syria. When France fell he deserted from the Vichy regime, made his way to Cairo and joined the Allied forces in the Middle East. Like Popski, he was commissioned in the General List and posted to the Libyan Arab Force, where we met. Itching to do something to restore the fair name of France and finding scope somewhat limited in the Libyan Arab Force (detailed for guard duties on the L. of C.), he transferred to Special Operations and for the past few months had been trying to sink ships in Benghazi harbour. Humorous, a trifle cynical, hard-working, able to cut through to the heart of a problem with his logical French brain,

Jan gradually assumed control of the administrative side of P.P.A. and, as we grew, ran the unit with meticulous efficiency. He was twenty-seven years old, unmarried, five foot nine, of athletic build and physically fit, with steady, unwavering eyes which weighed you up while you talked; he wasn't a man you could fool easily.

'How did you get on, Jan?' I asked, eager to hear what he'd done.

He laughed, threw back his head, opened his hands French fashion and ejaculated, 'Pough.

'Look, Bob,' he explained deprecatingly, 'we'd to come in from the Jebel at night, get into the harbour, crawl past the sentries, swim out to the ships under water, attach the limpets under the water-line, set the time-fuses, swim back, crawl past the sentries again, walk through the town and get back into the Jebel before daylight.'

'Did you sink any ships?'

'Pough. Of course not. The harbour was too well-guarded.'

Jan wiped his hands French fashion, dismissing the subject.

'Tell me about P.P.A.'

I told him about our antics since leaving Cairo.

'We hold the record, Jan. Eleven days to Kufra.'

'Eleven days! Popski must 'ave been furious.'

'He was.'

Pause.

'What's Popski planning to do, Bob?'

'Raids behind the Mareth Line.'

'Pough.'

I nodded in the direction of the 3-tonners.

'We've got enough eight-o-eight to blow up the whole of Tunisia.'

'Pough.'

We were silent for a time, lost in contemplation of the infinite destructive power wrapped up in quarter-pound, grease-papered rolls in the 3-tonners.

'We struck a mine coming into the oasis. . . .'

I told him about Weldon's truck and about blowing up the mine dump and breaking the windows in the quartermaster stores.

'You wouldn't be very popular, Bob,' he laughed when I'd finished.

'I wasn't.'

30

The shadows crept out from the date-palms and the strange hush of sunset settled over the oasis, rendering everything mysterious in the marching change of colours.

'I've got a bottle of wiski,' Jan inconsequently announced.

'What are we waiting for?' I asked.

Jan fumbled with the straps of his haversack and produced a bottle of Johnnie Walker. He unscrewed the metal cap and held the bottle under my nose.

'Cheers,' I said, taking a swig.

'*Santé*,' said Jan, taking a mouthful.

It was sun-downer time and we weren't on duty.

'All the best,' I said, taking another swig.

'*À Popski*,' Jan toasted, putting the bottle to his lips.

We were getting into our stride.

'*À la Huitième Armée*,' Jan proposed, taking another pull.

'To the Eighth Army,' I replied, following his example.

Now we were off.

'*À Monty*,' swig.

'To Monty,' swig.

'*À la victoire*,' swig.

'To victory,' swig.

'*À le Pey Pey Ah*,' swig.

'To P.P.A.,' swig.

'*À le L.R.D.G.*,' swig.

'To the L.R.D.G.,' swig.

We regarded the inch of whisky left in the bottle.

'Not worth keeping,' I suggested.

Jan nodded and passed the bottle to me.

'To Jan Caneri,' swig.

'*À Bob Yunnie*,' swig.

We shared the last mouthful, stuck the empty bottle in the sand and walked unsteadily through the oasis towards the L.R.D.G. Mess for dinner.

Eighth Army was still gathering momentum on the coast, carrying all before it. Zella, in turn, became obsolete and L.R.D.G. headquarters moved up to Hon, the next oasis, 100 miles further west; the tail of P.P.A. went also, tagged on like a spare part to an L.R.D.G. patrol.

We drove through an alien land. Gone were the billiard-table smooth stretches of virgin sand over which we could zoom at speed; gone were the glorious crested dunes through which we could plunge like ships at sea. We drove through a land of rough, black rock, of scorching, flinty plateaux, of sultry, airless ravines, an evil, abandoned, inhospitable country of sharp, knife-edged boulders which ripped and punctured our tyres. We had blow-outs all the way and it took us nearly as long to jolt the 100 miles from Zella to Hon as to skim the 500 between Kufra and Zella.

We had news of Popski at Hon, and met him later at Shweref. He'd been in trouble. Patrolling up the wadi Zemzem towards the coast they'd been stalked from the rear by German armoured cars ('Oh, Popski!'). In the running fight which developed the patrol was scattered, one man, Binney, was captured and they lost a P.P.A. jeep and an L.R.D.G. 30-cwt. Chevrolet truck. Popski wasn't a bit depressed. The men had had valuable battle experience and Waterson, justifying Popski's faith in him, had proved himself a tower of strength in a tight corner. The loss of the jeep was annoying—jeeps were precious things in those days—but the loss of valuable equipment never worried Popski. 'War is wasteful,' he used to say. 'You can replace jeeps and equipment, Bob. You can't replace experienced men.'

Further north, Locke, also, had proved himself when his jeep fell over an escarpment and he rescued it with all its equipment in the face of enemy machine-gun fire; with a fresh scar on his cheek to keep the black eye-patch company, he looked more like a pirate than ever.

And now there was a worthwhile job to do. General Montgomery planned to outflank the Mareth Line—his famous 'Left Hook'—and urgently required a reconnaissance made of the route for the armour; when that was accomplished P.P.A. would remain in the area to carry out raids on enemy airfields and landing-grounds in southern Tunisia.

We reorganized quickly and set out—P.P.A. and an L.R.D.G. patrol of New Zealanders commanded by Lieutenant Tinker—thirteen vehicles in all, an ill-fated number.

From where we stood smoking and talking amongst the acacia bushes of the wadi Shweref, Mareth was 400 miles north-west as the crow flies, but we couldn't go as the crow flew; we had to take a wider sweep westwards in order to cross the Tunisian border between enemy-held Ghadames and Nalut, and then curve north towards Mareth, a total distance of 500 miles to the southern tip of the Mareth defences.

Our route lay across unknown, uncharted country; we were the first wheeled patrol ever to pass that way—across the great plateau of the Homada el Homra, the Red Desert, so called because of its gravel formation of reddish granules which turn blood-red in the rays of the setting sun, a breathtaking, incredible, unforgettable picture as the sun goes down. Imagine a vast lake of venous blood overshadowed by crepusculating waves of violet light touching a burnished horizon of flashing gold and racing banners of scarlet; imagine black towers of basalt rearing nightmarish shapes above the stagnant ocean of blood—bent old men, crouching tigers, charging horsemen, lone scouting wolves, witches' hats; imagine an overhanging dome of palest duck-egg blue tinged with apple-green lavishly studded with scintillating diamonds; imagine an all-enveloping deathly hush, an empty, terrifying, universal silence and you have some idea of the incredible Homada el Homra at sunset; a place of awe and majesty.

We came to the edge of this plateau late in the afternoon and crawled along its bloody escarpment searching for a way to the plain below. Five hundred feet lower, the shadowy Tunisian plain stretched towards the sand-dunes of the Grand Erg Oriental and the limitless sands of the vast Sahara Desert. A writhing spume of dust rose from the plain, denoting a German or Italian armoured car moving north from Ghadames towards Tripoli.

Bathed in reflected blood-red light we walked along the edge of the Homada, looking for an exit.

'There must be a way down, Tinker,' Popski said.

Eventually Tinker found one, a fearsome gully, an open gash in the steep cliffs of the escarpment blocked by scree and fallen rocks.

'If we clear the rubble away, Popski, this'll just about do.'

Caneri and I peered over Tinker's shoulder into the dark maw of the gully and looked at one another. What must be, must be. . . .

Spades scraped, pick-axes clinked and boulders crashed in the ravine, booming and echoing loudly as they bounced from rock to rock. . . .

'What a mucking din,' panted Waterson. 'They'll hear us in Nalut.'

The men sweated and heaved in the blood-red glow like figures in a Wagnerian scene. . . . When the last obstructing boulder had thundered down the gully and the mounds of scree had been levelled, Popski turned to Bill Wilson.

'Right, Wilson. Down you go.'

Bill Wilson swallowed hard and nosed his jeep gingerly over the escarpment. . . . From the bed of the gully where I was standing, looking up, it seemed impossible that the jeep could remain on its four wheels, but must nose-dive and topple over; all I could see was a dark jeep-like shape canted at a frightful angle in silhouette against the stars with Bill Wilson's bodyless head and shoulders hanging from the sky. 'Christ,' I thought, 'he'll topple over,' and I waited for the crash. . . .

But Bill Wilson kept his head and that jeep came down on all four wheels inch by screeching inch without a thing going wrong. In perfect traction—lowest low booster gear with brakes half on— he crawled down the gully like a fly on a wall. . . .

I backed down in front of him, step by step, until he was past the steepest part, then I stood aside and waved him on.

'Well done, Bill,' I whispered as he scrunched darkly past.

'Muckin' good things these jeeps, sirr,' he whispered back, pleased as punch with his effort.

'Take your time, Bill. Go a couple of hundred yards at the bottom and wait. Look out for boulders coming down.'

I watched Wilson fade into the abyss and climbed up the scree to guide the next jeep down . . . the thin screech of half-applied brakes echoed from below like the wailing of a soul in torment. . . .

The jeeps crawled safely down, followed by the manœuvrable L.R.D.G. 30-cwt. trucks, expertly handled by their experienced New Zealand drivers; then the two overloaded P.P.A. 3-tonners.

Weldon's came first . . . suspended from the stars . . . filling the mouth of the gully with its dark bulk . . . screeching . . . slipping . . . slithering . . . stopping . . . poised for one mad, hurtling, screaming dive into the plain. . . . I watched nervously, ready to jump quickly aside if it got out of control . . . it was full of eight-o-eight . . . screech . . . slither . . . sideslip. ('Oh, God. He's had it.') One of the rear wheels bumped over a sharp rock and glanced off . . . the truck swayed dangerously . . . almost toppling. . . . Weldon braked and gripped the steering-wheel, gritting his teeth . . . the heavy truck steadied in its path and came down inch by inch . . . screech . . . scrunch . . . slither . . . inch by agonizing inch. . . .

It was dark by the time we were all gathered at the base of the escarpment. Had we been heard coming down? Would an enemy patrol be lying in wait for us on the road? We each had our private fears and kept them to ourselves.

Muted whispers floated from truck to truck, mingling with the softly popping note of the exhausts.

'Ready, Tinker?'

'O.K., Popski.'

'All set, Jan?'

'Ready, Weldon?'

'O.K., Sarge.'

'All ready, sir.'

Engines revved quietly, gears snicked, men settled comfortably into their seats. . . .

Tinker led, followed by Popski, then Jan Caneri with an L.R.D.G. jeep behind him; then the five L.R.D.G. 30-cwt. trucks, followed by the two lumbering P.P.A. 3-tonners trailed by Waterson; Bill Wilson and I brought up the rear with the eagle-eyed Mohammed Mustapha sitting at our backs making sure no German armoured cars surprised us from the rear. . . .

We moved across the uneven surface of the dark Tunisian plain, a ghost-train of shadowy, blacked-out, creaking trucks, ten yards apart, swishing past bushes, lurching into hollows, jolting over hummocks and stones. . . .

The drivers sat hunched behind their steering-wheels peering at the jogging tailboard of the shadowy vehicle in front; gunners and spare men searched the surrounding darkness, looking and listening for signs of the enemy. Nobody spoke. There wasn't a sound but the drooling note of exhausts, the creak and bump of chassis, the swish of scratching bushes. There was no moon. Overhead in an inky vault, a million points of winking light faintly illumined our way; we sat taut, keyed-up, alert, apprehensive, but enjoying the excitement of a dangerous situation. . . . When we reached the desert road between Ghadames and Tripoli, Tinker held up a hand and the column halted behind him, the rear trucks crowding up on those in front. Tinker scouted ahead in the darkness and we sat in our trucks waiting and watching, tensed for the

35

burst of machine-gun fire which might come tearing out of the night. . . .

But nothing happened. The road was deserted. Tinker returned, took his place at the head of the column and we followed him across the sandy road one at a time, feeling like boys stealing a march when the teacher's back is turned. When the last truck was across, the column halted again and waited, on tenterhooks, whilst the three Senussi ran back to the road and obliterated our tracks with their *jerds*. . . .

We drove all night, hour after hour, in unrelieved concentration.

Visibility was limited to the blurred outline of the truck in front and to about twenty yards of shadowy scrub-desert on either side. Thorn bushes clutched at us out of the gloom or suddenly appeared directly in front and vanished under our prancing radiators, smacking and tugging at the undercarriage as we rode over them. We halted for a few minutes about midnight to change drivers and stretch cramped muscles, then on again, mile after mile, lurching and jolting and creaking, nodding with fatigue in the small hours and jerking ourselves awake. . . .

Dawn surged out of the east, a rapid paling of the darkness, a fading of the stars, followed by a quick uprush of flashing, golden light and we found ourselves adrift in a grey sea of rolling white-flecked waves, a vast expanse of undulating scrub about a foot high set in wave-like motion by the gentle dawn wind which came out of the east like a giant's breath.

'Camouflage nets, everybody,' Popski warned. 'They may have aircraft about. Keep a sharp look-out.'

We draped green and khaki fishermen's nets over the trucks to break up the give-away shadow seen from the air, filled up petrol tanks, breakfasted and snatched a few hours' uneasy sleep; then on again with look-out men on the backs of the trucks searching the cloudless sky for enemy aircraft. . . .

The scrub grew thicker and taller as we advanced across the uninhabited plain. It was tough and wiry, dry as tinder. It didn't interfere with the bigger trucks but played havoc with the low-slung jeeps, catching round the driving shaft and collecting in the hot space between gear-box and exhaust pipe.

'Bob! Your jeep's on fire,' cried Jan Caneri, pointing to the smoke pouring from under my jeep. We were travelling in

36

V-formation with Tinker and Popski at the apex and Jan and I tailing opposite legs.

'So's yours!' I yelled back, indicating the smoke coming from his own jeep. Then we noticed that smoke was spewing from all the jeeps.

We stopped and located the trouble—an accumulation of tindery stalks between gear-box and hot exhaust pipe, smoking furiously, ready to ignite. . . .

Before we had covered a mile, smoke was pouring from the jeeps again. Every mile or so we were forced to stop and clean out the accumulation of brittle stalks (lest they ignite and set the jeeps on fire), lying on our backs on the scorching scrub, getting dust in our eyes and burning our hands on the exhaust pipes. . . .

And then we came to the dunes of the Grand Erg, the Tunisian outriders of the great Sahara sand sea. We saw the dunes ahead of us one morning as we brushed across the scrub, a tumultuous sea of crested ochre waves dancing in the heat-haze. We stopped to look at them, shading our eyes from the glare. They stretched to the far horizon, wave upon wave of them, like a giant ploughed field lying athwart our advance.

'Cor blimey,' exclaimed Driver Bell (no longer Popski's driver), 'do we have to cross that lot?'

'Don't like the look of them dunes,' observed Driver Davies from the seat of his heavy 3-tonner.

'This'll make 'em sweat,' grinned Sergeant Waterson, rubbing his hands. 'Plenty of spade-work.'

The crossing was a nightmare. The dunes weren't high, but the sand was soft and the distance between crests just sufficient to belly the trucks so that we progressed in jerks, like this: front wheels over crest . . . lurch . . . bump . . . chassis bellied . . . dig away sand. . . . 'Take 'er away' . . . lurch forward . . . front wheels over the next crest . . . bump. . . . 'Muck it' . . . chassis bellied . . . dig away sand. . . .

So we progressed throughout a never-ending day. Wind blew, swirling the loosened sand into our eyes, up our nostrils, down our parched throats. A pitiless sun blazed, scorching our bent backs, burning our hands, when we forgot and touched blistering metal; and there was no respite, only an endless repetition of lurch . . . bump . . . dig . . . sweat, from sand-dune to sand-dune. . . . And when we'd bellied through the final crest and were released from the agony, there was the rolling scrub again and stopping every mile to de-scrub the smoking jeeps. . . .

Why did we do it? Why, though we cursed and swore outwardly, did we enjoy every minute of it inwardly? Why? Because it was different, because it was adventure, because it was something no one else had done; we were right up in front, in advance of the main army, undertaking a difficult and dangerous task. Not one of us would willingly have been anywhere else.

A hundred miles south of the Mareth Line we met our first Tunisian Arabs, the first human beings we had encountered since leaving Shweref, poorly clad, half-starved, miserable, shifty-eyed wretches who peered at us suspiciously through glaucomatous eyes and held out their hands for food; quite different from the proud Senussi of Libya. Our Senussi talked to them in dialect and it was interesting to observe the undisguised contempt in which they held their Tunisian brethren. '*Basas*,' Mohammed Mustapha whispered to me when we drove on (informers, spies). The Tunisian Arabs under French colonial rule were disaffected and we soon had proof of their disaffection.

Later that same day we leaguered in a wadi sixty miles south of Matmata, the southern apex of the Mareth defences. The wadi was only a fissure in the flat plain, a shallow crack between sandstone walls with a sandy bottom and a few stunted bushes, but it offered cover. We dispersed the trucks close to the bushes and draped them in their camouflage nets.

Popski beckoned and we gathered round him.

'We are sixty miles from the Mareth Line,' he said. 'Tinker, Jan Caneri and I in three jeeps will make the reconnaissance. The rest of you will remain here until we return. Captain Yunnie is in charge. Stay by your trucks and don't move about. Remember you are in enemy territory.'

The men serviced their trucks and cleaned guns. The cooks prepared a meal. The reconnaissance party got ready to move out.

I had words with Popski.

'It isn't fair, Popski,' I complained, 'I stayed behind last time. It's my turn to go. I'm missing all the fun.'

'You'll get plenty of fun later, Bob,' he assured me. 'More than you bargain for. In the meantime, I want you to make up a supply of Lewis bombs.'

'Why can't Jan Caneri do it?'

'Because you're second-in-command and because I say so.'
Popski became a trifle nettled. I saw I'd gone far enough and
desisted. I watched the three jeeps drive away. 'One day,' I
promised myself as I waved good luck to Caneri, 'I'll have my own
patrol and go out by myself and have fun.'

Lewis bombs were the invention of a special operations officer
in the Middle East, Captain Lewis, and were used for blowing up
enemy aircraft on airfields and landing-grounds. They were simple
to make and very effective.

> Recipe: 1 lb. of plastic 808.
> 1 cupful of motor oil.
> 3 ounces of phosphorous.

Mix plastic and motor oil into a thick dough, sprinkle with
phosphorous and mould into a ball. Put into an army ration bag,
add detonator and delayed time-fuse. Place on wing of enemy aircraft close to fuselage (above petrol tank) at dead of night, set time-
fuse and be miles away from landing-ground when bomb explodes.

As the exhaust-notes of the reconnaissance jeeps died away
Sergeant Waterson and I sat down in the shade of Weldon's
3-tonner and started to make Lewis bombs.

We unwrapped a hundred sticks of eight-o-eight on to an
army ground-sheet, poured a canful of old motor oil over them
and squeezed and walloped and pressed and kneaded the filthy
mess into a thick, evil-smelling dough.

'Like treacle toffee,' I remarked, picking up a lump and
slapping it down.

'What would happen if you ate a piece by mistake?' Waterson
wanted to know.

'Don't know, Sarge. Probably make you sick. Safer to be a
non-smoker, I should think.'

We pounded and patted the putty-like dough, tearing it apart,
joining it together like plasticine, rubbing and rolling it into a
black, oily consistency.

'That'll do, I think, Sarge. Get the ration bags and the incendiaries.'

Waterson emptied the contents of half a dozen incendiary
bombs on to the ground-sheet. I made the dough into balls of
approximately 1 lb. in weight. Waterson held the mouths of the
ration bags open; I dabbed the plastic balls in the phosphorous

and dropped them inside. Later, we tied the necks of the bags and made up an equal number of time-fuses.

'Right, Sarge,' I said when we'd finished, 'stow these in a safe place. If we blow up a plane with each one we'll do well.'

Sergeant Waterson put the twenty-five Lewis bombs in one 3-tonner and the twenty-five time-fuses in the other.

An hour later I had a blinding headache, a most unusual thing for me.

'Have you got a headache, Sarge?' I asked Waterson.

'Yes, sir. Bloody awful.'

'Anybody else got one?'

We asked the crews.

'Got a headache, Jock?'

'No, sir.'

'Got a headache, Wilson?'

'No, sir.'

'Got a headache, Davies?'

'No, sir.'

The men looked at us, wondering why we were suddenly so solicitous of their welfare. I looked at Waterson, holding his head in his hands.

'Must be that bloody eight-o-eight, Sarge.'

I smelt my hands. They had a curious, cloying, metallic odour and when I put them close to my nose my head throbbed all the more.

'It's that bloody eight-o-eight. Smell it.'

Sergeant Waterson smelt his hands, and reeled back.

'Does it make your head throb?' I asked him.

Waterson nodded painfully.

'By Christ, it does.'

As the afternoon wore on our headaches grew steadily worse—a blinding, throbbing, splitting kind of headache which throbbed whenever we moved.

'This'll send me crackers,' Waterson groaned, rocking backwards and forwards on his heels in the shade of a bush.

'Think how you'd feel if you'd eaten a bit, Sarge. There's your answer.'

Towards evening the throbbing subsided and we woke next morning with clear heads; nor had we any after-effects.

· · · · ·

'Plastic eight-o-eight,' the Middle East Special Operations Training School instructor was saying in Cairo, 'never touch it with your bare hands. Gives you a vile headache. Always use rubber gloves.'

Time hung heavily. Having made up a supply of Lewis bombs, cleaned guns and serviced the vehicles there was nothing for us to do but wait. We couldn't move about for fear of being discovered and the wadi was a sun-trap; sitting in it was like sitting in an oven, being baked.

I felt uneasy.

Arabs from the encampment we'd passed the previous morning had come to take a look at us. They didn't venture into the wadi, but remained at some distance, watching.

I saw their heads bobbing on the skyline every time I looked up; not that there was anything particularly unusual about Arabs looking at us. At different times and in different places, Arabs had been looking at us ever since we'd left Cairo, but I remembered Mohammed Mustapha's whispered warning that these Arabs were probably spies and informers. I called Mohammed over to my bush.

'These bedouin, Mohammed,' I said. 'What should we do about them?'

The best thing to do, Mohammed thought, was to cut their throats, but we couldn't do that, he said, because there would be more bedouin in the vicinity and if we killed these ones or held them prisoner their relatives would come looking for them and we couldn't kill or imprison all the bedouin in southern Tunisia. 'Ignore them, Captain,' he advised. 'They are spies and informers, but what can we do? If we hold these, more will take their place. Less harm will come from ignoring than from antagonizing them. Leave well alone.'

It was sound advice and I took it. I had no desire to be attacked by hostile Arabs. In any case the damage had already been done.

We were having breakfast early the following morning, sitting by our camouflaged trucks eating fried bacon and biscuit when Waterson stopped chewing, put up a warning finger and listened intently.

'Aircraft, sir,' he intoned ominously.

We all stopped eating and listened intently. We heard the unmistakable drone . . . drone . . . drone of aircraft engines.

'Quick!' I cried. 'Push everything under cover.'

An enamel mug, a mess-tin, anything with a bright, shiny surface glints in the sun and can be seen from a searching aeroplane. We gathered up all cooking and eating utensils, all pieces of equipment and pushed them beneath the trucks. Upturned human faces can also be seen from the air.

'Under your camouflage nets,' I said, 'keep your faces down.'

Our rule in enemy territory was not to fire at aircraft unless fired upon. If we kept still and they didn't see us all would be well.

Drone . . . drone . . . drone. . . .

We sat under our camouflage nets listening to the Messerschmitts coming closer and closer . . . keeping our heads down. . . . We could have saved ourselves the trouble. Informed of our presence by the bedouin, the Luftwaffe pilots knew exactly where to find us. They zoomed overhead at a thousand feet, turned steeply and dived out of the sun.

D-r-r-r-r-r-r. . . . D-r-r-r-r-r-r-r. Bullets spattered in the wadi, kicking up sand . . . little scarlet darts pinged viciously past our ears and ricocheted off the sides of the trucks . . . incendiary bullets pierced petrol tanks and petrol-cans. . . . Weldon's 3-tonner was loaded with eight-o-eight . . . two Messerschmitts roared past, swaying the bushes with the wind of their passage. . . .

Tearing off camouflage nets, we leapt to our well-oiled guns. . . . Brrrrrrrrt . . . brrrrrrrrt. . . . D-r-r-r-r-r-r-r. . . . D-r-r-r-r-r-r-r . . . we didn't stand a chance . . . as soon as one plane cannoned its way out of the wadi the second one came in, keeping our heads down. . . . D-r-r-r-r-r-r-r-r. One by one our trucks burst into flames . . . out of the corner of my eye I saw a New Zealand gunner aim his captured 20-mm. Breda at an oncoming Messerschmitt. . . . D-r-r-r-r-r-r. . . . I saw him leap aside as his truck caught fire . . . blazing petrol-cans somersaulted through the air . . . ammunition popped . . . spare wheels, water-cans, tins of bully-beef, pieces of engine fell about our dodging heads. . . . I tried to save the wireless jeep, but a blazing petrol-can tumbled into it. I heard Waterson's commanding 'Look out, sir,' just in time . . . later, I couldn't get near it for the heat. . . . D-r-r-r-r-r-r.

... D-r-r-r-r-r ... the Messerschmitts roared up and down the wadi, pumping tracer and incendiary bullets into our trucks . . . we fired wildly at them and ducked out of the way. . . .

It was all over in ten minutes. In less time than it has taken me to write this passage, the Messerschmitts were heading for home. Every one of our nine trucks was a blazing wreck and nine columns of black smoke rose into the still morning air proclaiming our position for miles around. . . .

Following upon the clatter of machine-gun fire and the roar of aircraft engines a deathly silence now filled the wadi, broken only by the sultry crackling of the burning trucks.

'Christ Almighty,' ejaculated Waterson, surveying the scene. 'What a mucking picnic!'

'Jesus!' breathed Driver Davies emerging from a bush.

'The mucking bastards,' swore Fitter Welsh indignantly when he saw the burning remains of his prized 3-tonners.

'Anybody wounded?' I shouted.

'Yes,' Sergeant Garven (L.R.D.G.) called out. 'Two jokers down here.'

Two of the New Zealanders were wounded in the legs. We applied field dressings and made them comfortable in the shade of a bush. . . .

The wadi was a shambles. Smoke billowed from the crackling trucks, filling the air with an acrid stench. Charred bits and pieces lay everywhere, like a room which has been looted— tins of bully-beef, meat and veg, blackened petrol- and water-cans, compo boxes, spare wheels, Tommy-guns, ammunition clips, boots, driving-seats, sweaters, cap comforters, pieces of webbing. . . .

'Christ Almighty,' Waterson repeated, 'what a bloody mess!'

'No raids behind the Mareth Line now,' I groaned. 'Popski'll be furious.'

We'd lost everything. All the tons of demolition kit I'd drawn in Cairo and been at such pains to transport across three deserts, nearly 2000 miles, all gone, all gone up in smoke before we'd had a chance to use it. It was galling. . . . Looking up I saw heads bobbing on the skyline and a bitter rage seized me.

'It's those bastards . . . where's a rifle?'

I looked wildly round and saw one lying on the ground. I grabbed it . . . cocked it . . . put it to my shoulder . . . and fired . . .

43

phut. . . . I cocked and fired again . . . phut. . . . The bobbing heads vanished.

Waterson and I walked about the wadi kicking at blackened bully-beef tins, tins of condensed milk, water-cans, ammunition clips . . . and fear laid hold of me.

'This smoke'll be seen for miles, Sarge. The next thing'll be an armoured-car patrol to pick us up. We'd better get into the dunes.'

At the top end of the wadi, about a mile away, the sand-dunes of the Grand Erg began again. Armoured cars couldn't follow us there. Inside the dunes we'd be safe; we could fight off an attack on foot.

'Get the blokes to gather up the salvage,' I said, eager to get out of the wadi.

There wasn't much to salvage apart from bully-beef, meat and veg and condensed milk, a few cans of water; but there was some petrol—off-loaded from one of the New Zealand trucks the previous night and shaded under a bush—eight cans, about thirty-five gallons.

I called Mohammed Mustapha, and noticed he was looking glum.

'Cheer up, Mohammed,' I teased him, 'it isn't the end of the world.'

But Mohammed wasn't worrying about his personal safety. He was thinking of all the tea and sugar which had been destroyed on the 3-tonners—pounds and pounds of precious substances as valuable to the Arabs as currency and used by them as such.

'*Shay! Sucre!*' he mourned. '*Ayeeeeeeee.*'

We gathered the salvage and trudged up the scorching wadi, helping the limping New Zealanders. The petrol-cans were heavy, dragging at our arms. We wouldn't need petrol in the dunes.

'Bury them, Sarge,' I said to Waterson.

We cached them under a bush half-way up the wadi.

I took a last look round. What a dismal scene! Nine charred, smoking skeletons with their blackened entrails lying about. A desert kill. Only vultures were required to complete the picture. I looked up, half-expecting to see them wheeling in the sky. . . .

I sat in the dunes, thinking. There would be hell to pay over this and I would have to pay it. Popski would return full of plans

44

for raids behind the Mareth Line and when he found there was nothing left to raid with he'd be furious. I couldn't see that it was my fault; a strafing could happen to anybody. If Popski had been in my place, I asked myself, could he have done any better? That wasn't the point. I had been left in charge of the convoy and now there was no convoy. It had been my responsibility and I would be the scapegoat. I wasn't looking forward to meeting Popski. . . .

We sat in the dunes and waited. We waited a day and a night . . . and another endless day. No enemy patrol came to capture us; the bedouin didn't trouble us. I began to feel a little foolish; my fears had been groundless. But where was Popski? Had the reconnaissance party been strafed, shot-up, captured, killed or what? How long should we wait for them? We couldn't sit in the dunes indefinitely. . . . I decided to wait for another twenty-four hours and then, if there was still no sign of the jeeps, set out on foot for Tozeur—the nearest desert outpost occupied by the Allied forces operating in North Africa. It was a journey of 180 miles across blistering sand-dunes, but I had walked 400 miles across the Libyan Desert the previous year and survived the ordeal; I thought I could manage the 180 to Tozeur; the only problem was the two wounded New Zealanders, how far could they walk?

Night fell and we saw lights flashing in the sky.

'Is that Popski, Sarge, or an enemy patrol?'

Waterson and I crouched in the shelter of the dunes under the inky, star-lit sky watching the flashing lights drawing closer . . . closer. . . .

'Jeep headlamps,' said Waterson.

'Looks like it,' I muttered, focusing binoculars.

The twin beams dipped and danced, disappeared and reappeared, glaring out of the night like the eyes of a giant owl. . . .

We watched them swing into the wadi, bouncing and plunging, rearing and flashing, dimming . . . vanishing . . . flickering . . . glaring again . . . and finally staring. . . .

The stationary eyes blinked off and on . . . off and on . . . off and on. . . .

Popski or a clever Nazi officer; I wondered.

I was pretty sure it was Popski, but I was still suspicious.

The head-lights went out and didn't come on again. A few minutes later a hand-torch flashed and a thin pencil of light moved up the wadi towards the dunes. . . .

The torch flashed nearer and nearer. Waterson and I crouched on the sand, gripping our Tommy-guns, peering over the crest of the dunes . . . we saw two dark figures rise against the sky-line. . . . I clicked the safety-catch and challenged.

'Halt! Who goes there?'

A well-known voice came out of the night:

'Popski,' it growled.

My heart went down to my boots and I walked forward to meet him.

He already knew most of the story. At Kosar Rhilane, an old Roman fort twenty miles further north, they had met a party of Free French commandos who reported having seen Messerschmitts diving on the wadi and columns of black smoke rising from it after they'd gone. Fearing the worst, Popski had come post-haste to investigate—leaving Tinker and Caneri at the fort—and the worst was worse than he'd feared. Couldn't I have saved the wireless jeep, just that one little jeep out of all those trucks? I felt the sting of his sarcasm. The reconnaissance had been eminently successful, he told me, they'd found the route for the armour and been right up to the Mareth defences. He had the very information General Montgomery was waiting for, information of the most vital importance, and now through my failure to save the wireless jeep he couldn't communicate it. I was a fool, an incompetent, unfit for command, second or otherwise. Popski was livid. He lashed me unmercifully with his tongue, his eyes machine-gunned me from above his grey-black beard. I hung my head in shame. What could I say?

But worse was to come.

'Is there anything left?' he asked.

I nodded miserably.

'Some rations and water, a few cans of petrol.'

'I'll take the petrol.'

We walked down the wadi to the petrol cache. The petrol wasn't there . . . only the empty holes where the cans had been. The bedouin had looted it during the night. Popski looked at me. His eyes were hard. I felt him crack my shell and squash me into the sand with his heel.

46

'Can't even look after a few cans of petrol,' he shot at me with withering scorn.

I prayed for the wadi to open and swallow me.

Popski looked grimly into dark space. He was thinking furiously. His plans had collapsed like a house of cards. There would be no raiding behind the Mareth Line now. The chance of making a name for his unit had gone, snatched from his hands by a couple of Messerschmitts. That was bad enough, but now through the blundering incompetence of Bob Yunnie there wasn't enough petrol to get all the jeeps to Tozeur. What was to be done? First and foremost he must get a report through to General Montgomery's headquarters as quickly as possible. Secondly, he must extricate his men. He came to his decision, staring into the darkness above the mocking void of the looted petrol cache.

'Caneri and Tinker will go to Tozeur. The rest of us'll walk. I'll speak to the men.'

We walked back to the dunes in silence. I felt the size of a pea.

Mohammed Mustapha brought Popski a glass of shay. He tossed it off and smacked his lips appreciatively. Sergeant Waterson called the men to attention and Popski addressed them in clipped, vibrant undertones.

'Caneri and Tinker are at Ksar Rhilane. We found the route for the armour. A report must get through to General Montgomery's headquarters. We've no wireless communication. Tozeur is the nearest Allied outpost. It is 180 miles away. There isn't enough petrol for all the jeeps. Caneri and Tinker will proceed to Tozeur. The rest of us will walk.'

He paused to let his words sink in and continued:

'I am going back to Ksar Rhilane now. I will take the wounded with me. They will go with Caneri and Tinker. I will be back here by dawn and we'll start right away. There is nothing to worry about. We'll all get through.'

Mustapha's tea-fire flickered redly and a breath escaped from the group of dark figures huddled in the dunes. The wounded men moved their stiff limbs and groaned, biting their lips. We gave them each a shot of morphia and carried them down the wadi to Popski's jeep.

Nothing more was said.

Popski slid into the driving-seat, Yunes, his Senussi guide, clambered in beside him, the headlamps blazed and he drove into the night.

At Ksar Rhilane, three hours later, the wounded were transfered to Caneri's and Tinker's jeeps and they set off for Tozeur, through 180 miles of unknown enemy territory inhabited by hostile bedouin. Their orders were to contact the British or American forces in North Africa, get a report wirelessed to General Montgomery's headquarters and return with spare jeeps to pick up the walking party.

Popski drove into the wadi again as dawn was breaking. We gathered round his jeep in a forlorn group amidst the charred wreckage of our brave hopes. How pathetic they looked in the pale morning light, those twisted, blackened skeletons, like the abandoned ruins of a broken ideal.

'Caneri and Tinker have gone to Tozeur,' Popski said. 'If they get through, they'll get jeeps from the Americans and come back to pick us up——'

He broke off to glare at me.

'. . . I've only enough petrol for eighty miles. I'll shepherd you as long as it lasts.'

We started to pile the salvaged rations and water into the back of his jeep.

'There's another possibility,' he continued. 'L.R.D.G. may send a patrol to Tozeur. I want a volunteer to remain behind to intercept it if it comes.'

My heart sang. Here was an opportunity to wipe the escutcheon clean.

'I'll stay, Popski,' I said. 'Leave Mohammed Mustapha with me.'

I looked at Mohammed and he flashed me a smile, mouthing '*Aywah*' to indicate his agreement.

Popski gave me a long, direct look.

'Thank you, Bob,' he said at length.

While Waterson got everything ready to move, Popski drew me to one side and gave me instructions.

'You'll remain here for five days, Bob. If the L.R.D.G. patrol hasn't shown up by then, you make your own way to Tozeur. Good luck.'

48

I nodded and we shook hands. Popski gave me another searching look. I think he hardly expected to see me again.

Sergeant Garven suddenly spoke up:

'I'll stay too, Popski.'

In the end, four of us remained—Sergeant Garven, Mohammed Mustapha Abdel, Salem and myself.

Waterson gave me a generous supply of rations and water ('Good luck, sir') and we watched the party move off, wondering if we'd ever see any of them again. Shepherded by Popski in his jeep, they disappeared down the wadi like a serpent tail—twenty-odd ragged, bearded, unwashed, sun-scorched men dressed in an odd assortment of khaki shirts and shorts, black berets, cap comforters, pullovers, leather jerkins, battledress blouses, army greatcoats, with Sergeant Waterson walking on the flank under his peaked New Zealand hat calling 'Lef . . . Ri . . . Lef . . . Ri . . . Lef . . . Ri. . . .'

I watched the last man, little Jock Welsh, disappear round a bend and sighed with relief, feeling suddenly at peace.

I turned to find Mohammed standing behind me. Almost exactly a year previously, he and I set out from Mersa Brega on our long trek to Tobruk in the wake of a retreating Eighth Army.

'Do you remember what happened a year ago, Mohammed?'

'*Aywah*,' he grinned, showing perfect teeth, 'Benghazi—Tobruk,' and he cut the air with a hand.

'We got through last time. We'll get through this time.'

'*Inshallah*.'

Mohammed was quite unperturbed. The desperate situation presented no problem so far as he was concerned. A short wait in the dunes and then, if no trucks came, a longish walk to Tozeur, a walk no longer than many he'd taken between the oases of his native Libya. Hostile bedouin? He had a good British rifle, clips of ammunition; the rest was in the hands of Allah.

'*Ouse shay?*' he grinned at me.

Syrupy, astringent, heart-warming Arab tea; just the very thing.

'*Aywah*,' I smiled, and clapped him on the shoulder.

Mohammed found a more comfortable place in the dunes, near a shady acacia bush, and we settled down to our vigil. I snapped a twig from the acacia bush and broke it into four unequal lengths. We drew lots for look-out duty and Garven was first. I gave him my binoculars and he crawled to the top of the dune. Relaxing in the shade, I watched Mohammed make tea.

Shay (tea) is more than a drink in the desert; it is a ceremony, and the desert Arab is every whit as pernickety about the rules of his tea-making as the veriest London clubman about the rules of his club. A traditional pattern is followed and any *gaucherie* in execution is the mark of ill-breeding; the Senussi who misses the diminutive tea-glass when pouring at arm's length is regarded as the rankest outsider.

Three brews are made. The first is fairly weak, the second stronger, whilst the third is very strong and flavoured with mint. I watched Mohammed's lean, brown hands putting tea and sugar into a small, blue enamel teapot (made in Birmingham), fill it up with water and set it to boil on the red-hot embers of a fire made from dead acacia branches. I watched him sit back on his haunches and twirl his silky black moustache, looking through the fire with the remote, penetrating gaze possessed only by those accustomed to searching distant horizons; his skin was smooth, fine-textured, dark brown, his body lithe and muscular and his head rose proudly from straight shoulders to show an aquiline nose and a high, intelligent forehead. Mohammed, the son of a sheik, was well-built and good-looking; he looked every bit the proud desert warrior and I thought as I quietly observed him what a hit he would make in Hollywood garbed in traditional dress. . . .

When the teapot boiled, Mohammed set out four little tea-glasses, lifted the teapot from the embers and poured a sample of tea. He set the teapot on the embers and tasted the tea he'd poured; it didn't quite satisfy him. He lifted the lid of the teapot and poured back the sample. A few moments later he sipped again. This time it pleased him and he filled the four glasses, pouring expertly from a height, handing one to each of us. We sipped the syrupy, astringent amber liquid and smacked our lips in appreciation. . . .

Mohammed added more tea and more sugar, filled up with water and set the teapot to boil again, frequently sampling the brew and returning it to the pot. The final brew was poured from a good height and a glassful handed to each of us; we sucked and smacked, Arab fashion. . . .

Then came the third brew, the crowning glory of the tea-maker's art. Mohammed added a little more tea and a lot more sugar, dropped in some sprigs of dried mint and topped up with water. . . . A brownish foam spluttered about the lid, overflowed and coursed down the side of the teapot, making the embers sizzle. Mohammed watched it, eased the lid a little and poured a sample of tea. No good. He lifted the lid and poured it back. The teapot hotted for another five minutes and Mohammed poured another sample. Still no good. He waited three minutes and poured a third. Better, but not just right. He set the teapot on the embers for another minute and savoured a fourth time. Ah! He smacked his lips, tasted again to be certain and then, holding the teapot at extreme arm's height, he poured a thin spout of golden liquid into each glass, filling it to the brim without spilling a drop, a masterly performance. The tea was syrupy and very sweet, but the tangy mint flavour prevented it from being sickly. We sucked at the glasses appreciatively, showering Mohammed with praise.

We sucked in glorious isolation surrounded by sand, sand lying silently under the sun. Northwards, towards Mareth, the dunes of the Erg filled the horizon, curving away from us in turbulent waves which broke, 100 miles later, on the shores of the Shott Jerid; eastwards, beyond a mile of razor-backed slopes, there was the drab, scrub-filled plain which we searched continuously for a line of bobbing, sand-coloured 30-cwt. Chevrolet trucks; southwards, the dunes of the Erg again, wave upon wave of foaming breakers; and to the west, a limitless ocean of tossing yellow-ochre sand-waves beating against an azure sky; wherever we looked we saw sand, sand which shimmered and danced in the heat of the blazing sun.

We remained in our isolated sand-castle for five incredible days, watching the pageant of the hourly changing sand-scene. There is nothing but sand in the desert, but sand in beautiful shapes. The wind is the desert sculptor moulding and fashioning the sand into long, tapering curves, uprearing razor-back slopes, knife-edged prancing bows, softly rounded hummocks, smooth as a woman's breasts. The sun rises in the morning, spreading orange and yellow, shortening the shadows till noon. For a brief hour, at midday when the sun is high in the sky, no change takes place in the sand-scene, but with the westering sun the shadows creep out from the dunes again, becoming longer and longer. Red comes into the sky and colours play in the dunes, mauve and purple and gold, flying streamers of violet. And mirage is always

51

about you, changing the desert face. Ahead of you on the horizon
are pools of blue water, palm-trees, minarets, towers, which
shimmer and dance tantalizingly, right in front of your eyes; but
you never manage to touch them, they always stay just out of
reach. And all around you is silence, the silence of empty space;
but the silence isn't a dead one, it throbs and it pulses with life.
The desert is empty and lifeless and yet it is full of life, a life
which calls to you, bewitches you, lays its hold on your heart.
What is the call of the desert? The pull of its empty space? The sob
and the cry and the hurt of it? The awe of its mighty waste? No
man knows, but to some the desert is magic, like the pied piper's
music, holding them ever enthralled.

Five times the pageant unfolded. Five times, for a brief hour
at dawn, we watched the rising sun transform the drab eastern
plain into a dancing field of golden glory; five times we watched
the velvet shadows of the dunes tiptoe into their crests, mysteriously vanish for an hour and then glide silently out again, down
their opposite slopes, following the sun's passage across the Erg
like a master-painter's brush; five times we sat enthralled, watching the setting sun transform the Erg into a magic carpet of
creeping rainbow light; five times we watched a silver scimitar cut
a pathway through the stars.

A hundred times the question went 'See anything?' and a
hundred times the answer came, 'Not a bloody thing.' A hundred
times Mohammed asked *'Ouse shay?'* and a hundred times I
answered *'Aywah.'* At least 100 times I climbed to the top of our
dune and stared at the eastern horizon—and saw nothing but
mirage. We weren't attacked by hostile bedouin. I don't think the
bedouin knew we were there. No enemy patrols came to look for
us. Nothing happened at all. We simply sat in the dunes in the
sweltering sun cut off from the world, watching the eastern
horizon and drinking Mohammed's incessant *shay*.

'They're not coming,' I said to Sergeant Garven when dusk
obliterated the plain for the fifth time. 'We'll leave tonight.
Tozeur,' I said to Mohammed, cutting the air with my hand in a
north-westerly direction. . . .

The dunes ran north–south in curving parallel waves. We
walked along the trough between the spume-blown crests, like
children of Israel crossing between the waves of the Red Sea.

It was cool in the soft light cast by the quarter-moon and the twinkling stars, cool, mysterious and very lovely walking in a silver sea with the muted voice of the night-wind singing a lullaby to the waves and blowing silver spray.

We walked all night and when dawn came, bringing the pitiless sun, we were thirty miles nearer Tozeur.

'Look for a bush, Mohammed,' I said. 'We'll lie up by day and walk at night. It's cooler.'

'*Aywah.*'

Mohammed and Abdel Salem climbed to the top of a dune and waved to us. Garven and I waded up to them.

Two dunes away there was a spreading acacia bush growing out of a crest. We floundered ankle-deep down loose, powdery sand, crossed a hard, wind-blown trough, waded up to another crest, ploughed down another slope and gained the shade of the bush. Mohammed produced his ubiquitous teapot and glasses; Abdel Salem gathered dead branches and made a fire down in the trough. We had three rounds of *shay* and drew lots for look-out. It fell to Mohammed. I gave him my binoculars and he sat near the crest watching the plain while the rest of us crawled under the bush and went to sleep. . . .

Shortly after midday Garven was on look-out.

'Trucks!' he bawled. 'L.R.D.G. patrol.'

I was instantly awake and plunged up to him. He handed me the binoculars. Five tiny sand-coloured trucks danced across my line of vision. They were at least five miles away, going slowly through the soft sand along the eastern edge of the Erg.

'Quick,' I shouted excitedly. 'Catch them before they get out of the soft sand.'

Mohammed grabbed his teapot and glasses and we plunged wildly down the slope. . . . Blazing, sweltering sun . . . up one cloying slope . . . through a feathery crest . . . down the other side . . . running across the hard trough . . . panting up the next slope . . . stopping on the crest to wave and shout . . . plunging down . . . dune after dune. . . .

We stood on top of a high dune and waved frantically. We shouted until we were hoarse. The trucks went slowly past. We were a mile nearer to them and we could hear them grinding through the sand in low gear; but they couldn't hear us, the wind was blowing in the wrong direction, blowing our voices back to us; and they didn't see us wave.

It was maddening, heart-breaking, to see the trucks so close and have to watch them go. . . .

I watched the last truck disappear round the northern tip of the Erg and sat down wearily in the sand.

'Oh, muck it,' I groaned, 'after waiting all this time, to see them go past like that.'

And then I had an idea.

It was after three o'clock. In a couple of hours it would be dusk and the L.R.D.G. patrol would pull into leaguer for the night. When they turned the northern tip of the Erg they would go due west along its northern flank. If we cut diagonally across the dunes in a north-westerly direction and kept going, we should walk into their leaguer during the night.

I turned to Garven excitedly.

'Garven. Whose patrol is that?'

'Probably Henry's.'

'Well, look. They'll leaguer-up at dusk, won't they? What sort of a bloke's Henry?'

'Should do, but Henry's a goer, if it's him. He sometimes goes on and on.'

'But he'll leaguer sometime, surely. He won't go on all night.'

'He'll probably leaguer at dusk,' Garven admitted.

'Well, look,' I said, pulling out my map and pointing, 'if we cut across the dunes we should walk into him about there.'

Garven nodded his agreement and we set off, plunging through the dunes, back the way we had come. . . .

We stumbled through the scorching dunes . . . up one slope . . . down the next . . . mile after mile, panting and puffing, longing to sit down for a rest, but urging our aching legs with the thought that it was better to half-kill ourselves for twenty miles than to take it easy for 150; we could rest in Henry's trucks. The hot wind seared our gasping lungs, sand swirled about our feet and blew into our eyes. . . .

The sun went down and we plodded on through the creeping waves of violet light, too intent upon catching up with Henry to appreciate the ethereal beauty of the purple banners fluttering from the crests of the dunes.

When darkness cloaked the Erg I stopped to take a compass-bearing, guessing where Henry would leaguer.

'*Min hic*,' I said to Mohammed, cutting the air in the direction

I wanted to go. Mohammed looked up to the heavens, fixed a winking star in line with his shoulder and set off again at a cracking pace, more accurate than any compass.

We plunged after him.

Over one dune . . . across the trough . . . up to the next crest . . . plunging down the dragging sand . . . dune after dune . . . mile after mile . . . hour after hour. . . .

We didn't try to keep in line or in any kind of formation, but just panted on behind the tireless Mohammed, keeping up with him as best we could, hurrying when his dark head disappeared over a crest, slowing thankfully when we saw it down in the next trough. . . . About ten o'clock the dunes began to thin out. We came to the last straggling outriders and felt scrub scratching against our ankles.

'Henry should be somewhere near here,' I panted to Garven.

Mohammed halted and knelt down to peer against the skyline. I went close to him and saw only the dark outline of bushes . . . and then darker, square outlines when my eyes became properly focused.

'Trucks?' I breathed.

Mohammed nodded. '*Aywah.*'

I touched Garven's sleeve and pointed.

'Henry,' I chuckled. 'Bloody good guess.'

We walked through the low bushes towards the leaguered trucks. . . . A rifle-bolt clicked in the darkness.

'Don't shoot,' I called, 'Popski.'

Dark figures moved amongst the bushes and a surprised voice exclaimed:

'What the hell——?'

'Is this Henry's patrol?' I called out.

More dark figures moved.

'Yes,' said Henry, 'who are you?'

'Bob Yunnie, and Garven from Tinker's patrol.'

A safety-catch clicked.

'Where's Popski and Tinker?' Henry asked when we walked into his leaguer and shook hands.

'Let me get my breath and I'll tell you the story,' I said. 'We saw you on the other side of the Erg twelve hours ago and shouted ourselves hoarse. We've been running after you ever since.'

Henry took us under his wing and fed us. We rode on the back

55

of his trucks. It was a wonderful feeling just to lie and be jolted towards Tozeur without having to use your legs.

'Better than walking, eh, Mohammed?' I chuckled as we rode along.

Mohammed grinned broadly and smoothed his silky moustache. '*Aywah.*'

Two days later, crossing the dried salt-pan of the Shott Jerid, we saw a patrol of jeeps approaching. It was Jan Caneri coming to look for us.

'Hallo, Jan,' I called when he came alongside, 'where's Popski?'

' 'E's in Tozeur. We picked them all up.'

I thanked Henry for the lift and transferred to Jan's jeeps.

'What happened?' I asked as we raced across the hard white pan.

Whipped by the wind, Jan's story came in snatches.

'We left Ksar Rhilane at 0200 hours . . . helluva journey in the dark . . . got into Tozeur the following night . . . no wireless link . . . had to drive all through the night to Tabessa and then to Laverdure . . . sleeping at the wheel . . . got jeeps from the Yanks in Tabessa . . . picked up Popski and his party near . . . the Shott.'

'Damned good show,' I shouted above the wind.

'What happened to you?' Jan shouted back.

'Sat in the dunes for five days and drank tea . . . crossed the dunes and walked into Henry's leaguer.'

'Pough. . . .'

We left the white, frost-like surface of the shott for a smooth tarmac road and zoomed into Tozeur at sixty miles an hour. Jan drew up with a flourish before the ornate entrance of the luxurious Hotel Transatlantique set amongst waving green palm-trees and a garden of flowers with tinkling water fountains. Is this real or mirage? I wondered, after five days in the dunes of the Erg.

'Who's that?' I asked, drawing Jan's attention to the smartly dressed officer who came to the entrance. . . . 'Good God, it's Popski. . . .'

I barely recognized my own commanding officer. He was transformed. He'd shaved off his grey-black beard and discarded his New Zealander's hat. He was dressed in yellow-ochre suède

56

desert boots, cream corduroy slacks, well-pressed khaki drill tunic with epaulettes and ribbons.

'You look very prosperous, Popski,' I greeted him.

He smiled and we shook hands.

'Have a good trip, Bob?'

'Yes, thanks.'

But it wasn't the same. There was a strained atmosphere between us and months elapsed before it wore off. For a long time I had the feeling that Popski held the loss of the convoy against me.

'Extraordinary story,' exclaimed the war correspondent. 'Popski's Private Army . . . and you've come all the way from Cairo in jeeps . . . had a battle with the Germans behind the Mareth Line . . . destroyed twenty German aircraft . . . five tanks . . . and you fought your way out alone and saved the jeeps . . . .'

'All part of a day's work in P.P.A.,' said Corporal Locke modestly, adjusting his piratical eye-patch.

The correspondent wrote furiously. . . .

4

OUR position was somewhat irregular. We were Eighth Army troops operating in First Army administrative area. According to the rules, the unit should have returned to Cairo for a refit, but we knew what that meant—the end of the war for P.P.A. Popski solved the problem by attaching us to the Americans in Tabessa.

We drove to Tabessa in Caneri's borrowed jeeps. Dressed for the desert in khaki shorts we froze going north to Tabessa in the icy wind blowing down from the snow-bound Atlas Mountains. There was snow and mud in Tabessa. Snow! We hadn't seen snow for years.

The first Eighth Army patrol to link up with the Americans, we were made much of. Colonel Myres, their warm-hearted quartermaster, took us under his paternal wing and equipped us American Army style with warm winter vests, woollen shirts, gaberdine trousers, pullovers, windproof jackets, thick woollen socks, brown leather boots—and gloves! We retained our black berets with the little silver astrolabe badge and looked quite cosmopolitan.

The Americans fed us like kings, initiating us into the mysteries of spam, peanut-butter, pineapple juice. After three years on bully beef and biscuits it all seemed like a miracle. Sergeant Waterson went to draw rations for P.P.A. and stood hypnotized while a sack of flour, a bag of sugar, a side of bacon, half a cartwheel cheese, tins of coffee, spam, peanut-butter, peaches, tomato and pineapple juice, chewing gum and cartons of choice Philip Morris cigarettes were loaded on to his jeep. A British Army regular, Waterson had never seen anything like it, even in peace-time. In the warm barn off the main street where our men were billeted he showed me the rich haul.

'Look at this, sir,' he said in an awed voice, going over the rations item by item, 'a whole mucking side of bacon . . . a *sack* of flour . . . a *bag* of sugar . . . half a mucking cheese . . . *pineapple* juice, bloody tins of it . . . chewing gum . . . and look at the fags, sir, *cartons* of 'em. . . .'

Nor did the American generosity stop there. We took our desert-battered jeeps into 2nd Corps' magnificently equipped workshops ('Bloody factories on wheels') and Captain Montgomery (no relation), casting a critical eye over them, drawled: 'Say, Cap'n, these here jeeps are sure worn out. You need nu ones.'

Within a few days we were driving about Tabessa in brand-new jeeps altered to our desert specification and mounted with quick-firing American Browning machine-guns.

We felt we must do something to show our appreciation. In different jeeps on different days Popski and I drove to the British Army NAAFI in Constantine. Popski drew a case of whisky for O.C. Popski's Private Army. A day later I drew two cases for O.C. No. 1 Demolition Squadron, Middle East. Back in Tabessa, after dark, we went visiting our American friends with bottles of Scotch stuck in the pockets of our windproof jackets. The American Army in North Africa was no longer dry!

Popski, Jan Caneri and I were billeted in a villa in the town. At 0300 hours one dark and stormy morning I felt a rough hand on my shoulder.

'Get six jeeps ready to move at 0500 hours,' Popski barked, 'German tanks are attacking at Kasserine.'

I leapt out of bed and pulled on clothing. Outside, it was pouring rain, mud and slush and a biting wind, ugh! I slithered down to the barn and shook Waterson's blanketed shoulder.

'Wasamarrer?'

'Wake up, Sarge. There's a flap on. Jerry's attacking at Kasserine. Get six jeeps ready to move at once.'

Waterson was wide awake before I had finished speaking. He threw off his blankets and jumped up, strode round the barn bellowing in his parade-ground voice: 'Wakey, wakeey. Flap on. Wakey, wakeey.'

'Full loads, Sarge,' I said. 'Five days' rations, spare petrol-cans, ammo and mines. Send Popski's jeep round at once.'

While the men were rousing and loading jeeps I dashed back to the villa. Popski and Jan were conversing in French.

'Your jeep'll be round in a minute, Popski,' I announced.

Von Arnim, the German commander in Tunisia, had suddenly counter-attacked at the Kasserine Pass. If he broke through the narrow gap in the mountains and fanned out, Tabessa would become untenable and the American 2nd Corps would be forced to retreat. In his perusal of intelligence reports at Corps H.Q. Popski had foreseen this possibility and had been studying maps of the area. The enemy was using the Gafsa–Feriana road below Kasserine, massing tanks for a break-through; by making a wide detour across country we could come in on the flank and mine the road, do something to hold up the advance.

Popski's jeep skidded to a standstill outside the door. Popski hurried out to it through the drenching rain, got in and drove to Corps Headquarters where a harassed American general gave him the latest situation report. Popski was back at the villa within the hour and we set off immediately on the worst journey I ever made in P.P.A. This time Jan Caneri stayed behind.

Our route lay through rough, scrub-covered country. Passing through the British First Army outpost at Bir el Atar in lashing rain we commenced the thirty-mile cross-country drive to the enemy-held Gafsa–Feriana–Kasserine road.

Dampness was everywhere. The sky was filled with heavy dark clouds and it rained incessantly. In our open jeeps without wind-screens there was no protection from the elements and we were soon waterlogged. Rain-water ran down our necks and collected in pools on our seats. An icy wind blew. Fingers became numb and feet felt like blocks of ice as we lurched and bumped at a snail's pace over the cruel terrain. The surface was covered with tough prickly scrub which hid runnels and ditches, great cracks and fissures which banged and bellied the jeeps. Never able to rise above low-booster gear we crawled jerkily through the sodden dawn at three miserable miles an hour, inwardly cursing our fate. Every few hundred yards one or other of the heavily loaded jeeps bellied and we had to stop to push and heave it out of the mud.

'This is bloody silly,' groused Driver Davies, crawling from under his anchored jeep, soaked to the skin and covered in mud.

'The old man's mad,' muttered Fitter Welsh through chattering teeth. 'You can't take jeeps through this.'

'The things we do for England,' intoned Sapper Curtis, a new recruit we'd picked up in Tabessa.

Water was pouring off the brim of Sergeant Waterson's New Zealand hat. He winked a piercing blue eye and blew drips from his nose.

'Grand weather for ducks, sir.'

Sergeant Waterson was a tonic. Nothing ever depressed him. The more difficult things became the more he seemed to enjoy them.

Davies' jeep was unbellied and we crawled on again only to stop a few minutes later when Popski nose-dived into a deep, scrub-hidden hole. 'Blast,' said Popski irritably.

'Don't worry, sir,' said Waterson cheerily. 'We'll soon have you out.'

Hour after hour we struggled on, cold, wet, miserable and ill-tempered; all but Sergeant Waterson, who chirped to keep up our morale. We halted for a rest in the lee of some bushes and tried to make tea, but the wet, petrol-soaked branches wouldn't burn properly. We compromised by taking a mouthful of whisky instead and lurched on again mile after weary mile.

By late afternoon we were close to the Gafsa–Feriana road, worried about betrayal by unfriendly looking Arabs whose encampment we'd recently passed. Jeeps under cover of dripping bushes, crews crouching beside them out of sight, Popski and I climbed to the crest of a knoll and looked down upon the tarmac road and the single-line railway beside it, and upon the little station of Borj. Through binoculars we saw vehicles parked near the station buildings and soldiers moving about.

'Germans,' I breathed into Popski's ear.

He nodded.

'Stay here and watch, Bob.'

I nodded, keeping my eyes glued on the station.

Popski ducked away and walked back to the jeeps to speak to Waterson. The crews got busy priming road-mines.

A bare ten minutes had passed when, out of the tail of my eye, I saw a party of ragged Arabs hurrying across the bottom of the hillside towards the station.

'The bastards,' I muttered, backing down the knoll and beckoning frantically to Popski.

'Bloody Arabs making for the station,' I cursed when he came up to me. 'We're betrayed again, look.'

We both snaked up to the crest and looked over. The Arabs

had reached the station and were talking to a jack-booted German officer, pointing and gesticulating towards our knoll.

'Damn!' said Popski.

The uniformed figure turned and disappeared into the building.

'Gone to telephone,' I muttered.

'Damn!' said Popski again.

Dusk was falling. It would be dark in half an hour.

'We'll mine the road and get out, Bob.'

'O.K., Popski.'

As we turned to go, a party of soldiers appeared in the station yard and with the gesticulating Arabs started to climb the hill.

'We've been spotted,' Popski informed Waterson. 'Get the road mined quickly.'

The news was received quietly, matter-of-factly. There was no panic amongst the men, but joking ceased and faces grew serious.

In the gathering dusk we drove towards the road, bumping over the uneven ground. Fifty yards from the tarmac we ran on to a wide, unmetalled by-pass rutted by tank tracks. We stopped to examine the reddish, patterned mud.

'Recent, sir,' opined Waterson.

The Germans were obviously using the by-pass for tanks—to save wear and tear of tracks on the hard, tarmac surface.

'This is the place to mine,' Popski said.

We faced the jeeps the other way ready for a quick exit, and proceeded to mine the by-pass.

It was an easy matter to bury mines in the soft, churned-up mud. One thrust with the machete . . . another to deepen and shape the hole . . . lay the mine gently . . . scrape mud over it carefully . . . and the job was done. Working methodically in jeep-crew pairs (one digging, the other laying) we soon laid thirty-six mines along a 300-yards' stretch of by-pass towards Kasserine.

The last mine laid, Popski loud-whispered: 'Right. Off we go.' And Sapper Curtis clambering into his jeep had just chortled *sotto voce*, 'That'll fix the bastards,' when Sergeant Waterson gave a sudden warning cry.

'Look out, sir! Behind you.'

Waterson's new American Browning fifty-calibre clattered in the darkness and tracer streaked past my head in vicious red darts.

'What the hell?' I gasped, and looked round.

What I saw was the dark outline of a German armoured car .. and another one creeping up behind it. . . .

Brrrrrrt. . . . Brrrrrrt. Tracer spat from Waterson's gun and curved into the nearest armoured car in fiery red jets . . . jeep engines revved . . . gears crashed desperately. 'Christ!'

The leading armoured car burst into flames.

'Got the bastard!' Waterson yelled triumphantly. He had swung his gun round and was sitting, precariously balanced, on the dancing bonnet of his jeep, firing tracer-aimed bursts past his ducking driver's ear and punctuating them with: 'Take that, ye bastard' . . . Brrrrrt . . . 'and that' . . . Brrrrrrt . . . 'and that' . . . and giving forth a loud 'Woowho' Red Indian whoop every time he registered a hit. He was thoroughly enjoying himself.

The burning armoured car held up the others (there were three of them) and gave us our chance to escape. Flashing scarlet streamers filled the air, criss-crossing in the darkness like a firework display. We didn't attempt to set a course or even look where we were going, but just drove madly westwards away from the death-dealing armoured cars . . . bouncing over hummocks . . . thudding across hidden runnels and ditches . . . crashing through prickly thorn bushes . . . firing wildly over the backs of our prancing jeeps. . . .

Edging past the burning hulk of the leading armoured car the remainder of the troop gave chase, pumping tracer after our rapidly retreating forms; but their lumbering bulk was no match for our fast little jeeps on that dark, broken ground and the distance between us lengthened. The armoured car crews could scarcely have seen our low-slung jeeps in the deepening gloom, but only the flashes of tracer spouting from our bouncing guns.

The armoured cars fell further and further behind. . . . Brrrrrrt. . . . Brrrrrt. . . . Brrrrrrt . . . scarlet streamers streaked the dark sky . . . the jeeps crashed through the malevolent undergrowth . . . racing in top booster gear.

'Muck it!' screamed Curtis as he nose-dived into a deep hole seen a fraction too late. He and his driver jumped clear as the jeep crumpled and overturned.

We all stopped . . . the armoured cars closed up . . . tracer thrashed the air above our heads.

'No time to salvage it, Curtis,' Popski grunted. 'Take the guns and set fire to it. Quickly.'

Helping hands tugged the Browning guns from their mounts and dumped them into other jeeps while Curtis banged the top of an incendiary bomb and stuck it close to the petrol tank of the crashed jeep.

'Sorry, sir,' he apologized to Popski.

The armoured cars closed up . . . tracer hissed dangerously near . . . jeep engines revved. Curtis laid a hand on a moving jeep and leapt aboard; his driver jumped on to the back of another. Brrrrrt. . . . Brrrrrrt . . . tracer spat back at the armoured cars, streaming over the tails of the flying jeeps.

Bucking like broncos at a rodeo we topped a dark rise . . . crashed blindly through a line of low bushes . . . thudded down a black hillside . . . and saw the sky light up behind us as Curtis' abandoned jeep exploded and took fire . . . heard the armoured cars stop and give up the chase.

'Whew!' Curtis breathed from the back of Locke's jeep when the mad rush was over and we were picking our way carefully. 'That was a mucking close shave. . . . Pity about the jeep, though,' he added in a worried tone. 'I suppose the old man'll sack me.'

'Gosh, sirr, I wis scairt,' Bill Wilson secretly admitted.

'Don't worry, Bill,' I reassured him. 'So was I.'

'Got the bastard first shot,' a gleeful voice floated back from Waterson's shadowy jeep.

'How many armoured cars were there, Sarge?' a quavering voice asked.

We drove on through the wet, drizzling, pitch-black night, jolting and lurching and creaking over the vile terrain. Our front wheels dropped into gaping pot-holes, thorn bushes tore at the sides of the jeeps and branches smacked in our faces, mud squelched ominously under the chassis as we ploughed through morass. Visibility wasn't five yards and we strained our eyes trying to keep one another's dark shadow in sight.

Black shapes loomed ahead . . . shrill voices cackled . . . dogs barked . . . ghostly figures appeared beside our jeeps.

'Bloody Arab encampment,' somebody muttered. 'Give 'em a burst.'

The temptation was too great; after all, they'd betrayed us twice.

64

'Over their heads, Bill,' I whispered.

Brrrrrt. . . . Brrrrrrt. A stream of tracer cut a flashing red path through the darkness and the night was filled with a pandemonium of shouts and screams. Brrrrrt. . . . Brrrrrrrt. Other jeeps opened up. More tracer flashed in the sky. . . . Brrrrrt . . . brrrrrt.

Popski switched on his headlamps.

Wild, ragged, half-human, staring-eyed creatures scuttled in the searching beams, running in all directions. Black tents were all about us. We'd driven into the heart of an Arab encampment.

One after another the jeep crews switched on lights. Popski swerved and we followed him between a line of dirty, flapping tents . . . children whimpered . . . dogs snapped and yapped . . . men shouted . . . women screamed. . . . Brrrrrt. . . . Brrrrrt . . . tracer sailed colourfully over the tent-tops. . . . '*Ayeeeeee*,' shrieked the enraged Arabs.

A half-starved, wolf-like dog with gleaming eyes leapt at Waterson's jeep. Waterson had a rubber truncheon handy and as the dog came at him with snarling, snapping fangs he hit it a smart blow on its sensitive, pointed snout. The dog howled in pain and slunk off . . . a black-faced, wild-eyed Arab brandished a stick. . . . Brrrrrt . . . the Arab ran into the night.

'No more firing,' Popski shouted.

The encampment disappeared behind us, the shrill voices faded, dogs no longer barked. We kept our lights on and found the going easier, being able to avoid pot-holes and bushes, but after a while, hearing the rumble of tanks in the distance, Popski decided it was too risky and we reverted to black-out, driving blindly for a while until our eyes became accustomed to the dark again.

Lurch . . . side-slip . . . creak . . . thud . . . sccccccccrsh. Hour after hour we thrust westwards, scratched and torn by the thorn bushes which clawed at us out of the night, crashing into holes and hollows, sinking deeply into patches of evil-smelling bog, bouncing over tufts and stones and hummocks. We were tired now and longed to put our heads down, anything to break the torment of the continuous jolting and tossing, but Bir el Atar was still twenty long miles away and we had no wish to be strafed by enemy aircraft at dawn. There was no alternative but to drive on and on and on, mile after agonizing mile . . . talking ceased . . . heads nodded with fatigue and lack of sleep . . . the swaying crews barely kept awake. . . .

About 3 a.m. we dipped into a wadi and Popski halted for a short rest. Silently, we blessed him.

Popski got out of his jeep and shook Waterson's hand. 'Thank you, Waterson,' he said, 'your quick action saved us. Have a drink.'

The whisky bottle was passed round and we all drank Waterson's health.

'Cheers, Sarge.'

'Good old Sarge.'

'Up the K.D.G.s.'

'To Waterson, God bless 'im.'

And so on until we'd all toasted him.

'Right,' said Popski, clambering into his jeep. 'On we go.'

Some of the crews changed drivers and the column thrust on again.

'On, Stanley, on,' quoth Curtis as Locke's jeep lurched across the stony wadi bed and climbed the other side.

Dawn was breaking as we drove into the Derbyshire Yeomanry's outpost at Bir el Atar, an outpost alerted and apprehensive, having heard machine-gun fire and seen flashing lights. We reassured the commander, breakfasted in the drizzle and returned to Tabessa wet and muddy, yawning our heads off.

We found our American friends relaxed and smiling. The attack had been held, or rather it had dissolved, Von Arnim's tanks having suddenly withdrawn during the night. (They were switched to stem Eighth Army pressure at Mareth and it was the rumble of their movement we heard as we made our way back to Bir el Atar.) Our men made the most of the coincidence.

'Look, chum, use your loaf,' they said to the raw American G.I.s gathered round the bullet-scarred, mud-encrusted jeeps. 'Jerry attacks at Kasserine. P.P.A. attacks on the flank. Jerry withdraws. Well, I mean . . .' They broke off and shrugged meaningly, leaving it to their goggle-eyed, gum-chewing audience to draw its own conclusions.

Thus, half true, half exaggerated, our reputation grew.

5

Eighth Army pushed hard at Mareth and the Americans reoccupied Gafsa. Tabessa became a backwater and Popski's Private Army, like migrating swallows, joyfully returned to the sunny south.

A curious situation had arisen at Gafsa affording a heaven-sent opportunity for the unorthodox use of jeeps. A long, serrated, rocky ridge, 2000 feet high, crawls like a snake from sandy, date-palmed Gafsa across the Tunisian plain towards the sea at Sfax forming two fertile valleys patterned by green olive and almond groves, waving yellow cornfields and white-walled, red-roofed homesteads sweltering under a sky of deepest blue.

The American 2nd Corps had pushed a column along the northern valley as far as Maknassy where they were held by the enemy within a bulwark of retaining hills. The enemy controlled the southern valley as far west as El Qettar, a town on the other side of the ridge near Gafsa, so that the high ridge formed a natural defensive salient with the Americans on one side and the Germans and Italians on the other.

Popski had gone to First Army Headquarters in Laverdure, Jan Caneri was at P.P.A. H.Q. in Gafsa, and I was sitting with a patrol of jeeps on a green hillside watching a battery of American field artillery pumping screaming shells into the small Arab village of Sened, tucked into the base of the ridge half-way between Gafsa and Maknassy, where a garrison of chicken-hearted Italians was marooned.

A white flag fluttered pathetically and the shelling stopped.

'Come on, Sarge,' I said to Waterson, 'let's get in first. There may be some loot.'

We crossed the dusty main road and rattled along the track to Sened. The way was tortuous, with many bends, and it narrowed to a bottle-neck on the outskirts of the village. I turned a sharp corner and saw a vaguely familiar sand-coloured truck jammed against the verge.

'Muckin' 'ell!' I heard Waterson exclaim from the jeep immediately behind me. 'That's the L.R.D.G. truck we lost in Wadi Zemzem. Stop, sir.' But I had already stopped.

'By God, Sarge, this is a find,' I cried. 'Popski'll be tickled pink.'

The remaining jeeps crowded to a halt and we all jumped out to examine the prize. Welsh clambered into the driving-seat and ground at the self-starter. The engine refused to start. Lifting the bonnet, Welsh fiddled expertly with distributor, coil, points, carburettor, plugs, battery terminals, but couldn't persuade the engine to change its mind.

'We'll tow it,' I said to Waterson.

We heard footsteps and looked up. A party of Italian soldiers headed by an officer appeared on the track. They held their hands high above their heads when they saw us. 'To hell with Italian prisoners,' I muttered. 'This truck's more important.'

I waved the party on and pointed down the track.

'*Americani,*' I shouted. '*Avanti.*'

The Italians burst into song and ran past us, glad to be out of the war.

While Waterson was fixing the tow-rope I had an idea there might be something else in the village.

'Wait till I come back, Sarge. I'll go up to the village and have a shufty.'

The track narrowed to the width of a footpath and Bill Wilson found difficulty in driving into the village, but the effort was repaid by the sight of a little Fiat staff-car tucked into an alleyway.

'Hold it, Bill,' I called out and jumped into the dusty main street. I squeezed into the Fiat and pressed the self-starter. To my great surprise the engine purred sweetly. I engaged reverse and backed jerkily out of the alley. A broad grin split Bill Wilson's face.

'Take the jeep down, Bill,' I called. 'I'll go down in this.'

The little green Fiat went like a bird and I was back at the stranded L.R.D.G. Chevrolet long before Wilson in his wider jeep.

'Good God!' Waterson exclaimed when he saw me. 'A mucking staff-car. Ha, ha, ha.'

68

I saw a file of American infantry coming up the track.

'Ready? Let's get out before any questions are asked.'

I led off down the winding track in my little staff-car followed by Waterson's jeep towing the L.R.D.G. truck with Welsh at the wheel and the remaining jeeps behind him.

The American lieutenant was about to stop me when I distracted his attention by pointing wildly over my shoulder in the direction of Sened and putting on speed. . . .

Our strange procession passed on. The American infantry looked grim, cocked their rifles at the ready and went manfully into the empty village.

Back in our shady villa in Gafsa I said to Jan Caneri:

'How much will you give me for a staff-car and a 30-cwt. truck?'

He looked at me, puzzled.

'What d'you mean, Bob?'

'Come outside and see.'

I took him to the vehicle-park at the rear of the villa and proudly displayed my wares.

'Captured from the enemy,' I lied.

'It's an L.R.D.G. truck, Bob.'

'Quite.'

'Where did you get it?'

'At the Battle of Sened.'

Jan looked at me and smiled.

'Come off it, Bob.'

I laughed and told him the truth.

Later, Jock Welsh enticed the engine to start and we went for a run in the cool of the evening. The chassis was a bit rattly but the motor ran perfectly.

'Quite like old days, eh, Jan?' I laughed as we zoomed along. But Jan Caneri wasn't thinking of the old days. His practical brain was more concerned with present-day possibilities.

'I'll get an American six-wheeler for this, Bob.' I looked at him. His eyes twinkled behind his glasses.

Early the next morning Caneri and Welsh took the road for Tabessa. They were back two days later—driving a brand-new Chevrolet six-wheeled covered-in supply truck.

'How on earth did you manage it, Jan?' I asked.

'Simple arithmetic, Bob.' He smiled enigmatically. 'One 30-cwt. truck plus one case of whisky equals one Chevrolet six-wheeler.'

'You're a genius,' I said, regarding him with frank admiration. P.P.A. had to live by its wits in those days.

'The ridge, Bob,' said Popski when he returned from Laverdure in one of his tearing hurries. 'I want it recced from end to end. We must find a way through.'

In rock-climbing parties of two and three we scaled the ridge in the sweltering sun and looked down upon the heat-filled southern valley. Two roads wound through its Lilliputian olive groves towards frustrating El Qettar, and we sat for a day watching the writhing dust-wakes of enemy transport moving along the ochre ribbons. Eastwards, the valley widened and merged into the blue heat-haze of the flat Tunisian plain across which unseen German convoys rumbled to and from the Mareth Line.

For some extraordinary reason the enemy didn't trouble to guard the ridge. They hadn't a sentry or a look-out anywhere and our rock-rambling reconnaissance was completely unmolested. Waterson and I explored the section above Sened and followed a well-trodden goat-track which led us through an awesome cleft between the high black rocks of the summit. The cleft was jammed with boulders and fallen rocks, but when we scrambled over them we found ourselves on a narrow ledge which widened as we walked along it and gradually became a jeepable track descending steep scree slopes into the valley. Waterson and I looked at one another, the same thought in mind.

'If we cleared those boulders away, Sarge . . . '

'We could just about make it, sir, if . . .'

The ledge was terribly narrow, just wide enough for a jeep but no more, and there was a hideous drop into a ravine on the right-hand side. I visualized the jeeps crawling along that fearsome ledge, saw one of them edge just a little too far over. . . . I shuddered and thought of something else.

'It's risky, sir,' said Waterson as we walked back.

'Bloody risky, Sarge, but we'll make it. Let's go back and talk to Popski.'

Popski came with us to inspect the ledge. He regarded it with practised eyes and let his gaze travel further afield, to the heat-

70

hazed plain where the German convoys ran towards Mareth—a tempting target.

'How long will it take you to clear those boulders, Bob?'

I glanced at Sergeant Waterson.

'A day? Two days?'

'We could do it in a day if we worked hard, sir.'

'Right,' said Popski. 'Twenty-four hours to clear and widen the track. Get cracking.'

We worked like galley slaves the whole of the next day, heaving boulders, shovelling scree, pick-axing the rock walls of the ledge to make it as safe as possible.

'Wooah!' mimicked Curtis in a frightened voice, imitating a jeep driver going dangerously near the edge.

'Christ!' muttered Driver Davies when he saw the ledge. 'We're not taking jeeps along here, are we?'

'Jesus!' exclaimed Fitter Welsh when he saw the drop.

By six o'clock the track was ready. Bill Wilson drove a jeep very gingerly along the ledge in the dusk, guided by Waterson, went down the steep scree slope, turned and came back.

'What's it like, Bill?' the drivers asked.

'O.K. if you keep close in.'

Popski had spent the day at Corps Headquarters studying the latest situation reports and had moved P.P.A. into a convenient almond grove at the foot of the ridge.

'The track's all yours, Popski,' I informed him at eight o'clock that evening. 'We've had a jeep along the ledge and back. It's O.K.'

Popski looked at me in the soft moonlight, a smile playing about his lips.

'Feel like a moonlight Cook's tour, Bob?'

'You mean through the pass?'

He nodded.

'O.K., Popski,' I said delightedly. 'But let me get something to eat first. I'm famished.'

'You and Waterson have a meal, Bob. We'll leave in an hour's time.'

Two hours later Popski, Sergeant Waterson and I in three jeeps were crawling along the goat-track high up on the moonlit ridge with Jock Cameron, Popski's new driver, walking in front. We crept stealthily between the fierce black rocks of the cleft, feeling suspended between heaven and earth, and moved gingerly along the fearsome ledge hugging the left-hand wall and averting our eyes from the yawning chasm whose awful nakedness was mercifully clothed in dark shadow . . . slithered down the steep scree slopes . . . splashed through a shallow stream . . . lurched along a rough pathway . . . downhill . . . downhill . . . to a well-defined track. The valley was softly mysterious in silver light and the scent of almond trees wafted with the gentle breeze. As we approached the dark trees of an olive grove a dog barked and Popski's jeep halted. Waterson and I braked behind him and sat with bated breath. . . . Popski's jeep moved on again and we followed, toe pressing lightly on the accelerator.

A shuttered homestead appeared in a clearing and the dog barked again. We halted in the shadows and Sergeant Waterson stalked towards the moonlit walls, gripping a Tommy-gun. The dog growled. Waterson murmured soothing doggy words. The growling ceased and a tail wagged. The household slept or the house was empty for no one appeared. Waterson patted the dog's head and returned to the jeeps.

'O.K., sir,' he whispered to Popski.

The track led us through miles of silent, shadowy olive groves. In top gear, going slightly downhill all the way, with engines just ticking over we made hardly a sound, slipping through the groves like the shadows of the trees themselves.

As we approached the first of the two roads Popski drew up in the shadow of an olive tree and switched off his engine. Waterson and I each selected a tree and switched off.

A hundred yards away lay the road. We padded up to it and stood in the moonlight examining the wheel-tracks clearly patterned in the thick dust. Above the distant rumble of the guns at Mareth we heard the sound of an approaching truck.

'Under the trees,' Popski whispered.

We each stood behind an olive tree and watched a covered supply wagon rumble past towards El Qettar, feeling its dust tickling our nostrils and willing ourselves not to sneeze. Waterson fought manfully with finger pressed on upper lip but was unable to prevent the escape of a smothered 'Tisshoo' fortunately blanketed by the noise of the passing truck.

The dust settled and the rumble of the wheels faded into the night. We stood for a time listening intently, hearing our own heartbeats, but nothing else seemed to be coming and Popski whispered:

'Right. Back to the jeeps. We'll go a bit further.'

Ten yards apart, we drove along the dusty enemy L. of C. in the moonlight. I kept pinching myself to make sure I wasn't dreaming and thought inconsequently of my father retired in far-away Cape Town, wondering what he would think if he knew what his only son was doing at that particular moment. I glanced sideways at Bill Wilson. His face was grim and taut, his body unnaturally rigid.

'Relax, Bill,' I whispered.

A deep sigh escaped him. 'Gosh, sirr. . . .' He breathed and relaxed a little.

Popski drove on and on. It was only a couple of miles but seemed much further.

'Where the hell's he going?' I muttered under my breath. 'Mareth?'

I saw Waterson put up a hand. His jeep slowed and I braked. Popski swung into a side-track and we followed, choking in his dust.

We came to the second road on the far side of the valley and drew up in the shadows of an almond grove; again we bent to examine patterned wheel-tracks in the moonlit dust; again we heard the rumble of an approaching enemy vehicle and stood in the shadows with bated breath watching it go past. 'This is tempting fate too far,' I thought. 'We'll get nabbed if we don't watch out.'

But Popski had made up his mind to have a good look round and off he drove down the second main road as soon as the truck was past, with Waterson and I tailing him, quaking in our seats.

It seemed that Popski was heading straight for the Tunisian plain and I began to feel jittery. 'This is really asking for trouble,' I thought. But a mile or so down the road we swung into another side-track and headed back towards the first road. 'Thank God,' I breathed, and felt better . . . but only for a moment.

When we reached the road junction Popski turned *right* and drove towards the plain again. 'Hell's teeth,' I groaned as I followed Waterson's jeep into the main road, 'he'll have us all in the bag.'

But nothing went wrong. It seemed that everything was specially arranged for the occasion. The two main roads remained empty of enemy traffic whilst we were on them. Supply trucks conveniently passed when we were hidden in side-tracks. There were no road blocks and we didn't run into any sentries. Had I not done it myself, I wouldn't have believed the thing was possible.

At three o'clock in the morning when the moon had gone to bed, having led us on a criss-cross treasure hunt all over the southern valley, Popski headed for home; and when a hurrying enemy despatch rider whizzed past towards El Qettar a few minutes after we had turned into the security of our mountain-track I said to myself, 'The Gods are smiling on Popski tonight.'

Relaxed and at peace, hugging myself with delight, I followed Waterson's shadowy tail through the olive groves. What an incredible adventure! Who would have thought we could have driven unmolested all over the enemy L. of C. like that? Certainly not I.

'What a night!' I chuckled to Bill Wilson.

'Gosh, sirr, what a man!' referring to Popski.

Not a thing went wrong that night. Even Waterson's dog was waiting for him at the shuttered homestead and wagged his tail and jumped beside the jeep with delight as he passed. . . .

The pass was heavily dark. Cameron jumped from Popski's jeep and walked backwards along the ledge, guiding the jeeps safely through the cleft. . . .

'Right, Bob,' said Popski as we drove into the almond grove. 'We'll take a patrol through tonight and do some damage. A very pleasant trip. Good night.'

Waterson and I crossed ourselves and made for our respective almond trees.

Six jeeps went through the pass the following night, three of them boldly, three of them a trifle nervously . . . along the narrow ledge . . . down the steep scree . . . across the shallow stream . . . downhill . . . downhill to a barking, welcoming dog . . . through the moonlit olive groves like shadows chasing one another . . . up to the first main road.

'Follow me and do exactly as I do,' said Popski. 'No talking.'

Follow-my-leader in line astern we tailed Popski down the

main road towards the plain, six ghostly jeeps gliding almost silently over the soft road surface. We had no idea where he was going, but we all had complete faith in him.

Popski didn't turn into the first side-track as he had done the previous night, but carried straight on, doing a steady twenty miles an hour. In the last jeep my thoughts were with Popski in the leading one, trying to visualize what was formulating in his mind, trying to anticipate what he was likely to do. What would he do if we ran into a convoy or a single truck? What would I do in such circumstances? If a sentry challenged would Popski stop or drive straight on? I gave up speculating and kept my eyes on the dusty tail of the jeep in front. . . .

Popski drove steadily on. He had spent the day poring over his maps and knew exactly where he was going—the main German L. of C. between Tunis and the Mareth Line. . . .

Olive groves, almond groves, fruit orchards, cornfields, homesteads slipped past our flanks, shadowy and mysterious in the transforming moonlight. I saw a uniformed figure walk round the side of a house and enter a door as we swished past . . . a minute later my mind registered: 'Good God, that was a German soldier. He must have seen us go past.' I glanced back, expecting a rifle-shot, but the house was out of sight behind an almond grove. In those inexperienced early days, full of fears and apprehension, I failed to realize that when a German soldier saw a convoy of blacked-out vehicles passing along the road at night he naturally assumed it was his own troops and thought nothing of it.

Presently we left the main road and choked in one another's dust through a labyrinth of country lanes, going steadily eastwards. The high, sheltering, comforting ridge (its other side spelt safety) fell behind us. We were out in the open plain with the enemy all around us, sitting or sleeping in homesteads, leaguered in olive or almond grove, bedded down for the night, unaware of our presence in his midst. If the enemy knew . . . I fought down a rising panic. . . . Popski knew what he was doing . . . we would be all right.

The jeep in front of me slowed. I braked and heard the rumble of moving vehicles. I saw a torch flashing beside trees. A voice shouted something in German. My stomach turned over.

Popski swung off the road into an almond grove. We followed, bumping over a ditch, and dispersed under individual trees. Three hundred yards away, on the other side of the road, a German convoy was pulling into leaguer for the night.

Waterson stood by my jeep. 'Popski wants you, sir,' he breathed.

I tip-toed to Popski's jeep.

'Yes, Popski?'

'We'll shoot up this convoy, Bob. Pull out when I give the signal. Lay mines behind you as you go. Take Curtis on the back of your jeep.'

'O.K., Popski.'

The heavily loaded German supply trucks lurched over the ditch on the far side of the road and crashed into the olive grove, breaking the branches. Torches flashed and voices were raised.

I padded across to Curtis' jeep. He was three up with Porter (another new recruit) and Robinson. 'Come on my jeep, Curtis,' I whispered. 'We've got to lay mines on the way out.'

Curtis jumped from his jeep with a whispered 'O.K., sir,' and followed me through the trees. We passed a jubilant Sergeant Waterson going from jeep to jeep giving the crews Popski's orders.

The fantastic quality of the situation suddenly struck me. Here we were, a British patrol, sitting 300 yards from a German convoy on their own L. of C., quietly making plans to machine-gun them into kingdom come and they thinking of food and sleep blissfully unaware of our close presence. Was I dreaming?

Popski's self-starter rasped and his jeep moved forward through the trees . . . one by one the jeeps started up and followed him, each jeep taking up a position giving a clear field of fire until six long, black-barrelled Brownings were pointing across the ditch at the shadowy bulks of the German supply trucks dispersed in the opposite olive grove. . . .

Brrrrrrrrt. Popski jabbed the firing-button of his fifty and a long stream of scarlet tracer zipped through the branches and disappeared into the olive grove. Brrrrrrrrt. . . . Brrrrrrrt. . . . Brrrrrrrt. . . . Brrrrrrrt. . . . Brrrrrrrrrt. The remaining jeeps opened up and a searching, searing, annihilating stream of death poured across the road. . . . Brrrrrrt. . . . Brrrrrt. . . . Brrrrrrrt. . . . Flames appeared in the olive grove. . . . Hoarse shouts arose and shadowy figures moved in the light of the leaping flames. . . . Brrrrrrt. . . . Brrrrrrt. . . . Brrrrrrt. . . . Truck after truck took fire. Black smoke curled upwards through the crackling branches and the acrid smell of cordite stung our nostrils. . . . Brrrrrrt. . . . Brrrrrrt. . . . Brrrrrrt. . . . Pandemonium reigned in the olive grove as the terrified German transport drivers ran hither and thither trying desperately to escape our thrashing, tearing bullets. . . . Brrrrrrt. . . . Brrrrrrrt. . . . Brrrrrrrt. . . . More trucks bursting into flame. . . . D-r-r-r-r-r-t. . . . D-r-r-r-r-r-r-t . . . the slower chatter of a Spandau sounded above the clatter of our Brownings and we ducked as bullets swept the branches above our heads, dropping leaves. . . . Brrrrrrrrrrrrt. . . . Popski sent a vicious burst across the road . . . his engine revved and I saw his jeep reverse.

'Pull out!' he shouted above the din. His driver wheeled and the jeep disappeared amongst the trees.

Brrrrrrrrrt . . . another jeep fired a last burst and reversed, turned and followed Popski.

Brrrrrrrrt . . . another jeep pulling out. . . . Brrrrrrrrrt . . . another. . . . There was only Waterson and I left. Waterson was pumping tracer into the flaming olive grove in joyful, telling bursts, swinging his gun from truck to truck now clearly visible in the blazing leaguer. Brrrrrrrt. . . . Brrrrrrrrt. . . . Brrrrrrt. . . .

'Come on, Sarge,' I shouted.

'O.K., sir. Out you go.' . . . Brrrrrrrt. . . . Brrrrrrrt. . . . D-r-r-r-r-r-r-t. . . . D-r-r-r-r-r-r-t. Bursts of Spandau fire smacked into the trees dangerously near our heads. We ducked and reversed out together. . . . Brrrrrrrrrrrrrrrrrrrrrrrt. Waterson sent a last sustained burst by way of good-bye as his driver swung through the trees. . . .

Locke waited for us at the edge of the grove, to point the way the others had gone. He raced away as soon as he saw we'd seen him. . . . Lurch . . . bump . . . we were over the ditch and away . . . choking in the powdery dust thrown up by the jeep in front.

I braked violently when we'd gone half a mile.

'Mines, Curtis,' I panted. My mouth was dry.

Curtis jumped down and laid a string of mines across the road.

'O.K., sir,' he gasped and clambered aboard.

I revved after Waterson, screaming in low gear, snicking into second gear without taking my foot from the accelerator.

Across the flat Tunisian plain we raced, following Popski along one side-track after another, keeping direction by the dark outline of the ridge. Behind us the sky was lit up by the blazing inferno our guns had created in the olive grove. No one spoke. Drivers gripped their steering-wheels and kept their eyes glued to the tail of the jeep in front. Gunners and spare men looked furtively from side to side, fearing an enemy counter-attack.

The ridge was on our flank now, high and dark and comforting as we tore up the main road towards El Qettar. . . . 'Better lay more mines,' I thought. I braked.

'More mines, Curtis.'

'Got them ready, sir.'

Curtis jumped off and laid another line of mines in the road, hastily kicking dust over them with his boot.

'O.K., sir. Off you go.'

I revved and let in the clutch. Curtis swung aboard as the jeep thrust forward. On again at speed, catching up with Waterson's dust and his cheery backward wave when he saw us . . . some uniformed figures ran down the track from a farmhouse as we raced past. . . .

The ridge was a long pencil of darkness on our flank. . . . I saw Waterson's jeep slow and swing sharply out of sight. We'd reached the entrance to our mountain pass. We were safe. I breathed a sigh of relief, braked and swung into the shadowy olive grove.

'O.K., sir?' Waterson's voice asked.

'O.K., Sarge. On you go. We'll lay some more mines.'

Waterson's jeep disappeared and I called to Curtis.

'Put a line of mines across the mouth of the track, Curtis.'

Curtis got down and started to lay mines in the dusty dip. I heard the noise of vehicles in the distance.

'Hurry, Curtis. We're being followed.'

The rumble of wheels grew louder . . . there was a flash of light in the sky and the reverberation of an explosion . . . the rumble of wheels ceased.

'They've hit our mines, Curtis,' I chuckled. 'Come on.'

Curtis laid his last mine, kicked dust over it and jumped aboard rubbing his hands with glee. We raced through the dark olive grove, barely seeing the track. . . .

Popski and the other four jeeps were waiting for us in the clearing beside the empty, shuttered house. Waterson's dog was there, wagging its tail.

'All right, Bob?' Popski asked.

78

'Yes,' I replied breathlessly. 'We laid three lots of mines. I think a truck went up on one. There was a flash and we heard an explosion.'

'Good. Well done.'

We were jubilant, elated, thrilled with the results of the night's work. Vibrant whispers floated from the jeeps.

'Must have shaken Jerry to the bloody core.'

'Poor bastards, eh? I wonder how many we killed?'

'Must have set fire to at least twenty trucks.'

'Twenty? More like thirty, mate.'

'That was something like.'

Popski revved. . . . Six slinky jeeps crawled up the mountainside . . . splashed through the shallow stream . . . scrunched up the scree . . . nosed their way along the dangerous ledge, hung from the stars . . . disappeared between the black jaws of the cleft . . . reappeared on the other side of the ridge . . . jolted down the stony track to the safety of the moonlit almond grove in the northern valley where Popski said in cultured tones:

'Very satisfactory. Thank you all very much. Good night.'

The jeeps dispersed under their almond trees and for a time the grove hummed with the sound of undertones, like bees swarming in the branches, as the men unrolled their sleeping-bags and settled down for the night.

I was keyed up and couldn't sleep. I lay in my sleeping-bag looking up at the winking stars. What an experience! No casualties. Not a scratch! Three hours ago I'd been pumping tracer into a German leaguer on the other side of the ridge and now here I was lying safe and sound in my sleeping-bag. . . . What an incredible man Popski was. . . . How lucky I was to have met him. . . . Was it chance or did Fate guide you to meet people? . . . Popski's Private Army. . . . Kufra. . . . Zella . . . the sand-dunes of the Grand Erg. . . . Tozeur . . . fast little jeeps . . . bags of sugar . . . lay more mines, Curtis. . . . My thoughts became incoherent and I drifted off to sleep.

'Post a look-out on the ridge, Bob,' Popski said at breakfast time. 'They may have followed us.'

'I'll go up, Popski,' I said.

After a leisurely breakfast I strolled over to Waterson's jeep.

'Come up to the ridge, Sarge?'

'O.K., sir.'

We drove up to the ridge in Waterson's jeep, parked it below the summit and walked up to the pass.

Phut. . . . Phut. Two rifle-shots rang out as we showed ourselves and bullets pinged uncomfortably close. We drew back hurriedly and lay flat behind protective rocks.

'The bastards!' exclaimed Waterson indignantly.

'That's that, Sarge,' I muttered. 'No more jeeping trips. Jerry's wise to us.'

Wriggling on our bellies like snakes we crawled along the ridge away from the pass and cautiously raised our heads. Peering between the topmost rocks we were just in time to see a truck disappearing into the olive grove near the shuttered house, leaving a rising wake of swirling dust.

'They've put an outpost, Sarge. I wonder where those snipers are?' Wruuuuuuumph. A loud explosion shook the ridge . . . a mushroom of smoke rose high in the air, billowing up from the southern valley.

'Aw, hell, sir. They've blown up the track.'

'Sounds like it.'

'After all the work we did on it.' Waterson groaned.

'Where the hell are those snipers?' I muttered.

Moving cautiously on our stomachs we crawled along the ridge from rock to rock, searching for a German head. We couldn't see one anywhere, but every time we became a little rash and showed ourselves . . . Phut. . . . Phut. . . . Ping. . . . Ping . . . came the snipers' bullets.

'Where the mucking hell are they?' we asked ourselves in exasperation.

Determined to locate the snipers, we stayed on the ridge all day, foregoing lunch, and had our reward just before dusk when two helmeted heads bobbed on a green knoll opposite the cleft.

'There they are. Look!' Waterson grabbed my arm.

'I see them. On top of the knoll.'

Waterson raised his rifle, changed his mind and lowered it.

'Look, sir,' he said excitedly. 'If we get into position before dawn we could capture those bastards.'

I looked at him.

'You mean come up early in the morning?'

'Yes, sir.'

'O.K., Sarge. We'll do that.'

An hour before dawn the following morning Waterson, Porter and I crawled over the ridge and lowered ourselves into the ravine, wondering if we were altogether wise in putting our heads into the lion's mouth. By the time we sat at the bottom, on the German side, with the sun coming up I was quite sure we weren't. We crouched behind boulders at the bottom of the ravine, watching the grassy knoll become flooded in golden light. . . .

Waterson nodded and we started to climb up the steep, dew-soaked grass. . . . I went too far to the right, Porter too far to the left. Waterson judged it accurately and pulled himself over a hillock . . . to find himself looking into the surprised faces of two German snipers dug-in behind it. Quicker than they, Waterson pulled the trigger twice. . . . Bang. . . . Bang . . . and shot both snipers through the head at point-blank range, blew their brains out, grabbed their field-telephone, pulled off the wires and shouted to us to get out. Porter and I could see nothing; all we heard were the two shots and Waterson shouting to us to get out.

We slithered down the wet grass into the ravine, raced up the other side to the top of the ridge and threw ourselves behind its protecting rocks, panting. . . .

'What happened, Sarge?' I gasped as soon as I could speak.

Waterson was breathing heavily.

'Walked straight into the bastards' . . . gasp . . . 'saw two of 'em' . . . gasp . . . 'shot 'em both through the head' . . . gasp. . . . 'Bang. . . . Bang' . . . gasp. Sergeant Waterson had only one good eye, but it was a very good one, blue, and piercing, like a gimlet. He could stare any of us out, unblinking. He fixed his unwinking stare on me and mimed firing with finger and thumb 'Bang, bang'.

'You hypnotized them with your beady eye, Sarge,' I laughed.

Porter nodded his agreement.

We sat watching the knoll while we recovered our breath. Two uniformed figures presently appeared on the crest. Waterson took careful aim and fired.

'Got 'im,' he chuckled gleefully as one of the figures collapsed out of sight.

Porter and I both missed the other one, but it vanished from the skyline.

We waited and watched but no other figures appeared. At midday I said, 'Come on, let's go back.'

Our jeep was parked a mile below the pass. We heard the sound of aircraft engines as we reached it, and took cover. . . .

A flight of Stukas ridge-hopped over our heads, flying low in the direction of our almond grove. As they passed over it we saw little black objects drop from their shining bellies.

'Bombs. Look!'

Clouds of dust rose from the valley and the rumbling sound of explosions came to our ears. . . . Wruuuuumph . . . wruuuuumph.

'Looks like our almond grove.'

It was. When we reached camp we found the place in a shambles. Two sticks of bombs had dropped across the grove, making three large craters. One jeep had received a direct hit and there was nothing left of it but small pieces of twisted metal. One of the bombs hadn't exploded and lay on the greensward like a mine washed up at sea. Popski and Jan Caneri were at Corps Headquarters. There were no casualties.

We looked at the unexploded bomb and from the bomb to one another. Was it a dud or a delay? If we walked up to examine the thing would it suddenly explode in our faces? We couldn't leave the bomb there, but would have to dispose of it ourselves somehow because we were, after all, a demolition squadron and it would hardly do for demolition experts to ask American Corps Headquarters to send a bomb-disposal squad. Popski would never live it down.

Eventually we plucked up enough courage to shoot at it with rifles from 500 yards. Nothing happened. A little closer, we tried again. The bomb still didn't explode.

'It's a dud, sir,' announced Sapper Curtis confidently and walked right up to it. The rest of P.P.A. watched apprehensively, expecting to see him blown skywards. Nothing happened.

Curtis was our demolition expert and knew more about the ins and outs of demolition than the rest of us put together. An R.E. on detachment, he was in Gafsa when the Americans retreated and went with them to Tabessa where he heard of P.P.A. and offered his services. He turned out to be one of our best recruits. He wore glasses (one of the few), had a loud, horsy laugh, irrepressible high spirits and was a born mimic. Popular with the men, they christened him 'Bum'. I don't know why.

Curtis walked round the bomb, looked at it with an appraising eye, patted it affectionately and then, to our horror and delight, sat down upon it and waved to us.

'Jesus!' exclaimed Waterson in admiration.

Shamed by this exhibition of cold-blooded courage, we all walked up to the bomb.

Curtis gave it another affectionate pat.

'Don't tempt Fate, Curtis,' I admonished.

'It's quite safe, sir,' he said, giving the bomb a loud slap which made my blood run cold.

'Blow it with eight-o-eight,' Waterson suggested.

Curtis rose from the bomb and hurried to his jeep for eight-o-eight, detonators and fuse. The rest of us walked to a safe distance.

When he'd laid the charge, Curtis ran out 300 feet of instantaneous fuse and set it off . . . it petered out—at a kink—ten feet from the charge.

'Muck it,' said Curtis and walked up to connect a new fuse— the most dangerous part of demolition. As his officer I felt I must set an example and walked with him. I would much rather have stayed away.

Quaking inwardly, expecting to be blown to pieces, I helped Curtis to break the kinked fuse and set a new one. Curtis crimped the detonator with his *teeth*! I shuddered and closed my eyes. . . .

'O.K., sir.'

We walked back to the others and Curtis bent down. . . .

Wruuuuuuuuuuumph! The bomb exploded with an ear-splitting, ground-shaking roar which rocked the almond grove. Soil pattered on the leaves and divots of earth fell on our heads.

'Like the Italian mine dump at Zella,' I remarked to Waterson.

'Better, sir,' he laughed, wiping ochre clay from his hair.

A jeep drove into the grove as the dust of the explosion settled. Popski and Jan Caneri climbed out.

I explained what had happened and told them about events up on the ridge.

'Ah, ha,' smiled Popski, 'I thought they'd follow us.'

Waterson repeated the story in his own words.

'. . . fixed them with my beady eye, sir . . . shot them both through the head . . . bang . . . bang.'

A few days later Sergeant Waterson pinned the ribbon of the Military Medal to his tunic.

Unable, now, to drive our jeeps through the pass we were imprisoned in the northern valley and spent our days playing sniper's hide and seek on the ridge, with very little scoring on either side.

Time passed. Eighth Army turned the Mareth defences—by the route Popski and Tinker had recced—and the Americans cheered, but were still held at Maknassy by a handful of determined Germans. Eighth Army pushed again at Wadi Akarit and the beaten Afrika Korps turned and ran. . . .

From the top of the ridge, through binoculars, we saw a great cloud of ochre dust moving across the Tunisian plain. It could mean only one thing—Eighth Army.

'Everybody up to the ridge,' cried Popski. 'Get the track repaired.'

There was a huge hole to fill in, but there was plenty of rock and scree and no lack of enthusiasm. The jeeps were moving through the pass again in a matter of hours . . . through the cleft . . . along the perilous ledge . . . down the sliding scree . . . through the water splash. 'Look out for mines.' We found them, telemines, buried in the sand—downhill to the shuttered house . . . no welcoming dog . . . through the olive groves . . . on to the road . . . down to the plain. . . .

We waited and came in on the flank, not wishing to be shot at.

What a heart-gladdening sight they made, those victorious tanks and armoured cars sweeping across the flat Tunisian plain with their pennants proudly flying. We watched the leading squadrons surge past, feeling like orphans returning to the fold, proud to think we were a unit, if a very small and insignificant one, of this great and gallant Eighth Army. What a triumph it had been. Nearly 2000 miles of non-stop advance, right from the gates of Cairo. Brave Desert Rats! Good old Monty! We stood on the bonnets of our stationary jeeps and waved to the tank-men standing in their open turrets; tears stood unashamedly in our eyes and there were lumps in our throats. . . .

Later, we leaguered in the plain with one of the forward formations. We lay in our sleeping-bags talking, swapping yarns, looking up at the stars, listening to the friendly buzz and crackle of the wireless inter-com, feeling happy and triumphant, at one with the great desert family.

Waterson found old friends amongst the tank-men. As I drifted off to sleep I heard him telling the old, old story . . . 'fixed 'em with my beady eye . . . shot 'em both through the head . . . bang, bang. . . .'

Next morning we advanced with the armour, feeling very small and vulnerable beside the big, lumbering tanks, but there was little opposition and we weren't in the slightest danger; it felt good to be up in the van, scouting ahead in our fast little jeeps and coming back to report. . . .

The courageous Rommel made a last desperate stand at Enfidaville. Montgomery attacked. . . . Tunis fell on May 7th. . . . Von Arnim surrendered in the Cap Bon Peninsula.

The desert war was over.

6

Wᴴᴀᴛ was to be our fate?

The purpose for which we'd originally been formed—desert raiding—no longer existed. Would Popski's Private Army now be disbanded? Perish the thought! Surely there was something we could do, some special service role we could fill? Where would the war go next? To Sicily? To Italy?

We Cook's toured through North Africa looking for a suitable training ground and found one near Philippeville in a sandy, sunlit cove on the Barbary Coast.

'Right, Bob,' said Popski. 'Train for seaborne landings on the Italian mainland. Keep the men busy,' and off he went to Allied Force Headquarters in Algiers to make sure we remained in the war.

'Cheerio, Bob,' said Jan Caneri, and set out for Cairo by jeep to settle up our chaotic administrative affairs.

I drove to the nearest C.R.E. and drew 'Boats, assault, training, men, for the use of'.

P.P.A. had grown. Some of the originals had dropped out— Bell, Weldon and one or two others, and our faithful Senussi had returned to their homes in the Libyan Desert—but new blood had come in: Curtis, Dave Porter, Jock Cameron, Saunders, Beautyman, Riches and a number of others. We now had about twenty really good men. Left to my own devices, I set about training them for raids on the Italian mainland.

Our camp was on the beach and we lived practically naked, becoming as brown as niggers. Sergeant Waterson's boisterous 'Wakey, wakeey' rent the air at crack of dawn. We pulled on bathing-trunks (or didn't bother) and dived into the surf, swam around for five minutes, raced each other up and down the beach and then sat hungrily down to breakfast in the blazing sun. . . .

An hour later we were hauling the heavy assault boats through the bucketing, dancing surf, tumbling laughingly aboard and rowing 'Oh, ho . . . heave-o' through the swelling blue-green waves to the tune of the Volga Boat Song conducted by Trooper Riches . . . then overboard one by one for long-distance swimming, paced by the boats . . . all aboard again by noon and paddling hard for the shore. 'Oh, ho . . . heave-o' . . . crashing through the creaming, smothering surf . . . hauling the boats up the beach.

Lunch—bully beef, biscuits, cheese, fresh salad, fresh fruit, tea. Then a siesta in the flapping bell-tents for most of the afternoon.

Tea at five o'clock.

As soon as it was dark, we shouldered heavy demolition-packs, picked up Tommy-guns and took to the boats again . . . rowing out to sea . . . turning and coming silently in as though landing on an Italian coast . . . walking noiselessly inland to lay demolition charges in an imaginary power-station . . . returning silently to the enemy beach . . . splashing through the surf . . . rowing back to the (imaginary) waiting submarine . . . inshore again, listening to the reverberations of the exploding charges.

Sleepily to bed in the small hours . . . and up again at crack of dawn.

So the days passed, varied, to break the monotony, by cross-country running, treasure hunts, long-distance jeeping, jeeprobatics, navigation exercises, unarmed combat, revolver and machine-gun practice, map-reading.

In addition to training, my objective was to keep healthy, high-spirited men out of mischief and in the main I succeeded, but there were lapses. There was trouble over the matter of a prize-winning pig which had died in obscure circumstances and mysteriously found its way into a hotelier's pantry in exchange for wine.

I had Curtis up.

'Curtis,' I demanded, looking him straight in the eye, 'the truth.'

Curtis had his answer pat.

'Well, sir, if a bloody pig comes barging in and blows itself up on a charge, you can't blame me, sir. . . .'

And the French colonial geese were peculiar. They had almost unfortunate predilection for eight-o-eight and would put their ravenous, grasping beaks towards our charges just at the time they exploded. . . . 'Most unfortunate, sir,' said Curtis. 'We tried to shoo them away but . . .'

Charges, too, sometimes exploded under the windows of colonial homesteads in the small hours of the morning when we were all in camp, asleep. . . . 'Did it, sir?' (incredulously). '. . . Must 'ave laid the charge a bit too close, sir. Couldn't see properly in the dark. . . .'

I lapsed myself one evening.

Sergeant Waterson had made friends with the petty officer in charge of the naval canteen in Philippeville. He invited me for a beer one evening. Innocently I went, suspecting nothing.

When we entered the canteen, Sam, the petty officer, greeted us affably and we sat down at a wooden table upon which reposed a case of beer and three glasses. I noticed a zinc bucket under the table, but thought nothing of it.

' 'Evening, Skipper,' says Sam.

'Good evening, Sam,' says I.

'Have a beer, Skipper?'

'Thanks, Sam. I will.'

Sam poured me a beer.

'Beer, Sarge?' he says, looking at Waterson.

'Thanks, Sam.'

When our glasses were full Sam raised his to me.

'Good 'ealth, Skipper.'

'Your very good health, Sam,' I replied, raising my glass to him. We all drank. . . .

Sam produced a tin of navy Woodbines, the thick, duty-free ones, like Players, and passed it round.

'Smoke, Skipper?'

'Thanks, Sam.'

I took a Woodbine. Sam held a lighter for me.

We smoked and sipped our beer and chatted amiably about this and that. It was all very friendly and democratic. Presently, Sam asked:

'Can you play Cardinal Puff, Skipper?'

'Cardinal Puff?' I asked stupidly. I had never heard of Cardinal Puff.

Sam looked innocently at Sergeant Waterson and if I had been watching Waterson's beady eye (I wasn't) I would have seen it wink.

88

'Don't know Cardinal Puff, Skipper?' exclaimed Sam, aghast at my ignorance.

'Don't know Cardinal Puff, sir?' Waterson chimed in, equally aghast.

'Cardinal Puff's a great game,' says Sam. 'We must teach you Cardinal Puff.'

Feeling that my education had been sadly neglected and wishing to rectify the matter as quickly as possible, I put my head into the open noose.

'Please teach me, Sam.'

Sam topped up my glass, his own and Sergeant Waterson's.

'Repeat after me, Skipper,' intoned Sam, 'Cardinal Puff. . . .'

The game consisted of repeating a formula in which the word 'Puff' frequently occurred, repeating it in a certain sequence and punctuating it with finger-taps to the table and to different parts of your anatomy. If you made a mistake you were required to drink a pint of beer as forfeit and start all over again. It seemed simple enough.

'That's easy, Sam,' I said confidently.

But I found it wasn't.

'Cardinal Puff . . .' I began, and tapped the edge of the table with my forefinger, then the side of my nose.

'Wrong!' yelled Sam. 'Drink a pint of beer.'

'What did I do wrong, Sam?'

'Tapped the table first, instead of your nose. Start again.'

I drained the glass to its dregs and began again.

'Cardinal Puff . . .'

Before I had gone very far Sam yelled:

'Wrong, Skipper. Start again. Drink a pint of beer.'

I had tapped my nose twice instead of thrice. Sam handed me a brimful glass of beer. I lowered it and started again.

'Wrong!' Sam yelled delightedly before a minute had passed.

I drank another pint of beer—my fourth in quick succession—and began once more.

'Cardinal Puff' . . . nose-tap . . . table-tap. . . .

'Wrong, Skipper. Try again. Drink a pint of beer.'

I drank my fifth pint and my clouding mind dimly registered the reason for the bucket under the table. Grimly, I started again; not for anything would I admit defeat in front of Sergeant Waterson.

'Cardinal Puff . . .' I commenced hesitantly and to my horror I noticed that my reactions were becoming sluggish. My mind was confused. I couldn't remember the sequence. Did the table-taps or the nose-taps come first? The table, I thought. . . .

'Wrong!' bawled Sam delightedly. 'Start again. Drink a pint of beer.'

Too late, I realized I should have tapped my nose first. I swallowed my sixth pint of beer and felt queazy. My head was beginning to swim. I started again.

'Cardinal Puff' . . . table-tap . . . nose-tap. . . .

'Wrong, Skipper. Start again. Drink a pint of beer.'

I drank my seventh pint . . . my head was swimming. . . . I couldn't see straight. . . . Sam's face became blurred . . . my thoughts were jumbled . . . my fingers wouldn't do what I told them. . . . I was all mixed up. . . . Cardinal Puff. . . . Puff . . . Pufff . . . nose-tap . . . table-tap. . . . Puff. . . . Pufff. . . . Puffff. . . . I no longer knew what I was doing. . . . I was going to be sick. . . . I fought it down. . . . I was damned if I was going to use the bucket in front of Waterson . . . air. . . . I wanted air . . . fresh air. . . .

I swayed away from the table and staggered drunkenly out of the canteen. I breathed deep gulps of the cool night air and felt better. I had parked the jeep at the back of the building and made towards it, feeling a wild desire to get into it and put my foot down. . . . I clambered noisily into the driver's seat and pressed the self-starter. . . . I felt the engine rev. . . . I was dimly aware of Waterson piling into the seat beside me. . . . I crashed into first gear and revved away . . . changed into second and put my foot down . . . felt the rush of wind in my face. . . . We were doing about forty. . . . I heard Waterson shout frantically:

'Stop . . . stop . . . for muck's sake . . . stop . . . !'

I felt suddenly sobered and applied the brakes. The jeep came to a halt with the two front wheels hanging over the top of a flight of stone steps leading down to the harbour. Dark, oily water lapped ominously twelve feet below. . . .

'Whew!' gasped Waterson, mopping his brow with a handkerchief.

'Cardinal Puff,' I laughed shakily, stone cold sober, and reversed away from the danger. . . .

.   .   .   .   .

The days became weeks and May gave place to June. Mosquitoes bred in a nearby marsh and we all went down with malaria, undermining our perfect health. For a time, not a day passed but one of us complained of high temperature and burning eye-balls; a duty jeep ran daily between our camp in the cove and the General Hospital outside Philippeville. We all recovered. 'Benign tertiary,' they said it was. 'Keep taking mepocrine.'

Popski paid us a flying visit, contracted malaria too, went to hospital, recovered, and returned to Algiers.

We moved camp into the mountains, away from the mosquitoes, and continued to train for landings in Italy, minus the assault boats; but we acquired new military toys in their place—'Walkie-Talkie' wireless inter-communication sets—and spent our days and nights wandering about the wooded Tunisian hills talking to one another round corners.

In Algiers, Popski was busy ensuring our continued independence. He didn't find it easy. Private armies were frowned upon by the Sam-Browned, spit-and-polished General Staff newly out from England, who regarded anything not in the text-book as 'frightfully infradig'; but on the hill above the town where the Combined Operations Planning Staff worked in quiet isolation Popski discovered a few kindred spirits and one day I received a signal instructing me to meet him there.

'You're in charge till I come back,' I told Waterson. 'No pigs and no Cardinal Puff.'

Bill Wilson drove me to Algiers in a jeep.

I found Popski comfortably installed in a villa overlooking the town.

'Well, Bob,' he greeted me, 'how are the men?'

'All fit again, Popski. Training hard.'

We sat on the cool terrace looking down upon the jumbled buildings of the port, the crowded harbour and the blue Mediterranean beyond.

'Where do we go from here, Popski?' I asked.

'Gliding, Bob.'

'Gliding!' I was all attention.

'You know,' Popski made bird-like flapping motions with his hands, 'little aeroplanes.'

'Where to?' I asked eagerly.

'Italy.'

91

'Tell me more.'

There being no more deserts to fight in, Popski explained, P.P.A. would now take to the air. We would put our jeeps into gliders in North Africa, be towed across the Med by the R.A.F. and dropped into central Italy where, having destroyed the gliders upon landing, we would dash about in our jeeps cutting telephone wires, blowing up bridges and power-stations and 'creating alarm and despondency' behind the enemy lines.

I digested this for a minute and saw a snag.

'How do we come back, Popski?'

'We don't.'

I gulped. 'I beg your pardon?'

'We don't come back, Bob. We stay there.'

I looked at him. He was quite serious.

'You mean . . . we just . . . stay there?' I faltered.

'There will be Allied landings in Italy, Bob. Eventually we will link up with our own troops.'

'Eventually . . . we will . . . link up . . . with our own troops.'

I visualized myself looking into an empty petrol tank on a bare mountainside in Italy and sitting despondently by it waiting for our own troops to link up. . . .

'When do we glide?' I quavered.

'Training first, Bob. We'll be attached to the 1st Airborne Div. They're at M'saken, near Sousse. You'll move there right away. I'll join you in a day or two.'

Bill Wilson and I raced back to our camp in the Tunisian mountains.

'What's the form, sir?' Waterson asked.

'You'll never guess, Sarge. We're moving. Tell the men to pack up.'

Waterson bellowed his orders.

'Where are we going, sir?'

'G-l-i-d-i-n-g.' I spelt out the letters.

'Gliding?'

'Where to?'

'Across the Med.'

'In jeeps?'

I nodded and waited for it. It came.

'How do we get back?'

'We don't come back, Sergeant. Eventually we will link up with our own troops.'

Sergeant Waterson's remarks are unprintable.

Two days later we were comfortably installed in an olive grove near M'saken in the Tunisian plain, next grove to the British 1st Airborne Division, the famous Red Devils of Arnhem. Popski joined us from Algiers, and Jan Caneri at the end of another 2000-mile jeep-drive from Cairo.

New recruits came—Lieutenant McGillivray from the Derbyshire Yeomanry, Sergeant Brooks, a wireless operator, Sonley, Barnes, Williamson, Mee and others—a lieutenant (Maclaine of Lochbuie) and twelve staff-sergeant glider pilots from the 1st Airborne Glider Pilot Regiment were attached to us for glider operations in Italy.

Training commenced at once.

On the R.A.F. landing-ground a mile outside M'saken we were introduced to Waco gliders, tiny aeroplanes (without an engine) with a fibre-glass nose which lifted up and a fuselage just big enough to hold a jeep. Lying in the sun with their noses raised they looked like giant birds of prey with beaks agape.

'Christ!' muttered Waterson when he saw them. 'We're not going up in those, are we?'

We walked round the gliders like a well-conducted party of sightseeing tourists, asking questions, touching parts, examining mechanism.

'What if the nose jams and you can't get out?' Curtis asked.

'You hack your way out,' said the glider pilot, pointing to an axe clamped inside the fuselage.

Curtis went through the motions of hacking a way out and his horsy laugh rang across the landing-ground.

Popski turned to me. 'Bring up your jeep, Bob.'

I hurried to my parked jeep and drove it up to the nose of a glider.

'Other way round.'

I reversed.

'We'll need ramps,' Popski said.

The bottom lip of the fuselage was about six inches off the ground.

'Use sand-channels, sir,' Waterson suggested.

93

He unclamped my desert-battered sand-channels and set them against the bottom jaw of the fuselage, guided my wheels on to them and I reversed into the glider. One of the glider pilots followed me in and closed the nose. It was a snug fit—just nice room for jeep, guns, crew and pilot.

'How do you open the nose to get out?' I asked.

'That's easy, sir.'

From a hook in the front of the nose the pilot led a strong wire through a series of rings and fixed it to the tow swivel at the back of the jeep, testing it to make sure it was properly fixed.

'Put her into low gear and drive out, sir. Try not to jerk.'

I looked at him and at the closed nose.

'You mean drive into the nose?'

'Yes, sir. It'll open as you move forward.'

'Quite sure?'

The pilot laughed.

'It'll open, sir.'

I swallowed hard, waved to the group outside to get out of the way, revved, let in the clutch and drove into the closed nose. . . . Miraculously, it opened and swung up as I went forward. . . . Instinctively, I ducked as the nose yanked up above my head . . . but I needn't have worried, it was perfectly safe.

I bumped out, missing the sand-channels.

'Cor blimey,' goggled Sammy Barnes, 'just like Jonah and the bloody whale.'

Curtis' horsy laugh rang out.

'Cut yer blooming 'ead off if it fell.'

'All right, Bob?' Popski asked.

'Nothing to it, Popski,' I assured him. 'Simple as A B C.'

'Right,' he said, turning to Sergeant Waterson, 'bring up the rest of the jeeps. One to each glider.'

For the next few days gliders filled our waking thoughts and were with us in our dreams. Immediately after a six-o'clock breakfast, engines revved in our olive grove and a line of jeeps tore up the dusty road to the landing-ground, leaving a wake of ochre dust to settle on the olive leaves.

We laboured until dusk, driving the jeeps into and out of the gliders, time and time again, until we could all do it in a matter of seconds, with Popski, after perfecting his own technique, going from glider to glider with a stop-watch, cutting the seconds off our time.

Driving into the closed nose was rather frightening at first, it didn't seem possible that the nose could open in time, but it always did and you bumped out without cracking your head; and when you'd driven out a number of times it ceased worry to you, but I noticed that everybody (myself included) continued to duck their heads as they came out.

'Right,' said Popski one evening when he was satisfied he couldn't chop any more seconds off our time, 'tomorrow we'll go up.' It was a thrilling experience.

The great birds, beaks agape, glinted in the early morning sun. We reversed into their throats, closed beaks and secured the opening mechanism to the rear of the jeeps. The pilots took their seats at the controls and the jeep drivers and gunners sat in their accustomed places looking out upon the world like goldfish from a bowl.

A long nylon tow-rope snaked between each glider and its towing plane. Aero engines roared and dust spun on the landing-ground . . . the nylon snakes straightened their coils and became taut . . . the gliders jerked and moved gently forward . . . scraping and bumping a little with spumes of dust springing away from either side of the nose like foam from a ship's bows . . . a last bump . . . a gentle scrape . . . and we were airborne, tied to our mother planes by our nylon umbilical cords.

Up . . . up . . . up in wide circles to 5000 feet with the landing-ground a diminutive ochre square amongst dark green patches of olive grove, a glinting salt-marsh on the flank and the blue Mediterranean stretching to the far horizon. Craning our necks, we looked down upon Lilliput, upon toy encampments, toy houses and toy transport moving slowly along narrow ribbons of road. . . .

Something slapped against the nose and we were cast off, orphaned in mid-air without an engine, bucketing in the air pockets . . . circling round and round . . . gradually losing height . . . volplaning silently like giant hawks with only the sound of the wind tearing past our outstretched wings as we sailed down . . . down . . . down . . . with the burnished salt-marsh angling nearer and nearer. . . .

'Have you ever crashed?' I asked the pilot.

He laughed, pulling on the stick.

'These things are pretty safe, sir,' he assured me.

Beside me, Bill Wilson was whistling to keep up his courage; it was the first time he'd ever been aloft.

Down . . . down . . . down. The salt-marsh rushed towards us. . . . Bill Wilson and I gripped the sides of the jeep and pressed hard with our feet . . . the pilot pulled and pushed at the stick . . . gave the glider a bit of rudder . . . and settled it down . . . bump . . . scrape . . . bump . . . scrape . . . bumpumpump . . . scruuuuuuunch.

We were down, breathing freely again.

'Very nice landing,' I congratulated the pilot, drying my sweating hands.

'A bit rough, sir.'

'Thank God, we're doon, sirr,' Bill Wilson breathed.

The pilot transferred to the back of the jeep. Bill Wilson removed the wheel chocks. I engaged low booster gear.

'Is the wire O.K.?' I asked.

The pilot tested it.

'O.K., sir. Out you go.'

I drove at the nose. It yanked jerkily up and hung poised above our heads like the sword of Damocles as we bumped out on to the crusted marsh.

I looked for the others. They were landing graciously, like sea-birds, one after the other. I watched them skid along the hard pan. The minute they came to rest their beaks opened and the jeeps spewed forth.

I drove to the nearest glider. Waterson's jeep shot out.

'How did you enjoy that, Sarge?' I greeted him.

He regarded me unhappily. His stomach had been misbehaving aloft. He looked white about the gills and his beady eye had lost its brightness.

'Crazy bloody game this, sir,' he groaned.

'Don't you like gliding, Sergeant?' I twitted him.

'No, sir. I bloody don't' (emphatically).

I laughed heartlessly and drove on to see how the others had fared.

Popski was jubilant. I had never seen him so excited, for normally he never showed his feelings.

'This is the answer, Bob,' he enthused. 'Back to the landing-ground and up again.'

96

Popski kept us at it day after day, loading and unloading, taking off from the airstrip and landing in the salt-marsh; and thanks to the Airborne glider pilots we never had a crash, nothing, no accidents of any kind.

A night-landing exercise came next.

We took off one evening at ten o'clock when the moon was full, sitting in our jeeps in the glistening bowls listening to the towing planes racing their engines . . . a tug at the nose . . . a quick jerk forward and . . . we were off . . . skimming over the luminous dust and up . . . up . . . up into the inky, star-filled night.

The Mediterranean glinted under our port wings, dark blotches marked the olive groves of Sousse and under our bellies the widespread salt-marsh, patterned by our moving shadows, shone like a silver platter.

The planes cast off at 5000 feet and we volplaned silently down, wheeling and banking in wide turns, feeling the wind tugging at the wings. We were out of the world of men, silvered shadows high up in the sky playing hide-and-seek with the stars. How peaceful it was up there! Not a sound reached our ears but the creaking of the wheel-blocked jeep and the swish of the wind on the fuselage. . . . If this were the real thing, I thought, we'd still be on tow, heading across the Med. My thoughts ran ahead. I pictured us circling nervously above the Apennines, looking for the right place to land. . . . I saw some of the gliders crashing into the mountainside. . . . I heard Curtis' horsy laugh as he hacked his way out. . . .

We were banking steeply, wheeling over the gleaming salt-marsh like vultures . . . the jeep strained against the wheel-blocks, trying to run forward into the nose . . . the marsh was rushing towards us, terrifyingly close . . . the pilot muttered under his breath . . . pulled hard on the stick . . . ruddered frantically . . . bump . . . slap . . . bumpumpump . . . scruuuuuuuuunch!

We were down.

'Sorry, sir,' the pilot apologized.

'What happened?'

'Misjudged the height. It's difficult at night.'

'Any damage done?'

'I don't think so, sir.'

The pilot clambered on to the jeep. Bill Wilson removed the wheel-blocks. I engaged low booster gear and ran at the nose. . . .

The engine stalled. 'Blast!' I muttered and tried again. The engine stalled a second time.

'The nose won't lift,' I said to the pilot.

He got out and fumbled with the catch. 'This is what'll happen in Italy,' I thought.

'Try that, sir.'

The nose creaked and the pilot remounted the jeep.

I revved and let in the clutch . . . the nose shot up and we crashed out on to the moonlit marsh, instinctively ducking our heads. I made straight for the rendezvous.

Popski was already there.

'Get out all right, Bob?'

'Nose got stuck, Popski, but we managed. We'll have trouble with jammed noses.'

Popski nodded. 'We'll have to work out something for that.'

I wondered what.

One by one the jeeps came to the rendezvous. One jeep was missing—Locke's. We went to look for him and found the crew imprisoned in their glass bowl, unable to get out. The glider had landed badly and the nose was twisted.

Experienced glider pilot hands laid hold of the glider and manhandled it into a level position, pulled and pushed at the jammed nose and finally Locke drove out.

'We must find an answer to jamming noses, Bob,' Popski grunted on the way back to camp. 'Keep thinking about it.'

It was Curtis who eventually found the answer.

'We could blow the nose with eight-o-eight, sir,' he informed me one day.

I looked at him, interested.

'But won't it injure the crew, Bum?'

'No, sir, not if it's done properly.'

There was a crashed glider (not ours) on the aerodrome. I got permission to experiment. Curtis tamped very small pieces of eight-o-eight into the cracks beside the hinges and detonated them. The hinges burst and the nose lifted off.

'First rate, Curtis,' we congratulated him, 'you've solved the problem.'

'Nothing to it, sir,' he said modestly, blushing, and adjusted his glasses: then his horsy laugh rang out.

·   ·   ·   ·   ·

98

'I'm not too sure of my perimeter guard,' the R.A.F. commanding officer confided to Popski over drinks. 'Would you stage a mock raid to test it?'

'Certainly,' said Popski, always willing to oblige. 'Good training for the men. We'll chalk "P.P.A." on the plane—equivalent to putting a time-bomb in the fuselage.'

'Capital. Which night?'

'Tomorrow?'

'Fine.'

Popski and the C.O. raised their glasses and drank.

In twos and threes we crept up to the landing-ground perimeter, lay quietly in the starlit scrub until the R.A.F. guards went past, crawled under the wire and wormed our way towards the parked Spitfires and transport planes. In place of Tommy-guns we clutched pieces of coloured chalk in our hands. Taking our time, lying motionless whenever a sentry came near, we crawled from plane to plane, chalking the letters 'P.P.A.' clearly on wing, rudder or fuselage. By 4 a.m. we were back in our olive grove, chuckling happily.

'Well, how did the raid go?' the C.O. asked his adjutant at breakfast time. 'Popski's chaps manage to chalk any planes?'

The adjutant coloured and looked uncomfortable.

'Yes, sir.'

The C.O. looked at him.

'How many?'

'Twenty-nine out of thirty, sir.' (We'd overlooked one.)

'What?' the C.O. exploded. 'Good God. Double the guard. We'll ask Popski to try again.'

Two nights later Sergeant Waterson staged a very realistic attack on one side of the landing-ground. The alarm sounded and searchlights flashed. All the R.A.F. personnel rushed to stop the rot. Completely unmolested, the rest of P.P.A. slipped under the unguarded wire on the other side of the perimeter, 'destroyed' the communications block and 'captured' the Operations Room. Snaking past the officers' latrines at 2 a.m., Bum Curtis had one of his original ideas. He stopped, put a hand in his pocket and drew out a six-hour delay time-pencil. (The time-pencil was a device for setting off delayed demolition charges. Shaped like a pencil, it incorporated a glass phial containing acid which ate through a copper spring-wire to explode the charge.) Crimping a detonator to the end of it with his teeth, Curtis grinned wickedly in the star-light, lifted the well-scrubbed lid of the C.O.s private latrine and dropped his surprise packet down the hatch. 'That'll shake 'im,' he breathed and crawled away smothering a horsy laugh.

Time-pencils can be very accurate and this particular one was specially so.

At eight o'clock precisely the C.O. went to morning devotion, lifted the heart-shaped lid and sat down. Wruuuumph. The muffled explosion ten feet below didn't injure him, but . . . sweet violets!

'We'll throw a party,' said Popski. 'Everybody's been very kind to us. It's time we showed our appreciation.'

Loud murmurs of assent.

Jan haggled with an Arab merchant in M'saken. We roasted a sheep whole on a pit and broached a barrel of wine. Curtis transformed our olive grove with streamers of coloured lights and, with Popski's consent, hid small charges of eight-o-eight in the branches, connected to press-switches in the ground.

The guests arrived.

'By George, Popski,' said a young Airborne major. 'This looks nice. Just like fairy——'

Flash . . . bang!

The major was about to say 'fairyland' but he trod on a press-switch and exploded a charge of eight-o-eight in the branches above his head. He changed it to a muttered 'Good God', ducked, laughed nervously, and sidled towards Popski.

'Come in. Don't be shy,' Popski called to a suspicious flying officer who followed the major. The F.O. edged warily past the tree, keeping an eye on its branches.

Flash . . . bang!

He trod on another press-switch and exploded a charge in the next tree.

The vehicle park filled up and presently there was a crowd of uniformed figures standing round the crackling fire in the olive grove.

'Help yourselves,' said Popski hospitably, indicating the roasted sheep and the barrel of wine. 'Don't wait to be asked.'

The guests helped themselves to meat and wine.

'Nice piece of mutton. Damned good wine,' an Airborne

captain said appreciatively, and stood back to allow a brother officer to hack at the carcase. . . .

Flash . . . bang! A charge exploded above his head.

'Christ,' he muttered, dropping both meat and wine.

Curtis had booby-trapped the path to the latrines and as the wine-level in the barrel dropped, guests enquired directions and swayed down the path, fumbling with buttons. . . .

Flash . . . bang. . . . Flash . . . bang. . . . Flash . . . bang. . . . Many of the guests changed their minds and exercised will-power nearer the fire.

In the meantime Curtis was at work in the vehicle park, and when the time came for our guests to leave—about one o'clock in the morning—their nerves were further strained by the loud bangs which went off under their vehicles the minute they let in the clutch.

'Well, cheerio, Popski, and thanks very much,' said the R.A.F. commanding officer, shaking Popski's hand and stepping into his truck. 'Been a most delight——'

Flash . . . bang!

A P.P.A. jeep drew up beside a crowded Arab melon stall in the main street of M'saken. The time was 10.45 a.m.

Curtis jumped out and walked towards the stall, carrying a water melon under his arm.

He elbowed his way through the press of Arab customers, felt a number of the melons as though intending to buy, and surreptitiously placed the one he carried amongst the others on the stall. He stood for a moment as if trying to decide, then shook his head, pushed through the crowd and returned to the jeep.

He didn't immediately drive away, but sat at the wheel looking at the minute hand of his watch and chortling quietly to Riches, Davies and Locke. . . .

At ten seconds to eleven o'clock Curtis looked across the street towards the melon stall, still crowded by Arabs.

At five seconds past eleven the water melon he had placed on the stall suddenly exploded. . . .

'*Ayeeeeeeeeee*,' screamed the Arabs and ran in all directions, tripping over the melons falling off the stall. . . .

A horsy laugh rang out from the other side of the street . . . an engine revved. . . . ' "Melons, explosive, stalls, Arab, for the use of",' quoth Curtis, and a P.P.A. jeep disappeared in a cloud of dust.

We were in the first days of September now, edgy, keyed-up and touchy, suffering from pre-operation nerves, apprehensive of what lay ahead, imagining the worst, longing for action to put an end to our suspense.

Trained to the limit, operationally ready, we hung about the olive grove waiting for the right moon, snapping at each other, treading upon one another's toes, taking offence where none was intended. Even Sergeant Waterson was on edge.

'Bloody crazy operation,' he muttered repeatedly, 'we'll all get put in the bag.'

There was trouble over a jeep and the sequel made a deep impression.

First, the trouble.

Our six operational jeeps had gone to workshops for overhaul and when they came back Lieutenant McGillivray, our new officer in charge of transport, allotted one jeep to each crew without troubling to check that each crew received its own particular jeep.

Crews were fussy about their jeeps in P.P.A. and developed feelings for them like cavalrymen for their horses and, like cavalrymen, preferred their own mounts. New to the unit, McGillivray could hardly have been expected to understand these finer points of jeeping.

'This isna oor jeep, sirr,' Bill Wilson informed me with dismay.

'It isn't, Bill,' I said when I saw it, and I went in search of McGillivray.

It so happened that he had my jeep and I asked him to exchange.

'But what does it matter?' he jibbed. 'One jeep's as good as another.'

We had words, and Popski strolled over when he heard us arguing.

'What's the trouble, Bob?'

'McGillivray's got my jeep. I want him to exchange.'

Popski was inclined to favour his new protégé and listened sympathetically to his explanation. The jeeps had come back from workshops, McGillivray said, and he'd allotted one to each crew. One jeep was the same as another, they'd all been carefully overhauled, and he couldn't see what the fuss was about.

Popski turned to me.

'Aren't you being rather childish, Bob?'

I bristled.

'No, Popski,' I said heatedly, 'I'm not being childish at all. I simply want my own jeep.'

In the end I had my way, but it created a deal of ill-feeling.

Now for the uncanny sequel.

News of the Italian surrender came suddenly, unexpectedly. There was a rapid change of plans, a mad rush to Bizerta to board an American destroyer and in the rush McGillivray's jeep (the one he'd allotted to me) ran a big end with the result that McGillivray was delayed for a number of hours and sailed for Taranto in a different ship—the *only* ship which blew up on a mine and was lost with all hands.

7

THE destroyer nosed her way up to the quay. Dusk was falling, softening the harsh outline of bomb-scarred Taranto. A strange hush lay over the port, a tense expectancy. We sat in our jeeps on the open deck fingering the trigger-guards of our cocked Browning guns, waiting for the signal to land. What kind of reception would we get?

Around us on deck were the red-bereted men of the 1st Airborne Division (not yet blooded in battle). They would occupy Taranto and put a perimeter round the town. Our job lay further afield. We were the eyes and ears of the invasion. Our job was to get inland as fast and as far as possible to find where the enemy hid. Where were the Germans? In Taranto? In Bari? In Brindisi?

I had my eyes on Popski's broad back. He turned and gave me the signal. I passed it to Waterson, once more his old, cheery self.

'Right, Bill,' I muttered, 'here goes.'

Five eager toes pressed five starter-buttons and five highly tuned engines purred into life.

We drove on to the landing-nets. They tightened round us like string shopping bags when the cranes took the strain, lifted us up . . . swung us overboard and down . . . down . . . down. . . . As soon as our wheels touched the dock we were off, five dusky jeeps follow-my-leader in line, with their long, black-barrelled Brownings protruding in front. . . .

No lights showed. The town was completely blacked-out. We snaked out of the harbour and into the empty streets. Not a soul was in sight, but behind shuttered windows thousands of pairs of Italian eyes peeped fearfully at their new masters, wondering what the dawn would bring.

We snarled through the cobbled streets in the dark, our gun-mounts clanging in their sockets as we bumped over the uneven surface.

'Keep your eyes peeled for snipers,' I whispered to Bill Wilson, who was tense, gripping his gun. But there was no opposition. No one fired a shot. We just drove through the streets in procession and on out into the night. . . .

St. Giorgio, Grottaglie, smelly villages, fell behind us in the darkness and we approached Francavilla. . . . .

Lights flashed in the inky sky. Popski pulled up and we halted behind him, staggering our jeeps by the sides of the road. The lights were converging upon Francavilla from the north. I stared at them through binoculars. Was it an Italian convoy coming in to surrender or a German one coming out to attack?

Popski signalled me alongside.

'This is a bad position if we're attacked, Bob. Waterson and I will go forward. Wait here.'

Two jeeps vanished into the night.

It seemed strange to be sitting by a dark roadside in Italy after fighting the Italians for three years in the desert. We waited, quietly, watching the lights. . . .

A jeep appeared and Waterson's voice whispered, 'Move up, sir.'

We followed him to the shadow of a covert of trees where a side road ran off under a railway bridge.

'Under the bridge, Bob,' said Popski, 'train your guns on the road.'

An hour passed, the lights gradually went out and nothing came down the road.

'Itie convoy, sir,' Waterson said.

Popski nodded and we tip-tyred into the town.

Francavilla was asleep even to the Italian sentry nodding at the end of his beat. He was sitting in a doorway, chin on chest, his rifle over his knees as we drove quietly past. Popski stopped and Waterson padded across to the sentry, snatched his rifle and bawled into his ear:

'*Attenzione!*'

The bewildered sentry leapt to his feet. Waterson twisted his arm behind his back and frog-marched him to Popski's jeep where he stood rigidly to attention, terrified out of his wits, while

Popski interrogated him. The sentry's replies were a little incoherent, but Popski found where the barracks were and the sentry guided us there.

Popski entered a long, dark building and lights came on. The rest of us sat in our jeeps guarding the approaches, feeling we were coming to grips with something at last.

I walked across to Waterson's jeep.

'Better than gliding, Sarge?'

Waterson eased the tight chin-strap of his battered New Zealander's hat and his beady eye fixed me in the darkness. Gliding was a sore point with him. I grinned and went round the other jeeps. Bum Curtis wanted to set off a few charges outside the barracks. 'Just to wake them up, sir' (muted horsy laugh). Al Locke thought we should go and shoot up the town; Beautyman, in the wireless jeep, was concerned about his call time.

For an hour we waited, talking in undertones, listening to the sounds of the balmy night, the barking of a dog, the soughing of the wind in the trees. . . .

Popski strode out of the barracks.

'Brindisi,' he said.

'What's the form, Popski?' I asked.

In the barracks, he'd had a long talk with the Italian general, Popski informed me. There weren't many German troops in the area, mostly technicians on the airfields. The rest had withdrawn northwards. Popski had instructed the general to telephone through to Brindisi and the admiral in command of the port was now waiting to surrender to us.

'Beautyman's worried about his call time, Popski.'

'We'll stop nearer Brindisi, Bob.'

Popski revved and we followed him along the dark road towards Brindisi. . . .

We passed through sleeping Latiano and Mesagne and Popski stopped to let Beautyman call divisional headquarters in Taranto. He encyphered a short situation report and Sergeant Waterson took advantage of the halt to brew a welcome mug of hot tea— our first in Italy. Dawn was breaking as we entered Brindisi, revealing the masts of many ships in the harbour.

A testy admiral waited to surrender his fleet. Dressed in a spotless white uniform with gold epaulettes and carrying a magnificent scabbarded sword at his paunchy waist, he stood under the chandelier in a vast baronial hall, supported by his staff. He'd been standing there since 3 a.m. and was thoroughly brassed-off. 'Italian opera,' I whispered to Popski as we walked up the carpeted stairs.

The situation was ludicrous, like a scene from Italian opera staged in its native setting—the gilded baronial hall with shafts of golden light streaming through the mullioned windows, the ceremonial-dressed admiral complete with quivering paunch, the attendant, sycophant staff, the emotional monologue, the dramatic moment when the Italian fleet was surrendered to two unshaven, dust-begrimed Eighth Army officers representing His Britannic Majesty's Forces in Italy to the extent of five little jeeps and a handful of men laughing their heads off in the courtyard below.

The ceremony over, we paraded through the streets, proud conquerors of the port. The inhabitants thought we were Germans and vanished from sight!

One of them shouted, '*Inglesi!*'

The word acted like magic.

The population poured upon us from doorways and alleyways shouting:

'*Inglesi. Inglesi. Bravo. Viva Inglesi. Viva.*'

A yelling, cheering, gesticulating crowd surged through the narrow streets, blocking our passage. Men, women and children clambered on to our jeeps, threw their arms round our necks, kissed us and garlicked us, thrust wine, fruit and eggs into our laps. Little Union Jacks miraculously appeared, garlands of flowers fell upon us from balconies, hot-eyed *signorini* threw kisses from upper windows. It was heady and unsettling after three years in an empty desert.

'Shufty bint,' goggled Driver Davies in vulgar Cairene, eyeing a dark-haired beauty with pointed breasts and a flashing smile.

'*Bella, signorina,*' chortled Bum Curtis, pinching the bottom of a saucy lass who ventured too close to his jeep. '*Mama mia,*' shrieked the girl, backing away, and immediately came back for more.

Sergeant Waterson's beady eye surveyed the milling throng. 'Chuff chuff,' he warbled contentedly and held out his glass for more wine.

'But we were fighting the Ities,' exclaimed a puzzled Sammy Barnes. '*Tchach!*' ejaculated Popski, wiping the spittle from his cheek where an hysterical Sicilian had kissed him.

'*Alleati. Bravo. Viva Churchill. Viva Stalin. Viva!*' The vociferating crowd bobbed around our jeeps, deafening us with their chatter, embarrassing us with their fulsome laudations. We revved loudly and they parted to let us through, running alongside, holding on to the sides and backs of the jeeps, trying to jump on. . . .

We crawled through the noisy press and drove into the quiet countryside. Our ears were buzzing and our heads swam. Not one of us was entirely sober.

Curtis' horsy laugh rang out as we took the road to Lecce. '*Bella, signorina . . . mama mia . . . ha . . . ha . . . ha. . . .*'

We drove through a land of enchantment, enchantment to us after years of ochre sand, a green, sun-kissed land of vineyards and fruit orchards, of cosy white villas set amongst trees, of tall stately cypresses, of hedges and bushes and flowers. It was the time of the wine harvest. Clusters of gleaming black grapes hung from the vines. Men and women, boys and girls filled them into wicker baskets and waved to us as we passed. . . .

At Tuturano we turned through the barbed-wire gates of a P.O.W. camp. We were just a little too late; the prisoners had all been taken north, all except two South African medical orderlies who had somehow managed to remain behind. We took them under our wing, ignoring the tears in their eyes.

The Italian colonel in charge of the camp invited us to lunch, expressed his admiration for all things British and spat on the German name. How quickly an ally can change! Immediately after the coffee (real coffee) we left, taking the two South Africans perched on the back of our jeeps, the two happiest men in Italy. Tailing Popski's flying jeep, smothered in his dust, we sped through the fruit-laden countryside, visiting aerodromes. The Germans had abandoned them all. Runways were cratered, control-rooms wrecked, buildings demolished, but all the landing-grounds could quickly be made serviceable for the R.A.F. Popski gave each station commander his orders and raced on to the next. . . .

Late at night we drove into an orchard near Oria and Beautyman erected his aerial. Popski encyphered a long *sitrep* (situation report) and Beautyman tapped for an hour. After a meal we crawled thankfully into our sleeping-bags. We'd been on the go for thirty-six hours.

'Peaches for breakfast, sir,' Waterson announced the following morning. 'Help yourself.'

We had parked in a grove of peach-trees. Breakfast hung above our heads in yellow, juicy orbs and we had only to stretch out our hands.

'Back to Taranto,' said Popski ere we had eaten our fill.

The port was transformed. Ships filled the harbour and stood out in the bay. A continuous stream of loaded trucks rumbled through the dock gates and honked its way through the crowded streets. Gangs of Italian labourers cleared away the rubble of bombed buildings, ice-cream vendors called their wares and everywhere you looked you saw red-bereted figures standing or walking about.

'Are you Airborne?' Sergeant Waterson shouted to an Airborne sergeant passing along the street.

'No, ye bastard—stillborn!' the sizzling retort came back.

'Stillborn!' echoed Curtis. 'Ha . . . ha . . . ha . . . ha . . . ha!' his horsy laugh.

Popski's jeep appeared amongst the traffic and drew up beside us with a flourish.

'Bari,' he mouthed, wheeled and made off.

We whooped with delight, piled into our seats and revved madly after him, scattering the civilians on to the pavements as we swerved past the convoys of trucks. . . .

Unreal it was, that journey to Bari, like a dream. We drove upon a tarmac road, smooth as a billiard table. The sun shone from a blue-blue sky with never a hint of cloud. Doll's-house villas, cuddled by groves of vivid-green trees daubed in yellow, lined both sides of the route. In every village or township *carabinieri* stood at the inter-sections handing us through streets bedecked with Allied flags and waving, cheering crowds: '*Viva Inglesi. Viva Americani.*' Garlands of flowers, bunches of grapes fell into our jeeps as we passed. . . .

'Look at that smasher, Dave,' enthused Beautyman, eyeing a curvaceous piece as he took a corner in Locorotondo, bumping against the kerb.

'Hey, look out, Beaut!' warned Davies, fearing their jeep would overturn.

'It was that "beaut" that caused it,' punned Beautyman, straightening up, and turned his head for another look. 'What a bloody smasher!'

Popski slowed to consult his map. We slackened to a walking pace behind him. A thoughtful man ran out from the crowd and trotted beside us splashing wine from a bottle into a glass.

'*Beve . . . beve*,' he urged hospitably, handing up the glass. (Drink . . . drink.)

The crews grabbed at the glass in turn, drained the contents and handed it back.

'*Grazia*,' they called.

'*Bravo!*' roared the crowd.

Locorotondo fell behind us, then Fasano, and we drove downhill to the shores of the blue Adriatic with never a sign of the Germans . . . along by the side of the dancing waves . . . through Monopoli ('Shufty that one, Al') . . . Polignano ('. . . *bella, signorina* . . . ha . . . ha . . . ha') . . . Mola di Bari ('*Niente bint*') . . . and so to Bari, where Mussolini's outworn Fascist slogan stared at us from the wall of a factory building—*Credere. Obedire. Combatere.* (Believe. Obey. Fight.)

Bari was different. The people were jumpy and nervous. We felt the tension the minute we entered the town. Not that the people didn't welcome us when we drew up in the piazza in front of the barracks. They cheered and they waved, they kissed and hugged us, brought us cheese, wine and fruit, but these things they did a little subdued, with a wary eye over the shoulder. We soon discovered why—the Germans were just round the corner, in Molfetta and Trani, a few miles up the coast.

Popski went into the barracks to talk to the Italian commander.

'*Bella, signorina* . . .' Curtis began, but the girls of Bari were more timid than their sisters in Brindisi and stood out of reach.

'*Tedeschi . . . tedeschi.*' A frightened murmur ran through the crowd and the piazza emptied.

'They say the Germans are coming,' Al Locke translated.

'The Battle of Bari,' I thought and shouted to Waterson to stagger the jeeps. . . .

No Germans appeared and after a while the populace came back cheering and laughing. Their informant (a man on a bicycle from Mola di Bari) had seen us pass through and thought *we* were Germans!

Brrrrrrrt. Clearing his gun in case of accidents, Curtis inadvertently (or deliberately) fired a burst into the air. The piazza emptied again . . . inside the barracks an aged general blanched and all but fell to the floor. Poor lovable Italians. You never wanted a war. Music, not arms, is your forte.

'We'll stay in Bari tonight, Bob,' Popski said when he came out.

'What about the jeeps, Popski?'

'Inside the barracks. I've made arrangements.'

The barrack gates swung open and we revved inside, eyed uncertainly by Italian soldiers who had at one time been in Tobruk. 'How droll!' I thought. 'We've been fighting these blighters for years and here we are driving into their barracks, telling them to guard our jeeps.'

'Nothing will be touched,' an English-speaking Italian officer assured Driver Davies, who was dubious about leaving his kit.

Driver Davies blushed and looked embarrassed.

P.P.A. repaired to a nearby hotel and knew, for the first time in years, the luxury of wash-hand basins, spring mattresses and sheets. 'Sheets! Cor blimey.' (Barnes.)

Popski took his private army out to dinner. Twelve of us sat down at a long table in the crowded Ristorante Bella Vista, the cynosure of all eyes. No two of us were dressed alike. Popski sported his cream corduroy slacks and khaki-drill tunic; I wore American Army gaberdine trousers and a British Army battle-dress blouse; Curtis was in battledress, Riches wore a parachute jumping-jacket, Beautyman and Saunders wore khaki pullovers, Davies had a leather jerkin; some of the men donned ties, like officers, others had open-necked shirts. Riches had a beard; Locke wore his black eye-patch. And we were all sun-burned, exuberant, bursting with health and vitality. No wonder the diners turned to stare—especially when Curtis' horsy laugh reverberated round the walls.

'But officers and men dining together,' muttered two elegantly uniformed Italian officers from the barracks, horrified at the spectacle of a British major sitting down to dinner with his men.

.   .   .   .   .

Jeep engines revved noisily through the streets of Bari at crack of dawn and the Brrrrrt . . . brrrrrt . . . of testing guns struck terror into many Italian hearts.

We made contact with the enemy at Bitetto. Our five jeeps and two German armoured scout cars eyed one another down the length of the dusty village main street until Sergeant Waterson, in his element again, chortled, 'Chuff, chuff,' and opened up with his fifty. Brrrrrrrrrt. . . . A stream of scarlet tracer filled the narrow street . . . the Germans turned and fled . . . the Italians ran out of the village.

An hour later Popski made a startling discovery. A water company's private telephone line to its various control points upcountry had been overlooked by the retreating German Army and the wires hadn't been cut. By the simple procedure of entering the company's main office near Bari and ringing up its country control offices one after the other, Popski soon had an accurate picture of the German dispositions.

There were German troops in Trani and Barletta on the coast, and in Gravina, Altamura and Matera inland. Temporarily there was a fluid front, and if we were quick about it we could slip behind the lines before the German forces moving south to contain the Allied bridgeheads at Taranto and Salerno formed a solid front across Italy.

'Look, Bob,' said Popski, spreading out a map on the bonnet of his jeep and pointing to the hilly area behind Gravina, 'if we can get into the Murge without being seen we can work across country and sit astride the main German L. of C. . . .'

We hurried back to Bari, choking in the fine white dust which lies inches deep on the secondary roads of southern Italy, commandeered petrol from the Italian barracks, filled up to capacity and raced for the Murge follow-my-leader in line, foot hard down on the accelerator . . . through Modugno . . . Bitetto . . . Toritto . . . along narrow country lanes . . . through olive groves . . . over ditches . . . across fields . . . up hillsides . . . up . . . up into the hills overlooking the main roads coming in from Naples to Taranto.

The Murge was a saboteur's paradise (it was long the haunt of Italian *banditti*), lonely hill country affording excellent cover, easy jeep access to road and rail communications, well-disposed local inhabitants, food and water in plenty, complete secrecy.

Popski had been praying for such an opportunity for months and now his prayer was answered.

We lurched into a hollow on the plateau and Popski held up a hand. I drove alongside him.

'This'll do, Bob. We'll wait till dark. Keep an eye on the road.'

'O.K., Popski.'

I signalled to Waterson to disperse the jeeps under cover.

The crews filled up petrol tanks and cleaned guns. Popski pored over maps, for which he had an obsession. I slung binoculars round my neck and walked to the top of a rocky knoll where I lay in the warm sun watching German traffic moving between Foggia and Gravina. There wasn't a great deal of it on that secondary road; within the space of two hours only one staff-car, a convoy of lorried infantry and a couple of despatch riders went past. I watched until dusk and returned to the jeeps.

'Any traffic, Bob?' Popski enquired.

'Very little, Popski.'

I told him what I'd seen.

'Right. We'll move as soon as it's dark.'

Behind the lines, each jeep was self-contained and the crews did their own cooking. Bill Wilson handed me a messtinful of bully stew and I sat down to eat it with my back against a wheel. When I'd gobbled the last mouthful he handed me a mug of steaming tea.

'Mair, sirr?'

'No thanks, Bill.'

He took the empty mess-tin and I sipped the hot tea. . . .

Darkness enveloped the plateau and the moon rose. Popski climbed into his jeep and pressed the self-starter. The rasp of the pinion echoed shrilly in the dark silence. Four more self-starters rasped in unison, jarring taut nerves. 'Hell's teeth,' I muttered, 'they'll hear us in Gravina.'

Five dark shadows lurched out of the hollow and were momentarily etched against the skyline as we felt for the sheep-track leading down the ravine towards the road.

The track was steep and very rough. Sharp stones jutted every few yards threatening to rip the low-slung engine sumps and we jolted painstakingly downhill with our fingers crossed . . . lurch . . . scrape ('Hell!') . . . scrape . . . bump . . . scrape . . . scrape . . .

('Muck it!') . . . bump . . . lurch . . . scruuuuuuuunch ('Christ, we'll rip the bloody sump off!') . . . stopping to see if any damage was done . . . moving on again gingerly . . . lurch . . . bump . . . scrape. . . .

The valley took shape in the waxing moonlight. A white ribbon of road stretched like a tape measure between the dark shadows of occasional trees; the twin metals of a single-line railway gleamed beside it and a signalman's box stood out clearly, like a sentry guarding the line. Beyond road and railway silver-shadowed hills lay jumbled against the starry sky.

At the bottom of the ravine the track widened and the surface improved. Popski changed into higher gear and shot ahead. One by one we put on speed and hurried to catch up. . . .

The railway lines gleamed between us and the white road. Popski stopped in the middle of the track and the other jeeps halted behind him. A thousand yards away a despatch rider raced towards Gravina shattering the still air with the popping noise of his exhaust. There wasn't a breath of wind. The motor-cyclist's dust rose and fell in his wake, and hush followed his noisy passage. Somewhere a sheep-dog barked.

Popski drove on. We followed slowly, keeping distance. . . . Trees lined the track near the railway and we braked in their shadow. Waterson jumped out with a Tommy-gun and went to make sure the signalman's box was empty.

'O.K., sir,' he whispered (to Popski).

The road was deserted. We listened intently. There wasn't a sound.

'Bob,' Popski called softly.

I walked to his jeep.

'We go along the road for about a mile and then turn off,' he whispered. 'Ready?'

'O.K., Popski.'

I slid into my jeep and Popski revved quietly.

Five jeeps creaked over the level-crossing, bumpity-bump, and turned into the dusty road.

The German convoy was on top of us before I quite realized what was happening. Twenty trucks rumbled round a bend and bore down upon us in the moonlight. My mouth went dry and I felt my stomach turn over. 'What the hell do we do now?' I heard my mind ask. I'd been expecting this to happen ever since I'd taken to following Popski around enemy lines of communication, and here it was. . . .

Popski had nerves of steel. He never batted an eyelid. Realizing there wasn't time to turn back he put on speed and drove boldly on . . . and waved (yes, waved!) to the German drivers as the convoy thundered past at arm's length. We took our cue from him and followed his example, quaking in our seats, waving wildly and choking in the billowing dust which mercifully screened us from too close a scrutiny . . . and the German drivers waved back from the high cabins of their trucks. . . .

'No one will believe it,' I chortled to Bill Wilson when the danger was past.

'God, sirr, I wis scairt.'

'*Mama mia*,' came from Gino, an Italian interpreter we carried on the back.

Popski reached the turn-off, put out a hand, swung right and disappeared up a sheep-track. The rest of us couldn't get there quick enough.

Behind a hill, a mile from the road, Popski halted to give us a breather.

'That was a narrow squeak, Popski,' I whispered.

Popski chuckled happily. He enjoyed such situations.

'I hoped nobody would open fire. I hadn't time to warn you.'

Sergeant Waterson grinned in the moonlight and eased his chin-strap. Most of the men were quiet. It had given them all a turn. Even Curtis was silent.

We drove on again, winding our way through the moonlit hills of the Murge till we reached the Basentello River about one o'clock in the morning. Miles behind us another convoy of lorried infantry rumbled up to the front.

'There should be a bridge somewhere,' Popski said.

One jeep went downstream . . . another upstream . . . searching for the bridge.

'Found it, sir,' said Waterson, coming back.

Over a humpbacked bridge with the exhaust echoing between the stone parapets . . . along a winding sandy track . . . up a hill . . . into a dip with sheep scattering . . . up a long pull in low booster gear . . . into a secluded hollow in the hills overlooking the main road from Naples to Taranto.

'We'll stop here, Bob,' said Popski.

Waterson dispersed the jeeps and Beautyman put up his aerial. An hour later Airborne in Taranto, 100 miles away, knew what enemy reinforcements were moving up to the front.

Guard duty by crews. Sleep.

I dreamt I was driving down a long tunnel in the opposite direction to a German convoy which came on . . . and on . . . and on. . . . One of the trucks swerved and I crashed into it. . . .

I woke with a start. The sun was hot on my face, making me sweat. Popski was flicking pebbles at me.

'Road-watch, Bob,' he reminded me.

I nodded, wriggled out and looked about.

We were leaguered in a cup within a cluster of hill-tops, completely hidden from prying eyes. Under a cloudless, azure sky dewdrops sparkled like jewels in the grass and the air was sweet and clean. It felt good to be alive. I walked across the drying grass to a little spring of crystal water which bubbled up beside a moss-grown boulder and swallowed mouthful after mouthful of its pure nectar. On my way back I passed close to Curtis' jeep and overheard him say:

'. . . bloody German convoy and he never turned a hair . . . shook me.'

'Did you get a fright, Bum?' I asked, laughing.

'Not 'arf, sir. Shook me to the bloody core . . . cor.'

Bill Wilson handed me a mug of tea and I put some biscuits in my pocket.

'I'm off, then,' I said to Popski.

He nodded. 'Be back at dark.'

I strolled happily down the hillside towards the main road, glad to be off on my own. I liked road-watch. It was interesting, called for little physical effort and was just dangerous enough to prevent boredom.

Half-way down the hillside I sat down and searched the valley through binoculars, selected a clump of bushes near the road and made cautiously towards them, stopping frequently to make sure I wasn't being watched.

Thirty yards from the deserted tarmac I settled down in the shade of a bush, made myself comfortable and pulled out my little note-book and pencil. I ruled a number of pages down the middle, headed one column 'Up Traffic', the other 'Down Traffic', and waited patiently for things to happen.

116

There was a village on a hill-top across the valley and I could see the *contadini* working in the vineyards on the slopes. . . . A distant rumble grew louder. Fixing my eyes on a bend in the road I waited with pencil poised . . . a lumbering half-track appeared pulling a long-barrelled gun. . . . I watched it go past and wrote in my 'Up' column:

0815 Hrs.   1 P

signifying that one portee had gone in the direction of Gravina at a quarter past eight. A few minutes later another portee lumbered past and I added another '1 P' to my 'Up' column. 'Poor Airborne,' I thought.

Then there was a popping, banging noise . . . a despatch rider cornered in classic style and roared towards Gravina, leaving a smell of burned oil in the air. I wrote in my 'Up' column:

0830 Hrs.   1 D.R.

Twenty minutes later a staff-car swished past, making for Potenza. Two German officers sat stiffly in the back seat (I could almost see their monocles). 'Ha, ha, good Nazis,' I chuckled, 'you don't know I am here and wouldn't you be bloody annoyed if you did.' I watched the car disappear and pencilled in my 'Down' column:

0850 Hrs.   1 S.C.

There was a lull in the traffic for a while and I fell to thinking how funny it was that Bob Yunnie from Aberdeen, Scotland, should be sitting behind a bush on an Italian mountainside in September 1943 watching German traffic moving up to the front. Who would have thought it in September 1939? Certainly not Bob Yunnie. I was in Aldershot then, peeling potatoes and hating it. My thoughts went back to the early days of the war. From Aldershot we'd gone to Cheshire and then, just before Christmas, out to Palestine with the 1st Cavalry Division R.A.S.C. We'd crossed France by train from Cherbourg to Marseille in the days of the phoney war and then by troopship (the old *Devonshire*) to Haifa. Palestine in 1940 . . . sloping arms on the scorching square

117

at Sarafand . . . stealing oranges from the groves at Rishon-le-Zion. . . . Jerusalem. . . . Force Headquarters in the King David Hotel. . . . Swimming in the Dead Sea. . . . Moascar . . . the O.C.T.U. in Kasr-el-Nil Barracks in Cairo. . . . Commissioned. . . . Kilo 9 on the road to Alexandria . . . the Libyan Arab Force. . . . Captain Peniakoff and Lieutenant Jan Caneri . . . training in the desert . . . guarding aerodromes. . . . Mana House Hotel . . . the motor-cycle accident. . . . Ameryia. . . . Tobruk. . . . Benghazi. . . . Mersa Brega. . . . Rommel's sudden attack . . . cut off . . . the long walk to Tobruk. . . . Cairo. . . . Popski and P.P.A. Like pictures on a cinema screen the train of events since 1939 flashed through my mind.

Was it only four years? It seemed a lifetime, so much had happened. What did the future hold? The war would be over one day and then what? An office desk? How did one readjust oneself to an office desk and regular hours after the roving, adventurous life we led in P.P.A.? Could one readjust to that humdrum existence? I couldn't see myself doing it and began to worry. . . . 'This is bloody silly,' I admonished myself. 'Here you are sitting on the German L. of C. worrying about what will happen when the war's over. You might never get back. Forget it.' But the idea took root and worried me. . . .

The popping of an exhaust brought me back to earth. Another despatch rider cornered classically and raced, head down, towards Gravina. I noted it in my 'Up' column:

1015 Hrs.   1 D.R.

At eleven o'clock a couple of supply trucks rattled past followed by another long pause. . . . I felt hungry and chewed at a biscuit . . . took a pull at my water-bottle . . . then the sun was directly overhead and I moved closer into my bush.

Traffic became a little more brisk in the afternoon. Shortly after two o'clock a troop of armoured cars rumbled past. I scrawled in the 'Up' column:

1420 Hrs.   3 A.C.

At half past two another despatch rider zoomed past and shortly afterwards another staff-car . . . then an ambulance hurried towards Potenza. . . . I heard the rumble of trucks. . . .

I had my eyes on the bend and saw a convoy of lorried infantry come into the straight. I watched the trucks sweeping round one after the other, and counted them as they came . . . one . . . two . . . three . . . four . . . five . . . they seemed to be going very slowly . . . there was a screech of brakes . . . the leading truck stopped opposite me . . . the others drew up close behind . . . my heart beat fast. . . . I 'froze'. . . . To my horror, German infantry jumped out of the trucks . . . crossed the ditch . . . and walked towards my bush.

'Oh, God,' I thought, 'I've been given away. They're coming for me.' . . . And then I thought: 'No. It's not me they're after. They wouldn't send five truck-loads of infantry for one man. It's the jeeps they're after. Somebody's betrayed us. It's a mopping-up party. . . . I must warn Popski . . . but they'll see me and shoot me in the back as I run up the hill.' The soldiers stopped twenty yards from the bushes and began to unbutton their trousers. . . . I crouched, making myself as small as possible, and shook with silent laughter.

I watched the German infantry fasten their buttons and go back to their trucks. . . . I watched them clamber over the tail-boards. . . . I watched the sergeant come round the trucks checking that no one was left behind. . . . I watched the convoy start up . . . and rumble towards Gravina. . . .

In my 'Up' column I noted:

1500 Hrs.   5 L.I. (P)

and a deep sigh of relief escaped me. 'Whew!' What a fright I'd got!

The traffic thinned out again and there was nothing until four o'clock when a supply convoy went past . . . then another. D.R. . . . a small staff-car. . . . At five o'clock the sun dropped behind the hills . . . the shadows lengthened . . . a hush settled over the valley . . . stars twinkled . . . dusk.

Putting away my note-book and pencil I rose stiffly, ducked away from the bush, turned my back on the road and walked up the hill.

'Well, Bob,' Popski greeted me, 'how did you get on?'

'Fine,' I said, 'quite a lot of traffic.'

'Any tanks?'

'Not a tank. A couple of guns and five trucks of lorried infantry.'

I gave him my note-book and went to my jeep. I was ravenous. Bill Wilson put a messtinful of stew into my hands. I devoured it quickly.

'Any more, Bill?'

'Yes, sirr.'

I ate another messtinful and followed it with half a dozen biscuits and jam and three mugs of tea.

'Bob,' I heard Popski call.

Popski was mercurial. His moods changed like the weather and I never knew when he called me whether to expect a bouquet or a rocket. I tried to think of anything I'd done wrong as I groped towards his jeep.

He was busy encyphering my traffic census in the light of a shaded torch.

'Yes, Popski?' (expecting a rocket).

'What does the bracketed P after Lorried Infantry stand for?'

I chuckled, remembering why I'd put it there.

'Pissed.'

Popski stopped writing and looked up.

'I beg your pardon?'

'P for pissed. The convoy stopped for the men to have a piss. I thought they were coming for me. I got the fright of my life.'

Popski started to laugh and I told him the details.

'The same thing happened to me in the Jebel,' he said when I'd finished, and he related how nearly he'd been caught in the very same way, sitting in the scrub on the edge of the desert watching the Benghazi road.

'That deserves a drink, Bob,' he said when he'd finished encyphering. 'Give this to Beautyman and come back.'

I stumbled across to Beautyman's wireless jeep with the signal.

'Send this off, Beaut.'

'O.K., sir.'

Beautyman put on his headphones and started to tap. . . .

I picked my way back to Popski's jeep.

'Good luck, Bob,' he said, handing me an enamel mug with an inch of whisky in the bottom.

'All the best, Popski.' I swallowed the fiery stuff and coughed.

From that moment Popski and I were better friends. The fact that we'd both shared the same nerve-racking experience drew us closer together and seemed to form a bond between us.

Popski was a complex character. Half Russian, half Belgian, he was a curious mixture of traits. He was arrogant and humble, shy and confident, fearless and hesitant, cold-blooded and warm-hearted, a harsh commander, a wonderful friend. He was both intuitive and pig-headed, extraordinarily far-sighted in some things, quite naïve in others. A genius in his own line (unorthodox warfare), he had a determination and persistency of purpose which drove himself and his men to the farthest limits of human endurance, and there were times when it was quite impossible to reason with him. But charm! The Popski charm had to be experienced to be believed. Popski could turn on charm like turning on a tap. And how effective it was! He would have irate generals eating out of his hand in five minutes. Shy of women, unsure of them, they hung on his every word. Popski was P.P.A. and P.P.A. was Popski, the instrument through which he expressed his powerful personality. Feared rather than loved, respected by all, Popski left the imprint of his personality upon all who came in contact with him. He surprised me the following morning when I was preparing to continue the road-watch by saying:

'Locke will do road-watch today, Bob. Show him where to go and come back here. I've got a job for you.'

Wondering what was in store for me, I took Locke to the top of the hill, showed him the bush I'd sat behind the previous day and returned to Popski's jeep.

'Yes, Popski?'

'I want you to go up here,' pointing to the map, 'and see what's going towards Salerno.'

'Here' was a lateral road linking Barletta on the Adriatic with Salerno on the Tyrrhenian.

'Road-watch?' I asked.

'Yes. Take Waterson with you. Two jeeps.'

'D'you want me to go now?'

'No. Wait till dusk. Twenty-four-hour watch. Come back tomorrow night.'

I nodded, feeling elated.

'I'll see you before you go,' Popski said, and he and Cameron climbed into their jeep to spend the day visiting the local sheep farmers, gleaning information and swearing them to secrecy, the latter not a difficult task since the *contadini* already hated the Germans for stealing their sheep.

Locke went to his lonely vigil by the roadside. Beautyman watched his call times. The crews dozed in the shade of their jeeps and moved about as little as possible. Sergeant Waterson and I studied the map.

'He wants us to go up here, Sarge,' I said, pointing to the thick red line linking Barletta with Potenza and Salerno. 'Wants to know what traffic's going to Salerno.'

'We'll have to be careful here, sir,' Waterson pointed to the criss-cross of roads near Venosa.

'We will,' I agreed and added, 'we don't want to meet any more convoys do we, Sarge?'

Waterson thought of the previous night's narrow escape.

'God, the old man's terrific, sir. Never turned a hair.'

'Did you get a fright?'

Waterson chuckled reminiscently.

'Nearly pissed myself, sir,' he confided.

The day passed. I shaved . . . went up the hill to see how Locke was getting on. I could see the bush, but not Locke. There was little traffic on the road and I assumed Locke was safe . . . had lunch . . . studied the map . . . dozed for an hour . . . had tea . . . chatted to Waterson . . . got ready.

Popski and Cameron lurched into the leaguer as dusk fell.

'I'm off, then, Popski,' I said.

'Quite happy about it, Bob?'

I nodded.

'When d'you want me back?'

'Be back not later than midnight tomorrow night.'

'O.K., Popski.'

We shook hands.

'Good luck, Bob.'

Sergeant Waterson followed me along miles of winding sheep-track to the trees and vineyards of Gensano lying hushed and mysterious under the moon. I drew up before I came to the first of the criss-cross roads, jumped out and ran back to speak to him.

'We'll park the jeeps and go and have a shufty on foot.'

Waterson nodded and followed me into an adjoining vineyard where we parked the jeeps in shadow, ready for a quick exit.

'Sit tight,' I instructed Bill Wilson. 'Use your loaf if Jerry comes along.'

'O.K., sirr.'

I padded along the side of the road in the white, moonlit dust with Waterson close behind. At 10 p.m. the *contadini* slept behind locked doors and Gensano was as quiet as the grave. There was no wind and the leaves of the vines and their sheltering trees hung limp and motionless, covered by a film of dust which gleamed in the moonlight and gave them a ghostly appearance. The nostalgic scent of honeysuckle burdened the air. . . .

We approached the first road junction, stopping in the shadows to listen before walking into the open road. The thick, flour-like dust was grooved and channelled by narrow wheeltracks. We bent to examine them.

'Cart wheels,' I whispered.

Waterson nodded.

Silent, corridored vineyards lined the roads. We walked through them from road junction to road junction, helping ourselves to grapes. Dogs barked near homesteads, betraying our passage, and once, passing close to a cottage, we heard the sound of Italian voices raised in anger. All the roads were patterned by the wheels of bicycles and farm-carts, but there was no sign of enemy traffic.

'Right, Sarge,' I said when we'd examined most of the roads, 'let's go back to the jeeps and carry on.'

We retraced our steps, followed by the sound of barking dogs, and found Wilson and Barnes standing by their fifties eating grapes.

'Gutsy muckers,' Waterson commented.

The thick dust cushioned our wheels, making hardly a sound as we sped along the moonlit lanes towards the lateral road beyond Venosa. I felt happy and uplifted and wished this free, adventurous life could go on for ever.

A pedal cyclist appeared . . . gave a frightened stare . . . touched his cap, obviously thinking we were Germans . . . and pedalled furiously as soon as we were past . . . a yapping dog ran out of a gateway . . . snapped viciously at the wheels . . . tired of the game and trotted home.

The first buildings of Venosa appeared, quiet and peaceful in the soft light. Turning into a vineyard, Waterson and I repeated our previous tactics on foot. . . . An hour later, having prowled all round the sleeping village, we drove along by-pass lanes towards the lateral road.

I drove on to it before I realized where we were and panicked when I heard the rumble of vehicles. 'Christ,' I muttered, braking violently and throwing Bill Wilson's nose against the fifty, 'we're on the lateral road.' I reversed blindly, missing Waterson's jeep by inches.

'We're on the lateral road,' I whispered hoarsely, 'there's a convoy coming.'

I looked wildly around. Vineyards shadowed both sides of the road but there was a ditch on either side. 'We'll have to risk it,' I thought, snicked into low booster gear and put the jeep at the ditch like a horseman putting his horse at a water-jump . . . lurch . . . thud . . . smack . . . crash. . . . I was over the ditch and running smoothly between the trellises. . . . I heard Waterson's jeep crash through the ditch behind me. Temporarily, we were safe.

The rumble grew louder.

'Tanks,' Waterson breathed.

My heart missed a beat. . . .

From behind a dusty, grape-laden vine trellis Waterson and I watched a convoy of German tanks thunder towards Salerno, grey, iron-clad monsters with clattering tracks and vicious 88-mm. guns poking their noses in front. . . . We looked at one another and grinned, feeling prickly shivers running up and down our spines . . . the last tank disappeared . . . the clatter subsided . . . the dust settled . . . the rumble faded into the night.

'That was a close shave,' I breathed shakily.

Waterson pulled at his chin-strap and breathed 'Chuff, chuff.'

I glanced at my wrist-watch. It was twenty minutes past two. In another three hours it would be daylight. Could we spend a whole day in the vineyard without being discovered? Would *contadini* come to work, see us and betray us by their gossip?

'D'you think we're safe here, Sarge?'

Waterson's mouth was full of grapes. He shrugged and swallowed.

'Where else can we go?'

'Let's take a look.'

Telling Wilson and Barnes to stay put, Waterson and I tip-toed into the lateral road and stood on the floury tracks, looking and listening. There wasn't a sound. Soft, heart-aching, silver light poured down upon the slumbering countryside, upon the bare hillside which stretched skywards on the northern side of the road and upon the silent vineyards which filled the southern vista.

'Not much cover up there, Sarge,' I whispered, indicating the bare moonlit hillside, 'we'd better stay where we are and risk it.'

Waterson's beady eye glinted and he eased his tight chin-strap. We turned and walked back to the vineyard, prepared for a trying day.

'We'd better do something about this, sir.' Waterson indicated our wheel-marks in the ditch.

'Hell, yes.'

Waterson picked up a dead branch and swept the dusty road, the flattened grass, the soil between the trellises. Sherlock Holmes would have known jeeps had entered the vineyard, but it wouldn't have been obvious to less observant men.

'We're spending the day here,' I told Wilson and Barnes. 'No talking and no moving about.'

'O.K., sir,' they both whispered, pinning their faith on Waterson and me.

Waterson took up a look-out stance near the lateral road. I felt suddenly tired and sat down with my back against a wheel . . . the next thing I knew, it was broad daylight with Waterson whispering urgently in my ear: 'Hey, wake up, sir. Ities coming.'

I was instantly awake, feeling alert and refreshed.

Italian voices sounded from the far end of the vineyard where the *contadini* were beginning the day's work of harvesting the grapes. They were a good distance away. . . .

I regarded Waterson's serious face. His beady eye bored questioningly into my soul.

'Sit tight,' I whispered, 'they mightn't come here.'

The sun rose above the trellises, flooding the vineyard with golden light, stripping us naked. . . . A motor-cycle sounded on the lateral road and Waterson reached his look-out stance just in time to see a German despatch rider roar past in a cloud of billowing dust.

An hour passed . . . two hours . . . the voices were nearer . . . waves of laughter rippled through the vineyard. . . .

125

Dust rose from the lateral road as a convoy of lorried infantry rumbled past close enough for Bill Wilson to see 'the white 'o their een, sir. . . .'

The Italian voices came closer.

Waterson sniggered and touched my arm. 'Look, sir,' he whispered.

I looked and sniggered also. At the far end of our corridor a *contadina* crouched with her back to us, holding up her black skirts. Ungentlemanly, we didn't avert our eyes, but glued them on the woman's back, both thinking the same thought. Would she look round when she'd finished? If she did, the cat would be out of the bag and then what? Fascinated, we watched her rise . . . drop her skirts . . . and walk away without looking round.

At noon the *contadini* ceased work, repaired to the shade of some trees and ate their midday snack. There was chattering and laughter for a while . . . then silence when they took their siesta . . . Voices again about two o'clock when work recommenced. . . . Little children played hide-and-seek while their parents and elder brothers and sisters worked . . . there was a rustle of leaves beside us and a little body wriggled under the trellis. . . . Sammy Barnes looked into a pair of startled brown eyes in a flushed, cherubic face. With great presence of mind he smiled, put a hand into his pocket and held out a piece of chocolate to the little girl. She smiled bewitchingly, grabbed the chocolate with a dirty hand and popped it into her mouth. . . . Sammy Barnes crooned softly to her, invited her on to his knee and plied her with more chocolate. . . .

All would have been well if the child hadn't looked up to see Waterson's piercing blue eye. . . . She uttered a heart-rending shriek and ran for her life. . . .

'That's done it,' I groaned.

We waited to see what would happen, listening to the sounds of German transport passing along the road 100 yards away. . . . Nothing happened for a time. Italian voices were hushed . . . we heard stealthy movements behind the trellises . . . heads appeared at the end of the corridor and were quickly withdrawn. . . .

'They'll think we're Germans, Sarge,' I whispered.

'Hope they do, sir. Safer for us.'

A bold *contadino* appeared in the corridor. Waterson pointed his Tommy-gun and took a couple of strides forward . . . the *contadino* vanished . . . no more heads appeared. . . .

The sun sank, shadows crept out from the trellises and a deep hush settled over the vineyard. A sigh of relief escaped us; in another hour our vigil would be over. . . .

The *contadini* went to their homes, stars twinkled in the sky and darkness settled over the countryside, cloaking our movements.

'O.K., Sarge? Let's go.'

Self-starters rasped, making me jittery . . . two dark shadows moving between the trellised vines . . . quiet burble of exhausts . . . lurch . . . creak . . . lurch . . . the snick of gear changes . . . two jeeps moving quickly along the dust-cushioned lane . . . a terrified cyclist dropping his bicycle in the ditch and running for cover (smiles in the jeeps) . . . a yapping dog scampering beside the wheels . . . desisting with a final, frustrated yap . . . hesitation at a cross-roads, unsure of the way ('Look for our wheel-tracks, sir') . . . on again confidently, following our tyre-prints in the dust . . . past the lamplit windows of Venosa in a wide detour . . . past a group of cyclists . . . staring hard . . . . pedalling furiously . . . across the last road-junction beyond Gensano . . . safely on to the familiar sheep-track. . . .

Miles later a shadowy figure rose from the ditch, pointing a Tommy-gun. 'O.K., Dave. Don't shoot.'

Driver Davies grinned in the moonlight and waved us on. . . .

'Popski and Cameron have gone to Gravina, sir,' Curtis informed me, 'you're to wait here.'

'They've gone where, Curtis?' I asked incredulously.

'To Gravina, sir.'

'Good God,' I muttered. 'What on earth's Popski up to?'

Curtis didn't know. 'He just said you were to wait for him here, sir.'

I waited, wondering what Popski was doing in German-occupied Gravina, wondering what the hell I would do if he didn't come back. . . .

A jeep drew up at the road-block outside Gravina. The German sentry, warned to expect the vehicle, raised the barrier and waved it through. . . . 'So far, so good, Jock,' Popski muttered to Cameron as they sped down the moonlit road into Gravina. . . .

The jeep pulled up in the shadow of a house in the piazza. The street door was open and a light shone through the shutters of an upstairs window. Popski spoke an authoritative word of command to the German sentry who approached and watched him turn and walk away. Cameron leant over the side of the jeep and hauled at a heavy box. Popski grabbed an end and the two of them carried it upstairs to the lighted room. . . .

Major Schulz dozed at his desk, back to the door. Cameron lowered the box to the floor and Popski hit the major a sharp wallop with a rubber truncheon. Major Schulz fell sideways and slumped to the floor. Cameron ran downstairs for another box and Popski's eyes popped—spread out on the major's desk were the ration-strength returns of the German forces opposing Taranto. What a scoop! Popski stuffed the returns inside his battledress jacket and he and Cameron hurried downstairs, climbed into their jeep, returned the sentry's salute and drove through the road-block. . . .

I heard Popski's jeep coming up the hill and went forward to meet him as he drove into the leaguer.

'Hallo, Bob,' he greeted me with suppressed excitement. 'How did you get on?'

'Fine, Popski,' I said. 'How did you get on?'

He brandished a file of papers in my face.

'Strength returns,' he crowed. 'Tell Beautyman I want him.'

The story came out later. While Waterson and I were sitting in our vineyard watching the German traffic pass, Popski had made friends with a local farmer who supplied Major Schulz, the German supply officer in Gravina, with wine, eggs and meat for the Officers' Mess, and learned something of the major's habits.

Posing as an Italian quartermaster-sergeant Popski telephoned Major Schulz from a deserted railway station and told him he had some cases of Napoleon brandy for disposal, they were black-market goods and did the illustrious major want to buy them for the general's mess? Major Schultz thought of kudos, fell for the tale and haggled over the price. Eventually he agreed to buy the brandy. Speaking in a calculated mixture of good Italian and bad German, Popski told the major he would deliver the brandy after dark in a small captured American car, would the good major please tell the guards to let him through the road-block? Yes, yes, said the major and rang off. . . .

Some hours later, Major Schulz shook an aching head and

128

hunted high and low for his strength returns. Fifteen miles away, Beautyman tapped out the précis in code to 1st Airborne Division. 'But this can't be right,' said a puzzled Intelligence officer in Taranto. 'Ask Popski to confirm.'

'Message from Airborne for you, sir,' said Beautyman at dawn. Popski read the Divisional Intelligence Officer's 'Please confirm' signal.

'So,' he muttered, 'they don't believe me, eh? I'll show them,' and he sat down by his jeep in the rising sun and encyphered page after page of verbatim details from Major Schulz' strength returns, numbers and ranks of officers, numbers of other ranks, locations of each unit; surely the most detailed intelligence report ever sent from behind the lines. Later, at the wireless jeep, Beautyman cursed volubly and tapped for hours, not realizing he was making history. . . .

'Right,' said Popski when a limp Beautyman told him the cypher had been transmitted, 'pack up your wireless. We're moving.'

Popski led us out of the leaguer at dusk. We followed him along the sheep-track Waterson and I had taken two days previously . . . down a side-track towards the river . . . along the river bank for a mile or two . . . across a bleak hillside in the dark before the moon came up . . . on to another sheep-track . . . past a large farm where barking dogs rushed out . . . through a ploughed field in low booster gear . . . up to a ruined castle on a hill-top . . . down into a valley. . . .'Where the hell's he going?' I wondered, nodding with fatigue in the last jeep. Popski was laying a false scent for Major Schulz to follow (if he ever did), but didn't trouble to tell me . . . up to another hill-top in the moonlight . . . down the other side smothered in shadow . . . into a secluded hollow as dawn broke.

'Breakfast and sleep, Bob,' Popski announced. 'Two men on look-out.'

'O.K., Popski,' I yawned sleepily, and implemented his orders. . . .

'Truck coming, sir,' I heard a voice say and awoke with a start. My horizons were limited by the grassy banks of the hollow in which the jeeps were dispersed. Popski was looking grim, standing by his jeep with a Tommy-gun under his arm. Waterson, carrying a rifle, was striding towards a knoll where one of the look-outs lay. Elsewhere the jeep crews stood expectantly by their guns. I noticed that the sun was in the west and glanced at my watch. It was half past three.

Curious to know what was happening I picked up a Tommy-gun, ducked up to Waterson's knoll and lay down beside him.

'False alarm,' he muttered. 'It's a foraging truck.'

I watched a truck raising dust on a farm road half a mile away. It disappeared round a bend in the direction of Foggia. We watched its dust subside.

'Flap over,' grinned Waterson and backed down the knoll. Everybody relaxed and we brewed-up.

An hour later, we were jolting down a gully towards the Gravina road, feeling our way towards the sheep-track which would take us back to Bari and petrol supplies before our tanks ran dry.

Popski gave a farmhouse a wide berth and shortly afterwards Saunders announced, 'Two jokers trying to catch up.'

We looked round. Two *contadini* were running along the side of the track obviously trying to catch up with us. Popski halted and we watched the men approach. . . . What did they want? A lift somewhere or were they running to warn us of Germans in the vicinity?

As they came closer it became obvious that they weren't *contadini*.

'Escaped prisoners of war,' I thought.

They had high cheek-bones and spoke Italian with a curious sing-song intonation.

'We are Russians,' the taller of the two announced.

'Russians?' exclaimed Popski and spoke to them in Russian. When they heard their mother-tongue, Ivan and Nicolai, captured at Smolensk in 1942, escaped from the Todt labour organization in Italy in 1943, broke down. Tears coursed down their faces. Delirious with happiness, completely overcome by emotion, they fawned upon Popski like a long-lost brother and begged to be taken along. No, no, said Popski, he couldn't take them along, there wasn't room.

'But, sir,' urged Ivan, 'we are Russian soldiers. We want to fight the Germans.'

'No, no,' Popski repeated, not wishing to be burdened with two complete strangers however keen to fight the Germans, 'I can't take you with me.'

Ivan was six foot three, blond, blue-eyed, ox-chested and very determined. Eventually Popski gave way and said:

'All right. I'll take one of you. One only. I can't take both.'

Ivan turned to say a tearful good-bye to Nicolai and Nicolai looked so utterly heartbroken—he and Ivan had been captured together, escaped together, gone through hell together—that Popski relented and said in Russian:

'All right, Ivan. You can both come. Hop on.'

Wild joy took the place of tears. Ivan leapt on to the back of Popski's jeep and fondled a Tommy-gun like a mother fondling a child. Nicolai, stocky and tough, jumped on the back of Waterson's jeep and caressed the rear 30-calibre Browning.

'Hey, steady, mate,' said Waterson, slightly alarmed. Nicolai looked hurt.

Popski's Private Army was rapidly becoming international— Russians, Englishmen, Scotsmen, Frenchmen, New Zealanders, Italians, South Africans, American jeeps. We were getting on.

Darkness fell and we floundered in a morass of deep, squelchy mud a mile from the Gravina road. Engines revved loudly as the cursing drivers tried to extricate their jeeps from the black, sucking, evil-smelling bog.

'Christ, what a din!' Waterson muttered. 'We'll be heard on the road.'

'Look out, sir,' a voice warned, 'there's a convoy on the road.' Above the noise of the revving jeeps I could hear the rumble of passing trucks.

'Quiet there,' Waterson called to the drivers.

'What?' they shouted back, unable to hear above the noise of their racing engines.

'Over here, Popski!' Saunders yelled from the flank.

It was bedlam. I put my fingers in my ears and hoped for the best.

Hours later, encrusted with black mud, we turned into the main road and raced for the turn-off beside the signalman's box . . . crossed the railway line, bumpity-bump . . . and felt safe.

'Mine the road, Bob,' said Popski. 'We'll wait and shoot up a convoy.'

Before leaving Tunisia Popski had acquired supplies of a new type of road-mine named 'Turds, Calabrian', intended for use on the mountain roads of Calabria. Made of plastic material containing high explosive which detonated on contact, 'Turds, Calabrian', had the appearance of mule droppings and when placed upon a road at night resembled the genuine article so closely as to deceive a stable boy. Holding these innocent-looking objects gingerly in their arms the crews walked up and down the road, placing them strategically in the shadows of trees in clumps and single lumps.

When the last turd had been laid, we stood back to survey the result.

'It's a bloody good likeness, Popski,' I chuckled.

'Turds, Calabrian, roads, for the use of,' chortled Curtis.

'Looks just like horse-shit,' tittered Sammy Barnes.

'Back to the jeeps,' said Popski.

The jeeps were staggered in the shadows of trees with their guns trained on the mine-field. Each crew stood by its guns itching to pull the triggers. . . .

An hour passed . . . nothing came along the road.

We waited, impatiently.

Another hour went by. . . .

Popski looked at his watch. It was half past eleven.

'Another half hour, Bob. We can't wait longer. We must be across the Murge before dawn.'

The minutes ticked slowly by . . . the road remained bereft of traffic. At midnight Popski said:

'Sorry, Bob. Can't wait any longer.'

'Another half hour, Popski,' I urged.

'Ten minutes,' he compromised.

The ten minutes passed. . . . I prayed for a convoy to come . . . the road remained deserted.

'Right, Bob,' said Popski at ten minutes past twelve, 'out we go.'

'Just a minute, Popski,' Saunders requested, 'I've got a Union Jack.'

'What are you going to do with it?'

'Shin up the telephone pole.'

'All right,' Popski nodded, 'be quick!'

Saunders, ex-L.R.D.G. New Zealander, crossed the railway line and shinned up the nearest telephone pole, clung like a monkey at the top, fixed the Union Jack and slid quickly down.

The flag fluttered bravely, defiantly, and a muted cheer burst involuntarily from the watching crews.

Self-starters rasped . . . engines revved. The noise no longer worried us. We'd grown blasé and were on our way out. Reluctantly, with many a backward glance, we followed Popski up the track towards the dark ravine.

Jolt . . . bump . . . lurch . . . scrape . . . up the awful track, droning at a snail's pace, fearful for our sumps . . . cursing . . . swaying . . . glancing back . . . looking down at the valley from the top of the ravine . . . watching red flashes . . . leaping flames . . . hearing the reverberations of explosions. . . .

'Good old Turds, Calabrian.'

'We should have waited.'

'That shook 'em.'

'Got a bloody convoy after all.'

Whispered comments floated up from the barely discernible jeeps halted in the dark jaws of the ravine as the crews looked down upon their handiwork—three fires burning fiercely by the roadside.

Up on the plateau a sea wind blew in our faces, clouds obscured the moon and tenuous wraiths of mist eddied about the jeeps as we lurched across the uneven surface, jolting over stones, bumping into hummocks, scraping the undercarriage on the wiry grass, feeling rather than seeing our way across the bleak mountain.

Approaching an opening through a low stone dyke we were challenged by a German sentry who suddenly appeared by the side of the track, pointing a rifle. Popski switched on his headlamps and barked a command in German. The dazzled sentry stood rigidly to attention thinking it to be one of his own officers.

Popski accelerated . . . braked level with the unsuspecting soldier . . . leaned out and snatched the rifle from his hands. Cameron jumped down and tackled the sentry from behind . . . not quite quickly enough to prevent him giving the alarm.

A confused jumble of querulous, questioning voices rose from behind the dyke and a number of heads bobbed up and down . . . a rifle-shot rang out . . . strong-man Ivan grabbed the struggling, terrified sentry and lifted him bodily on to the jeep where he sat paralysed with fear, gazing down the black muzzle of a Tommy-gun held two inches from his face. . . . Sergeant Waterson yelled

133

'*Charge!*', put his jeep at the opening and went through with his guns blazing, clearing a passage.

Brrrrrrt . . . brrrrrrrrt. Streams of tracer raked the dyke, flashing over in searching red points, smacking into it and leaping high into the air in scarlet richochet . . . engines revved . . . headlamps flashed . . . bullets whined . . . hoarse cries filled the night. Brrrrt . . . brrrrrrt . . . one after the other the jeeps tore through the opening, spraying a searing curtain of death on either side . . . hobnailed boots scraped against stones and sparks flew as the German infantry scattered and fled.

'Mucking hell,' grinned Curtis when we were through the German front line and jogging happily down the lower slopes of the Murge, 'you never know your luck.'

'Never even saw the bastard' (Sammy Barnes).

'Bloody bullet went pinging past my ear . . . ducked just in time' (Driver Davies).

'How many Jerries were there?' (unknown voice).

'Gosh, sirr. . . .' (Bill Wilson).

As dawn broke over the Murge and the sun rose in the sky, dispelling the mist, we crossed the last German-patrolled road and drove into a farmyard for breakfast. Weary in body, bloodshot in eye, happy, exuberant, triumphant, ravenous—all but for our prisoner, who sat dejectedly by Popski's jeep with a vacuous expression in his eyes and refused to be comforted.

'Cuppa, old man?' Curtis hospitably offered a mug of steaming tea to show there was no ill-feeling. The dispirited prisoner made no attempt to take it but continued to stare blankly into space. Curtis took umbrage. 'If the mucker doesn't want it,' he swore, turning to Sammy Barnes, 'he can mucking well do without it. Muck 'im.'

Poor German sentry! What sort of a war was this when the enemy advanced upon you from behind, speaking your own language?

8

Bari was no longer a P.P.A. preserve. Occupying forces had moved in during our absence. There were brass hats in the hotels, naval types in the harbour, military police at street corners. After one horrified look at the scene we turned and revved out of town. Bari was no place for us.

A country villa was more in our line, a place of comfort where we could relax and be on our own. On the road to Foggia, near Andria, we found one.

'This looks a likely place,' I said as we passed a wooded property glimpsed through iron gates and an avenue of tall cypress trees. Turning through the massive gates the jeeps scrunched up the well-kept drive to a white-walled villa set amongst green lawns and shady oak trees.

'Just the job,' said Waterson as we drew up in front of a pillared portico.

A fawning *contadino*, cap in hand, informed us that the villa belonged to his master, the Conte Spagnoletti, who lived in the palazzo in Andria. That's all right, we said, we'll call on the count later, in the meantime we're moving in. The poor caretaker was very upset, but sensing that argument would be useless he stood philosophically aside and watched us move in.

'Not bad, eh?' quoth Driver Davies, sitting down on a brocaded Renaissance chair which would have fetched a price at Christie's.

'Just the job,' said Waterson again, testing the springs of a double four-poster bed.

'Do all right there with a *bella signorina*, eh, Sarge?' Curtis' horsy laugh echoed down the passage.

Popski and I journeyed to Andria to pay our respects to the count.

From the main street of the town we drove through the iron-studded doors of a magnificent fifteenth-century palace built round a central, cobbled courtyard. A white-gloved, uniformed flunkey bowed us into an ante-room where we sat for a respectful few minutes before being bowed through a series of gilt and plush reception-rooms to an inner *salon* where a suave young man of thirty greeted us affably and introduced us to a severe, elderly lady, his mother, and to a breath-takingly lovely young woman, his countess.

'*S'accomodo, Signor Commandante,*' said the count, indicating a couple of gilded chairs. (Please sit down.)

Popski and I sat.

'*Poss offrire qual cosa? Liquore?*' the count asked hospitably. (Can I offer you something? A liqueur?)

'*Grazia,*' said Popski.

The count pulled an ancient bell-rope and somewhere in the caverns of the palace a bell rang. Presently a flunkey appeared bearing a silver tray, bottle and glasses. The count went to a side-table and poured an amber-coloured liquid into exquisite miniature glasses. The flunkey took them from him and handed them round.

'*Salute,*' said the count, raising his glass. (Good health.)

'*Salute,*' we responded and sipped.

Popski, who spoke fluent Italian, entered into a long conversation with the count. The lovely young countess politely tried to make conversation with me, but as my knowledge of the Italian language then consisted of some three phrases—*Bon giorno* (Good morning), *Grazia* (Thank you) and *Come sta?* (How are you?)—our conversation was a little one-sided, but what my share of it lacked in verbosity I made up for in silent admiration for the countess was very beautiful and there are things a man can say to a woman which do not require the medium of words. Mother, in the background, sent me severely disapproving glances, which I ignored. . . .

We were invited to luncheon.

In the centre of a vast panelled hall hung with the gloomy oil-paintings of departed Spagnolettis we sat at an oval table agleam with silver and stiff white napery. A uniformed flunkey stood behind every chair.

A huge dish of *pasta* was placed before me, yards of coiled and

136

twisted macaroni. How on earth, I thought, do I eat this? Surreptitiously, I watched the countess. . . . She picked up a fork, inserted it into the steaming white coils and with a deft twist delicately transferred a portion to her vivid red mouth. That's easy, I thought, and tried to emulate her. . . . I forked myself into a terrible mess. There was no end to the clinging white coils. I turned my fork round and round as I'd watched the countess do but instead of coming to an end in a nice-sized mouthful the coils went on . . . and on . . . and on. . . . And when I tried to take a mouthful they festooned from my mouth to the plate like streamers at a Christmas party. . . . I felt myself growing red in the face.

'*Piace, Capitano?*' the countess enquired kindly, pretending not to notice the mess I was making. 'You like macaroni?'

'*Si, si,*' I hissed desperately, forking hard and blushing to the roots of my hair.

I felt Popski's critical eye upon me and daren't look at him.

Mother threw me a withering glance down her aquiline nose and I was conscious of the flunkey behind my chair thinking, 'What sort of conquerors are these who can't eat macaroni?'

Mercifully, the next course was served. A disdainful gloved hand removed my plate, wiped away the overflow and placed scallops of veal before me. This was familiar ground. I picked up knife and fork and tackled the course with confidence.

'*Piace, Capitano?*' the lovely voice enquired.

'*Si, si,*' I sibilated happily and raised my glass to lovely eyes. '*Salute.*

'*Come sta?*' I ventured after a minute.

'*Bene, grazia, Capitano.*'

Mother gave me a haughty look. I raised my glass to her.

'*Bon giorno. Come sta?*'

The dowager smiled frigidly and informed me she was well.

The countess hid a smile. I raised my glass to her again. What heavenly eyes, I thought.

'*Come sta?*' I repeated, parrot-like.

'*Bene, grazia, Capitano.*' (Did the countess wink or did I imagine it?)

I applied myself to a nicely browned scallop. . . .

The lovely countess brought me luck for later that same day my dream came true.

137

As Popski and I drove up to the villa I blinked and rubbed my eyes, unable to believe their evidence. Jeeps, brand new ones, littered the lawn.

'Our jeeps have had kittens, Popski,' I exclaimed.

'Yes,' he laughed, 'Jan's arrived.'

Jan Caneri had indeed arrived. In addition to more jeeps he had brought more men, more Browning machine-guns, another wireless set, an adjutant's pick-up and a truckful of special equipment.

'Hallo, Jan,' we greeted him and shook his hand.

Popski congratulated him later when he'd seen his prodigious haul.

'Well done, Jan,' he enthused, 'I couldn't have done better myself,' which, coming from Popski, was praise indeed.

'Now, Bob,' said Popski, turning to me, 'I can give you your own patrol.'

I absorbed the nectar falling from his lips.

'I'll give you four jeeps and you can pick your own men.'

I was too overjoyed to speak and Popski mistook my reticence for doubt.

'What's the matter, Bob? Don't you want a patrol of your own?'

'Yes, p-please, Popski,' I stammered and dashed off to select my men before he had time to change his mind.

I chose Curtis, Riches, Locke, Porter, Barnes, Wilson, Stewart (wireless operator) and Gino (Italian interpreter). Counting myself, that made a patrol of nine, three times three, a lucky number I thought. Curtis was promoted to sergeant, Riches to lance-corporal.

Curtis drew jeeps, guns and equipment; ammunition, mines, demolition kit, rations.

I reported.

' "B" Patrol operationally ready, sir.'

'That was quick work, Bob,' Popski laughed.

A few days later I was off on my own.

Eighth Army, pushing up from Calabria, linked up with the bridgeheads at Taranto and Salerno. On the Adriatic, Foggia fell and Fourth Armoured Brigade—landed at Bari—pressed on towards San Severo in the plain. Menacing their right flank, a prickly thorn in the side if defended by the enemy, was the mountainous Gargano Peninsula, the spur on the heel of the Italian boot. It was jeep country. Would P.P.A. make the reconnaissance?

'Here you are, Bob,' said Popski. 'A nice job for you. Off you go.'

'B' Patrol couldn't get away quick enough!

We drove to Manfredonia on the coast, hair-pinned up the tortuous mountain road to Monte S. Angelo and sat in the piazza in the sun drinking wine, listening to Gino interrogating the excited, gesticulating *contadini* who crowded round our jeeps. Where were the Germans? In Vico? In San Marco? *Si, si,* many Germans, many guns. How many? *Molti, molti.* Tanks? Armoured cars? Machine-guns? *Si, si,* hundreds of tanks, hundreds of machine-guns. According to the *contadini* the Gargano was bristling with guns, a veritable fortress.

'What do they say, Gino?' I asked.

Gino looked sceptical.

'*Capitano*, they say the Germans are in Vico and San Marco.'

Vico was down on the coastal flat near the Lake of Varano where the Italians had a seaplane base; San Marco was over the hills towards San Severo where Fourth Armoured Brigade was attacking.

'We'll take a look at San Marco first, Gino.'

I signalled to Curtis.

'O.K., Skipper,' he acknowledged, emptying a wine glass and tossing it to the crowd.

Engines revved, scattering the crowd. We wheeled hard about and snarled out of the piazza, through the narrow streets and down the corkscrew road to the fork where one road led over the hill-tops to San Giovanni and San Marco, the other down to Vieste, Vico and Rodi at sea-level.

'Left,' I shouted to Bill Wilson as we approached the fork at speed. . . . Racing in line, dust flying, we tore across the hills to San Giovanni, slowed down on the outskirts and crawled warily into the town.

The *contadini* gathered about the throbbing jeeps.

'*Dove tedeschi?*' Gino asked. (Where are the Germans?)

Shrugs and doubtful looks from the *contadini*.

'In San Marco?' I asked impatiently.

'*Si, si,*' chorused the crowd.

'*Quanti?*' Gino enquired. (How many?)

'*Molti, molti.*'

'Come on, Gino,' I said, exasperated. 'This is a waste of time. There's only one way to find out.'

We revved through the cobbled streets. . . .

I crept up to the bend in the road outside San Marco with the other jeeps tailing me . . . nosed gingerly round . . . saw people walking in the main street of the town.

'*Niente tedeschi, Capitano,*' Gino assured me. (No Germans.) We drove into the piazza.

'*Dove tedeschi?*' Gino asked the crowd which quickly gathered. Shrugs and noncommittal replies.

Three miles beyond the town we stood in the dusty road beside a demolished bridge and looked down upon the shattered roofs of San Severo in the plain, watching the puffs of smoke raised by the guns of Fourth Armoured Brigade.

'Back and down to the coast road, Bum,' I called to Curtis.

Reversing in the narrow road, we raced back the way we had come . . . through sleepy San Marco. . . . San Giovanni, exhausts hammering as we gear-changed in the narrow, cobbled streets . . . left-fork at the cross-roads below Monte S. Angelo . . . down the twisty road to Vico and Vieste. . . . No Germans. . . . Along the tree-girt side of blue Lake Varano. . . . No seaplanes, no Germans. . . . On madly to Sannicandro . . . Apricena . . . Poggio Imperiale . . . Lesina . . . through dusty, dirty, cobbled streets . . . scattering grunting pigs . . . squawking hens . . . terrified *contadini*. . . .

'*Dove tedeschi?*' Gino asked a dull-witted *contadino* on a bicycle.

'*Si, si, tedeschi,* 'the yokel agreed, touching his cap and pedalling for dear life.

There wasn't a German soldier in the whole of the Gargano Peninsula. I stopped at a farmhouse and Stewart tapped out in code:

BOB TO POPSKI   GARGANO CLEAR

The message was picked up by our wireless link in the villa near Andria and transmitted to Fourth Armoured Brigade.

Late in the afternoon we caught up with the enemy—a party of sappers laying mines in a ford on the River Fortore. I saw uniformed figures bending over the sand as I drove quietly up to the ford.

140

'Quick, Bill,' I whispered, braking, 'Jerry mining the ford. Give 'em a burst.'

Brrrrrrt. . . . Brrrrrrt. Tracer flicked away from the forward fifty . . . the uniformed figures dropped their mines and ran into the bushes which lined the north bank. . . . Brrrrrrt. . . . Brrrrrrt. Bill sprayed the bushes, swinging his gun in a wide arc . . . bodies crashed through the undergrowth. . . . Brrrrrt. . . . Brrrrrrt. Gino grasped a Tommy-gun, jumped from the back of the jeep and waded through the ford. The water came below his knees. He bent and picked up the mines, deprimed them and flung them on to the bank, out of harm's way. Then he turned and waved.

'*Avanti, Capitano*,' his voice floated across the water.

I snicked into booster gear and drove into the river. The water swirled about the jeep wheels and rose up . . . up . . . up to the floor-boards . . . the engine faltered and spluttered as the racing fan picked up water and threw it over the plugs. . . . 'Hell,' I thought, 'I'm going to strand in midstream. What a disgrace on my first patrol!' But the engine kept running and I chugged up the far bank.

I looked back. The other jeeps were staggered round the mouth of the ford with eager faces grinning over their bonnets. I signalled them to come across.

'Take it easy,' I shouted. 'Don't race your engines.'

The jeeps crossed one at a time without stalling and we drove through the bushes on to a bare, grassy hillside with a wood on the skyline and a ruined tower on a knoll in the foreground.

We advanced up the hill in V-formation.

Wheeeeeeeee. . . . Wruuuuuumph. A mortar bomb crashed between the legs of our V, throwing up divots of black earth.

'Spread out,' I yelled, waving my arms outwards.

Wheeeeeeeee . . . wruuuuuumph . . . wruuuuuumph. Two more mortar bombs exploded near, doing no damage, but making us swerve wildly.

'There's an O.P. in that tower,' I muttered. 'Give it a burst, Bill.'

Brrrrrrt. . . . Brrrrrrrrt. Tracer curved into the grey stone walls and disappeared through the glassless windows. . . . Brrrrrt. . . . Brrrrrt. . . . Brrrrrt. The other jeeps opened up. Sparks and dust, stabbing jets of scarlet, enveloped the ancient watch-tower.

Wheeeeeeeeee . . . wruuuuumph . . . wruuuuumph . . . wruuuuumph. Mortar bombs crashed on the hillside, making us zigzag, swerve, brake and accelerate madly. Brrrrrrt . . . brrrrrrt . . . brrrrrrrt. Streams of tracer spattered the crumbling walls of the tower. . . . Wruuuuuuumph. A salvo of bombs fell viciously, bracketing Curtis' jeep.

'*Mama mia,*' he cried in mock terror, ducked and swerved. Black earth thudded on the bonnet of his jeep.

'This is getting a bit dangerous,' I thought when another salvo, exploding close, threw mud in my face, and I signalled to Curtis to pull out.

We swung obliquely across the hillside with mortar bombs following our bumpy passage . . . doubled back . . . ran through an exploding salvo undamaged . . . recrossed the ford as dusk began to fall.

'Bloody near thing, Skipper,' Riches panted, laughing, twirling the points of his handlebar moustache.

'Missed us by bloody inches,' gasped Stewart.

'Whew!' whistled Curtis, wiping his clouded, mud-flecked glasses. 'Thought we'd mucking had it,' and burst into his loud laugh.

I breathed a sigh of relief. By good luck I had brought my men safely through our first patrol action.

On the high ground behind us, overlooking the river, a mansion-house squatted sentinel-like, surrounded by its attendant farm buildings. It was marked 'Ripalta' on the map.

'Keep an eye on the ford, Bum,' I instructed Curtis. 'I'm going up to have a look at that casa.'

Two jeeps moved into position to guard the ford with their guns. Riches' jeep followed mine up the hill to Ripalta. . . .

The house had the appearance of a mediaeval castle with its adjoining high-walled garden and heavy, iron-studded oak door set in a gothic arch. I pulled up in the driveway, jumped out and hammered imperiously on the great door. Riches covered the house with his guns.

I heard footsteps inside . . . the door creaked open to reveal a golden-haired beauty with cornflower-blue eyes, peach complexion, red mouth, a well-shaped bust and silk-stockinged legs who smiled at me intoxicatingly and said in perfect London-English:

'Good evening, Captain. Won't you come in?'

You could have knocked me down with a feather.

Of course I went in, endeavouring to cover up by polite conversation the severe bout of coughing which suddenly afflicted my men.

Princess Charming closed the door and led me into a spacious lounge where my hypnotized mind dimly registered white pillars, rugs, chintz-covered settees, bowls of red roses and a polished mahogany table in an alcove.

'Please sit down, Captain.'

I sat while Princess Charming went to a side-table and brought me a glass of red wine in a crystal glass on a silver tray.

'Your very good health,' I beamed, raising the glass.

'Good luck,' said the Princess.

I sipped the genuine Chianti and felt a luxurious warmth course through my veins.

'Is this a dream?' I asked. 'Or did it really happen?'

Princess Charming smiled bewitchingly. I took a sip of wine.

'It is real, Captain. My name is Dorothy. I'm a London girl. I married an Italian.'

'How do you do, Dorothy,' I said, holding out a hand. 'Bob's the name.'

'How d'you do, Bob,' said Dorothy, smiling.

We shook hands, and were friends.

We looked at one another, and laughed spontaneously . . . and then the spell was broken. People came into the room, crowding it. Dorothy introduced me to husband, sister-in-law, brother-in-law, the Parlato family.

'*Come sta?*' I addressed the pretty sister-in-law, airing my limited Italian, and immediately regretted my folly when the Parlato family, thinking I could speak Italian, deluged me with fast-spoken questions. I couldn't understand a word and looked appealingly at Dorothy.

'I can't speak Italian properly,' I confessed. 'I know only a few words.'

Dorothy interpreted and the barrage died.

'You'll stay the night, Captain?' Dorothy asked hospitably.

'Yes, please,' I enthused. 'Can you accommodate my men— eight of them?'

'Of course.'

'I'll tell them.'

Excusing myself, I went outside to speak to Riches. The coughing began the minute I opened the great door.

'Bad coughs you've got, Rich,' I smiled. 'Been out in the rain?'

'Yes, Skipper,' said Riches demurely.

The coughing stopped.

'Go down to the ford, Rich, and tell Bum to come up. We're staying the night here. I've fixed accommodation for you. Tell Stew to put up his aerial.'

Riches roared his engine and revved away, whooping like a Red Indian.

I sat in my jeep and encyphered a wireless message to brigade telling them I held a ford across the river.

'Give that to Stew, Bill,' I said, handing the message to Wilson. 'Tell him it's urgent.'

'O.K., sirr.'

We stayed at Ripalta for three nights and had a wonderful time. The Parlato family fed us like kings. The men had a storage barn to themselves in the outbuildings. I had a feather-bed in the mansion. Each morning, at dawn, we sallied forth in our jeeps to skirmish with the Hun on the other side of the river and returned, elated, to Ripalta at dusk ready for the glass of wine, the hot bath and the excellent dinner which awaited us. Dorothy was the perfect hostess.

Naturally, such ideal conditions couldn't last. They never do. Our sojourn in paradise was cut short by an urgent message from brigade, asking if the ford was suitable for the passage of armour. I wirelessed back 'Yes'.

Ripalta, isolated behind the spur on the heel of the Italian boot, had escaped the war. Practically self-contained on their lonely estate the Parlatos had been left in peace, their only contact with the Germans being a recent visit from S.S. men who had commandeered their only motor-car. The party of sappers we had surprised at the ford hadn't troubled them, being in too great a hurry. But now the war engulfed the Parlato family, throwing them into confusion. Heavy tanks ploughed a destructive path through their well-tended olive groves; bren-carriers tore up their lawns; wireless trucks parked in the midst of their walled vegetable garden; the shattering boom of artillery racked their nerves and rattled and cracked their window-panes; booted officers and men invaded the privacy of their rooms, leaving mud-stains wherever they trod. Dorothy welcomed her countrymen and did everything she could to help but the eyes of the Parlato men were sad. It took years for an olive tree to bear; a tank crushed it in a matter of seconds.

'Never mind,' I consoled Dorothy, thinking of some of the other war damage I had seen, 'nature will repair the damage. You've got off lighter than most.'

Recruiting the Parlato estate labour, we widened the ford with pick-axes and shovels and led the armour across. It was a lovely morning. The sun shone, glinting on the river, emphasizing the vivid green of grass and trees, and when a German shell exploded inside a bren-carrier, killing all of its laughing occupants and spattering their flesh and blood, it seemed incongruous that Death should gate-crash into so much vibrant Life. The carrier was just behind our jeeps and we felt the blast of the explosion; a few seconds earlier and we would have got it. 'Poor bastards,' I muttered, glancing round at the quivering heap of smoking, twisted metal and the blood and the mangled flesh strewn over the glistening, diamond-studded grass. Further down the slope, carriers, tanks and armoured cars were pouring across the river and fanning out towards Serracapriola, the town we were attack-ing on the top of the hill. Shells and mortar bombs crashed on the hillside, flashing and banging, throwing up cascades of black earth. Some'll be hit and some'll escape, I reflected, and accelerated, secure in the soldier's belief that it could happen to others but not to me.

'Thanks, Yunnie,' said the brigadier when Serracapriola fell. 'You've helped us a lot.'

'Don't thank me, sir,' I replied. 'Thank Popski. The original idea was his.'

We shook hands and parted company.

According to the rules I should have returned to P.P.A. head-quarters in the villa near Andria, but Freedom whispered in my ever-willing ear, 'Why go back?' The coastal flank was no man's land. We'd rations and petrol. 'We'll have a field day, first,' I thought.

'Bum,' I said to Curtis. 'We'll take a trip towards the coast and see what cooks.'

Whoops, grins and a horsy laugh. . . .

A few miles from Serracapriola bridges were blown and we made a detour through the lovely woods, blazing a path in single file between the boles of the silent trees. Floundering in thick undergrowth I was surprised to see a German staff-car drive through the wood 100 yards ahead.

'There must be a road there,' I observed to Gino.

We went to investigate and came upon a woodland track, a curving green tunnel illumined by filtered sunlight. A thought struck me.

'That car went *south*, Gino. Jerry's retreating *north*. They'll be coming back. Quick! We'll ambush the car and capture a staff-officer.'

It was the work of a few moments to manœuvre two jeeps under cover on either side of the track, guns trained on a bend, and we sat, excitedly, waiting for the staff-car to appear.

An hour passed and I began to think I was wasting time when Gino put a warning finger to his lips. His keen ears had detected sounds. We listened intently . . . voices sounded in the wood, coming from the direction of the bend . . . a group of *contadini* appeared on the track, about twenty men, women and children, with the German staff-car behind them.

'What the hell?' I muttered and held my fire.

The *contadini* approached, gesticulating and jabbering excitedly, looking apprehensively over their shoulders at the staff-car . . . a sharp-eyed youth saw the black barrels of our Brownings and stopped in his tracks. His eyes dilated and his mouth fell open. He pointed stupidly and the other *contadini* piled up behind him. Panic ran through the group. A few courageous spirits took a chance and dived between the trees, but the majority came on like terrified sheep, urged by the staff-car behind. . . .

'*Scapare! Scapare!*' Gino yelled. (Run! Run!)

But the poor creatures were too dumbfounded to understand. They just looked at us desperately, pleadingly, with dull eyes, and came on like sheep to the slaughter. Germans behind them, machine-guns in front of them. What could they think but that this was their end?

The staff-car stopped, went into reverse and started to turn

146

round. We pranced beside our jeeps in an agony of frustration, waving and yelling frantically to the terror-stricken *contadini: 'Scapare! Yallah! Imshi!'* (Muck off! Get out of the bloody way!) It was a waste of breath. The *contadini* just stood in the middle of the track, right in our line of fire, paralysed with fright, staring at us with wild eyes. We couldn't murder innocent civilians. In dismay, I watched our prize escape. . . .

'After it,' I shouted. 'After the staff-car.'

Self-starters rasped . . . engines revved . . . the jeeps broke from cover and bumped on to the track, scattering the petrified *contadini*. We tore after the rapidly disappearing staff-car, firing as we went. . . . Brrrrrrt. . . . Brrrrrrrt. The target was småll and the bouncing jeep upset Bill Wilson's aim, but some of the scarlet tracer found its mark. . . . Round the bend, we came upon the staff-car, abandoned and bullet-holed. The windscreen was shattered and there was blood on the seat. . . . We listened. From the depths of the wood, some distance away, came the sounds of stumbling feet. 'After them,' I thought, 'they're wounded. They can't get far.' And then I thought: 'No. The fortunes of war. It might be our turn next,' and let them escape.

It was long after midday and we'd been on the move since dawn. I felt hungry.

'Gino,' I said. '*Pasta*. Those *contadini* owe us a meal. Let's go and find them.'

We roared up the green tunnel, feeling the joy of the leaf-cooled sun-breeze on our hot faces. The *contadini* looked round when they heard us coming and ran into the trees. We braked and waved to them. Nervously, tentatively, they gathered round the jeeps and Gino explained.

'*Inglesi! Inglesi! Liberatori! Viva! Viva!*

The overjoyed *contadini* burst into tears and laughter and threw themselves upon us with outstretched hands.

'Hop in, mother,' I called to a fat-legged, wide-girthed peasant woman dressed in unrelieved black. 'Oh, *grazia*,' she puffed as Gino hauled her aboard. The jeep sank under her weight. The others clambered on to the remaining jeeps.

'O.K., Bum?' I called back to Curtis in the last jeep.

'*Avanti*, Skipper,' he sang out, laughing his horsy laugh. He had one arm round the waist of a buxom lass who was blushing furiously.

The *contadini* guided us to a large farmhouse in a clearing and Gino told them to prepare a meal. Wine was brought. . . .

'We'll recce the wood up to the coast, Bum, and come back.'

'O.K., Skipper.'

It was an unforgettable drive. The afternoon sun was low in the sky and its slanting beams fell upon the autumn-tinted upper leaves creating a rippling ocean of burnished copper and gold under which, cushioned by moss and a carpet of leaves, our jeeps sped silently through quiet green tunnels vibrant with shimmering golden light. Russet, bushy-tailed squirrels leapt across our path and peeped at us suspiciously out of bright, beady eyes as we splashed through pools of molten gold. . . .

At Tre Fantina, on the coast, the Germans had blown up the station and most of the railway line. Trucks lay sickly on their sides, riven and wrecked; the jagged ends of rusty, writhing, twisted rails reared drunkenly and a gusty wind blowing in from the sea swirled sheets of paper from the doorway of a shattered, looted house. On impulse, I entered, and stood aghast at the senseless destruction German soldiers had wrought. Furniture was smashed, ornaments broken, curtains ripped, cushions torn, photographs holed, drawers and cupboards rifled and disarrayed as if some giant had stood in the rooms and lashed out in every direction, venting his spleen. In one room, a child's blue-eyed china doll lay broken in a corner where it had been tossed against the wall. 'Why?' I thought, regarding its cracked, pink cheek. 'Why destroy a little child's china doll?' and visualized the little owner coming back to find her favourite doll, holding it to her breast and sobbing over it. I shook my head and turned to leave . . . and stood upon a folded, muddied, printed document. I bent and picked it up. It was a Life Insurance policy for 1000 lire payable in 1961. 'What a hope!' I thought. The Italian lire was then arbitrarily pegged at 400 to the £. What would it be worth in 1961? (Current value 1958 is approximately 1800 lire to the £.)

Pasta was waiting for us at the farmhouse in the clearing. Fat Maria bid us welcome and we sat down at a spotlessly clean, well-scrubbed kitchen table. Women and girls bustled about laying plates and cutlery; men and boys brought bottles of wine and filled our glasses.

'*Salute.* . . . *Viva Inglesi.* . . . *Viva Italia.* . . . *Viva Churchill.* . . . *Viva Stalin.* . . . *Viva Pey Pey Ah.*'

The buxom lass who'd been on Curtis' jeep turned out to be Maria's daughter, Rosa. She fell for Bum's breezy manner and hovered about his chair like a moth round a candle. What did the letters 'P.P.A.' stand for, she wanted to know.

'Army Privato de Popski,' said Bum, following immediately with his shattering horse-laugh.

Rosa looked enquiringly at Gino.

'*Da vero, Gino?*' she asked, showing lovely teeth between her ruby lips. (Is it true?)

'*Si, si, signorina,*' Gino assured her. '*Armata Privata de Popski.*'

Rosa asked if we'd come from the Libyan Desert. Her brother had been killed at Tobruk. 'Yes,' we nodded, and I saw Maria wipe a tear from her eye and felt embarrassed, an embarrassment I was to feel in many an Italian home as we made our way through Italy. How could I be sure that it wasn't a bullet of mine which had taken the life of a beloved husband or son?

Maria placed a huge bowl of steaming *pasta* in the centre of the table, *pasta* made the way only the Italian housewife can make it, from flour and eggs and milk rolled into a thick dough flattened and cut into streamers with a sharp knife, plunged into boiling, salted water and served thick and creamy, soft and mouth-watering with a rich brown sauce made from chopped chicken liver, tomato *purée* and aromatic herbs, and grated Parmesan cheese sprinkled generously over the top. Mmmmmmm! Lovely. Washed down with red wine. We all had second helpings and sat back replete, patting our swollen bellies.

By the time we'd finished, it was dark outside. Damn it, I thought, we'll spend the night here.

'Gino,' I said. 'Ask Maria what accommodation there is.'

There was a room upstairs for the *capitano* and a big barn outside for the *soldati*, Maria informed him.

Bum Curtis' eyes gleamed behind his spectacles.

'*Me dormire here questa noche,*' he informed Rosa meaningly in his half-English, kitchen-Italian. Rosa blushed and glanced at her mother. 'If your mother's wise she'll lock you up for the night,' I thought.

'Up with your aerial,' I told Stewart, 'I have a message for Popski.' I encyphered:

BOB TO POPSKI   MISSION COMPLETE   WHAT NEXT

The message was transmitted through the dark ether and we sat round the lamplit table drinking wine and singing songs. Bruno, one of the sons, was a budding Mario Lanza. He opened his broad chest and thrilled us with arias from the operas—*Tosca*, *Pagliacci*, *La Bohème*. I hoped that one day a talent-spotter would hear him and give him his chance. Riches, a great music-lover, was enraptured and repeated after each aria, 'Christ, what a voice!' It is wholly wrong to assume that soldiers like only jazz and bawdy songs. Give the lowliest private access to what is best in classical music, to Brahms rhapsodies, to the concertos of Rachmaninoff and Grieg, to the soul-lifting symphonies of Beethoven, and he will sit enthralled for hours, transported to another world. Great music sends its message to the heart, to the heart of the hardened soldier no less than to the heart of the sensitive composer.

At nine o'clock Stewart went out to the wireless jeep to take his routine H.Q. call. A few minutes later he hurried in with a message which read:

POPSKI TO BOB   COME IN AT ONCE

I looked across the table at Curtis. He was nicely settled, savouring a glass of wine, with the love-struck Rosa hovering near.

'Happy, Bum?' I asked him.

'*Molto benissimo*, Skipper.' He horse-laughed, giving Rosa's rounded bottom a playful pat. 'Just the job.'

I smiled at him and dropped my bombshell.

'Right. Well, pack up. We're leaving.'

Bum's face fell.

'Aw, Jesus, Skipper. Have a heart.'

'Come on, Bum. Get jeeping. We're going back to H.Q.'

Groans went round the table, glasses were emptied and chairs scraped back. Fear came into the eyes of the *contadini*. 'What's the matter?' they asked Gino. 'Are the Germans coming back?' No, no, he assured them, the Germans weren't coming back, but we had to go.

Outside in the darkness Rosa clung to Bum Curtis whispering: '*Amore mio. . . . Amore mio*,' imploring him to return.

Engines revved noisily, gun-mounts clanged, brutalizing the stillness of the forest night, headlamps flashed. Amidst a bedlam of *vivas*, cheerios, *retornos*, good-byes, *arivederlas*, we wheeled and raced into the night, cutting a pathway of dancing light through the dark tunnel made by the trees.

Against the wall of a silent farmhouse a little Italian girl sobbed her heart out.

When we came to the blown bridges I had an idea. A map reference had followed Popski's message. P.P.A. had moved H.Q. to Lucera. Why not go *via* Ripalta and say good-bye to Dorothy?

I turned left through the wood, speeding silently over its soft carpet of dead leaves and moss . . . past the ruined watch-tower . . . down the shell-and-bomb-scarred hillside to the muddy ford . . . across the river with dipping, flashing headlamp beams . . . up the tank-churned slope to Ripalta.

Italians dine late. A chink of light showed through the curtains of the dining-room windows. Still at dinner, I thought . . . and then I saw the staff-car parked in the driveway. 'Ho, ho,' I muttered, 'somebody muscling in. I'll shake 'im.'

I drove past the gothic door and pulled up in the shadows of the walled garden, signalling to the others to follow. I got out and walked over to Curtis' jeep.

'Bum,' I whispered, pointing to the staff-car. 'One burst in the air from each jeep. *One* burst only. *Capito?*'

'O.K., Skipper.' Bum suppressed a horsy laugh.

I tip-toed up to the front door, knocked loudly and put my fingers to my ears. . . . Brrrrrrt. . . . Brrrrrrt. . . . Brrrrrrt. . . . Brrrrrt.

Four staccato bursts, separately fired, shattered the silence of the autumn night. A woman screamed inside the house. I rat-a-tatted on the door and heard footsteps in the passage. A red-faced, sam-browned major opened to me.

'Good evening, Major,' I greeted him affably. 'How are you?'

The major looked crestfallen and confused, like a boy caught in the pantry.

'Who's that firing outside?' he demanded irately.

'Just the patrol clearing guns, Major. Did it give you a fright?'

I saw Dorothy and the Parlato family hovering in the background. I walked past the fuming major.

'Hallo, Dorothy,' I greeted her. 'We're just passing through. Thought I'd drop in to say good-bye.'

Dorothy put a hand to her heart.

'Bob, what a fright you gave us. We thought the Germans were attacking.'

I laughed and kissed her hand.

'I'm sorry. It was just the patrol clearing guns.'

I felt the major's eyes boring a hole in my back.

'Will you join us, Bob?' Dorothy indicated the half-eaten dinner.

'No thank you, Dorothy. We've just had a huge meal of *pasta* at a farmhouse across the river. I'm in a hurry.'

'A glass of wine, then.'

Yes, I thought, I'll have a glass of wine, just to annoy the major.

'Thank you, yes.'

Dorothy poured me a glass of Chianti. I raised it to her and to the Parlato family in turn.

'*Salute.*'

I raised it to the major.

'Good hunting, Major.'

The major glowered at me and said nothing.

I drank the wine and took my departure. Dorothy came with me to the door.

Dotted lines of venom ran from the major's eyes into the back of my head.

'Good-bye, Dorothy. Thanks for everything. It's been grand meeting you.'

'Come back whenever you like, Bob. You'll always find a welcome here.'

'Thanks, Dorothy. I'll remember that.'

I kissed her on the cheek, making sure the major could see me, turned and ran down the steps. The great door clanged behind me.

'Thanks, Bum,' I said to Curtis. 'You did that very nicely. Just what I wanted.'

'What happened, Skipper?'

'Shook 'em to the core, Bum. They thought the *tedeschi* had returned.'

Like a stallion's neigh, Bum Curtis' horse-laugh rang in the night and echoed shrilly from the walls of Ripalta as we took the rutted track for San Severo.

9

WE FOUND H.Q. in a villa on the outskirts of Lucera.

Popski and Jan were poring over maps spread out on a polished table. Popski and maps. I cannot separate the two. Whenever I think of Popski I see his swarthy, weather-beaten face and determined mouth suspended over a map-board. Jan Caneri and I consulted maps. Popski lived with them. Where we saw red and black lines, blue wiggles, buff splatches, dots, circles and squares, Popski saw tarmac roads, railway lines, winding rivers, escarpments, trees, villages and cities. Maps came to life before his eyes. When he looked at a red line crossing a blue one it didn't mean to him what it meant to us, merely that a road crossed over a river; Popski saw the dust on the road, the gravel by the verge, the stone parapets of the bridge, the grass and the bushes on the river banks, the flowing, swirling water, the cattle in the adjoining fields, the telephone poles and wires.

Popski looked up from the circle of lamplight as I entered the room.

'Ah, Bob. How did you get on?'

'Fine, Popski. Thoroughly enjoyed the trip.'

'No casualties?'

I shook my head.

'The brigadier sent me a glowing report.'

'Good.' (The major won't, I thought.)

'What's the form, Popski? Are we moving tonight?'

Popski shook his head.

'Just a minute, then. I'll tell Curtis to bed down.'

'There's a place for your patrol in the barn, Bob,' said Jan.

I went outside and spoke to Curtis.

'. . . and tell Bill Wilson to bring in my things.'

Back in the villa I asked:

'Where did you go, Popski?'

'The Alban Hills.'

'Where?'

'The Alban Hills. Near Rome.'

I looked at him uncertainly, incredulously.

'You're joking, Popski.'

Popski shook his head and laughed.

'Come round here, Bob, and I'll show you,' he invited.

I walked round the table and stood beside him. He smoothed the map and traced upon it with a stubby forefinger the mountainous route he had followed to within a few hours' jeep ride of Rome.

I sat down and looked at him, feeling I'd missed the boat.

'And all I did was to cross a bloody river,' I groaned.

Popski threw back his head and laughed.

'You would have your own patrol, Bob,' he twitted me.

'Drink, Bob?' Jan asked.

'Please, Jan.' I felt I needed one.

Jan poured three generous whiskies from a half-empty bottle of White Horse. We toasted one another.

'Now then,' said Popski, putting down his empty glass and orienting the large-scale map of Italy. 'The German front line is roughly here.' He traced a winding line from Naples through Campobasso to Vasto. 'You'll take the sector from Campobasso to Vasto, Bob. I'll take the sector from Campobasso to Naples.'

'When do we move?' I asked.

'Whenever you're ready. Make your own arrangements.'

'Object?'

'Probing. Intelligence. Try to slip behind the lines if you can. Keep going forward.'

We talked for an hour, discussing possibilities, future plans, men, jeeps, equipment.

When we began to yawn about 2.30 a.m. Popski folded his maps.

'Bed,' he said.

'Full loads,' I told Curtis next morning. 'As much petrol as you can carry. We'll be away for some time.'

'Where are we going, Skipper?'

'Into the mountains. Roving commission. Do as we like.'

'Woowho!' Curtis whooped, rubbed his hands gleefully, horse-laughed and rushed off to get the patrol ready.

'Bloody awful, isn't it, Bum?'

I blew the drips from my nose and felt icy raindrops trickle down my spine. 'Ugh!' I shivered.

Curtis grimaced, bent at the knees and pulled at the seat of his sopping battledress trousers.

'Your arse gets so bloody wet, Skipper,' he complained.

I nodded and grimaced too, pulling at the seat of my own soaking trousers.

'*Shay* ready, Rich?' I called to bearded Lance-Corporal Riches who was watching a primus stove.

The roar of the primus died as I spoke and the smell of un-burned paraffin filled the air.

'Oh, muck it,' Riches groaned. 'Anyone got a pricker?'

'Coming up, Rich,' called Bill Wilson, throwing a packet of primus prickers.

Riches caught the packet deftly and bent over the smoking primus, poking at the choked jet . . . poured methylated spirit into the groove . . . struck a match . . . was rewarded by a steady, satisfying blur-ur-ur-ur.

'Won't be long, Skipper.'

The jeeps were drawn up by the side of a muddy road in the mountains near Campobasso. Round a bend, the bridge spanning a deep ravine was blown and wet, rocky, almost perpendicular slopes pierced the leaden sky on either side, sides too precipitous for jeeps. Rain fell steadily in a solid driving curtain, lashed by the wind. In our open jeeps, devoid of weather protection, we absorbed every drop, up our sleeves, down our necks, through our waterproof (!) jackets until we sat in damp misery soaked to the skin, cold and shivery, squelching in pools of icy rainwater. Mud in heavy sienna clods clung gluelike to the jeep wheels and mud-guards, adding extra weight to their dripping, waterlogged over-loads; under their celluloid coverings our maps were streaked and pulpy. Hour after hour, since early dawn, we had forced a muddy way through the mountain pass and now after de-mining miles of road and successfully circumnavigating a dozen demolished bridges we were finally stuck at the top of the pass with no alternative but to go all the way back and try again in another direction. It was heartbreaking.

'*Shay* up!' Riches called.

We gathered round him in a wet, bedraggled, shivering group and held out our rain-washed mugs.

'B-bloody g-good,' stammered Sammy Barnes, taking a gulp of the steaming tea. The mug rattled against his chattering teeth and rain dripped into it from his freckled nose.

'I know what this needs,' I said, taking a gulp and reaching into the back of my jeep for the reserve bottle of whisky I always carried there (and seldom touched, preferring wine). A pool of rainwater gurgled and dripped when I moved the canvas sheet which covered the load.

I poured a double tot into each extended mug, screwed on the cap and put the half-empty bottle back in the jeep.

'Cheers, chaps.'

'Cheers, Skipper' (seven times), one '*Salute, Capitano*' from Gino.

'Right,' I said when we'd drained our mugs and felt better, 'back the way we came and try again. Ready, Bum?'

'O.K., Skipper.'

Riches tinned the primus . . . mugs clinked against metal . . . nine wet bottoms sat gingerly into nine sopping seats ('Mucking hell') . . . four engines revved . . . four jeeps wheeled and reversed . . . gear-changed down the skiddy, slithery road, flinging lumps of mud from their flying wheels. . . .

We had our first brush with the enemy on the banks of the Trigno.

Early one morning we nosed our way along the mountain road to San Bartolemeo, a tiny dead-end village on a mountain-top overlooking the Trigno Valley. The rain had stopped, but the sky was full of racing clouds and a gusty wind blew. Grassy slopes led steeply down to the valley where a white road followed the winding, glinting river towards Vasto, on the Adriatic.

The *contadini* gathered round us in the cobbled piazza and whilst Gino gleaned what information he could from them Curtis and I walked into a house and searched the valley through binoculars from an upstairs window.

156

'If we can get the jeeps down to that road and across the river Bum——'

'The bridge'll be blown, Skipper.'

I examined the bridge. It was blown. I could see the gap in the parapet; but the road winding up the opposite hillside intrigued me. 'If only we can get across,' I thought. . . . I couldn't see a trace of the enemy.

'Those grass slopes look feasible, Bum,' I said. 'We'll go down and recce that bridge. Come on.'

Curtis looked doubtful.

'It's a bit tricky, Skipper.'

'I know, but we must try to slip through.'

We returned to the jeeps.

'What do they say, Gino?'

'*Capitano*, they say the Germans have all withdrawn across the river.'

I nodded.

'Can you get me a guide, Gino? A *contadino* who knows the country?'

There was no rush of volunteers, but eventually a stalwart, stocky peasant offered his services.

'Tell him to hop on, Gino.'

The *contadino*, Alfredo by name, clambered on to the back of Locke's jeep and we drove along the mountain road until we found a way on to the slope leading down to the river.

'This'll do,' I said to Bill Wilson and held up a hand. The patrol halted. I braked beside a grassy verge, reversed, squared up, engaged lowest booster gear and crawled over, scraping the under-carriage on the ridge of tufty grass. The slope was steep and Bill Wilson and I braced our bodies as the jeep crept almost perpendicularly downhill like a fly on a wall . . . down . . . down . . . down, with the other three jeeps crawling behind us. Half-way down the 1000-foot slope I crossed my fingers and prayed that we'd be able to get up again if we had to. . . .

The slope eased towards the valley and we bumped over rough grass on to the riverside road.

The bridge was destroyed. There was a wide gap between the jagged ends where the span had been blown out and frothy, blue-green water eddied about a pile of broken masonry in the middle of the river.

157

The white, winding road mocked us from beyond the impassable gulf.

'*Capitano.*' Gino's voice broke into my thoughts. 'Alfredo says there is another bridge a few miles upstream.'

'Bet you it's blown, Skipper,' said Curtis.

'Probably is, Bum, but we'll just make sure.'

We wheeled and drove upriver. . . .

I saw the bridge as I turned a bend in the road. It, too, had a wide gap in the middle and the water was too turbulent to ford. 'Blast!' I muttered. 'We'll have to go back.'

Rain started to fall, a few big, ominous drops followed by a sharp shower as we drove back to our point of descent.

'This isn't going to be easy, Bill,' I muttered.

Wheeeeeeeeeeee. . . . Wruuuuuuumph! A ranging mortar bomb crashed on the slope, throwing up a flurry of earth.

'*Tedeschi!*' Gino grunted in my ear.

'*Madonna mia,*' cried Alfredo as he leapt from Locke's jeep and ran up the hill, away from the jeeps.

'Rush it,' I shouted to the jeeps behind me, hearing the whistle of another bomb. . . .

The jeeps fanned out and raced for the slope. From their ringside seat in the piazza the people of San Bartolemeo watched the fun.

Wheeeeeeee . . . wruuuuuumph . . . wruuuuumph . . . wruuuu mph . . wruuuumph. A salvo of bombs exploded between our floundering jeeps.

'Zigzag !' I yelled.

But we couldn't. We had reached the steep part of the slope and were dismayed to feel our wheels spinning on the wet grass. Even in four-wheel drive our four wheels spun. . . .

Panic laid its icy hand on my heart. 'Oh, God,' I thought, 'we're going to be wiped out and it's all my fault. We should have left the jeeps in the piazza and come down on foot. . . . Why didn't I think of chains. . . . We'll be wiped out . . . we'll be wiped out. . . .'

Out of the corner of my eye I saw Alfredo running up the slope and envied him; it never occurred to me that we could leave our jeeps and run for it, so much did I feel that the jeeps were part and parcel of us.

Engines stalled and we began to slip back. . . .

Wruuuuuumph! A mortar bomb exploded close at hand,

spattering wet earth. The German mortarmen had us bracketed and would wipe us out one by one. . . . We were a sitting target. . . . 'Back,' I yelled desperately. 'Back. Down to the river.'

I crashed into reverse and swung the wheel wildly. The jeep rocked perilously. I felt Gino clutch the back of my seat and heard Bill Wilson mutter a frightened 'Christ!'

The jeep was round. I declutched, snicked into first gear and let in the clutch as the wheels gathered momentum. The engine started, slowed our pace, and we crawled downhill, zigzagging, swerving out of the path of the bombs. I glanced back. The other jeeps were zigzagging behind me.

Wruuuumph . . . wruuuuumph . . . wruuuumph. A cluster of bombs fell on the slope where we'd been stuck a minute earlier.

'Missed!' we yelled jubilantly and raced down the slope to the river road. On the road and on the lower slopes the wheels didn't spin and we had the advantage of mobility. For a couple of hours we played a thrilling game of 'mortar chess', like this:

'Rush it!'

Four jeeps, thirty yards or so apart, rushed up the slope, zig-zagging, swerving, braking, accelerating. . . . Wruuuumph. . . . A mortar bomb crashed beside Curtis' jeep . . . the crew ducked as the driver swerved wildly and a triumphant 'Missed, ye bastard' echoed above the noise of the racing engine. . . . Wruuuuumph . . . wruuuuumph . . . wruuuumph. . . . Another cluster exploding close . . . a wild swerve . . . a muttered 'Christ' . . . earth spattering . . . a sibilant 'Missed' . . . Jeeps losing speed . . . engines labouring . . . wheels spinning. . . . 'Back to the road.'

Jeeps reversing . . . wheeling hard . . . almost overturning . . . zigzagging . . . swerving desperately to avoid a crashing bomb . . . wruuuumph . . . racing downhill. . . . 'Missed again' . . . horsy laugh. . . .

As we turned on the steep part of the slope, the enemy mortar-men altered their range and followed us downhill to the road . . . wruuumph . . . we bumped on to the road and raced upstream . . . wruuuumph . . . on the verge . . . wruuuuumph . . . behind Curtis' jeep . . . splaaaash . . . in the river throwing up a spout of water. . . . Four jeeps going at top speed, thumbs to noses in the direction of the enemy slopes. . . . Short pause at the blown bridge. . . . Wruuuuumph, when the mortarmen got our range . . . racing down the road again. I was playing for time, desperately. The rain had ceased and a kindly if wintry sun was drying the grass. If the rain held off . . .

Wheeeeeeeeee . . . wruuuuuumph. A bomb crashed in the rubble of the demolished bridge. . . . Splaaaash . . . another one fell in the river, throwing water over the jeeps. . . .

'Back to the slope.'

Four jeeps with ducking crews racing down the riverside road closely followed by crashing mortar bombs . . . wruuuumph . . . wruuuumph . . . wruuuumph. . . . Off the road and on to the grass.

'Go like hell.'

Up the slope . . . higher . . . higher . . . wheels gripping better . . . hope rising . . . wruuuuuuumph . . . swerve . . . zigzag . . . up . . . up . . . past our previous best . . . up . . . up . . . engines labouring . . . wheels spinning . . . 'Muck it' . . . engines pinking and stalling . . . a bare 100 yards from the top . . . so near and yet so far . . . wruuuuumph . . . wruuuumph . . . wruuuumph. . . . 'Christ' . . . ducking . . . reversing . . . zigzagging downhill again . . . accelerating . . . wruuuumph. . . . 'Missed' . . . But the grass was drying. We'd do it next time.

'Back to the road,' I yelled.

We raced downhill . . . bumped on to the hard road . . . raced up and down it for a good twenty minutes . . . swerving, braking, accelerating, missing the searching mortar bombs which followed our passage like an evil shadow. . . .

'The slope,' I shouted, when I thought the time was ripe, 'we'll make it this time.'

Over the verge . . . up the slope . . . wheels gripping firmly . . . confidence rising . . . up . . . up . . . up . . . wruuuuumph . . . swerve . . . up . . . up . . . higher . . . wheels continuing to grip . . . up . . . up . . . up . . . engines beginning to labour . . . wheels throwing out black mud . . . still going higher . . . engines straining . . . pinking loudly . . . wheels spinning . . . higher . . . higher. . . .

'We'll make it!' I shouted gleefully, sure we'd get up this time.

Still going . . . up . . . higher . . . fifty yards to go . . . forty . . . thirty. . . . 'Get off and push.'

Gino and Bill Wilson jumped off and pushed from behind . . . the butt of the fifty Browning swung loosely and smacked against my elbow. . . . 'Ouch, muck you.' . . . The gunners jumped from the other jeeps and pushed hard . . . black mud hit them in the face . . . up . . . up . . . ten yards to go . . . engine stalling . . . wheels spinning. . . .

'Push!' I yelled desperately. 'Push!' and rocked backwards and forwards in the driving-seat trying to help the straining jeep.

Wheeeeeeeeee . . . wruuuuumph . . . wruuuuumph . . . wruuuuumph. . . . Bombs crashed dangerously close, but we were almost up and didn't heed them.

'Push!' I bellowed hoarsely. 'Harder . . . harder . . . heave. . . .' I felt the front wheels bump over the crest.

'Heave,' I cried frantically. 'Heave. . . .'

The jeep bonnet was pointing heavenwards . . . the back wheels gripped on the verge . . . the bonnet sank. . . . I was on the road. . . . I was on the road. . . . I was on the road. . . .

'Help the others,' I shouted to Gino and Bill.

I drove 100 yards down the road, light of heart, parked the jeep round the first bend and ran back on foot.

One by one the jeeps bumped on to the road. . . .

'Keep going,' I shouted to the drivers, pointing towards the bend.

The wireless jeep stuck a few yards below the road. We rushed to Stewart's aid and manhandled him to safety.

Wheeeeeeeeeeeeeeeee . . . wruuuuumph . . . wruuuuuuumph . . . wruuuuuuumph . . . wruuuuuuumph. Seeing their quarry escaping, the enemy put down a vicious concentration, a salvo of hate. . . . We ducked and ran through it, wiping mud from our eyes, gained the parked jeeps, jumped aboard and raced away. . . .

I pulled up round a bend and looked back from jeep to jeep.

'Everybody O.K.?'

'O.K., Skipper,' Curtis called from the last jeep. '*Molto benissimo, Avanti.*' Wruuuuuuumph. A mortar bomb crashed round the corner.

'Balls to you!' Porter bawled derisively.

Engines revved . . . gears snicked. . . . Four jeeps zoomed down the twisting mountain road to the strains of 'Torno Sorrento' (our patrol signature tune) conducted by Riches. . . .

'Curtis,' I said an hour later when we were comfortably installed in a warm farmhouse miles from the danger zone, 'never, never, never take jeeps down steep grass slopes in the rain.'

'No, Skipper. Never.'
Sip of wine . . . horse-laugh.

Loud cheers greeted us when we drove into the piazza of San Bartolemeo the next morning.
'*Bravo Ingelesi! Viva!*'
Alfredo, our guide of the previous day, came up and shook my hand.
'*Oh, Capitano. Bon giorno.*'
'*Come sta*, Alfredo?' I greeted him. 'Do you want to try again?'
Alfredo looked puzzled. Gino interpreted.
'*Si, si*,' said Alfredo enthusiastically, much to my astonishment.
'You mean Alfredo liked it?' I asked Gino.
'*Si, Capitano.*' He laughed.
I regarded the grinning Alfredo with interest. A *contadino* who enjoyed mortaring was unique in my experience.
'Ask him if he knows of another way across the river, Gino.'
Gino and Alfredo jabbered in dialect for a time, then:
'*Capitano*, he says there is a sheep-track through the hills leading on to the Campobasso road.'
I oriented the map and Alfredo showed me where his sheep-track ran.
'Look, Bum,' I said to Curtis, 'if this sheep-track's jeepable we might be able to cross the Campobasso road   ad work inland towards Isernia.'
Curtis studied the map.
'Looks bloody mountainous, Skipper.'
'That's where we'll have the advantage, Bum. Jerry won't expect vehicles to come that way.'
We pored over the map, looking at the network of roads running from Isernia to Naples, Rome, Sulmona, Pescara. . . .
'We'll be right on the German L. of C., Bum.'
I put down the map-board.
'Wait here, Bum. Gino and I'll go with Alfredo and look at this track.'
Alfredo led us through a back alley and out on to the bare mountainside behind the village. I sat down and searched the opposite slopes through binoculars. I could see the turns and twists of the Campobasso road high up on the hillside, and nearer

at hand Alfredo's sheep-track, stony and narrow, straggling along the contours. If we could get jeeps along that track . . .

'Right, Alfredo. *Avanti*,' I said.

Gino and I followed the sturdy Alfredo along a tortuous foot-path which dipped into gullies, sprawled over hillocks, canted at a fearsome angle on scree slopes and was never more than a foot or two wide. Jagged rocks stuck up, boulders blocked the way, hummocky tufts caused sharp twists and bends. 'We'll never get jeeps along this,' I muttered as I picked my way behind Gino. . . . Later, when the track widened going through a deep ravine, I thought: 'I don't know, though, this bit's not too bad. We might just make it. . . .'

Alfredo halted in the ravine for a breather. Far down in the valley the blue-green River Trigno raced towards the Adriatic under a cloudy sky with the sun breaking through, making mirrors on the surface and patterning bright patches on the hillside. Somewhere in the peaceful-looking hills on the other side of the river German mortarmen and machine-gunners were crouched behind their death-dealing weapons, watching the slopes of San Bartolemeo.

'What do you think, Gino?' I asked. 'Is the track safe for jeeps?'

Gino shrugged.

'*E possible, Capitano.*'

'It'll need widening in places.'

I was uncertain what to do. The prospect was tempting . . . but at night, in the dark, if a driver made an error of judge-ment . . .

Alfredo looked at me. I nodded and he got up and walked on.

As soon as we emerged from the ravine I had the uneasy feeling we were under observation.

High up on the hillside, on the Campobasso road, the window-pane of a house blinked in the sun like a heliograph.

'There's an O.P. in that house, Gino. We're being watched. Tell Alfredo to come back.'

Alfredo was striding ahead. Gino called 'Alfredo'. Alfredo looked round and we signalled to him to come back.

Hidden from view in the ravine I said:

'Back to San Bartolemeo, Gino. We'll find the recce at night. If we're seen it'll give the show away.'

'*Si, Capitano.*'

All the way back to the village I visualized the jeeps crawling along the mountainside in the darkness. It would be terribly dangerous. The track shelved outwards in many places so that the moving jeeps would be canted at a fierce angle. One little slip and over a jeep would go, over and over, down into the valley, bodies, guns and equipment falling out as it crashed down the mountainside, hurtling from boulder to boulder. . . . It was too dangerous, I decided . . . but what a feather in our caps if we made it! Caution and rashness fought a silent battle within and I was still undecided when we walked through the alley into the piazza.

Curtis came out of a house when he saw us.

'What's the track like, Skipper?'

'Bad in places, Bum. I'm not too sure about it.'

'Did you go right across?'

I shook my head.

'There's an O.P. on the hillside. We'll go across tonight on foot.'

Curtis grinned and adjusted his spectacles.

'Like some *pasta*, Skipper?'

It was afternoon and I felt suddenly hungry.

'I would. Where?'

'In this casa.' Curtis jerked his thumb towards the house behind him. We entered.

I found Riches, Barnes, Porter, Stewart and Wilson seated round a table forking *pasta* into their mouths. A bowl of steaming *pasta* occupied the centre of the table, ringed by bottles of wine. An obese *contadina* and her two daughters stood by the kitchen range. An appetizing smell of cooking filled the room.

'*Questo, Capitano*,' said Curtis by way of introduction. 'This is the Skipper.'

'*S'accomodo, Signor Commandante*,' said the elder of the girls, curtseying and hastening to lay a place for me. She was a well-built girl of about eighteen with a firm bust and black, flashing eyes.

'Have some *vino*, Skipper.' Riches hospitably poured me a glass of red wine.

'You seem to have got yourselves organized,' I remarked, looking round the table at the happy faces of my men and then at the two girls.

A horse-laugh reverberated round the walls.

164

'Good casa, this, Skipper,' pronounced Curtis.

'Where's Locke?' I asked, noticing that he wasn't there.

'Feeding in another casa, Skipper,' Curtis informed me.

Al Locke was a lone wolf who preferred to hunt on his own.

Gino passed me a heaped plateful of *pasta* over which I sprinkled a garnishing of grated cheese from the dish held out to me by the elder girl. *'Grazia,'* I said, looking up at her. She gave me a dazzling smile and her black eyes flashed disturbingly.

I picked up a fork, took a sip of wine, and applied myself. Gone were the days of my *pasta*-complex. I was now an experienced virtuoso and could confidently cross forks with the best Italian. If the Countess Spagnoletti could see me now, I thought, as I deftly twirled a neat forkful from plate to mouth. . . .

Wheeeeeeeeeee. . . . Wruuuuuuumph. A shell exploded in the village with an ear-splitting, shattering clatter.

The fat *contadina's* hand flew to her quivering, outsize bust. *'Madonna mia,'* she breathed, terror-stricken. Her two daughters screamed and ran out of the kitchen. Alfredo blanched and hesitated, unsure whether to run or remain. He looked to Gino for a cue. Gino raised his glass, *'Salute, tedeschi,'* and forked unconcernedly at his *pasta*. Alfredo remained. I listened, wondering where the next shell would fall.

Wheeeeeeeeeee . . .

'Here she comes,' grinned Riches.

We waited.

Wruuuuuuumph. The shell landed closer this time, shaking the house. We heard a scream and the sounds of falling masonry.

'Some casa's got it,' laughed Curtis.

I remembered the parked jeeps.

'Get the jeeps out of the piazza. Quick!' I shouted.

Chairs scraped on the stone-flagged floor as we rushed from the house.

Al Locke was already at the wheel of his jeep, pressing the self-starter.

'Down the road, Al,' I shouted to him. 'Round the first corner.'

Locke wheeled and revved out of the piazza . . . the other jeeps roared after him. . . . Wruuuuuuumph . . . a shell exploded on the cobbles, making a hole and rattling the window-panes. . . .

We pulled up round the bend.

'Drivers stay with their jeeps,' I ordered.

165

Gripping Tommy-guns, Curtis, Porter, Riches, Gino and I walked back to the village. A shaken Alfredo joined us in the cratered piazza.

Wheeeeeeeeee . . .

'Look out!'

Wruuuuuuumph. A third shell banged through the roof of a house . . . terrified screams sounded from an alley, followed by cries of pain smothered by the crash of falling tiles . . . a cloud of dust rose into the air.

Then the barrage came down on San Bartolemeo.

Wheeeeeeeeeeeeee . . . wruuuuuumph . . . wruuuuuumph . . . wruuuuuumph. . . . The shells fell thick and fast. . . .Wruuuumph . . . on the mountainside . . . wruuuumph . . . in the piazza . . . wruuuumph . . . in an alleyway . . . more screams . . . wruuuumph . . . through a roof . . . clattering tiles . . . wruuuumph . . . in the piazza again . . . wruuuumph . . . another house. . . .

The shelling continued for twenty minutes and stopped as suddenly as it had begun. There was a last shattering bang as a shell exploded inside a house on the far side of the piazza, then an eerie silence.

One by one, the terrified *contadini* emerged from their hiding-places and furtively made their way to their homes, expecting the worst.

We returned to our casa. The table was just as we'd left it.

'Might as well finish our lunch,' I said.

We sat down and began to eat the cold *pasta*.

The back door opened and two wild-eyed girls entered nervously.

'*Avanti, signorini,*' said Gino.

'*Dove Mama?*' the elder girl asked. (Where's Mama?)

Fat Mama appeared in the doorway and waddled into the kitchen breathing heavily.

'*Bon giorno, Mama,*' we greeted her jocularly. '*Come sta?*'

Mama was too upset to appreciate the joke. '*Oh, Dio . . . paura,*' she gasped, pressing both hands to her heaving breasts. (Dear God . . . I'm frightened!)

A white-faced boy burst into the room and spoke urgently to Gino.

'What's the matter, Gino?' I asked.

'He says his mother is wounded. Will we please come?'

166

I nodded.

'We'll go and see her. Come on.'

The boy led us through a maze of cobbled alleyways to the broken shell of what had once been his home. Most of the roof was open to the sky and only one of the four walls was still undamaged. Everything else was rubble. Crunching upon broken glass, we stumbled through a havoc of smashed furniture and crockery to a sagging bed in a corner where a white-faced woman lay upon torn bedclothes, moaning piteously. A small group of relatives stood by wringing their red, work-worn hands. They moved to one side as we approached.

The woman's eyes were closed, her breathing catchy and shallow. I put my finger on her pulse. It was there, but thready, difficult to feel.

'Where's she hit, Gino?' I enquired.

Gino spoke to the relatives.

'In the back, *Capitano*,' he informed me.

I eased my hand under the woman's back and felt blood, warm and sticky. A low moan escaped from blanched lips as I withdrew my hand.

'Bring a first-aid kit, Rich,' I said, without looking up.

'He's gone for one, Skipper,' Curtis replied.

A loosened tile fell with a clatter. The woman on the bed moaned and twitched. Conscience pricked me. 'It's my fault this has happened,' I thought. 'If I hadn't come here and showed myself on the mountainside the village wouldn't have been shelled and this wouldn't have happened.' 'Nonsense,' said Commonsense. 'War is war. If you hadn't come somebody else would; besides, who started the war? Mussolini was keen enough to join in when he thought he couldn't lose. Serves the Ities right.' Conscience pricked again. Did this poor woman need serving right? I looked at the pain-drawn face, the bloodless lips, the dark shadows under the closed eyes, the hollow cheeks. Husband killed in Libya, life hadn't been easy for this poor creature and our coming had made it immeasurably worse. . . . How far-reaching are the consequences of a man's actions, I reflected. Mussolini declares war in Italy. Bob Yunnie joins up in England. Years later Bob Yunnie drives into an Italian village in an American jeep and an Italian woman is wounded by a German shell made in Czechoslovakia and . . . The woman on the bed gave a convulsive twitch and died.

'Here you are, Skipper,' said Riches, coming in with the first-aid kit.

'Too late, Rich, she's dead.'

Grown-ups can take it, or should be able to, but it is a terrible thing for a little boy to watch his mummy die. My heart bled for the little chap. He was no more than eight or nine. When he knew his mother was dead he didn't cry out for sympathy, but just stood by her bedside staring at her still form with pleading, unbelieving eyes. Then his little mouth trembled, tears coursed uncontrollably down his grimy cheeks, leaving little cleansed channels on the sun-burned skin, and the nails of his clenched fists bit into the flesh of his palms. A wailing, sniffing relative put a comforting arm round his shoulder but he shook it off, manfully . . . something broke inside him and he turned and ran out of his shattered home, an orphan in a cruel world. . . .

'Aye, aye, Bum,' I sighed as we stumbled from the scene. 'This is the other side of war, the side we don't often see. Poor little kid.'

For once, Curtis didn't wisecrack. None of us was entirely dry-eyed.

Dusk fell and we made up a foot party—Alfredo, Gino, Curtis and myself. We followed Alfredo's dark bulk along the rough track, stumbling over the outjutting rocks . . . rested for a few minutes in the silent ravine . . . emerged into the moonlight on the enemy side.

'There's the O.P.,' I whispered to Curtis, indicating the moon-lit window-panes of the house on the Campobasso road which blinked at us like giant's eyes.

The track dipped into a gully by the side of a rushing stream and we lost sight of the house for a while. I tapped Gino on the back.

'Tell Alfredo to stop.'

Gino spurted ahead.

'Ask Alfredo where the track comes out, Gino,' I whispered when we caught up with them.

Gino and Alfredo talked in undertones.

'*Capitano.*'

'Yes, Gino?'

'The track comes out very close to the house.'

'Damn,' I thought, 'that means the track'll be watched.'

'O.K.,' I said to Gino, 'on you go. Tell Alfredo to stop before he comes to the house.'

We walked on.

A chill wind arose and ragged clouds sailed across the face of the moon, casting moving shadows on the mountainside.

Into another gully . . . across an impatient stream . . . round the base of a knoll.

The house came into view again, much closer, blinking its baleful eyes. I guessed it to be half a mile away.

Alfredo halted and waited for instructions.

'We'll cut up to the road, Gino,' I whispered.

Alfredo changed course and led us up a steep slope to the Campobasso road where we crouched by the verge, listening and watching.

'You and Alfredo wait here,' I whispered to Gino after a while. 'Bum and I'll take a walk down to the house.'

Memorizing the place by a tall bush bent back by the prevailing wind, Curtis and I levered ourselves up to the road and padded softly towards the enemy-occupied house. The wheel-tracks of armoured cars showed in the dust.

Round a bend, the house came into view, squat, white-walled, eerie, guarded by trees ghostly in the intermittent moonlight.

Hugging the shadows of the verge, stopping to peer and listen every few yards, we closed up to it . . . closer . . . closer. . . . My heart thumped audibly . . . closer. . . .

We reached the shadows of the trees and stood close to their protective boles, holding breath, looking and listening. . . .

A familiar sound came to our ears—the buzz and crackle of wireless inter-com. Peeping round the trunk of my tree I saw the dark outline of an armoured car parked in the driveway close to the back wall of the house. 'So that's the set up,' I thought. 'O.P. upstairs with wireless communication to the guns.' What should we do? Attack the house and destroy the armoured car or lay mines in the road? So long as the Germans occupied the house we couldn't bring jeeps along the track. There were only the three of us (excluding Alfredo). Too small a party. Silly to make a botch of the job. Better to go back, I thought, plan the thing properly and capture the O.P. the following night.

I motioned to Curtis. . . . We backed away from the trees . . . turned and padded along the verge to the tall bush.

'Back to San Bartolomeo,' I whispered to Gino. 'We'll raid this joint tomorrow night.'

Ten minutes, later, jumping across the impatient stream, we heard the exhaust-note of an armoured car on the road. 'We'll get you tomorrow night,' I chuckled. . . .

'Where are we kipping, Skipper?' Curtis asked when we walked into the silent piazza.

I smiled to myself in the darkness, knowing what prompted the question.

'You know where the jeeps are, Bum?'

'Yes, Skipper.'

'Well, we're sleeping beside them in our sleeping-bags, taking turns of guard duty. Just in case. Jerry sometimes night-patrols.'

'It looks like rain, Skipper,' said Curtis artfully. 'Wouldn't we be better in casas?'

'No *bella signorinas* tonight, Bum,' I laughed.

Curtis was silent.

We said good night to Alfredo and walked down the road to the parked jeeps.

'I'll take the last hour of sentry-go,' I told Riches.

Spreading a ground-sheet on the grass verge close to my jeep, I unrolled my sleeping-bag and crawled into its fleecy comfort. Three jeeps away I heard Curtis muttering to Porter, '. . . mucking sleeping-bags. . . . I'd a warm bed all fixed up in that casa. . . .'

Riches woke me at 5 a.m.

Damp mist enshrouded the jeeps. I wriggled out of cosy warmth and shivered, pulling on sweater and duffle coat. It didn't seem five minutes since I'd put my head down. I tucked a Tommy-gun under my arm.

Walking up and down the misty road, I planned the details of the night's raid. We'd leave after dark . . . get into position near the house . . . mine the road on both sides to prevent reinforcements coming up . . . attack . . . a hand-grenade inside the turret of the armoured car . . . into the house with a rush . . . upstairs, spraying from the hip . . . a prisoner or two. . . .

Dawn broke and the sun struggled through, dispersing the mist. I went from jeep to jeep imitating Sergeant Waterson's 'Wakey, wakeey'.

Soon primus stoves were blaring by the side of the road and the morning air was filled with the lure of sizzling bacon.

'I want the *tedeschi* to think we've gone,' I said to Gino. 'We'll drive down the road in full view immediately after breakfast and come back after dark. I want you to stay in the village and keep an eye on things. Be ready with Alfredo at six o'clock.'

'*Si, Capitano.*'

As soon as breakfast was over, Gino walked into San Bartolemeo. The rest of us packed up and drove in the opposite direction, going very slowly round a bend in the road where we could be seen from the German O.P.

'Make sure they see you,' I shouted to the crews.

The day was spent in a secluded farmhouse five miles away. We exchanged a quantity of compo rations for wine, eggs and roasted poultry, slept most of the afternoon and drove back to San Bartolemeo after dark.

Gino and Alfredo waited for us in the piazza. There had been no more shelling and they had passed an uneventful day. It seemed my ruse had succeeded.

Leaving the jeeps at the first bend in the road in charge of Stewart and Sammy Barnes, we loaded ourselves with road mines, hand-grenades, Tommy-guns, spare ammunition clips and followed Alfredo along the winding sheep-track. . . . We rested in the dark ravine for ten minutes, sitting by the side of the track, looking up at the stormy sky or down into the valley where the river occasionally gleamed when the moon shone through a break in the racing clouds. The rolling boom of artillery wafted to us on the wind blowing up from the distant coast.

'We'll stop a thousand yards from the house,' I told Curtis. 'Riches and Locke will mine the road south of the house and you and Porter will mine it to the north. When you both come back, we'll attack.'

'O.K., Skipper,' Curtis whispered.

An hour later, Gino, Alfredo, Bill Wilson and I crouched in a damp hollow beside the impatient stream waiting for the road-mining parties to return. I was jittery, as I always was just before going into action, imagining the worst. . . .

Curtis and Porter were first back. Their dark silhouettes appeared on the skyline and they dropped into the hollow.

'O.K., Bum?'

'O.K., Skipper. No trouble at all.'

We waited for Riches and Locke. They were a long time coming, and I began to worry, thinking something had happened to them. When they eventually ducked into the hollow I whispered irritably:

'Where the hell have you been?'

'Jesus, Skipper!' Riches expostulated. 'We'd to climb up a bloody ravine to get to the road and crawl down it again when we'd finished laying the mines.'

'Sorry, Rich,' I apologized.

I collected my thoughts.

'Right,' I whispered, 'now listen carefully. We'll all walk quietly up to the house and stand under the trees. When I give the signal we rush the house. There's an armoured car parked near the back door. Curtis and Porter will deal with it. The rest of us will burst into the house and rush upstairs. Got that?'

Nods and grunts of assent.

'Right. Off we go.'

When we stood in the shadows of the trees bordering the driveway I couldn't see the armoured car nor could I hear the sound of the inter-com. 'Must be round the other side of the house,' I whispered in Bum Curtis' ear. He nodded. 'O.K.?' I breathed. 'In we go.'

I jumped between two trees and raced for the back door as fast as I could, with the others pelting after me. Our feet seemed to make a terrible din on the scrunchy gravel. . . . I reached the door . . . wrenched at the handle . . . forced the door open . . . rushed up the dark stairs, spraying from the hip. . . . Brrrrt. . . . Brrrrt . . . as I ran. The noise was deafening. I reached a landing . . . kicked a door open and sprayed the room. . . . Brrrrt. . . . Brrrrt. . . . Locke didn't trouble to open the door of the next room, but just sprayed through the panels, ripping them open. . . . Brrrrt. . . . Brrrrt. . . . Brrrrrrrrrrt. . . . No cries of pain came from the rooms, no loud shouts of '*Kamarade*' . . . the house seemed strangely silent when the echo of our shots died away.

It was empty.

10

W e remained in the mountains until the end of November, probing for a way through the German defences, but never found one. Day after day we thrust hopefully along little-used mountain-tracks only to find a raging torrent or an impassable ravine barring further progress after hours of boulder-shifting and track-widening. The enemy had observation posts on all the hill-tops and whenever we came within range we were greeted by a concentration of mortar bombs or machine-gun fire.

We repaired bridges, demined roads, made deviations and drove hundreds of miles. We slept in palaces and hovels, on hill-tops, in valleys and by roadsides. We got soaked to the skin and were dried by the sun and the wind. We made friends with the *contadini*, learned their dialect and became familiar with their simple mountainy ways. We took our jeeps through rivers, over mountains, down crazy slopes with never a thing going wrong with them. We were mortared and machine-gunned, shelled and sniped without any of us receiving a scratch. We became hardy and resilient, experienced and resourceful. War lost all its terrors and became an exciting adventure, a skilful game of outwitting a brave and cunning enemy. In our fast little jeeps we were difficult targets to hit, and as the weeks passed without casualties we developed a faith in our jeeps and ourselves which took away fear.

In place of fear we developed a zest, a zest for our independent, roving way of life, a zest for its hazards, excitements and thrills. Virtually our own masters, we were at liberty to come or to go as we pleased; our only duty was to harry the enemy, to keep advancing, to keep probing for a way to slip through his defences. What gave us our zest? What motive urged us deliberately to court danger, to keep slogging through the mud and the rain, and enjoy it? It was difficult to analyse. It was compounded of a desire to excel, to do something others hadn't done, a certain desire for fame, but mostly it was a simple enjoyment of adventure and the fun of being free and independent, able to think and to fend for ourselves. No moment was dull. If we weren't risking capture or annihilation, experiencing the satisfaction of taking our jeeps over impossible terrain or planning a raid on an outpost, we were enjoying the fun of being entertained by the *contadini*, listening to arias or flirting with the girls. At the end of a gruelling day we didn't *have* to sleep out in the cold and the wet because we could always drive the few miles to a comfortable farmhouse, villa or mansion and exchange our monotonous compo rations for comfortable beds, *pasta*, roast chickens and wine, a thing we invariably did.

By the end of November some twenty German divisions were securely entrenched from coast to coast—roughly along the line of the Garigliano and Sangro Rivers—and the Allied advance bogged down in the hell of Cassino. We were brewing up in a farmyard in the mountains near Castel di Sangro when Popski's withdrawal message came in. 'Return to base immediately,' it read unequivocally.

'Pack up, Bum,' I shouted to Curtis, 'we're going back to Lucera. There's something on.'

It was mud and slush, sleet and rain all the way. We were driving in the opposite direction to the supply convoys moving up to the front and we had long exasperating delays at single-span Bailey bridges while mile-long convoys clattered across the muddy slats. . . .

It was dark when we reached Lucera, wet through, numbed, mud-bespattered.

Sergeant Waterson walked out of the lighted barn as we drove into the yard.

"Evening, sir,' he greeted me regimentally. His voice had lost its joviality and boisterousness, his beady eye its glitter.

'What's the matter, Sarge? You sound browned-off.'

'I am, sir. I'm leaving P.P.A.'

'You're what?' I asked incredulously.

'Leaving P.P.A., sir. Going back to my regiment.'

I was dumbfounded. Waterson was a pillar of the P.P.A. edifice. One of the Cairo originals, he had been with us from the very beginning, seen us through our teething troubles, saved our lives on many occasions. What would P.P.A. do without him?

'What on earth for, Sarge?'

Waterson shrugged.

'I'm not fit, sir.'

'Balls!' I said rudely.

He didn't reply. An unhappy expression came into his face and he saluted and walked away.

'That's not like Waterson,' I muttered. 'There's something behind this. He's had a row with Popski.'

After seeing that the patrol had everything they required, I went into the villa to report my arrival.

Popski and Jan were finishing dinner.

'*Buona sera, Capitano,*' Jan greeted me with a broad smile.

'Well, Bob,' said Popski, X-raying me with his penetrating eyes, 'you didn't manage to slip through.'

'Sorry, Popski. I tried damned hard, but we just couldn't get through.'

'Don't worry, Bob,' Popski smiled. 'Neither could I.'

Jan Caneri bawled, 'Vincento!' and an Italian mess waiter came running in.

'*Cena per il Capitano,*' said Jan. (Bring supper for the captain.)

Vincento, a dark-skinned, close-cropped, obliging young man, said, '*Si, Capitano,*' and hurried out. He was back in a trice carrying a large dish of steaming *pasta.*

Jan poured me a glass of wine.

'*Salute,*' I said, raising my glass.

I applied myself ravenously to the appetizing dish. . . .

'What's the matter with Waterson, Popski?' I enquired when the first pangs of hunger were satisfied. 'He tells me he's leaving.'

Popski nodded.

'Battle-weary. He needs a rest.'

'But why's he leaving P.P.A. if he only needs a rest?'

'I suggested that, but he feels if he can't be in the thick of it he'd rather leave.'

I didn't know it then, but Waterson was the first case of a mysterious disease which attacked P.P.A. patrolmen. Curtis contracted it six months later and many more after him. An insidious thing, difficult to diagnose, it began with a chink in one's armour of faith, a sudden lack of confidence, a feeling that the luck couldn't last. Anything could promote it, the chance remark of a patrol-mate, a narrow escape from death, a wound, a nerve-racking experience, seeing a patrolman killed, anything which caused you to lose faith in your ability to survive. In many cases the disease took root without any outside factor being responsible, simply the growth of an idea in the mind that your luck couldn't last. The unfortunate part about the disease was that it attacked the cream of the patrolmen, the dare-devils, the ones who were best at the job; and there was no sure cure for it. Sometimes a rest, a period at base, was effective and the victim returned as good as ever; more often the disease was incurable, the patient never recovered his faith and he was no more use on patrol. It wasn't a lack of courage or bravery, simply a breakdown of faith.

'What's the next move, Popski?' I asked, changing the subject.

'We're going into winter quarters at Bisceglie for a rest and re-fit. Jan and I are flying to Algiers to get a bigger establishment for P.P.A. You'll be in charge of training, Bob.'

'Where's Bisceglie?'

'On the coast between Barletta and Bari,' said Jan. 'A nice place, Bob. We've got seven villas in a row.'

'Seven!' I exclaimed.

Jan laughed.

'P.P.A.'s going to grow, Bob.'

We discussed the proposed new establishment, strength, patrol formation, men, promotions, future plans, jeeps, equipment.

'We'll have to devise some sort of weather protection for the jeeps, Popski,' I said. 'It's bloody miserable in wet weather.'

Popski nodded.

'I agree, Bob. I've been thinking about it. The answer's either waterproof clothing or a waterproof jeep cover, like a kayak.'

'Suppose you want to jump out quickly?'

'Zippers,' said Jan.

'We'll do some experimenting when we get settled in at Bisceglie,' said Popski. 'The important thing is to get the new establishment passed.' And with that we said good night and went to bed.

'But why leave P.P.A., Sarge?' I argued with Waterson next morning. 'If you're not feeling well, take a holiday. God knows you deserve one.'

176

'No, sir. I've lost my grip. I don't see eye to eye with the old man about certain things. I'm going back to my regiment.'

Waterson's mind was made up and I couldn't change it. I know now that he made a wise decision, but I was sorry to see him go, for a braver, better, more honest sergeant never served the British Army.

P.P.A. moved to Bisceglie and Popski and Jan Caneri flew to Algiers, returning a week later grinning from ear to ear like a couple of successful armament salesmen.

'You're looking very pleased with yourselves,' I greeted them when they stepped from the jeep I'd sent to meet them at the airport. 'How did you get on?'

'Fine, Bob,' said Popski.

'Got everything we asked for,' grinned Jan, lugging a heavy brief-case. 'Jeeps, wireless truck, workshops, the lot.'

I rubbed my hands.

'That sounds something like.'

Jan told me the story later.

As a result of his Intelligence scoop at Gravina, Popski's personal stock had sky-rocketed. Almost overnight he had become the darling of the Staff, an Intelligence wizard, a legendary figure endowed with superhuman powers. His private army was no longer a joke. He had done what was deemed impossible—taken a patrol of jeeps behind the lines in Italy and come out unscathed. Did he want more jeeps, more men? Certainly. A wireless van for long-range inter-communication? By all means. A properly equipped unit workshop to handle jeep repairs? But of course. Was that all? It wasn't enough. Specialist personnel would be required—fitters, armourers, wireless operators, administrative clerks. A new P.P.A. War Establishment was hastily drawn up increasing our total strength to 120 officers and men, with priority for equipment and recruits. Officially, if not socially, P.P.A. had arrived.

Popski left almost immediately on a recruiting tour of base depots; Jan Caneri, armed with a new G1098 and a sheaf of carefully prepared priority indents, turned his Latin charm upon the quartermaster branch; I stayed at Bisceglie and trained the men.

From a loose, two-patrol, irregular formation we set about

transforming P.P.A. into an organized raiding force for special operations in Italy. We formed three operational patrols of six jeeps each, a small H.Q. patrol (called 'Blitz'), a workshops section, a wireless section, an equipment section and an adminstrative headquarters under Jan Caneri.

The patrols were my special concern and I thought about little else. Each patrol was manned by an officer, a sergeant, a corporal, a lance-corporal, a fitter, a wireless operator and six driver-gunners —twelve in all. Since the success of our operations depended upon the efficiency and resourcefulness of the patrols much care and attention went into their composition. Each patrolman had to be an experienced driver trained in what we called 'jeeprobatics'— able to take his jeep anywhere at any time over the most impossible terrain—and in addition he had to be a good navigator, a motor mechanic, a competent machine-gunner, a demolition expert, a keen and resourceful fighter able to look after himself in any situation and determined to accomplish whatever task he was given. The standard was high and we had difficulty in finding the right men. Out of every hundred volunteers Popski interviewed at base depot only fifteen or twenty were considered suitable; Jan Caneri whittled this number down to a round dozen at Bisceglie; and by the time the recruits had been through the mill of patrol training only about half the original number remained permanently with the unit, for it wasn't only a question of keenness and efficiency, the new recruit had to 'fit' into the patrol and be able to harmonize with other patrolmen more experienced than himself. Patrol suitability was the most difficult test the new recruit had to pass and if he failed to pass it he went to one of the base sections or was returned to his own unit. Experienced patrolmen were highly intuitive—their lives depended upon this intangible factor —and if they didn't take to the new recruit there was always a very good reason. Time and again a recruit who had passed all his efficiency tests with flying colours came up to me and asked why he was being taken out of the patrol. All I could say was: 'Sorry, old chap. Your face doesn't fit,' or 'The men don't like you,' not a very satisfactory reply to an enthusiast who had worked damned hard to make good; but experience proved intuition to be more reliable than reason.

You cannot teach men the craft of war; they have to learn it for themselves—in action. Danger does something to a man's mind. It either paralyses him with fear and makes a coward of him, or inspires him with an inner joy which brings the best out of him. The recruit's final test came in action and we had many surprises. The mediocre blossomed into towers of strength, the star-turns turned and ran.

Training was streamlined and completely realistic. We tried to reproduce in training the conditions the men would encounter in action and we used live ammunition. First-class machine-gunners were turned out in a fraction of the time required by the Regular Army. In P.P.A. we weren't concerned with the names of the parts, but only their use in the gun. The new recruit was given a Browning machine-gun and shown how to take it to bits. Under the eye of an experienced patrolman he sat in a room of the patrol villa dismantling and reassembling the gun day after day, faster and faster. At the end of a week he was blindfolded and made to do the same thing again, faster and faster, working by the feel of the parts. Then he went out to the range in a jeep with unlimited ammunition and if, by the end of the week, he couldn't knock a wine-bottle off a wall at a thousand yards, using tracer, he wasn't considered much good.

The same basic principle was applied to jeeprobatics, map-reading, navigation, jeep maintenance, demolition—practical, realistic training without any frills. Night after night the patrols went out on exercise, ranging across the whole of southern Italy, driving from map reference to map reference given by wireless from base, through rivers, across mountains, blowing up imaginary targets, staging mock raids, finding their way back 'through the lines'. The experienced patrolmen trained the recruits, discovered their weaknesses and strengths and decided whether or not they would feel happy with them in action.

Discipline was self-imposed. There was no guard room, no orderly room, no miserable docking of pay; no spit and polish, no rampaging sergeant-major, no jumping to attention when an officer passed. Each man was given a job to do and allowed to get on with it. He was well-fed, well-clothed and well-billeted, never pushed around. Every man felt he was one of a team, a privileged member of a unique organization which was difficult to join, and after experiencing the unbelievable absence of 'bull' at base, the free and happy comradeship of life in the patrols, he didn't willingly risk a return to Regular Army ways so that the constant threat of R.T.U. (Return To Unit) held over his head was a greater deterrent of misdemeanour than any King's Regulations.

Service with P.P.A. was voluntary and every recruit started from scratch. Corporals and sergeants reverted to priv? ɜ and it says much for the spirit of P.P.A. that so many N.C.O.ᵤ ɔined our ranks. We had more difficulty with officers, for they too had to forego their rank. Our new establishment allowed for one major, two captains, three lieutenants. Popski was the major, Jan Caneri and I were the two captains, so that there were vacancies for lieutenants only, without much hope of promotion. Promotion didn't worry the P.P.A. triumvirate—Popski, Jan and myself—because we had more independence than most generals, and freedom and independence meant more to us than rank, but it worried our officer recruits and we were always short of good lieutenants.

The weeks passed and the new organization gradually took shape. Corporal Moss, a rosy-cheeked, fair-haired, cheery, innocent-looking young man whose outward cherubic appearance completely belied an inner ruthless efficiency, was promoted to staff-quartermaster-sergeant and took over the stores and equipment section where, in the comfortable villa allotted to him, he neatly shelved and docketed the various items Jan Caneri wheedled out of unwilling quartermasters. Sergeants Beautyman and Brooks, our two genius wireless operators, built up a foolproof system of W/T communication in the villa next door to the Mess. Beautyman, fair, stocky, bulldoggish once he got his teeth into a problem, and Brooks, tall, thin-haired, ruddy-cheeked and unperturbable, made an excellent pair, carried out secret research work of their own, trained the patrol operators and were known as 'The Backroom Boys'. Their villa was sacrosanct and only the favoured few were allowed entrance into its wired and batteried precincts.

Corporal McDonald from R.E.M.E., soon promoted to sergeant-fitter, a lovely natured man with a soft-spoken Highland lilt and a perennial spot of grease on his rather pale cheek, quickly built up an efficient jeep workshops in the outbuildings and yard behind Moss' villa. Lights blazed there after dark and long after most of us were in bed McDonald's hammers still banged, his red-mouthed forge still glowed and streamers of ice-blue light darted from the spout of his oxy-acetylene plant as he welded a gun-mount or fitted an extra petrol-can bracket to a jeep.

In his Admin. villa adjoining the Officers' Mess, Jan Caneri worked into the small hours of the morning checking indents, filling in returns, bringing his logical French brain to bear upon the problem of P.P.A. logistics. Popski and I eschewed paperwork and the whole burden of administration fell upon Jan's obliging and capable shoulders. He worked longer hours than any of us. Feared rather than loved by the men, respected for his fairness, Jan became the recognized consultant to whom all took their problems, whether of pay or procedure.

New recruits reported for duty and were absorbed into the growing organization. Lieutenant Rickwood from the Tank Corps, a tall, flaxen-haired officer with a disarming smile, a swashbuckling manner and an utter contempt for orthodoxy; Lieutenant Reeve-Walker, a South African mining engineer with a flare for improvisation; Troopers O'Leary and Hodgson, an inseparable pair of rogues from a commando unit, men who would go anywhere and do anything provided they were together, fearless of wounds or death, first-class men in a scrap, but always in trouble at base. We dubbed them 'The Heavenly Twins'; Jock Simpson, a pawky-humoured Scot who grew a Christ-like beard and became known in patrol as 'J. C.'; George Sonley, a well-built, good-looking, devil-may-care type from a famous cavalry regiment, a man with a way with the women; Don Galloway, also from the cavalry, a shy young man who later broke through his shell and grew to greatness on patrol; Ben Owen, Sammy Sizer, Ron Cokes, Sloan, O'Neil, Burrows, Tindall and many others.

A few duds inevitably slipped through the mesh of our careful screening and two were discovered at Christmas time.

Popski was dozing in a chair in the Mess during after-lunch siesta when one of his new recruits tapped on the door, entered, stood smartly to attention, saluted, and asked, 'May I speak to you, sir?' Popski didn't stand on ceremony with his men. He opened one eye, looked Trooper Edwards up and down and told him to go ahead. Trooper Edwards pulled a hand-grenade from his pocket and solemnly asked Popski's permission to kill himself.

'I beg your pardon, Edwards?' said Popski, sitting bolt upright, opening his other eye and keeping both on the pin of the hand-grenade Edwards was fondling.

'It's like this, sir,' began Trooper Edwards, 'I want to be killed in action. I joined the Commandos for that reason and never went on a raid. Then I volunteered for the S.A.S. and the same thing happened. When I heard of P.P.A. I thought third time's lucky and I would get my chance, but here's another Christmas come round and I'm still at base. It's no good, sir, I can't go on like this any longer. I want your permission to kill myself.'

A crazy gleam shone in Trooper Edwards' eye. Realizing he was dealing with a madman, Popski humoured him and played for time.

'But not on Christmas Day, Edwards, please. Kill yourself by all means if you want to, but please don't spoil our Christmas dinner. Wait until tomorrow, as a special favour to me.'

Edwards appeared to consider this very reasonable request. Popski followed up his advantage with:

'If you're going to kill yourself, Edwards, be sure you make a proper job of it. Some of these grenades are defective. Let me check it for you.'

Fixing Edwards with an hypnotic eye, Popski held out a hand and Edwards meekly put the grenade into it. Popski unscrewed the cap, shook out the primer, rescrewed the cap and gave Edwards the harmless grenade.

'Just a minute, Edwards,' he said, 'I'll check this primer for you.'

Popski rose, walked into the passage and bawled for O'Leary and Hodgson.

Trooper Edwards gave no trouble. He sat like a lamb between The Heavenly Twins in the duty truck and was hurried to the psychiatry ward.

A special Christmas dinner had been arranged in the Mess for that evening. Some of the nurses from the New Zealand Hospital in Bari had been invited and Jan and I went in for them. . . .

We had cocktails and sat down to dinner.

One chair remained empty, that of a new officer-recruit whom (to spare his wife's feelings) we shall call Fenton. Half-way through the fish course, the door was suddenly thrust open and Fenton staggered in, unshaven, dishevelled, bleary-eyed, drunk as a coot.

' 'Appy Ishmus, Popshki.' Fenton slurred his words, swayed drunkenly, put a wavering finger to his lips and tottered towards his place at table.

Jan and I grew hot under the collar. Popski's eyes blazed.

One of the nurses wore a rather low evening gown. To our horror, Fenton fixed a glassy eye on her exposed back, planted a resounding kiss on the nape of her pink neck, slurred ' 'Appy Ishmus, Shweetie' and subsided into the empty chair next to her. There was a dead silence. . . .

Fenton sat hunched in his chair, mouth drooping, eyes closed. He sighed deeply, drew the back of an unmanicured hand across his mouth, hiccoughed loudly, opened his eyes and blinked like an owl . . . hiccoughed again . . . suddenly burst into ribald song:

'Oooooooooooh she widna' deet——'

He broke off abruptly, came to his senses, realized where he was, pushed back his chair, apologized profusely, bowed solemnly to the table in general and staggered from the room.

Three days later he was still drunk. He was a dipsomaniac. The duty truck took him away.

Ivan and Nicolai, our two Russian pets, thoroughly disgraced themselves that same night, but in a quiet way which embarrassed nobody but themselves. Unable to toast the nativity in their native vodka, they repaired to the local *trattoria* in Bisceglie with an empty four-and-a-quarter-gallon-capacity jerrycan, filled it with wine and drank it to the dregs between them. . . . They were found on the beach at dawn, snoring, with the tide coming in, lapping their feet.

'But how did you get here, Sarge?' asked the R.A.S.C. transport corporal. Sergeant Curtis looked suspiciously round the group of transport drivers gathered at the table in the *trattoria* and drew his questioner to one side.

'Look, chum,' he whispered conspiratorially, putting a cautioning finger to his lips, 'it's all very hush-hush and I'm not supposed to tell anybody, but I'll tell *you* if you promise to keep your trap shut.'

The lanky R.A.S.C. corporal crossed his breast and bent a dust-filled ear.

'We were parachuted into the Alps last Spring,' lied Curtis in a vibrant undertone. 'We fought our way down through the Apennines, right through the German lines.'

'Cor!' gasped the pop-eyed corporal, looking at Bum with veneration. 'Let me stand you a drink, Sarge.'

.   .   .   .   .

Jan Caneri and I were in trouble on Boxing Day. We were driving sedately through the main street of Bari when Jan's foot slipped off the clutch and banged down on the press-button of the smoke-discharger fitted to the rear of the jeep. The discharger was a new idea of Popski's, designed to give protection when escaping from enemy armoured cars, and was simply a row of smoke cylinders held in a bracket under the tail of the jeep and electrically operated by a press-button near the clutch.

There was a loud hissing sound from the rear of the jeep, like steam escaping from a railway engine. Jan realized at once what he'd done.

'Bob,' he said desperately, 'I've set the bloody discharger going.'

I looked round. A mushroom of smoke was welling up.

'Christ,' I muttered, knowing that having set the discharger going we were powerless to stop it. Four cylinders gave out a lot of smoke.

Bari was crowded that Boxing Day afternoon. Troops and civilians crowded the pavements. Seeing the smoke two red-bereted Airborne types stopped to watch the fun. I saw a military policeman approaching.

'We'd better get to hell out of it, quick,' I urged.

The discharger was beginning to function at pitch. The mushroom had grown to the size of a cloud and was billowing larger and larger. Jan pressed the accelerator and we picked up speed. There was a breeze blowing and as we swung out and revved past a convoy of trucks our billowing smoke-screen clawed sideways and enveloped it. . . .

We tore down the main street honking imperiously like a run-away fire-engine. Trucks gave way to us . . . civilian cars drew quickly into the kerb and stopped . . . the crowds on the pavements turned to stare . . . a brass-hat gave us an ugly look from the back seat of a staff-car before he was swallowed in smoke . . . traffic came to a standstill behind us, choked and blinded by the cloud of dense smoke which now filled the street.

'It's a bloody effective smoke-screen, Jan,' I observed, looking back. The street, the traffic, even the tramway wires were hidden. All I saw was a churning mass of grey-blue smoke connected to our tail by a writhing stem.

'Left, Bob,' Jan shouted as we approached an inter-section.

184

I stuck out an arm and we careened round, making for the open country. Our buoyant cloud followed us like a witch's curse.

'We'll have the M.P.s on our tail,' I laughed.

We zoomed under a railway bridge, filling it with smoke like a train going into a tunnel . . . oncoming traffic braked furiously. . . . Still spewing smoke, we reached the suburbs, but the cylinders had shot their bolt. The cloud began to disperse. There was a final choking sizzle, like a death-rattle, and the smoke-serpent died.

We breathed a sigh of relief.

'Dischargers, smoke, jeeps, for the use of,' quoth Jan.

We laughed till the tears ran down our cheeks.

A sergeant of military police awaited us at Bisceglie, deep in conversation with O'Leary. As we drove through the gateway to the Admin. villa O'Leary whispered to Hodgson, 'Here they are.' . . . Right heels banged on the gravel . . . two arms described extravagant salutes. . . .

'Military police to see you, sir,' O'Leary announced gleefully as we drew up.

We groaned and stepped from the jeep.

'Come inside, Sergeant,' said Jan, bounding up the steps of his villa.

I followed.

Two right heels banged . . . two right arms described a wide arc . . . two rigid hands quivered beside two black berets . . . two hands were closed and cut smartly to the trouser seams . . . a parade-ground voice (O'Leary's) bawled 'About . . .' . . . two pairs of legs high-stepped . . . two right heels banged on the gravel . . . 'Qui . . . ick' . . . two pairs of arms swung stiffly from front to rear at chest height. . . . 'Lef . . . Ri . . . Lef . . . Ri'. . . . Barely able to contain their laughter, The Heavenly Twins marched for ten yards and then broke into a run, bursting to tell the glad tidings. . . .

II

Early in January Popski went to Caserta where Allied Force Headquarters, luxuriously billeted in the historic palace of the Bourbon Kings of Naples, were planning the Anzio landing. A week later we received a top-secret cypher warning us to stand by for a sea-landing up the coast. Jan and I were sitting in the Admin. villa discussing ways and means of weather-protecting the jeeps when Beautyman brought the signal. Jan read it and passed it to me.

'Where d'you reckon it is, Jan?'

'No idea, Bob.'

The patrols were out in the mountains, training hard.

'The patrols will have to come in,' I said.

I encyphered a signal to each patrol and gave the forms to Beautyman.

When the patrols came in the following day there followed a period of intense activity. Jeeps went into workshops for overhaul, guns were tested and checked, equipment was made up to scale, escape kits were issued; all local leave was stopped and night passes were cancelled, patrol personnel were confined to the immediate vicinity of their villas.

Outside 'B' Patrol villa Sergeant Curtis walked up and down his row of highly tuned jeeps, rubbing his hands.

'Just the job, Skipper,' he beamed when I went to see how things were going.

'Have you checked everything, Bum?'

'Everything, Skipper.'

'Ammo?'

'Yes, Skipper.'

'Demolition kits?'

'Yes.'

'Jeep spares?'

'Yes.'

'Escape kits?'

'Yes.'

We checked the loads item by item. Curtis hadn't overlooked anything.

'Where are we going, Skipper?'

'I've no idea, Bum. Up the coast somewhere.'

'Adriatic?'

'I really don't know, Bum.'

I walked round the jeeps with him, watching the crews stowing their loads. There were new faces in the patrol. Don Galloway, quiet and reserved, giving no hint of the leadership quiescent in him; Jock Simpson ('J. C.') of the slumbrous brown eyes, the reddish beard, the misleading drawl; Toddy Sloan, the boyish-looking wireless operator in place of Stewart; Ben Owen, dark-haired and dark-eyed, thoughtful and intuitive; George Sonley in place of Bill Wilson (transferred to H.Q.); O'Neil, McAllister and Hunter.

'Quite happy about the new men, Bum?'

'Yes, Skipper.'

'What's Hunter like?'

'Good bloke, Skipper.'

'Ben Owen?'

'First class.'

'Simpson?'

'O.K.'

We went over the names of the new men. Curtis was satisfied we hadn't picked any duds.

'O.K., Bum. Keep everybody standing by.'

'O.K., Skipper.'

I walked through the hedge to 'S' Patrol commanded by Lieutenant Reeve-Walker and run by The Heavenly Twins. O'Leary and Hodgson were at the top of their form, overjoyed at the prospects of action.

'Happy, Twins?' I asked them.

They grinned, looked at each other and stuck their thumbs up. O'Leary had a heavy Colt revolver strapped to one side of his waist and a commando knife to the other. He was cleaning a Tommy-gun. Hodgson was similarly armed and was squinting down the barrel. I regarded the pair, warmed by their devil-may-care enthusiasm. They were dying to get into a fight.

I thought, 'God help the Germans they meet,' and walked through to the next hedge to workshops where McDonald, Frankensteinish behind shield and goggles, was welding brackets to a jeep. I watched the ice-blue light melting the metal. The pencil of flame blared from the spout, darting sparks of brilliance like the sparklers we used to light on Guy Fawkes' night. I watched him for a minute or two, walked on to 'R' Patrol villa, and then into the Admin. villa to speak to Jan.

He looked up from his desk as I entered, picked up a signal and held it out to me. I read it and groaned. 'Operation cancelled,' it read.

'When did this come in?'

'A few minutes ago.'

'The blokes'll go crazy, Jan.'

Jan shrugged.

'Nothing we can do about it, Bob.'

I toyed with the signal, trying to make up my mind how to put it to the patrols. . . .

'Better get it over,' I decided, and went out.

I told 'R' Patrol first. They were nearest.

'Operation's cancelled, Ricky,' I informed Lieutenant Rickwood. 'You can unload.'

Sergeant Saunders was standing near him. He made no comment. He was used to disappointments. He simply shouted 'Off-load' and started to take his equipment back to stores. . . .

I walked over to 'S' Patrol villa.

The Heavenly Twins were cleaning their fifty-calibre Browning.

'You're wasting your time, Twins,' I said.

They looked at me, puzzled. I dropped my bombshell in their lap.

'Operation's cancelled. Signal's just come in.'

Their spirits sank visibly to their boots. O'Leary pushed the gun away, flung his cleaning rag on the ground and swore heartbrokenly.

'Oh, Jesus. . . .'

Hodgson asked in a broken voice, 'What the hell for?'

I left them to their misery and went to break the news to my own patrol. I heard Curtis horse-laugh as I walked through the gap in the hedge and thought, 'Poor Bum, this is going to stop his laughter.' Curtis had just played his favourite trick on one of the new men (McAllister) and he and Jimmy Hunter were laughing at McAllister's discomfiture. Curtis always carried an odd assortment of demolition kit on his person—time-pencils, release-switches, press-buttons, primer cord, and the like—and, for safety, he carried detonators between the cigarettes in his cigarette-case. His trick, brought by practice to a fine art, consisted of exaggerating the destructive power of detonators. ('Blow your bloody head off . . . treat them with respect', whipping out his cigarette-case, flicking it open under the nose of the new recruit and saying nonchalantly as if offering a cigarette, 'Have a det, old man.' The recruit invariably jumped back and Curtis burst into his horsy guffaw.)

'Bad news, Bum,' I said when I stood beside him.

His face grew serious.

'What's the matter, Skipper?'

'The operation's cancelled. Signal's just come in. Off-load and take your equipment back to stores.'

Bum's face fell.

'Auh, Jesus, Skipper,' he groaned.

Laughter died away and depression settled over the crews like a cloud. Riches kicked a stone and looked out to sea. Locke adjusted his black eye-patch and mouthed a string of curses. George Sonley dropped a belt of ammunition with a clatter and said, 'Oh, muck it.'

I walked back to the Admin. villa feeling very depressed.

Reaction took different forms. The Heavenly Twins went into Bisceglie, got roaring drunk and wrecked a wine-shop; Bum Curtis went down to the beach and let off loud bangs with his demolition kit, a thing he often did when upset; the noise seemed to give him psychological release. Al Locke, the knife-thrower, took his throwing knives and vented his spleen on the trunks of trees. I sat morosely in the Mess and drank wine. Three days later another signal arrived:

POPSKI TO JAN   STAND BY FOR OPERATION

I dashed out to tell the patrols. The effect was miraculous. Within seconds everybody was laughing and singing. Happy men

189

rushed backwards and forwards from Moss' villa carrying guns, grenades, mines, ammunition belts, compo rations, escape kits. Engines revved, gun-breeches clicked, petrol-cans clanked into brackets. Outside 'B' Patrol villa the sunny morning air vibrated to the strains of 'Torno Sorrento' led by Riches. . . . At the front door of the next villa The Heavenly Twins were executing a fandango which terminated in a rude expletive and the motions of a Tommy-gunner spraying from the hip. . . .

Behind the next hedge Sergeant Saunders was whistling 'Waltzing Matilda'. . . .

We stood by with crossed fingers for nearly a week, keyed-up, edgy, keen to be off. . . .

The final blow fell unexpectedly in the small hours of a morning when Beautyman shook Jan's shoulder at 0200 hours and handed him Popski's signal which read 'Operation cancelled'.

I groaned when he told me at 0700 hours.

'What the hell's going on, Jan?'

'Bullshit baffles brains, Bob,' he said cynically. 'Too much brass at Caserta.'

It is one thing to train high-spirited, adventure-loving men for special operations behind the enemy lines. It is quite another to control them at base when an operation upon which they have set their heart is cancelled.

'We'll have to find something for the patrols to do, Jan,' I said one evening when yet another complaint came in from Bisceglie. 'That's the third wrecked *vino* joint this week.'

'Send them out on training exercises, Bob.'

I shook my head.

'That's not the answer, Jan. Training's lost its interest. The patrols are trained to the hilt. It's action they want. If I send them out on exercise they'll only go berserk in the mountains.'

Jan shrugged and said, 'Pough.'

Popski provided a partial answer to the problem when he returned from Caserta a few days later.

'We're attached to Fifth Div.,' he told us. 'They're attacking across the Garigliano. We'll move the patrols over tomorrow.'

'What happened at Caserta, Popski?' we asked.

Popski looked grim and shook his head.

'Muddle and red tape. Politics. Too many cooks.'

190

'Just what I told you, Bob,' Jan smiled. 'Bullshit baffles brains.'

'Exactly,' said Popski and painted for us a vivid word-picture of A.F.H.Q. in Caserta—the vast, thousand-roomed palace thronged with sam-browned generals, brigadiers, colonels, majors, captains, lieutenants, lieutenant-commanders, wing-commanders, group-captains, squadron-leaders, Fannys, Wrens, Waafs; Americans, British, Canadians, Poles, Free French, all squabbling and angling for promotion and precedence; Conferences and Planning Talks, form-filling, gossiping, bickering; cocktail parties and sight-seeing tours; crowded passages, packed vehicle parks, people coming and going, rushing hither and thither, everybody trying to pass the buck to somebody else. . . . 'Complete chaos, my dear sir,' Popski finished up.

'What are we going to do on the Garigliano?' I asked.

'Watching brief, Bob. The attack is timed to coincide with the Anzio landing. If Fifth Div. break through Cassino will be relieved and there will be a rush for Rome. It's the best I can do at the moment.'

The patrols drove across Italy from the cool winds of the Adriatic to the warm breezes of the Tyrrhenian and leaguered in the woods on the reverse slope of a ridge overlooking the Garigliano Valley.

From the hill-top, through binoculars, our backs comfortably supported by resiny fir trees, we watched the attack going in . . . crowded pontoons shooting out from the grassy bank . . . diminutive, khaki-clad figures running up the far bank and flinging themselves down . . . the flash and smoke of shell and mortar-bomb explosions . . . the scarlet streamers of machine-gun fire . . . tanks and bren-carriers moving forward . . . the twisting blue river . . . the blue Gulf of Gaeta . . . the white road stretching across the green valley . . . the cloudless, azure sky . . . the lone German aviator weaving desperately through the puffs of ack-ack . . . the spume of black smoke pouring from his spiralling wings . . . the opening parachute, white and fluttering . . . the shell-shattered houses of Minturno. . . .

The idea behind the attack, coincident with a paralysing thrust from Anzio (which never materialized), was to trap the German divisions in the Liri Valley, annihilate them, cut off reinforcements, break the Cassino deadlock and liberate Rome. The plan miscarried. The Anzio landing was a flop. Fifth Division's attack was held and the Cassino massacre continued.

'Division want us to blow a bridge, Bob,' Popski informed me later in the day. We went to look at it.

From Battalion H.Q. we followed the tape line to Company H.Q., ducking and wriggling on our stomachs on a shell-torn slope to the lea of a ridge over which we hoped to obtain a view of our target.

There was a lot of stuff coming over—shells, mortar bombs, rifle-grenades—and we crouched in a narrow slit-trench waiting for the hubbub to die down. Around us were the men of a north-country regiment, stolid farmer's sons from the hills and dales of Northumberland, dug-in with bren-guns and rifles. We were in 'A' Company lines; on the other side of the ridge precariously entrenched on the exposed forward slope the gallant men of 'B' Company bore the brunt of the German counter-attack. . . .

The din of battle increased . . . mortar bombs crashed furiously . . . viciously exploding shells threw divots of earth high into the air and they spattered down upon the riven, trembling hillside . . . hoarse cries and shouts drifted over the ridge, mingling with the rising crescendo of bren-gun and Spandau-fire . . . a white-faced company runner plunged over the crest . . . took momentary shelter at the foot of a splintered tree . . . shook the blood from a wounded hand . . . cursed . . . ducked down the slope. . . .

I knew a moment of panic, a moment of wild desire to get up and run away. . . . 'How bloody silly to sit here and be killed or taken prisoner,' I thought. . . . Popski smiled and winked at me . . . the moment of panic passed. . . . I winked back and gripped my revolver. . . .

The battle on the forward slope reached its height. The German infantry spent themselves on the rifles and bayonets of the steadfast north countrymen and withdrew their decimated ranks. The danger was over. The shelling subsided, the mortar bombs thinned, an irregular burst of Spandau-fire, a few desultory rifle-shots marked the end of the counter-attack.

A breath of relief rippled through 'A' Company lines, like the evening breeze moving through a cornfield. Bren-gunners relaxed their trigger-grips and wiped beads of sweat from muddied brows;

riflemen eased butts from aching shoulders; armbanded stretcher-bearers hurried on their errands of mercy.

'Quite an experience, Bob,' Popski smiled.

'I thought we'd had it,' I grinned.

'Right. On we go,' said Popski.

We heaved ourselves out of our slit-trench and crawled to the top of the ridge. Round the base of a shattered oak tree we looked down upon devastated no man's land, upon a gaunt and ghastly hillside of split and broken trees, shell-holes and bomb craters, upon a grove of undamaged trees in the valley and the winding blue river beyond them. A couple of miles up-stream our target single-spanned the moving water, looking peaceful and detached in the sunlight, like an onlooker at a drama. A white road curved from the bridge, twisted through green hills and disappeared over a ridge into the Liri Valley; beyond the ridge range upon range of blue mountains folded against the sky. . . .

Back in the safety of our leaguer I remonstrated with Popski.

'It's pointless,' I said. 'Even if we blow the bridge it won't make any difference. The sappers'll make a diversion in a few hours.'

'Division want it blown, Bob.'

'But I can't see any point in blowing it, Popski,' I reiterated. 'It isn't as if there was a ravine there and we could cut off re-inforcements. The valley's flat. It won't make any difference to Jerry whether there's a bridge there or not.'

Popski looked at me sternly.

'Don't argue, Bob. The bridge has to be blown.'

I shrugged and walked away. So far as I could see this was a suicide job. We had to walk through our own front line after dark, go down the forward slope, run the gauntlet of the enemy night-fire, pick our way through a mine-field, crawl past the German out-posts, reach the bridge, overpower the sentries (it was sure to be guarded), hold the bridge long enough to lay charges, crawl past the outposts again, through the mine-field and up the forward slope, risking a shot in the back from the enemy and one in the face from a jittery bren-gunner as we approached our own lines. Had there been any good reason for blowing the bridge I wouldn't have cared, but I couldn't see any. The risks were out of all pro-portion to the gains; we'd just be throwing away the lives of good men. I cursed the comfortably seated staff-officer who had thought up the idea and reluctantly prepared for the ordeal.

I chose Curtis, Locke, McAllister, Ben Owen and Jimmy Hunter from my own patrol. We put on gym shoes, emptied our pockets of valuables, blackened our faces with burnt cork, packed demolition charges into rucksacks and put the fuses inside our berets, out of harm's way, had a meal and climbed into a truck. . . .

We drove to Battalion H.Q. and sat by the roadside, waiting for darkness. I felt depressed, sure that disaster impended. As dusk fell Jimmy Hunter came up to me and put his wallet and wrist-watch into my hand.

'Please send these to my wife, Skipper,' he said, 'I'm not coming back from this job.'

'Don't be silly, Jimmy,' putting into my voice a confidence I didn't feel. 'Of course you'll come back. We'll all come back.'

But Jimmy refused to be comforted. He just looked at me dully, convinced he was going to be killed.

Darkness spread an inky cloak over the torn hillside. Shoulder-ing our heavy packs, we picked up Tommy-guns, nodded good-bye to Popski and Jan and picked our way silently up to the ridge. . . .

Below the crest, we paused for a breather. There was no moon. The night was heavily dark with only a handful of stars. Silence enveloped the front, a tense, watchful, brooding silence, broken only by the booming of the guns at Cassino.

'Ready?' I breathed. My heart was like a leaden weight.

We slunk over the crest, slipping like shadows between the split and gaping tree trunks . . . past the forward platoons gripping their weapons and peering into the night, crouched like animals in their earth-holes.

'Don't shoot us when we come back,' I stopped to whisper in the ear of a burly north-country sergeant.

'We'll look out for you, sir,' he assured me. 'Good luck, sir.'

I nodded my thanks and ducked down the cratered slope. . . .

When we entered the grove of trees I felt like a cat on hot bricks, apprehensive of mines, fearful of booby-traps. An over-grown footpath wound through the shadowy trees. We rested for a moment to ease our aching shoulder muscles and then padded along the grassy verge in single file. I led, followed by Ben Owen, then McAllister, Jimmy Hunter, Locke, Curtis. . . .

We'd gone a couple of hundred yards when there was a sudden blinding flash, a loud explosion, a strangled cry. I felt my heart contract, gripped as by an icy hand, and looked round. . . .

194

Major (later Lieutenant Colonel) Vladimir Peniakoff, a.k.a. 'Popski'. A master of five languages, including Arabic, his extensive knowledge of the Libyan desert gained him a much sought-after 'demolition unit' in October 1942. It was immediately named Popski's Private Army.

A P.P.A. jeep – the seminal transport of the unit. On the role of the jeep in P.P.A., Yunnie wrote: 'Crews were fussy about their jeeps ... and developed feelings for them like cavalrymen for their horses and, like cavalrymen, preferred their own mounts.' This is a rare, and possibly unique, photograph of a flamethrower on a jeep during World War Two.

Bob Yunnie (aka 'Park'; pictured right), the skipper of 'B' patrol, and his companion Ben Owen (below). Both are photographed while still serving with P.P.A.. Owen's tribute to his skipper appears on page 5, while Yunnie wrote in praise of 'the real Ben Owen' after accompanying him on several perilous patrols in Italy: 'a man of sterling character, intelligent, intuitive, quite fearless, and with a happy knack of making the best of things.'

Service with P.P.A. was voluntary, and demanded that officers and NCOs forego their former rank and start from scratch. Among the recruits to join P.P.A. during the Italian campaign were Ron Cokes (pictured above) and Don Galloway, MM with two bars (pictured adjacent), a shy individual who displayed surprising leadership whilst on patrol.

Jeep patrol in Southern Italy, 1943. Driving the leading jeep is Mike Mitchell. A black disk can be seen between the two men in the second jeep. This is a miniature searchlight, which was traditionally attached to the commanding officer's jeep (Popski is driving). The contraption was later discontinued after a number of jeeps were lost at Tenna Valley.

Ali Stewart, MBE. An ex-member of the Long Range Desert Group, he graduated easily to P.P.A., where he became a mechanic.

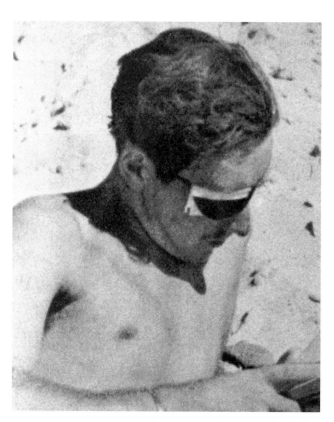

Corporal Alan Locke of 'B' Patrol, whose body was a mass of scars, and whose piratical eye-patch concealed a missing right eye.

Hector Simpson, nick-named 'J.C.' due to his Christ-like beard, had a laconic Scots drawl which belied a sharp, active wit.

Dave Porter, DCM of 'P' Patrol was an explosives expert who was killed in action in November 1944

Porter is pictured on campaign in Italy with (left to right): Arthur 'Dave' Davies, who was often the 'driver' on patrol; Lieutenant Bray and Mike Mitchell.

P.P.A. jeeps roll into St. Mark's Square, Venice, on the last day of World War Two. In the front jeep, Harold Varley (Caneri's gunner, of Blitz Patrol) drives Guillelmo 'Gigi' Guardone (left) and Jean Caneri. Guardone's story is prosaic. An Italian partisan hoping to join up with Eighth Army, he encountered Popski's army in the mountain village of Esanatoglia, and joined up immediately. He was to prove invaluable on patrol. He retired some years ago as a general in the Italian Army. Captain Jean Caneri was a Free French Officer who had struck up a friendship with Yunnie and Popski while all three served in the Libyan Arab Force. As the third founder member of P.P.A., Caneri was Yunnie's constant companion throughout the campaign. In the rear jeep, wireless operator Fred Yeoman (left) sits beside Paddy McAllister of 'B' Patrol, who recovered from serious injury at Cassino to see the end of the war.

Popski (left) is driven by Ron Cokes through St. Mark's Square on VE-Day. The jeeps were apparently the first wheeled vehicles to be seen in the city.

Popski pictured again with Driver Cokes in Vienna. Here, Popski's loss of his left hand, an injury sustained at Ravenna (the last Italian action Yunnie was to see), is clearly visible. This is Popski's older patrol jeep, with two Browning .50 MGs installed, as opposed to the usual deployment of one .50 MG and one .30 MG. A medical pack is being transported at the front of the vehicle.

Jimmy Hunter was lying on the path, blood gurgling and spurting from a gaping hole where his throat should have been. Ben Owen was leaning against a tree, holding his arm. McAllister lay crumpled on his side, groaning. Locke was hopping on one leg. Curtis and I were unhurt. Jimmy Hunter had stood on an S-mine. He died instantaneously and couldn't have felt a thing.

There was nothing we could do for Jimmy Hunter. Dropping our cumbersome packs, Curtis and I half carried, half dragged McAllister through the trees, away from the mine-field. We dumped him behind a tree and fumbled with his clothing. He was hit in the back. Clumsily, we applied a field dressing to the bloody wound. Ben Owen and Al Locke, able to walk, looked after themselves.

Then hell broke loose. . . .

The Germans had mortars and machine-guns trained on the mine-field; the flash of the explosion and Jimmy Hunter's death-cry were their signal to open fire. A hail of bullets thrashed through the branches of the trees, dropping twigs and leaves on our heads. 'Christ,' we muttered and ducked, squeezing ourselves as small as possible. Then mortar bombs whistled over, crashing and banging behind us, cutting off our retreat. We were caught like rats in a trap. . . .

We lived a lifetime of agony in the next few hours. The curtain of machine-gun fire lifted and fell upon the forward slopes; mortar bombs exploded in the wood. Wheeeeeeee . . . wruuuu-uuumph . . . wheeeeeeeeeeee . . . wruuuuuuuumph . . . wruuuuu-uuumph . . . wruuuuuuuumph. Over they came in singles and clumps, whistling through the branches, smacking against the boles, thudding into the damp earth, making us quiver and crouch. . . .

Wheeeeeeeeee . . . wruuuuuuuumph . . . wruuuuuuuuumph . . . wruuuuuuuuuuumph. The barrage went steadily on, pinning us to our respective trees, unable to move an inch. The minutes were like hours, nerve-racked points of time strung endlessly together in a dark eternity of cowering apprehension. It seemed that the German mortarmen played with us like cat and mouse, amused to torture and terrify until they felt disposed to kill, knowing we couldn't escape. Wruuuuuuuumph . . . wruuuuuuuumph . . . wruuuuumph. The bombs crashed closer and closer, searching for us with malevolent intent. 'Ha, ha,' they seemed to cry with fiendish glee, 'you think you won't be hit. You think you'll get away. Not a chance. We know exactly where you are. We'll kill you one by one.'

Wruuuuuuuuumph . . . wruuuuuuuuumph . . . wruuuuuuu-umph. Above our heads . . . close to our trees . . . in the mine-field, exploding other mines. Wruuuuuuuuumph . . . wruuuuuuuuumph . . . wruuuuuuuumph.

Our nerves were at breaking point, taut and screaming, ready to snap. I found relief in passionate, measured cursing every time a bomb exploded. Wheeeeeeeee . . . wruuuuuuuuuumph. One crashed against my tree making me reel with the force of its shattering explosion. . . . 'Muck you.' . . . I felt a sudden pain in my leg and put my hand down expecting to feel blood and splintered bone . . . it was only a divot of earth. Wruuuuuuuumph . . . wruuuuuuumph . . . wruuuuuuuuumph. 'Hell, blast, muck it.' . . .

They say that when a man is waiting for death the events of his life pass before his mind's eye like pictures on a cinema screen. I had no such experience. A single thought kept ringing in my head like the carking repetition of a cracked gramophone record . . . 'It'll pass' . . . 'It'll pass' . . . 'It'll pass.' . . . Wruuuuuuuuuuuumph . . . wruuuuuuuuumph . . . wruuuuuuuuumph. . . . 'It'll pass' . . . 'It'll pass' . . . 'It'll pass.' . . . 'Hell. . . . Muck. . . . Blast.' . . . Wruuuuuuuumph . . . wruuuuuuuuumph . . . wruuuuuuuuumph. . . .

The mortarmen were methodically quartering the wood, section by section, and when the barrage crept temporarily to one side I took advantage of the respite to speak to Curtis. He was crouched at the base of a thick tree ten yards from me. 'Bum,' I called softly, 'Bum.' He had his head down and didn't hear me. 'Bum,' I loud-whispered again. I don't know why I kept my voice low, because the German mortarmen on the other side of the river couldn't have heard me above the din of their exploding bombs if I'd shouted at the pitch of my lungs; fear, I suppose. Unable to attract Curtis' attention I plucked up enough courage to crawl over to his tree and reached it as the barrage began to creep over us again.

'Skipper!' Curtis made room for me and gave me a sickly smile.

'Bum,' I whispered, 'this is hopeless.' . . . I broke off until a whistling bomb exploded . . . wruuuuuuuuumph. . . . 'We'll all be killed if we stay here' . . . wruuuuuuuumph. . . . 'You and Locke try

196

to get out' . . . wruuuuuuumph. . . . 'Ben Owen and I'll stay with McAllister' . . . wruuuuuuuumph. . . . 'Get a stretcher-party' . . . wruuuuuuumph . . . 'come back when the barrage stops' . . . wruuuuuuumph . . . wruuuuuuuumph . . . wruuuuuuumph. . . . A cluster of bombs fell viciously. We hugged the shuddering earth. . . . 'Make a dash for it as soon as it lifts.'

'O.K., Skipper.'

We crouched at the base of the tree for a long time without speaking . . . holding on to Life with a grim determination while Death teased from the wings . . . wruuuuuuumph . . . wruuuuuuu-umph . . . wruuuuuuuuuumph. . . . 'Hell, muck, blast.' . . . 'It'll pass' . . . 'It'll pass' . . . 'It'll pass' . . . wruuuuuuumph . . . wruuuuuuumph . . . wruuuuuuumph. . . .

The barrage crept away again and the machine-gun fire ceased. 'Now's your chance, Bum,' I whispered hoarsely. 'Tell Locke and make a dash for it. Watch you don't get shot going in. Hurry!'

'O.K., Skipper.' Curtis' voice was tense. He gripped my hand . . . looked wildly round for Locke—pressed against a tree some yards away—and plunged towards him . . . wruuuuuuumph. . . .

I sat with my back to the tree and watched Curtis and Locke crouch . . . wruuuuuuumph . . . jump up . . . wave . . . zigzag from tree to tree and disappear. . . .

Having sent two reliable men to bring help, I felt better. There was hope. I looked round for Ben Owen and saw him watching me from his tree. He waved cheerily. I got up and ducked over to him . . . wruuuuuuumph. . . .

It is in desperate situations that you come to know a man. You can be friends with a man in peace-time and never discover the real man hidden beneath the exterior he presents to the world; but in the Valley of Death all pretence is thrown aside and the real man comes uppermost. Until that night in the wood by the Garigliano, Ben Owen was only a name to me, a new patrolman, but in the hours we sat by McAllister's side waiting for Curtis to return I discovered the real Ben Owen, a man of sterling character, intelligent, intuitive, quite fearless, and with a happy knack of making the best of things. I warmed to him from the moment I sat by his side and we formed a friendship then which has lasted to this day. Ben was sorely shrapnel-wounded in arms and legs and in considerable pain yet he made little of it, describing wounds which kept him in hospital for weeks as 'Only a scratch, Skipper.'

McAllister was in a bad way. He had lost much blood and his body was cold to the touch. I put my hand under his back and found his battledress sticky with blood. He groaned when I withdrew my hand.

'He's still alive, Ben,' I whispered.

The barrage crept towards us again. I was glad I'd sent Curtis and Locke when I did and wondered how they were getting on. . . .

'Another pasting coming, Skipper,' Ben Owen whispered.

I nodded and we crouched beside McAllister, holding his lifeless hands, trying to pump warmth and courage into his flagging spirit, listening to the bomb explosions coming closer . . . wruuuu-uumph . . . closer . . . wruuuuuuuumph . . . closer. . . .

Wheeeeeeeeeeee . . . wruuuuuuuumph. A bomb crashed very close, spattering us with dirt . . . wheeeeeeeeeee . . . a jagged piece of shrapnel whined through the air and smacked viciously against our tree. Instinctively, we ducked. . . .

'That was a near one, Ben,' I breathed when the danger was past. Ben grinned at me in the darkness.

'Bet you we don't get hit, Skipper.'

Wheeeeeeeeeeee . . . wruuuuuuuuuuumph . . . wruuuuuuu-umph . . . wruuuuuuuuuuumph. . . .

The barrage continued for another hour, ebbing and flowing about us like an angry sea and then, after a last nerve-shattering crescendo, died away and left us in peace.

'You're a good prophet, Ben,' I smiled, hoping I wasn't speaking too soon.

In the deathly silence which followed the end of the barrage a new fear gripped me. Would the enemy now launch an attack? I didn't think it was safe to move McAllister without a stretcher and we couldn't leave him. I urged Ben Owen to make his way back to our lines, but he flatly refused to go.

'No, Skipper,' he said, 'if you stay, I stay.'

I didn't persist, being glad of his company.

We sat peering into the murky darkness imagining stalking Germans in every dark shadow, jumping nervously whenever a branch creaked, uncomfortably conscious of Jimmy Hunter's dead body lying in the mine-field fifty yards in front of us. . . .

A broken branch, held in a cleft, fell to the ground when a gust

198

of wind prowled through the wood like a wraith. We 'froze', mistaking the noise for a footstep, and gripped our Tommy-guns, determined to resist capture.

'We're nervy, Ben,' I whispered when nothing happened.

McAllister grew weaker. His face a ghastly grey in the faint luminosity of starlight which filtered through the branches, he scarcely breathed. His hands were cold as ice and his pulse was barely discernible. We tried to make him more comfortable but he only moaned when we moved him so we left him alone, just holding his clammy hands. . . .

In the small hours of the morning voices sounded from the direction of the forward slopes and the barrage began again. . . . Wheeeeeeeeeeeee . . . wruuuuuuuumph . . . wruuuuuuuuumph . . . wruuuuuuumph. . . .

'God, why can't they keep quiet?' I muttered.

Between the whistle and bang of the falling bombs I heard Curtis' voice calling.

'Are you there, Skipper? . . . Where are you, Skipper?'

'Here, Bum' . . . wruuuuuuuumph. . . . 'Don't make so much noise.'

Figures loomed between the trees and came towards us—Bum Curtis . . . Jan Caneri . . . four stretcher-bearers.

' 'Ullo, Bob,' Jan greeted me.

I gripped his hand . . . wruuuuuuuuumph . . . wruuuuuuumph . . . wruuuuuuuumph. . . . 'Christ' . . . we ducked behind trees. . . . 'Quick!' I urged in the short interval between bombs, 'get McAllister on to that stretcher. Careful with him. He's badly hurt.'

As if the hand of God intervened to enable an act of mercy to be performed the barrage stopped long enough for us to lift McAllister on to the stretcher and carry him out of the wood . . . wruuuuuuuuuumph . . . wruuuuuuumph . . . wruuuuuuuumph. It came down again, behind us, the moment we were clear of the trees, a long, wicked concentration of hatred right in the place of our vigil.

'Just in time, Jan,' I breathed shakily, feeling we'd escaped by a miracle.

Panting hard, we reached the top of the starlit riven slope and I don't think I ever felt so safe as I did in that wonderful moment when I ducked past the forward bren-gunner; after our recent exposure that single machine-gun seemed like a mile-wide armoured Maginot Line.

Popski had an ambulance waiting into which we put the unconscious McAllister. Locke had already been taken to hospital. Quite unconcerned about his wounds, Ben Owen was reluctant to go, fearing he would become enmeshed in red tape and never see P.P.A. again. 'Don't worry, Ben,' I assured him, 'I'll come to see you in hospital and make sure you return to P.P.A.'

Popski drove to Divisional H.Q. Curtis, Jan Caneri and I went back to our leaguer.

I was bitter about the loss of Jimmy Hunter. For no good reason at all, merely to satisfy the whim of some self-opinionated staff-officer (who kept well away from the danger zone) we had thrown away the life of a highly trained patrolman, difficult to replace, and three others would be in hospital for an indefinite period. 'We're just wasting time, Jan,' I complained. 'We'll never do anything messing around the front line on foot. We're a specialized jeep force. Jeeping behind the lines is our job. What we want is a private landing of our own with nobody else mixed up in it.'

'I agree, Bob. So does Popski. We had a talk this evening.'

'Well, I hope something comes of it' (disconsolately).

Something did.

A day later Popski said to me, 'Would you like to go parachuting, Bob?'

My spirits rose. Ever since the end of the Libyan campaign I had been urging Popski to let me take the men on a parachute course. As a specialized raiding force working behind the enemy lines it had seemed to me essential that all P.P.A. personnel should be trained parachutists.

'When do we leave, Popski?' I asked eagerly.

Popski smiled at my enthusiasm.

'I'm going to Caserta to plan a landing of our own,' he told me confidentially. 'We'll move base from Bisceglie up into the Matese Mountains. It's a better training ground and nearer Caserta. In the meantime, you'll take the patrols on a parachute course to keep them occupied.'

I could have hugged him.

12

From the Tyrrhenian and the noise of battle back to the Adriatic and the quiet peace of green fields where, at the newly established Parachute Training School on the outskirts of Brindisi, we ran round and round an aerodrome in shorts, sweating in the warm spring sunshine; jumped into sand-pits from a height and rolled over and over, getting sand in our hair; swung backwards and forwards in parachute harness, like trapeze artists, suspended from the beams of a hangar; sat upright in 'stick' formation in the fuselage of a grounded bomber; and observed how carefully parachutes were packed in the packing room—a stroke of genius on the part of our instructor, I thought, because watching skilled feminine hands painstakingly stretching and folding the nylon panels on long wooden tables removed all fear from our minds that our parachutes might fail to open.

Then aloft, under the tutelage of our dynamic instructor, a Polish Army major with 400 jumps to his credit and consequently a man of tremendous stature in our eyes.

On a cloudless, windless day we strapped ourselves into harness and single-filed into the renovated bowels of a DC3, sitting uncomfortably upright in a row with our ripcords hooked like dog-chains to a rail. The door clanged and the engines roared and we taxied into the runway, sitting for a moment feeling the plane vibrate with the throb of the racing engines tugging against the braked wheels; then we were off, tearing along the concrete strip, bumping gently and lifting into the air. . . .

In semi-daylight, our hands resting on our knees, we sat feeling the parachute harness tight and uncomfortable, being borne aloft and not knowing where, apprehensive of our first jump. Curtis cracked a joke, but it fell flat, like a tactless remark at dinner.

Time passed and a red light shone by the door.

'Action stations.'

We stood up and the jump-master checked our static lines, making sure the ripcords were securely hooked to the rail, and shepherded us into a 'stick' by the door.

Hearts beating fast, we stood in file, swaying to the motion of the plane, waiting for the order to jump. . . . What was it like, that first jump into space before your parachute opened?

The red light blinked out and a green one blinked on. The door swung open. I was the first of my stick, nearest the door. I looked out and down, and gulped. Mother Earth seemed very far away. I felt a sharp slap on the back, a voice in my ear shouted '*Go*' and I went—out into the slipstream. . . .

A rush of wind took my breath and I knew nothing until I felt a painful jerk between the legs. My eyes opened and I looked up. There was my parachute, open, swaying above my head just as the instructor had said it would. 'So it does open,' I heard myself say and my voice sounded strangely out of place in that azure vault, like trying to converse with God.

The thing which impressed me most was the silence, the complete and utter tranquillity, the peace after the noisy rush of air when I jumped. It was heaven to dangle in the stillness and feel oneself safely airborne. . . . I began to twist. . . . How did one correct a twist? Ah, yes, I remembered. Pull on the cords. I reached up, took a firm grip, pulled myself up and let go. . . .

The descent was sheer delight. I felt like a part of eternity, light as thistledown, drifting with the gentle breeze. A great happiness and contentment filled my mind. What fun life was! Only yesterday I had been close to annihilation and had come through the ordeal unscathed, and now here I was falling through the blue Italian sky, suspended between heaven and earth by a few yards of white nylon, safe as safe could be. All one needed was a little courage. The idea took root in my mind that I bore a charmed life and would survive the war. . . .

I looked up. The rest of the stick were bobbing in the air like balloons at a Christmas party, eleven white umbrellas with kicking, khaki-clad figures hanging on to them. I waved, jerkily . . . and looked down.

I looked down upon Lilliput, upon a little toy aerodrome with toy buildings and toy aeroplanes, upon toy vehicles crawling along toy roads winding between toy houses and toy vineyards, upon diminutive figures gazing skywards from a field of green grass far, far away. . . .

I let everything go, relaxed completely, and let myself drift . . . drift . . . drift . . . azure sky . . . stillness and peace. . . . It was so peaceful up there I wished I could drift for ever. . . . I closed my eyes in bliss. . . . I became aware of a voice, the voice of our instructor. He was standing on the greensward bawling instructions through a megaphone. His voice floated up to me, thin and tenuous. . . . 'Pull on your harness, number one.' . . . 'Bend your knees, number three.' . . . 'Feet together, number eight.' . . . The voice grew louder, the diminutive figures on the grass grew visibly larger, the grass was rushing towards me at a terrifying speed. . . .'Pull on your harness, number one. . . . Number one, pull on your harness.' . . . Number one? . . . Hell, that was me, I was number one. I reached up and pulled, remembering the instructor's words: 'Draw up your knees, close and level your feet. Turn your feet to the drift.'

I drew up my knees, pulled hard on the cords, levelled my feet; the landing-ground was rushing up at me . . . faster . . . faster. . . . I turned my feet, pulled hard, let go, felt a jolt, put my hands over my face, elbows well in . . . rolled over and over, feeling the sweet smell of the grass. . . . I stood up, slapped at my harness lock . . . ran round my billowing 'chute.

I was down. Ye gods, I was down, unhurt and happy and breathless. 'So this is parachuting,' I said to myself. 'Hell, Yunnie, this is fun!'

The others were landing all round me, a scattered group of laughing men, slapping at harness locks, rolling on the grass, running round flapping white sails.

'*Piace, Gino?*' I called to Gino who was nearest to me.

'*Si, Capitano,*' he laughed. '*Molto.*'

Bum Curtis was grappling with his unruly 'chute. Without glasses he was a little short-sighted.

'O.K., Bum?' I called.

A sudden gust of wind wrapped the nylon panels round him and all I heard of his reply was '. . . mucking thing'.

Riches was down, and Sonley, Don Galloway, Danny O'Neil, all unhurt, elated, eager to jump again. Only Toddy Sloan was quiet; he'd landed badly, given himself a jolt, and decided he didn't care for parachuting.

The Heavenly Twins, landing with another stick, danced upon the grass, executing their private fandango. . . .

Up again in the afternoon, and again the following morning, following afternoon, following morning, then two night jumps to complete the seven jumps of the fortnight's course. . . . Proudly into Brindisi to buy little blue-and-white parachute wings to sew on our battledress.

In the meantime, Jan Caneri had moved our base from Bisceglie to San Gregorio, an isolated village above Piedemonte D'Alife, at the foot of the Matese Mountains, thirty miles from Caserta, where he requisitioned the local *albergo* (hotel) for the men and a nearby summer villa for the Officers' Mess. Three thousand feet above sea-level, we had a magnificent view of Vesuvius when it erupted that year in a leaping bonfire of gigantic proportions which vomited lava and covered the surrounding countryside with a film of thick, grey ash.

Training, training, training. We climbed the lovely Matese Mountains in jeeps and on foot. We laid ambushes, blew up bridges, cut telephone wires, mined roads and shot up imaginary German convoys. We struck terror into the hearts of the local *contadini* with our incessant machine-gun fire and loud bangs in the night. Occasionally we visited Naples, and once went to Pompeii to see human bodies preserved in lava two thousand years after their death.

Time dragged again. March passed, and April, and May, and we were still playing games round Lago Matese, longing to be doing the real thing.

Popski was at Caserta most of the time trying to convince a negative-minded Planning Staff, deflated by the failure of the Anzio landing, that it would be a profitable venture to land P.P.A. on the Adriatic coast a hundred miles behind the German front line and let their jeeps loose on the L. of C. where isolated groups of Italian partisans were beginning to rise against their masters. He succeeded in the end (when the opportunity was gone), but his task wasn't easy. There were too many form-fillers at Caserta, too little imagination, and politics had begun to creep in. Depressed and weary, Popski turned up at the villa at week-ends, pored over his inevitable array of maps, refreshed himself in the healing balm of our mountain retreat and returned to do battle at Caserta.

A flourishing black market had sprung up in Naples and we felt the back-wash in San Gregorio. Supplied by the Americans and run by the Neapolitans, it was organized on a very large scale and deals involving millions of lira were transacted in the back streets of Naples during the hours of darkness. Not only food and cigarettes were involved, but truck-loads of clothing, ammunition and even military vehicles changed hands.

In May 1944 a jeep tyre and tube was worth a mint of money in Naples, and when we went to our vehicle-park in San Gregorio one sunny morning we found a number of our jeeps denuded of their spare wheels. There was an immediate hue and cry.

'Fetch the *podestà*!' cried Jan Caneri and a few minutes later The Heavenly Twins dragged a trembling village headman into our seething presence.

'Where are our wheels?' we demanded of the innocent man.

The *podestà* didn't know and spread out his hands in a gesture of helplessness.

'The wheels must be found,' we bullied him. 'Every house must be searched. Somebody in San Gregorio must have stolen them.'

'No, no,' protested the *podestà*. San Gregorians weren't thieves. The wheels would be found in Piedemonte D'Alife. It was well known that all Piedemonte D'Alifians were thieves.

'We'll take your word for that,' said Jan. 'But we'll search San Gregorio first.'

The village was cordoned off and every house systematically searched from attic to cellar. No jeep wheels were found, but the search revealed an astonishing collection of hidden treasure. Food was scarce and much of the *podestà's* time was taken up in organizing food-relief schemes for his starving population. The *podestà* came with us on our search and his blood-pressure rose to dangerous heights when P.P.A. patrolmen unearthed secret hoards of flour and sugar, great hams and cart-wheel cheeses. 'Thieves and vagabonds,' roared the disillusioned *podestà*, enraged to find his 'starving' villagers better hoarders than himself. Drawing a blank in San Gregorio, we drove *en masse* to Piedemonte D'Alife.

'Jeep wheels have been stolen,' we informed the *podestà*. 'Every house in Piedemonte D'Alife must be searched.'

'You are more likely to find the wheels in San Gregorio,' smirked the *podestà* of Piedemonte D'Alife. 'It is well known that all San Gregorians are thieves.'

Hiding a smile, we searched the houses of Piedemonte D'Alife, bringing to light much hidden treasure, but no jeep wheels.

'They must be somewhere, Jan,' I said.

'Probably in Naples by this time, Bob'—cynically.

I didn't think so. I had a strong feeling the wheels were still in San Gregorio, and so did Ben Owen, now fully recovered from the effects of his wounds.

Ben and I put our heads together.

'The job was done by someone with local knowledge, Ben. Someone familiar with the vehicle park.'

We stood in the centre of the vehicle-park and tried to reconstruct the crime.

'If you were stealing jeep wheels for the black market, how would you set about it, Ben?'

Ben looked thoughtful for a moment.

'I'd hide them in a safe place till the hue and cry died down, Skipper.'

'Where would you hide them, Ben?'

'In some place where nobody would ever dream of looking, Skipper.'

'Where would that be, Ben?'

Ben Owen's dark eyes travelled from the vehicle-park to the road and along the dusty road until they came to rest upon the tombstones in the village cemetery, enclosed within their grey stone walls, their neatly trimmed cypresses and padlocked iron gate.

I saw a gleam come into Ben's eyes.

'What about the cemetery, Skipper?'

'That's an idea, Ben. Let's go and look.'

We hurried along the road to the cemetery, vaulted over the low stone wall and walked between the tombstones.

'The soil's been disturbed here, Skipper. Look.' Ben pointed to a patch of recently turned earth beside a heavy stone slab.

'Get a spade, Ben. Quick.'

Ben ran back to the vehicle park for a spade and we opened up the vault.

'Well, I'm damned, Ben!' I exclaimed when the slab was off.
'Look at that.'

The missing wheels were there, wrapped in damp-proof covering, keeping company with the corpses.

The thief was never found.

'Somebody from Piedemonte D'Alife,' said the *podestà* of San Gregorio.

'Somebody from San Gregorio,' said the *podestà* of Piedemonte D'Alife.

On an afternoon in June, Popski arrived unexpectedly.

His depression and weariness gone, he was bursting with drive and vitality.

'He's been successful at last,' I muttered when I saw his bulky figure heave out of the jeep, gather up a bundle of maps, and come striding purposefully towards the Mess. 'Landing' was written all over him.

'Jan,' I shouted, 'here's Popski!'

The three of us sat down at the Mess table and Popski spread out his maps. 'We'll land here,' he said, pointing to an inch of coastline eighty miles north of Pescara where Eighth Army were still battling to dislodge a stubborn enemy from strongly entrenched positions at the Adriatic end of the Cassino line.

I looked at the wiggly blue line marked 'R. Tenna', at the thick red line of the main road running close to the sea between Pescara and Ancona, at the little fishing village of Porto S. Giorgio a few miles south of the river mouth, at the town of Fermo a few miles inland, at the valley of the River Tenna and the crisscross of roads leading up into the mountains of Cingoli.

'My plan is to land on the coast at night,' said Popski. 'Drive inland and link up with the partisans in Cingoli.'

'Why Cingoli?' I asked.

'Because I'm in touch with partisans there through "A" Force and the beach is suitable for a landing. There's a track leading from it up to the coast road.'

'What about supplies after you land?' Jan asked.

'By air drop.'

'How many jeeps, Popski?' I enquired.

'Twelve, Bob. The L.C.T. won't hold more.'

'Which patrols?'

' "B" and "R". "S" will remain in reserve, but we'll take the best men from each patrol.'

'When's D-day?'

Popski looked directly at me and I knew what was coming. I felt butterflies in the pit of my stomach.

'An advance party will land first—you and Gino and Porter. Porter will go with you to recce the beach and come back to report to me. You and Gino will remain ashore, make sure it is safe to land and come down to the beach at night to signal us in.'

I saw myself sitting on a lonely enemy beach at dead of night desperately flashing a torch out to sea.

'When do we leave?' I asked, swallowing hard.

'The day after tomorrow—June 12th.'

I nodded.

Jan asked questions about supplies and equipment, and we sat for a couple of hours discussing the details of the landing, the selection of men, the best route into the mountains, what we should do if this or that situation arose, the arming and training of the partisans, the dropping of supplies by air, which targets to go for on the German L. of C. and so on.

When we'd covered the entire ground, Popski gathered up his maps and rose. He was returning to Caserta to make sure nothing misfired at the planning end.

'I'll be back tomorrow night,' he said.

'No likelihood of the landing being cancelled at the last moment, is there, Popski?'

Popski smiled ruefully.

'I can't guarantee it, Bob, but I don't think it's likely.'

Jan and I walked with him to the gate of the villa, watched him climb ponderously into his jeep, adjust his motoring goggles and drive away.

What an amazing man he was! Nearly fifty, over-weight, bald, handicapped by varicose veins which would have kept any other man out of the army, he had a drive and determination, a love of adventure which shamed men half his age. There had been no need for him to join up. Managing director of a sugar refinery in Cairo, he could have sat back and made money as so many did. Not Popski. He threw up his lucrative job the minute war was declared, divorced his wife, packed his children off to a boarding school in South Africa and looked around for the most dangerous role.

'Popski's an incredible man,' Jan remarked as we walked up the path to the Mess.

Popski's jeep hurtled down the twisty mountain road to Piedemonte D'Alife. Twenty minutes later, from the terrace of the villa, we saw a spume of dust rising from the plain as he raced towards Caserta.

I stood on the terrace and looked down on the green plain with the blue river winding through it, upon the grey and red roof-tops of Piedemonte D'Alife, at the sweep of green forest rising on its flank and the red-roofed monastery built into the hillside. A familiar scene. I'd looked at it every morning and evening for three solid months and grown tired of it, as of the view from a prison window. I hoped I was looking at it for the last time. Jan Caneri was standing beside me. I turned and pumped his hand.

'At last, Jan, at last,' I said emotionally. 'At long bloody last.'

13

On June 12th, Dave Porter, Gino and I drove to Manfredonia harbour and boarded a naval launch, what they called a P-boat. We had with us one Quinto, a partisan from the mountains of Cingoli. Quinto worked for 'A' Force, a secret organization which maintained wireless contact with partisan groups behind the lines and repatriated escaped allied prisoners of war. Quinto had come down the coast by boat a week previously and knew the landing beach. He was a surly little man with an unattractive personality. I didn't take to him and doubted his ability.

The pilot waited for sunset, cast off his moorings and chugged out of the harbour. Gino, Porter and Quinto went into the little cabin below-deck. I wanted to be alone and made my way to the bow where I stood gripping the rail, taking deep gulps of the clean, fresh air blowing down from the far Dalmatian mountains. Clear of the harbour mouth the pilot put on speed and the fast little boat rocked and plunged in the choppy sea. I watched the knife-edged bow splitting the water and folding it over in a creamy wake.

The sun went down in a blaze of glory, momentarily poured a crucible of molten copper over the heaving waters and scurried before the approach of night. A cold wind sprang up, but I wore a warm duffle coat which kept out the chill and I remained pressed against the rail, splashed and wetted by the spray, enjoying its tangy saltiness. There was no moon, but the stars shone brilliantly in a velvet sky and I watched the phosphorescence glinting in the water as it churned past.

We turned the spur of the Gargano Peninsula—shades of my first patrol and the Parlato family (I wondered how Dorothy was) —saw the winking lights of Vieste, passed between the lonely unseen islands of Tremiti and Pianosa and headed north, parallel with the coast, thirty miles out to sea. The launch was trailing a fathom-line, logging the exact distance before turning in to our landing point.

The dark sea miles surged past our plunging bows and became lost in the writhing white serpent which marked our passage. We throbbed steadily on past Termoli, Vesto, Pescara. North of Pescara we were in enemy waters and anything could happen. I kept a sharp look-out for mines and imagined a U-boat periscope in every breaking wave.

It was thrilling to stand in the bows of that trim little craft and thrust deeper and deeper into enemy territory. Vague longings tugged at my heart and long-forgotten memories, things which had happened in childhood, flashed through my mind. I hadn't done much in the war up till then except follow Popski around. Now, on my own, I felt I was doing something really worth-while. . . . A naval rating checked the fathom-line and presently we changed course. As we drew towards the coast I imagined that a German spy in Caserta had given warning of our approach, that a machine-gun would open up the minute we walked ashore. I had a mild attack of nerves and my subconscious mind began sending up excuses for not landing. I fought them down and the moment of fear passed as quickly as it had come.

A mile off-shore the pilot cut his engines and we drifted silently towards the beach, peering ahead, trying to pick up our landmark—two tall pine trees growing on a knoll. There was a thick bank of mist along the shore and all we could see was the dark line of the hills against the starry sky.

I called Quinto to the bows and gave him my night-glasses. He looked through them for a time, shook his head dubiously and grunted non-committally. Gino took a turn, and then I peered again. None of us could see any trees. Were we at the right place? Perhaps we were too far off-shore. I spoke to the pilot:

'Can we go in a bit further?'

The pilot nodded and started his engines. My nerves jumped, fearing we'd be heard from the shore.

The P-boat nosed quietly in-shore followed by the cadences of its water-burbling exhaust pipes. Wraiths of grey dampness clawed at the rail and the open sea vanished behind our stern. A naval rating kept testing the depth of the water. The mist-bank swirled about our heads and for a time we could see nothing at

all. . . . Gino suddenly gripped my arm and pointed. '*Capitano* . . .'
I looked along his outstretched arm and saw what we were
looking for—two tall pine trees—growing out of the mist. Our
landing-point was a mile upshore. The pilot went astern and made
for the open sea. He hugged the edge of the mist-bank, logging
the distance. When he'd covered the mile he cut his engines again
and the P-boat rocked gently on the waves. This was where
Yunnie and company got off.

An able-bodied seaman inflated a rubber dinghy and lowered
it over the side. It fell upon the scuttling waves with a flattening
splash and the A.B. held it close to the boat's side with a cord
while another A.B. slid into it and took up a pair of light metal
oars. The inflated yellow tub looked anything but safe upon the
slapping water and I eyed it diffidently as I shook hands with
the pilot—I never knew his name—and clambered overboard.
A whispered 'Good luck' followed me down.

I sat unsteadily, feeling the pressure of the water under the
thin rubber bottom, and waited for Gino, Porter and Quinto to
come down. Gino came first, nimbly, then Quinto, clumsily,
rocking the dinghy. Grinning, Dave Porter was last, scraping his
Tommy-gun against the rail. He felt for the dinghy with his
feet and lowered himself gently into it, a bit cramped for the five
of us with our Tommy-guns and rucksacks getting in the way.

The A.B. pushed off and paddled a sidling, crab-like course
through the mist. It was eerie, slithering through that fog-bank
to the beach. The weighted dinghy slewed and skewed and
flopped on the waves. The pea-soup fog engulfed us so that we
couldn't see where we were going, but just sat expectant and
apprehensive hoping all would be well. Would a burst of Spandau
fire tear into us the moment we scraped on the beach? We kept
our thoughts to ourselves and none of us spoke.

Our heads were suddenly clear of the mist and we saw sand-
dunes, a dark line of hills, tree-tops. An impatient surf tossed the
dinghy about, wetting our bottoms. Holding Tommy-guns high
in the air, we splashed overboard, waded thigh-deep through the
surf and pulled the dinghy up the beach behind us. I walked a
little way up the firm, gravelly sand and stood listening. The only
sounds were the beating of the surf and the pounding of my own
heart.

It was the right place. Through a gap in the dunes a sandy

track led towards the coast road. I set Gino and Quinto to guard the approach while Porter and I recced the beach. The A.B. stood by the dinghy.

The beach shelved gently, the sand was firm, there were no visible rocks and the sand-dunes hid us from the road. It seemed an ideal landing-place.

'Got it, Dave?' I whispered.

Porter grinned and nodded. 'O.K., Skipper.'

'Of you go, then.'

Porter and the A.B. lifted the dinghy down to the surf, waded in with it, steadied it on the bucketing foam and tumbled aboard. I watched them vanish into the mist, feeling like a man who has burned his boats.

The coast road was less than a mile away, with a railway line running between it and the beach. Quinto led up the sandy track and Gino and I padded softly along the grass verge behind him, gripping our Tommy-guns. We passed under the stone railway bridge and lay in the long grass a few yards from the road while Quinto went to make sure the way was clear. He was back in a trice, beckoning us to follow. Like thieves in the night, we crossed the deserted tarmac, stumbled over a ditch, slipped between the twanging wires of a fence and followed Quinto into a wheat-field.

The wheat was waist-high and swished and tatted against our clothes as we pushed our way through. I broke off a ripe head and chewed the milky grains as I walked. . . .

Across the field we came to a line of trees and followed Quinto through an iron gate on to a footpath by the river. The rusty gate squeaked when Quinto swung it, a dog barked in the distance and an owl hooted in the trees, making me jump.

The footpath followed the course of the crooning river, dipping and rising under the shadows of the trees. The night air was soft and balmy, a great peace lay over the valley. Was there really a war on? I asked myself. Was I really behind the German lines or taking an evening stroll through peace-time farmland in Kent?

Quinto walked steadily on and we followed him through another squeaking gate, through another wheat-field, along another footpath, past the dark outline of farm buildings clustered by tall trees and guarded by barking dogs, across a dusty farm road, under a fence and into a silent vineyard where we halted and Quinto and Gino talked in Italian whispers.

The vine trellises were six feet high, thick with dark leaves and bunches of grapes. I felt happy and secure in their shadowy presence, safe from prying eyes.

'*Capitano* . . .'

'Yes, Gino?'

'Quinto wants us to wait here. He'll go into the house first.'

I nodded my agreement.

Quinto disappeared into the night and we heard the dogs heralding his approach to the farmhouse. Gino and I waited, feeling our Tommy-guns heavy on the arm. . . .

'Gino,' I whispered, 'what do you think of Quinto?'

Gino considered for a moment, and summed Quinto up nicely. '*Huomo honesto ma non molto valoroso*,' he breathed in my ear. (An honest man but not very brave.)

'You think we can trust him, Gino?'

'*Si, Capitano.*'

Intuitively, I doubted Quinto, but felt reassured by Gino's summing up of his countryman's character.

Presently we heard footsteps and Quinto's stocky form appeared in the vineyard, beckoning. We followed him along the farm-road into the farmyard where two vicious-looking dogs rushed upon us, filling the air with their clamour. Quinto quietened the dogs and led us to the back door of the farmhouse. He knocked twice and the door was immediately opened, showing a splash of light. We filed into the kitchen and Quinto introduced us to our host, one Vincento.

'*Buono sera, Capitano. S'accomodo*,' said Vincento, pulling out a chair for me.

'*Grazia*, Vincento.' I sat down.

While Quinto, Gino and Vincento talked rapidly in dialect I looked round the typical Italian farmhouse kitchen—open fireplace, stone-flagged floor, scrubbed deal table and chairs, bunches of garlic and onions hanging from hooks in the ceiling.

Vincento, paunchy, dark of hair and eye, ruddy-cheeked, produced a bottle of wine, a loaf of bread and some cheese.

'*Prende*,' he urged hospitably. (Help yourself.)

I was hungry and required little urging.

The staccato, rapid-fire conversation in dialect continued, like machine-guns and waving hands. Gino translated from time to time. There were German troops in Fermo and in Porto S. Giorgio, not many, just a few. There was a steady flow of traffic on the roads, increasing of late. Parties of German soldiers came round the farms commandeering oxen and wagons and there were rumours of a German retreat from Cassino. The dialectal barrage came down again and I listened, trying to get the hang of the clipped phraseology, like a Londoner trying to understand Somerset yokels talking in a pub.

Presently, Vincento yawned and we all became infected.

'*Va bene*,' he said, scraping back his chair. (English equivalent 'All right'.)

I looked enquiringly at Gino.

'We sleep here tonight, *Capitano*.'

I nodded sleepily and smothered a yawn.

Vincento showed us to our sleeping quarters, an upstairs hayloft full of warm, sweet-smelling hay. Thankfully we sank into it and instantly fell asleep.

I was awakened by the cry of a baby in the room below. I opened my eyes. Hay-dust danced in the beams of sunlight streaming through cracks in the door. For a moment I couldn't think where I was . . . then I remembered, in an Italian hayloft, eighty miles behind the German front line. I sat up, wide awake.

Gino was still asleep. There was a well-pressed hollow in the hay beside him where Quinto had slept, but no Quinto.

I prodded Gino. 'Hey, Gino, wake up.'

Gino sat up, rubbed his eyes, yawned and passed a smooth brown hand through his tousled brown hair. His blue eyes smiled at me.

'*Buono giorno, Capitano*.'

'*Dove Quinto?*' I asked, pointing to the flattened hay. (Where's Quinto?)

Footsteps sounded on the stairs and before Gino could reply the loft door was flung open, admitting a flood of golden light and the head and shoulders of Vincento.

'*Buono giorno, buono giorno*,' he greeted us. '*Buono giorno, Capitano. Buono giorno, Gino.*'

'*Dove Quinto?*' Gino asked.

Vincento quick-fired an unintelligible reply and I looked

enquiringly at Gino. Quinto had left at daybreak, he told me. He'd gone to Cingoli and would be back in three days.

I shrugged and thought, 'I wonder.'

Vincento brought breakfast—wine, cheese and fruit. We ate it in the hayloft.

'When you've finished,' I said to Gino, 'borrow a bicycle and go into Fermo and Porto S. Giorgio. Have a good look round. Be back by dusk.'

'*Si, Capitano.*'

Gino was an Italian. Dressed in civilian clothes he resembled any other Italian and his presence wherever he went would cause no comment. I was in officer's uniform (irregular, I admit) and would have to watch my step. It wouldn't do for me to be seen walking about in British Army battledress blouse, American Army gaberdine trousers, and black Tank Corps beret. Italian tongues were apt to wag and there were German troops in the vicinity. I remained in the hayloft.

When Gino had gone I studied my map and did some thinking. It was the 13th of June. The L.C.T. (landing-craft) was due to beach on the night of the 15th. During the interval I had to form a clear picture of the situation in the Tenna Valley, the enemy strength and locations, the condition of the roads, and whether we could drive jeeps up to Cingoli. For the latter information I relied upon Quinto and hoped he wouldn't let me down.

The L.C.T. would lie off-shore on the night of the 15th. Unless I signalled from the beach, it wouldn't come in, but would rendezvous again on the nights of the 16th and 17th when, if there was still no signal from the beach, it would return to port, the landing would be cancelled and I would be presumed captured or killed. If I didn't think it safe to beach, I wasn't to signal. Popski left the decision to me and I felt the responsibility weigh heavily. Should I misjudge the situation either way, my career in P.P.A. would be at an end, for if I were too cautious opportunity might not knock again and if I were rash many good men, the cream of P.P.A., would lose their lives. The situation in Cingoli troubled me. I wanted to see for myself, but I couldn't be in two places at once. Should I send Gino on his bicycle? I didn't think he would have time to get there and back by the night of the 15th.

The day passed slowly. Vincento's pretty daughter, sworn to secrecy by her father, brought me food and wine at midday and, troubled by doubts about Quinto, I dozed fitfully in the afternoon. Dusk was falling as Gino cycled into the farmyard and I went out to stretch my legs.

'Well, Gino,' I greeted him, 'how did you get on?'

Gino's news was disturbing. He'd been into Fermo and Porto S. Giorgio. Troop movements were taking place and there was an abnormal amount of traffic on the coast road. In a *trattoria* in Fermo he had fallen into conversation with a man who'd cycled down from Ascoli. The roads inland were choked with German traffic; the Germans were retreating from Cassino, the man had said.

I listened to Gino's report with a falling spirit. 'Too late,' my mind kept repeating, 'too late . . . too late.'

Gino and I strolled down to the coast road after dark. We lay hidden in the wheat by the roadside watching the German transport go by. There wasn't much traffic before ten o'clock, but round about midnight the flow increased considerably and during the small hours of the morning there was a steady stream of staff-cars, motor-cycle combinations, army trucks, and commandeered civilian lorries passing almost nose to tail. The retreat from Cassino was on, there was no doubt about it, and Gino and I were caught right in the middle of it. I looked at the traffic-filled road ten yards in front of my nose and cursed the staff in Caserta. Delay had ruined our chances. The timing was out by a week.

'We're too late, Gino,' I breathed.

'*Si, Capitano,*' he nodded despondently.

When the sky began to pale we crawled through the wheat-field and walked back to the hayloft.

Vincento looked worried when he brought breakfast. I guessed what was troubling him. The Germans would visit his farm, take his oxen and wagons, his pigs and his poultry, and if a British officer was found in his hayloft both he and his wife would be shot. I felt sorry for him and told Gino to let him know that I would move from his hayloft into a wheat-field, the safest place I could think of.

Another long day passed. Gino went out on his bicycle again and returned at dusk with a long face. German troops were pouring into the Tenna Valley. Fermo and Porto S. Giorgio were filling up and foraging parties were visiting the farms.

'Too late, Gino,' I groaned again. 'We should have landed a week ago.'

Down to the coast road again after dark to lie hidden in the wheat-field. There was hardly a gap in the traffic. Peering between stools of wheat, we watched a stream of cars, motor-cycles, trucks, vans, lorries and ox-drawn wagons go past, even push-carts piled high with loot and soldiers on foot and on bicycles. 'If only we'd brought some turds, Calabrian,' I thought. What a perfect target!

I fell to thinking and worrying about the L.C.T. Should I or should I not bring it in? So far as I could see we hadn't a hope of getting to Cingoli with transport blocking the roads, and even if we could get through it was pointless now because Cingoli would soon be in front of, not behind, the German front line; but traffic-filled roads presented the perfect shoot-up target for P.P.A. jeeps. Twelve jeeps, twenty-four mobile machine-guns, let loose amongst the rabble with complete surprise—hell, it would be terrific! I visualized the jeeps emerging from the track, dashing up and down the coast road pouring tracer and incendiary bullets into the panic-stricken convoys (what a picnic for The Heavenly Twins!), then racing down the track to the beach, up the ramp of the L.C.T. and pulling out to sea. That was the answer. Forget about Cingoli. Shoot up the coast road, back to the waiting L.C.T. and away, leaving the road chock-a-block with burning German transport. Then plan another landing further north when the front line stabilized. . . .

I waited for a gap in the traffic and pulled Gino's sleeve. I'd seen enough.

'*Andiamo*,' I mouthed. (Let's go.)

We crawled away from the fence, rose and ducked towards the path by the river. I was at peace. I'd come to my decision and knew it was the right one. The following night Gino and I would go down to the beach and I would signal to the L.C.T. When it beached I would give Popski the picture of the situation inland, suggest a shoot-up and leave the decision to him. It was a pity we couldn't drive inland as planned. Popski would be bitterly disappointed, but I couldn't help that. It was the fortune of war. Better luck next time. At least I had proof that his idea was sound; I had seen with my own eyes how entirely possible it was to land jeeps on the coast and drive inland at night provided conditions were right. A week earlier, we could have done it. Blast those people at Caserta!

I slept like a top, ate a hearty breakfast and spent the day in the middle of Vincento's wheat-field convinced that it was the safest hiding-place behind the lines.

Gino spent another profitable day on his bicycle, pedalling through the cobbled streets of Fermo and Porto S. Giorgio, chatting to soldiers and civilians in the wine-shops, touring along the dusty country roads, taking a good look at the retreating Germans. He joined me in my wheat-field at sunset when the Tenna Valley was filled with soft golden light and red banners waved above the enclosing hills. I was lying on my back watching the colours play in the sky when I heard his softly repeated '*Capitano . . . Capitano . . . Capitano*' drifting over the field as he swished through the yellowing grain, looking for me. I stood up and showed myself.

Gino reported 'no change' in the situation.

'O.K., Gino,' I said. 'We'll bring in the L.C.T. Cingoli's out of the question with all this traffic, but we can shoot up the coast road and pull out. We'll have to plan another landing further north.'

When dusk fell we strolled up to the farmhouse to wait for Quinto. Six o'clock . . . seven o'clock . . . eight o'clock. No sign of Quinto.

'Come on, Gino,' I said at ten past eight, 'we can't wait any longer. Quinto isn't coming.'

Velvety darkness filled the Tenna Valley, cloaking our movements. We walked stealthily along the footpath by the river, keeping to the shadows of the trees, and entered the wheat-field. We walked half-way through it, then ducked, and finally crawled the last bit up to the fence where we lay for a time watching the transport moving along the coast road, waiting for an opportunity to cross. . . .

A long convoy of overloaded lorries rumbled past and the wind blowing in from the sea carried the acrid stench of diesel exhaust to our nostrils. 'Oh, God, don't let me sneeze,' I prayed, and pressed hard on my upper lip. The awful moment passed and I breathed freely again. . . .

A black saloon car swished past followed by a covey of pedal cyclists with rifles slung over their backs; then another long line of trucks. 'Christ,' I thought, 'we'll never get across. . . .'

Nearly an hour passed and I was beginning to despair when a convoy of covered wagons came to an end and there was a gap. . . . I heard the creaking of ox-wagons in the distance. I pressed Gino's arm.

'Quick, Gino,' I breathed, 'now's our chance.'

We slid under the fence, snake-bellied into the ditch, crouched like milers at the tape, dashed across the tarmac twenty yards in front of a team of blowing oxen. A car pulled out and revved past as we slid under the opposite fence and lay panting in the long grass. 'Just in time,' I thought.

Recovering our breath, we crawled through the dew-soaked grass until we were out of earshot of the road, then stood up and walked down to the track, under the railway bridge and down to the beach. I glanced at the luminous dial of my watch. It was just on ten o'clock.

'Keep an eye on the track, Gino,' I whispered.

Gino crouched in the sand-dunes near the mouth of the track and I tiptoed down to the water-front. The beach was dark and deserted. A thick fold of mist blanketed the creaming surf. Above it stretched an inky sky with stars strewn lavishly.

I drew an electric torch from my pocket, made sure the red glass filter was in place and sat back on my heels out of reach of the waves.

Dot—dash—dot . . . dot—dash—dot . . . dot—dash—dot. I flicked the torch on and off, signalling the letter 'R' out to sea and glancing nervously up and down the beach, feeling sure that every German soldier on the coast must see what I was doing. I signalled for a solid hour . . . dot—dash—dot . . . just as I was beginning to think that something had gone wrong and I was wasting my time a huge black thing took shape in the mist above my head, like a sea-monster rising from the ocean depths. There was a scrunching, tearing sound like teeth crushing bones; a shudder ran through the monster . . . its great mouth partially opened and snapped shut . . . I expected to see flames dart from its eyes and jumped hurriedly back. The L.C.T. had beached.

Popski was standing in the prow, waiting for me as I clambered aboard. Behind him, drawn up in rows ready to drive down the ramp, the twelve shadowy jeeps made a heart-gladdening sight with their eager crews standing beside them and their long-barrelled Brownings pointing in front. Muted wisecracks greeted me as I scrambled over the high gun'l.

'Watcha, Skipper'—Curtis.

'*Viva Capitano Bob*'—Riches.

'Up "B" Patrol'—J.C.

'Well, Bob,' said Popski, as if I'd been walking into the Mess in San Gregorio. We shook hands and I gave him a quick appreciation of the situation inland.

'We'll never get to Cingoli,' I told him. 'The roads are chock-a-block with transport. I suggest we shoot up the coast road and pull out. Plan another landing further north. We're a week too late.'

Popski's mouth hardened and he looked grim.

'Where's Gino?'

'On the beach, keeping an eye on the track.'

'I want to speak to him.'

I walked to the gun'l and hissed for Gino. A party of beaching commandos clambered overboard to take his place.

Popski questioned Gino in Italian about what he'd seen in Fermo and Porto S. Giorgio and on the roads in the Tenna Valley. I watched the struggle taking place in Popski as they spoke. Fascinated, I saw Popski make his decision, and loved him for it. It wasn't an easy decision to make.

Popski had staked his reputation on the landing. For months, single-handed, he had badgered the staff at Caserta and finally got his way. If he cancelled the operation he would have to go back and face the sneers and the jeers, the I-told-you-so's of the form-fillers and might never get another chance. If he let his jeeps loose on the coast road he could do some damage but he might lose both jeeps and men. Popski wasn't interested in destroying a few ramshackle enemy vehicles and killing a handful of Germans. He'd done that before. He was out for bigger game. He wanted to get behind the lines in jeeps and stay there, co-ordinate the Italian partisan movement in North Italy and do some real damage to the Germany Army. Rather than risk expending the cream of P.P.A. in a spectacular shoot-up which would certainly make headlines, but cause very little real damage, he preferred to face ridicule, bide his time and plan another landing further north. Popski's decision measured the stature of the man. Ridicule to a man of his calibre was more deadly than bullets. He had the courage to face it.

'Operation cancelled, Bob.' His voice was dead. I felt heart-sore for him and wanted to say something comforting to show that I understood, but I couldn't think of anything appropriate to say.

The word went round the ship, 'Operation cancelled'.

But it wasn't to be so easy as that. Whilst we'd been talking a cross wind had blown up, swinging the stern of the landing craft round to shore, and when Lieutenant Dale, R.N.V.R., rang to his engine-room to go astern, he found his craft was fast aground.

At first, I didn't realize there was anything wrong. Conscious of the noise of the threshing screw, I was talking to my men, trying to soften their bitter disappointment by the promise of another landing further north and fervently hoping we'd be well out to sea before the Germans came down to investigate the noise on the beach.

Of a sudden, voices were saying, 'The ship's aground!'

I saw Popski talking to Lieutenant Dale and went up to him.

'What's the matter, Popski?'

'We're aground on a sand-bank.'

'Oh, Lord,' I groaned.

An escorting motor-launch stood out to sea. Dale began signalling to her to come in to tow him off the sand-bank and it never occurred to me that we wouldn't get off. Presently the launch came inshore, grounded on the sand-bank also, refloated herself and refused to come any closer. Signalling lights flashed, tow-ropes splashed in the water, strident voices bawled through megaphones, engines raced, screws threshed, an awful hubbub took place and I kept looking over the gun'l towards the mouth of the track expecting to see an enemy force deploy on to the beach. But nothing of the kind happened, the hubbub continued unabated and the L.C.T. remained fast aground.

It was an ironical situation, one at which the gods must have held their heaving sides. There we were, come to destroy the enemy on his home ground, stuck fast upon his beach unable to advance or retreat and he, oblivious of our presence, passing along the coast road a thousand yards away.

'Can't we get the jeeps off, Popski?'

But when we tried we found the ramp was facing into the sea. . . .

At 2 a.m., still aground, the word went round 'Abandon ship'.

Popski took me by the arm. 'I've got a job for you, Bob.'

My heart went down to my boots. I knew what was coming and couldn't avoid it.

'I want you to take a foot-party ashore and remain in the area until you are over-run. Intelligence and bombing targets. Pick your own men.'

'O.K., Popski,' I replied without enthusiasm. Foot-slogging again, how I loathed it! If only I could have taken a jeep! My entire patrol wanted to come with me, but I couldn't take them all. Gino was a must. In addition, I chose Ben Owen, Danny O'Neil and Toddy Sloan, my wireless operator. Including myself, that made a party of five, quite large enough.

Whilst Curtis went 'mucking' and 'helling' round the jeeps, laying demolition charges, Gino, Ben Owen, Danny O'Neil, Toddy Sloan and I loaded ourselves with a suitcase wireless set, batteries, Tommy-guns and spare ammunition clips. It broke my heart to realize that all those finely tuned jeeps upon which I had lavished so much care and attention were shortly to be blown to bits. Like a cavalryman saying good-bye to his favourite charger I patted my jeep on the bonnet and said good-bye to it under my breath. I felt a presence behind me and heard two well-known voices ask in unison, 'Can we come with you, Skipper?'

I turned and looked into the hopeful faces of The Heavenly Twins. It was a shame to refuse them, their enthusiasm deserved a better fate, but I couldn't say 'No' to men of my own patrol and say 'Yes' to men of another.

I shook my head, and saw Hope die.

'Sorry, Twins. Can't be done.'

The Twins about-turned and went back to their jeep. For two pins, but for the thought of R.T.U., they would have gone ashore on their own.

When my foot-party was ready to leave I went in search of Popski and found him with Lieutenant Dale, destroying documents.

'I'm off, then, Popski.'

He turned at the sound of my voice and we shook hands.

'Good luck, Bob.'

Everybody was preparing to swim to the waiting launch. 'Here's where your training on the Barbary Coast comes in,' I thought. We said cheerio to the patrol, wished them a warm swim and clambered over the side into deep water. . . .

223

I looked back from the mouth of the track. The rectangular iron box with its chunky superstructure at one end was lying askew, side on to the beach, with the mist-bank hiding its nether regions. It looked lost and pathetic, like an unwanted child abandoned on a doorstep. I saw shadowy figures poise on the gun'l and disappear overboard. 'What a bloody disaster,' I thought, as I turned and led my small foot-party up the track, fully expecting to meet a German patrol coming down. . . .

Reaching the road without mishap we lay in the long grass waiting for an opportunity to cross. It came shortly, a break between teams of tired oxen.

'Quick, Ben,' I whispered.

Gino dashed across on his own. Ben and I went together and Danny O'Neil fathered Toddy Sloan looking like a tripper with his suitcase in his hand. We crawled under the fence into the dark security of the wheat and made for the path by the river. . . .

It was a long time before we reached it. R.A.F. fighter-bombers droned overhead and a few minutes after we crossed the road they dropped flares, looking for the bridge across the Tenna. Caught in the middle of the field, we went flat on our faces and pressed our bodies into the earth's dank comfort, feeling naked and exposed. . . .

Wheeeeeeeeeeeee . . . wruuuuuuuumph . . . wruuuuuuuumph. The first load of bombs fell. Vivid flashes showed through the trees near the bridge and the earth tremored under us. There were hoarse shouts from the direction of the road and the sound of twanging wires. . . . I stood up to see what was happening . . . and quickly sat down again.

'Don't look now, Ben,' I whispered to Ben Owen, jocularly hiding my panic, 'but Jerry's invading our wheat-field.'

Wheeeeeeeeeee . . . wruuuuuuuumph . . . wruuuuuuuumph. Another stick of bombs exploded near the bridge, illuminating flashes showed through the trees, the wheat-field shuddered and filled up with panic-stricken Germans. Thank God they were panic-stricken and took us for some of themselves, otherwise we must have been discovered.

The flares burned out and we breathed more freely, listening to the enemy crawling all round us. More flares dropped and burst into flame, turning night into day; the wheat-field was dotted with crouching bodies cursing the all-revealing light. . . .

Wheeeeeeeeeeee . . . wruuuuuuuuuumph . . . wruuuuuuuuumph . . . wruuuuuuuuumph . . . wruuuuuuumph. There was a terrific explosion behind the trees when two sticks of bombs fell together. A sheet of searing light lit the sky and the earth shuddered and shook, the droning grew fainter, the flares died out, blessed darkness enveloped the wheat-field; voices called, shadowy figures swished through the wheat. . . .

'Thank God,' I breathed. 'Now they'll go back to their transport.'

But it wasn't to be.

Puff . . . puff . . . puff . . . puff . . . puff . . . puff . . . puff . . . puff . . . puff . . . puff. A heavily laden goods train puffing northwards from Porto S. Giorgio hove in sight upon the raised embankment, a long dark pencil against the starry skyline. It was moving very slowly, panting like a runner out of breath, and to our amazement we saw tracer curve into it from the sea; the engine shrieked in steaming agony and stopped; scarlet tracer disappeared into the stationary trucks; some of the red darts soared over the railway and fell into the road, some into the wheat-field.

'Hell,' I whispered to Ben Owen. 'They're firing the Bofors from the launch.'

'Bloody inconsiderate of 'em, Skipper,' whispered Ben when a scarlet streamer sailed over the train and plunk . . . plunk . . . plunked into the wheat-field, too close to be pleasant.

But the unfortunate thing was that the German transport drivers returning to their transport panicked again and reinvaded the wheat-field.

'Here we go again, Ben,' I groaned.

Voices, thudding footsteps, swishing wheat-stalks, panting breaths . . . closer . . . closer. . . .

Act Three of the night's unexpected drama burst upon us without warning. Of a sudden, the sea-front was alight with leaping flames and a series of loud explosions reverberated along the shore and were echoed back from the hills as the L.C.T. and its precious cargo of jeeps blew up.

'God, what next?' I muttered under my breath and nudged Ben Owen, thinking it was time we made a move before anything else happened. I jerked my thumb in the direction of the footpath by the river and started to crawl through the wheat.

Before I'd crawled a few yards I thought: 'This is bloody silly. Why not stand up and walk?'

I stood up and the others followed my example. In single file, Toddy with his suitcase, we walked nonchalantly (feeling anything but) past a group of bomb-happy German soldiers laying face down in the flattened wheat . . . out of the field and on to the tree-lined path by the river.

'Can you beat it, Ben?' I asked when we were at a safe distance.

'What a night, Skipper!' chuckled Ben.

I led my little party towards Vincento's farm and conducted them into the vineyard where Quinto had originally taken Gino and me.

'Gino,' I whispered, 'go and tell Vincento what's happened. Ask him to find us somewhere to stay. We'll wait here for you.'

'*Si, Capitano.*'

Gino was swallowed up in the night; we heard the dogs announcing his arrival at the house. . . .

We squatted amongst the silent vines, feeling their calmness and peace. The air was cool and damp, redolent of dew-soaked earth. What an unexpected turn of events, I thought. The very last place I'd expected to be at 0400 hours on 16th June was back on Vincento's farm. . . . I wondered how Popski and the others fared and imagined them all nice and snug on the launch, scudding through the waves towards Manfredonia Harbour. Lucky devils, I thought . . . and yet I didn't really envy them.

Footsteps sounded and Gino and Vincento appeared between the trellises.

'Oh, *Capitano*,' said Vincento in a nervous whisper.

'What's the form?' I asked Gino.

'*Capitano*, Vincento will take us to another farm.'

'Good.'

As though eager to be rid of us, Vincento set off at a cracking pace and we followed him along the side of one wheat-field after another, across a farm road, through a vineyard, along the bottom of another wheat-field, through a gate in a hedge and into the yard in front of a white-walled farmhouse where two wolf-like dogs rose from their stance by the door and bounded across, growling dangerously. Vincento pacified them and motioned to us to remain by the hedge while he and Gino went to the house.

Vincento's knock, knock, knock, knock, knock broke the

stillness of the night. An upstairs window opened and a dark head popped out. Dialectal undertones ensued, punctuated by a sequence of '*Si, si, bene, bene, si, si . . .*' The head was withdrawn and the window squeaked shut. A few moments later the door opened and Vincento and Gino disappeared within. Standing in the shadow of the hedge we watched the two dogs watching us.

Presently the door opened again and Gino beckoned. We crossed the yard, chary of the growling dogs.

Inside the farmhouse, Gino introduced us to Roberto Scarlatti, stocky, black-haired, ruddy-cheeked, dark-eyed, paunchy, a typical *contadino* farmer of the best type, hard-working, healthy, honest as the day. I took to him at once. Yes, Roberto said, we could stay. There was an upstairs attic we could have. He was a partisan and wanted to help. He wasn't afraid of the *tedeschi*. He and his family would feed us and look after us. We would be quite safe. Nobody would give us away.

I looked into Roberto's honest face and was inwardly at peace. We would be all right here. We'd come to the right place.

Vincento took his leave and I thanked him, through Gino, for what he had done for us. He made a deprecating gesture with hands and mouth as though to say, 'It's nothing,' and hurried away.

Roberto took us upstairs to the attic. There were mattresses on the floor and the single window showed a faint paling in the sky. Roberto put blankets into our hands and we stretched out on the mattresses. I was asleep before he closed the door.

14

I WAS awake at 9 a.m., refreshed and alert. Golden sunlight streamed through the attic window. Ben Owen was asleep on his side, a lock of dark hair curling his brow. His folded arm showed a deep wound scar. Next to him, Toddy Sloan was lying on his back, snoring gently. His long eyelashes fluttered slightly. 'He's only a kid,' I thought. Beyond him, Danny O'Neil's strong, weather-beaten form lay motionless. Gino slept next to the wall, his back to me.

I lay, thinking. We shouldn't all stay in the farmhouse. It was too dangerous, and unfair to the Scarlattis. If the wreck of the L.C.T. were discovered, S.S. men might come round the farms searching for survivors and in any case there were sure to be requisitioning parties coming to the farms for oxen and wagons. Gino could stay in the house. It would be quite safe for him. He could pass as one of the family. The rest of us would move into a wheat-field.

I woke Gino and talked it over with him.

He agreed, and when Roberto entered the attic a few minutes later he told him. Roberto listened and shrugged, hunching his shoulders, opening his hands and pulling down the corners of his mouth, Italian fashion.

'Va bene,' he said. 'As the *Capitano* wishes.'

Downstairs in the big farm kitchen with its scrubbed deal table and onion-festooned ceiling Roberto introduced us to his family, to Signora Scarlatti, black-haired, dark-eyed, olive-skinned, buxom, dimpled, happy, nice; to Signorina Bianca, aged seventeen, dark-haired, black-eyed, olive-skinned, white teeth, ruby lips, firm-breasted, slim-waisted, lovely, nice; to Signorina Maria, aged fourteen, dark-haired, bright-eyed, rosy-cheeked, slim-figured, nice; to Signorina Elizabeta, aged ten, dark-haired, sloe-eyed, mischievous, nice. The whole family were nice and the more I saw of the Scarlatti family the more I liked them.

'*Niente figli?*' I asked the signora. (No sons?)

She blushed and shook her head.

'*Tuttie figli, Capitano,*' she laughed. (All girls.)

After breakfast, Gino and I went to look for a good hiding-place, and found one in a wheat-field bordered by trees near the river, a field corridored by thick, trailing vines trellised twenty feet apart with wheat growing between.

'Right in the middle of that wheat-field, Gino.' I pointed. 'The trellis will give us shade and hide the wireless aerial.'

Ben Owen, Danny O'Neil, Toddy Sloan and I moved in immediately. Toddy put up his aerial and I sent a message to Jan Caneri in San Gregorio, 150 miles away. The deceptive suitcase when opened revealed a high-powered transmitting and receiving set. I gave Jan our map reference and a short situation report and asked him to stand by for bombing targets. Gino borrowed Roberto's bicycle and rode off on a tour of inspection. The harvest is early in the favoured Tenna Valley and they were starting to cut the wheat at the top end of the field. Bianca appeared in our corridor at midday, carrying a basket of food—a bottle of wine, bread, cheese and salami wrapped in a spotless white napkin. Even if the Germans saw her, I thought, what could be more natural than a farm girl bringing a basket of food into a wheat-field at noon when the harvest was on? It was the perfect camouflage.

The Scarlattis' farm covered a triangular piece of flat ground between the ridge upon which the town of Fermo stood, the coast road and the River Tenna. The hill road from Ascoli ran down the other side of the river and was joined by another road from Fermo, over a bridge. A track ran through the middle of the farm linking the coast road with the Ascoli road through a ford, and dust began to rise when the enemy, blocked on the coast road by the bombed bridge, diverted their slow-moving traffic through the farm. Faster traffic took the Ascoli road from Fermo and we sat hidden in our wheat-field, munching grapes, within a rifle-shot of both streams of traffic, transmitting messages to Jan Caneri.

Gino kept me supplied with bombing targets. Jan Caneri got

a flight of fighter-bombers on tap and so good was the co-ordination between Toddy's suitcase, the Backroom Boys in San Gregorio and the fighter-bomber wing in Foggia that we were able to give targets in one message and bombing results in the next. Hunched against the trellis, framed in an arbour of luscious grapes, Toddy Sloan tapped like a trojan and Ben Owen, looking through binoculars at the circling, diving planes, kept up a running commentary on results while I enciphered the signals and Danny O'Neil kept guard.

Unaware of our presence in their midst, the retreating German forces cursed the R.A.F. and marvelled at the accuracy of their bombing.

When darkness fell we packed up the wireless set and repaired to the farmhouse for supper.

Signora Scarlatti was a superlative cook and we sat down at the lamp-lit family table to heaped platefuls of savoury *pasta* followed by plump roast ducklings, fresh green salad, cheese and fruit. Roberto plied us with wine which we drank, *contadino* fashion, diluted with water. '*Prende, prende*,' our hostess urged, offering us more *pasta*, more duckling. '*Basta, basta*,' we pleaded (Enough, enough), and drew our fingers across our throats to show that we couldn't eat more. Maria and Elizabeta giggled at our execrable Italian and Bianca cast disturbing glances at me with her flashing, black eyes.

Replete, we sat back and smoked American 'Camel' cigarettes, which delighted Roberto and then, by prior arrangement, Ben Owen and I went out on the prowl while O'Neil and Sloan climbed up to the attic and Gino remained in the kitchen conversing with the family.

I was never too happy behind the lines in daylight, apprehensive always of being seen by some informer, but as soon as darkness fell I was at peace. Hidden by night's well-fitting cloak I could move about at will and who was to know I was there?

Ben Owen liked night-prowling too. 'Happy, Ben?' I asked him when we sat in the bushes by the side of the Ascoli road watching the convoys go past.

'Just the job, this, Skipper.' He grinned.

By three o'clock in the morning we were back at the farmhouse, nipping upstairs to the dark attic, having prowled all over the valley and seen what the Germans were doing.

Sleep until eight or nine o'clock, then back to the wheat-field.

We narrowly escaped capture, and if it hadn't been for the quick-witted Bianca, bless her heart, I wouldn't be writing this story.

We'd breakfasted and gone out to our wheat-field when I remembered something I wanted to tell Gino before he set off on his bicycle. I was half-way to the farmhouse when Bianca ran round the gable and frantically signed to me to lie down in the wheat. I flopped down and lay quietly, feeling the sun hot on the back of my neck, wondering what was happening and hoping Owen, O'Neil and Sloan wouldn't show themselves. . . .

Presently I heard footsteps and a soft voice calling, '*Va bene, Capitano.*' I rose and followed Bianca into the house.

Gino told me what had happened.

Shortly after we'd gone down to the wheat-field a party of German soldiers came to the farmhouse demanding oxen and wagons. Gino, about to set out on Roberto's bicycle, changed his mind and ran upstairs to the attic, where he stood at the window with a cocked Tommy-gun while Roberto, agreeing to the German demands, drew the soldiers away from the house. Bianca, looking out of the kitchen window, saw me coming and immediately ran out to give warning; but for her quick action I would have walked round the gable and into the German arms. You saved my life, Bianca, and the lives of your parents too. You didn't have a university education or a wardrobe full of clothes, you hadn't travelled the world. You were only a simple farm-girl who'd never been further than Fermo, but you'd courage, intelligence, guts, a heart filled with gold. Thank you, Bianca.

Hearing a commotion at the ford one afternoon, Ben Owen and I ducked along the wooded river bank to see what cooked.

From the cover of a thicket, barely suppressing our laughter, we watched the antics of two German transport drivers trying to persuade a team of wide-horned, wild-eyed oxen to pull an over-loaded wagon through the river. There is a way of handling oxen—one must be born to it—and these German drivers just didn't have the knack. In mid-stream, pawing and threshing the water, straining and swinging sideways to avoid the whip, one of the oxen broke its trace rein, kicked out viciously and bolted. Splashing through the river, bellowing loudly, the heavy animal thundered up the bank and came pounding past our thicket. . . .

231

The German drivers cursed and gave chase and had they been less intent upon catching the terrified ox they must have seen us, so close did they pass by our thicket. Ben Owen and I fingered our Tommy-guns, itching to fire, but thought better of it.

Back in the wheat-field an hour later watching Toddy Sloan tapping out a cipher to Jan, I had the intuitive feeling that we should leave the Scarlattis' farm. We'd had two narrow escapes in two days and these things invariably went in threes. We mightn't be so lucky the third time; besides, it was never wise, behind the lines, to stay too long in one place.

The country was hilly and wooded on the other side of the river, dotted here and there with little white-walled cottages. 'We'll cross the river tonight,' I thought, 'and hide up in the woods.' The Ascoli road from Fermo was still chock-a-block with German transport, but the retreat couldn't go on for ever; sooner or later we must come to the enemy rearguard and then we'd be free. Ben Owen was doodling in the black soil with a piece of wheat-stalk.

'Ben,' I called softly.

He looked up. I signalled and he came over and sat beside me.

'I think we should move into the woods across the river, Ben. We've been here long enough.'

'Funny thing, Skipper. I was just thinking the same.'

'That settles it, then. We'll go tonight.'

Gino cycled into the farmyard at dusk and I told him to tell Roberto we were leaving.

The Scarlattis would never have asked us to go, but I don't think Roberto and his kind-hearted wife were sorry when we left, for our dangerous presence was telling on them both.

We had supper and took our leave.

I saw tears in Bianca's eyes when I said good-bye to her. She was young and romantic and sweet and lovely and had saved my life. How good that unpretentious Italian family had been to us! Complete strangers, we had come knocking at their door at dead of night, asking for succour, and they had taken us in, fed us and sheltered us and made us free of their farm knowing full well the risk they ran if we were discovered by the Germans. And they had helped us without any thought of monetary or other reward, but just out of the kindness of their simple hearts. In this, the Scarlatti family were no different from a thousand other Italian

232

families who likewise sheltered and cared for untold numbers of allied prisoners of war who escaped into the Apennines at the time of the Italian armistice. When we vilify the Italian nation let us forget the turn-coat politicians and remember the kindness of the *contadini* and the risks they ran to save our worthless lives.

The river was dark and mysterious in the starlight when we waded across and I thought how incongruous Toddy Sloan looked knee-deep in mid-stream carrying his little suitcase.

We spent the night in a thicket in the V of hilly country between Fermo and the Ascoli road, waking up damp and chilled in the misty dawn and wishing we were in Roberto's warm attic.

Gino strolled into Fermo during the day and returned late in the afternoon to report that the traffic was definitely thinning. 'Good,' I thought, when he told me, 'that means there's only the rearguard now. Our vigil will soon be over.'

But it dragged on for days.

I felt a growing disquiet about wireless transmission. Toddy Sloan complained that his signals were becoming weak. This was a serious matter because once our batteries went flat we'd no means of charging them and our wireless set would become just so much dead-weight to carry.

'Jan'll think we've been captured when we stop sending,' I remarked to Ben Owen.

'Somebody coming, Skipper,' said Ben, cocking his Tommy-gun.

I looked round to see a man dressed in civilian clothes approaching our thicket and cursed, not realizing I was regarding Tommy Atkins sent by Providence to solve our wireless problem.

'It's a *contadino*,' I observed. 'I wonder what he wants.'

Ben Owen shook his head and covered the man with his Tommy-gun.

'No, Skipper. He's either a spy or an escaped P.O.W.'

The man walked right up to us, looking a trifle embarrassed, I thought. He had fair hair and blue eyes and wasn't a *contadino*, but only dressed like one.

'Well?' I asked, eyeing him suspiciously.

'Eccles, J., sir. Captured at Tobruk.'

I sighed with relief and Ben Owen lowered his Tommy-gun.

'Sit down, Eccles,' I said.

Eccles squatted cross-legged in the thicket and related how

233

he'd been captured in Tobruk in '42 and taken to Italy, how he'd escaped from the P.O.W. camp when the armistice was declared and taken to the mountains where an Italian family hid him and fed him through the winter, how with the coming of spring he'd worked his way across country and was now working for his keep on the farm over the hill where he was friendly with the daughter.

'You didn't try to get back to your own side of the lines, Eccles?'

Eccles, J., dropped his eyes.

'Didn't see any point in it, sir,' he excused himself lamely. 'I knew Eighth Army would catch up sooner or later.'

Private Eccles was typical of thousands of prisoners who escaped into the Apennines at the time of the Italian armistice. Fed and clothed by the kind-hearted *contadini*, many of the prisoners worked on the farm for their keep, fell in love with the pretty daughter and stayed where they were, making no attempt to get back to their own side of the lines. Some were cowards, no doubt, and simply deserted, so to speak, but I fancy the motive which prompted many wasn't escape from military duty in Italy, but from a nagging wife at home.

I was about to deliver a homily on the subject of patriotism when I remembered our flagging wireless batteries. Wait a minute, Yunnie, I admonished myself, don't be so hasty. Perhaps this man can be useful.

I looked hard at Eccles, wondering how far I could trust him. He didn't look a bad sort, that mouth wasn't weak. I decided to take him into my confidence.

'Look, Eccles. I need your help. Our wireless batteries are flat. Can you get them charged or find us a replacement?'

'Yes, I think so, sir,' said Eccles, surprisingly.

Eccles stood up, made to salute (from habit), remembered he was in civilian clothes, nodded instead, and walked away.

I watched him go, wondering if I wasn't the biggest damn fool on earth.

'What do you think of friend Eccles?' I asked Ben Owen when Eccles had gone.

Ben was dubious.

'Something wrong with a bloke who doesn't try to get back, Skipper.'

I nodded, feeling depressed.

But we were both wrong in our judgement of Eccles, who turned out to be a most resourceful and intrepid man. A German H.Q. formation was temporarily leaguered on his farm. Eccles crawled into it at dead of night, pinched a spare wireless battery and delivered it to our thicket in the small hours of the morning with the bare comment, ' 'Ere's your battery, sir.' I was flabbergasted.

A day later, Eccles gave us all a fright.

We were having breakfast in a thicket—brought to us by the *contadino* from a nearby cottage—when we saw Eccles approaching with a German soldier. 'Betrayed,' we thought, and held our breath.

And then I noticed that the soldier wasn't armed.

'What the hell . . .' I muttered to Ben Owen. 'Has he come to ask for his battery back?'

The two figures approached. . . .

'This is Karl, sir,' said Eccles when the two of them stood before me. 'He's a deserter.'

Karl stood rigidly to attention and looked appealingly at me, like a stray dog asking to be taken in.

Karl was tired of the war, it transpired. He was from the formation H.Q. to which our battery belonged and had made friends with Eccles, remaining behind when his formation moved on. Eccles naturally enough brought him to me.

I was in a quandary. I didn't want to be burdened with a German deserter, and how could I be sure he wasn't a cleverly planted spy? But I must either keep him or kill him, for now that he knew of our presence I dare not send him away.

I regarded Karl's boyish face with the unshaven down fluffing his chin. He didn't look like a spy. Unable to kill him in cold blood, I decided to keep him.

'All right, Eccles,' I nodded. 'Karl can stay.'

Eccles returned to his farm and Karl remained with us. Still suspicious, I detailed Danny O'Neil to guard him with a Tommy-gun, but as the day wore on it became obvious that Karl was genuine and wanted to help so we relaxed our vigilance and took him on strength, unpaid, w.e.f. date.

Karl carried his own heavy wireless battery when we moved from thicket to thicket, shouldered my pack, brought me my meals, proved himself an excellent batman—Karl, a German soldier, fetching and carrying for a British officer, spying within his own divisional area. Surely a unique situation!

Traffic on the roads became almost negligible. Gino reported a field-gun moving into position on the ridge above Fermo and we observed a mushroom of smoke rising from the town when the Germans blew up the power-station.

'It won't be long now,' I thought, 'another day or two at most.'

I sent Jan Caneri the map reference of the field-gun, but no planes came to bomb it. Our flight of fighter-bombers were busy elsewhere and had gone off tap. Childishly, I felt alone and neglected.

Having escaped capture so far, I was now on tenterhooks lest misfortune overtake us at the last moment, as the jade has a habit of doing. It would be just too bad, I thought, to elude the clutches of a division and be caught by a rearguard platoon. I became edgy and irritable and kept moving from thicket to thicket, listening to the single gun booming defiance.

Another day passed and the gun no longer boomed. Something induced me to take a look at the river bridge on the road coming out from Fermo. Crawling to the top of a knoll, I looked down upon the bridge through binoculars and saw German sappers laying charges under the arches. 'Ah, no you don't,' I said to myself, 'that bridge is ours. You may mine it, but you won't blow it.'

I backed down the knoll and hurried to our thicket, calling breathlessly for Gino.

'They're mining the bridge,' I panted. 'We must prevent them blowing it. Can you rouse the *contadini*? We'll stage an attack.'

Gino went round the cottages that night and early the following morning, as the mist was rising from the hills, we raced down the knoll towards the bridge, about twenty in number, shouting and yelling, firing our Tommy-guns, shotguns and blunder-busses. The ruse succeeded. The German sappers took fright, dropped their charges and fled. . . .

The bridge was ours.

We walked into Fermo that afternoon—Toddy with his week-end suitcase and Karl following behind him, carrying the battery

—the first British troops to enter the town, and received a tremendous ovation. Standing on the plinth of a statue in the piazza, I named myself Military Governor of Fermo and declared the following day a public holiday.

'*Bravo! Viva Inglesi! Viva Capitano Bob! Viva!*'

At the Albergo Imperiale Toddy Sloan slung his wireless aerial between the chimney-pots and raved about the clear reception. I gave him a cipher for Jan:

PLEASE NOTE NEW ADDRESS   ALBERGO IMPERIALE FERMO

Karl, being German, caused a modicum of embarrassment and we had to hide him in a bedroom to prevent the crowd tearing him limb from limb.

I hadn't had my clothes off for more than a week and felt badly in need of a hot bath which, for some obscure reason, the *albergo* couldn't provide. I sent for the chief of the *carabinieri*.

He came, knocking at my bedroom door.

'*Avanti!*' I called from my reclining position on the bed.

The door opened and a servile, pot-bellied, uniformed figure stood stiffly to attention.

'*Signor Commandante?*'

'Find me a hot bath or I cut off your head. *Bagno. Caldo. Capito?*'

'*Si, Signor Commandante. Pronto!*'

The servile one grovelled, saluted extravagantly and was gone.

But he was efficient. Within the hour I lay in a bath such as I had never had before, hot, pine-scented, luxurious.

The chief of the *carabinieri* conducted me to a palace on the top of the hill, to the ancestral home of the Vinci family, descendants of the revered Leonardo da Vinci.

At the palace gates two black-visaged, wrought-iron churubim gazed at us through sightless eyes and rumbled majestically as we passed between their gaping mouths. A well-tended avenue bordered by stately cypress trees led us past a sunken rose garden ablaze with colour to white marble pillars supporting a cool terrace where a count and his countess waited.

'*Buona sera, Commandante,*' said the count. '*S'accomodo.*'

'*Grazia, Conte,*' I said, and bowed to the countess.

237

Wine was brought on a silver tray.

'*Salute!*' I raised my glass.

The count seemed ill at ease, his countess more composed. Little was said. I sat on the terrace sipping my wine, captivated by a view superb. Beyond the rose garden the ground fell steeply down vivid green slopes to a sandy shore and the eye came to rest on a vast expanse of blue Adriatic stretching unhindered to the shores of Yugoslavia. What a magnificent place in which to live! Who couldn't create in such inspired surroundings? The changing fortunes of war, I mused. A week ago I was crouched like a mole in a wheat-field while my Nazi counterpart sat on this terrace quaffing wine, talking to this count and countess. Now the positions were reversed. . . .

'*Pronto, Signor Commandante.*'

A pert maid in pre-war English black and white announced that my bath was ready. I excused myself to the count and countess and followed the maid into the palace, along a carpeted passage to a blue-tiled bathroom where she curtseyed and closed the door.

'*Grazia,*' I said.

Blue water steamed in a sunken bath, warmed towels of large dimension hung on a silver rail. There was soap, green and pine-scented, and blue bath-crystals in a fish-shaped jar. I caught a glimpse of myself in a silvered wall-mirror mercifully dulled by a film of steam. Good God, was that me? I recoiled and fingered my three days' growth, feeling grubby and uncouth, like a beast in Beauty's bathroom.

I stripped and stepped into the water. Just right. I sat down, feeling the soft, balmy luxury stealing over my body. I lay back, with the soothing water lapping my chin . . . and relaxed. This was heaven, sheer bliss! I closed my eyes and let go . . . lovely. . . .

I lay in the bath and soaked. Time was no object. No Germans to worry about. I could remain for hours if I wished. . . . Memory's screen began to flash . . . the P-boat in the mist . . . the flopping rubber dinghy . . . waving to Porter from the beach . . . Vincento's hayloft . . . the traffic on the coast road . . . dot—dash—dot . . . dot—dash—dot . . . the L.C.T. on the beach . . . Popski and the jeeps. . . . 'Bob, I've got a job for you.' . . . The Germans in the wheat-field . . . the awful, revealing flares . . . the bombs whistling down on the bridge . . . the scarlet tracer curving into the train . . .

the explosion on the beach . . . the flash of light . . . shadowy vineyards . . . the Scarlattis' farm . . . Bianca's firm young breasts . . . her warning signal when the Germans came . . . the runaway ox at the ford . . . Eccles at the thicket . . . Karl . . . the sappers at the bridge . . . the crowd in the piazza . . . the Albergo Imperiale . . . hot bath . . . hot bath . . . pine-scented water. . . .

I opened my eyes. Had I been dreaming? I splashed the water to make sure it was real. How much had happened in a short space of time! I had lived a lifetime in a week. And never a scratch! Incredible. I bore a charmed life. . . .

I stood up, soaped myself frothily, went under again and stepped out, dripping, grabbed a warmed towel from the rail and wrapped myself in its cosy fleece. . . . What sheer luxury!

I shaved.

Turning to dress, I picked up my soiled under-pants. 'No. I can't,' I said to myself. 'I can't put this disreputable garment on to this clean body. It's sacrilege.'

My eye fell on the bell-pull.

'What the heck,' I muttered. 'Am I not Military Governor of Fermo? My word is law.'

I yanked the bell-pull and wound a towel about my loins. . . .

A discreet knock came at the door.

'*Avanti!*' I bawled.

The door opened a crack and the appraising eyes of the pert maid swept over me. I held up my torn under-pants, shrugged my shoulders, opened my hands and pulled down the corners of my mouth, *contadino* fashion.

It was effective.

The maid nodded vigorously, sibilated '*Si, si, Signor Commandante*,' and hurriedly withdrew.

I hummed 'Torno Sorrento' and waited. . . .

Within a very few minutes the discreet knock came at the door again, the appraising eyes regarded my towel and an out-thrust hand dangled a set of the count's silk underwear.

'*Grazia*,' I said, and took them.

The door closed rapidly.

Ten minutes later I sat on the terrace, feeling like a real aristocrat. On the side of my under-pants, sewn in letters of gold, was the family crest of the time-honoured House of Vinci.

. . . . .

We enjoyed the amenities of Fermo for forty-eight hours, and then the Poles came rumbling in and we moved out.

An urgent message came from Jan Caneri, reading:

MEET POPSKI (map reference) EIGHTEEN HUNDRED HOURS
LOVE AND KISSES FROM UNCLE JAN

Popski, without casualties, had returned safely to San Gregorio. With ten jeeps, all that remained in base, he was now haring across country, trying to overtake the retreat.

I consulted the map.

The map reference was Sarnano, a small town in the mountains forty miles from Fermo. The time was 1300 hours.

'Forty miles in five hours!' I exclaimed. 'Without transport! The thing's impossible.'

But it wasn't.

Partisans drove into Fermo in captured enemy transport. I commandeered a battered staff-car, borrowed petrol from the Poles, handed over a terrified Karl with the horrible feeling that the poor devil would never see a P.O.W. camp, and we rattled into cobbled Sarnano with five minutes to spare.

A P.P.A. jeep was parked outside the *albergo*. I went in search of Popski and found him in the lounge, as large as life.

'Well done, Bob,' he greeted me.

I stood stiffly to attention and saluted in my best cadet-school manner.

'Mission accomplished, sir. No casualties.'

We gripped hands and laughed like drains.

15

I NOTICED the change in Curtis the moment I spoke to him.

His voice had lost its breeziness, the gleam had gone from his eyes, even his horse-laugh was subdued, as if nervous of being heard. What ailed the man? His spirit was dead.

'What's the matter with Bum?' I asked Riches.

Riches just shrugged and said nothing.

'What's biting Bum?' I asked J. C.

J. C. stroked his curly beard, regarded me with slumbrous eyes and said nothing.

'I'll get to the bottom of this,' I determined.

It was a serious matter. A worried patrol sergeant could undermine the morale of an entire patrol.

'What's worrying you, Bum?' I shot at Curtis, taking him off his guard.

'N-nothing, sir,' he stammered, and regarded his feet.

'Don't lie to me, Bum,' I reprimanded, more severely than I meant. 'Something's happened to you. You aren't the same.'

'I'm all right, Skipper,' he replied dispiritedly.

'You're not, Bum. Your spirit's dead. You've lost your drive. What is it, man? Tell me. I'm your friend.'

But all I could get out of him was a lifeless, 'I'm all right, Skipper.' I can't think why I was so dense, but it wasn't until the next day that I realized what ailed Curtis.

We split the jeeps into two patrols. Popski took command of one patrol and I the other.

From Sarnano we drove to San Genesio along smooth, twisting roads under trees. How good it felt to be again in jeeps after foot-slogging in the Tenna Valley! Jeeps were our lives, our *raison d'être*. We couldn't cope without them. Parted from our jeeps we were out of our element, like fish out of water. In our jeeps, behind our loved Browning guns, we felt sure of ourselves, invincible. Come what might, sunshine or rain, mountain or river, mortar bomb or machine-gun bullet, in jeeps we could cope. Jeeps were our means of attack and defence, of surprise penetration and quick withdrawal, our mobile homes in which we lived and fought and had our being, our private world about which all else revolved.

'This is the life, George,' I enthused to George Sonley, my driver-gunner. 'No more foot-slogging for me.'

I put my foot down, thrilling to the immediate response of the lively engine, and zoomed along the shady lane after Popski's five jeeps.

The Germans had withdrawn from San Genesio and we drove on, cautiously, towards Caldarola on the banks of the River Chiente.

Whenever we came to an Apennine town we could tell whether the Germans were in it, near it, or gone. If the Germans were in the town a tenseness pervaded, a blanketing silence of fear and suspicion. Windows were shuttered, doors closed and locked, streets empty, nobody moving about; even the birds in the trees were mute and dogs kept well out of sight. If the Germans were near, but not in the town, invariably on our approach, as soon as they knew we were British, one or more of the *contadini* would run up to us, agitatedly, and point where the Germans were. In towns from which the last German had gone, the populace openly welcomed us, filled the piazza and crowded about our jeeps.

The streets of Caldarola were empty. There wasn't a soul in sight and a pregnant silence, the stillness of fear, gripped the place. Staggering our jeeps, we crawled up both sides of the main street, guns cocked, nosing our way towards the bridge which was blown, with enemy machine-gunners sitting behind it, on the north bank of the river, waiting. . . .

Holding our fire, glancing from side to side at the locked and shuttered buildings, we advanced upon the demolished bridge feeling the intense emotion of action which is half fear, half excitement, a delirious enjoyment of danger. I glanced quickly round and noticed that Curtis' jeep was lagging behind.

'O.K., George?' I breathed.

Sonley nodded and didn't look up. He had his nose close to the fifty, squinting along its black barrel.

Closer . . . closer . . . the jeeps were barely moving now . . . the atmosphere was tense, electric . . . 300 yards to the broken parapets of the bridge . . . not a sound but the rushing water . . . 200 yards . . . annihilation impending. . . . I glanced across the street at Popski . . . he turned his goggled eyes towards me and signalled.

'O.K., George,' I hissed. 'Let 'em have it!'

Our jeep jerked and vibrated as a stream of burning tracer leapt towards the bridge, whining and ricocheting amongst the broken masonry, throwing up dust and scarlet sparks. Brrrrrrt . . . brrrrrrrt . . . brrrrrrrt. . . . One by one the other jeeps opened up. Stabbing scarlet jets flew past our ears and the cobbled piazza of sleepy Caldarola was transformed into an echoing inferno of flashing, flailing bullets. . . .

No answering fire came from the bridge. The concentrated fire of our fifties was so heavy that the German machine-gunners daren't raise their heads, but they had a field telephone to a mortar-post some distance behind and the first bomb landed fair and square in the middle of the piazza, rattling the window-panes and giving us all a fright because we didn't hear its whistling approach above the din of our clattering fifties.

Wruuuumph . . . wruuuuumph. Two more bombs fell in quick succession, one very close to Popski's jeep. I saw Popski duck . . . snick into reverse and begin to back away from the bridge. . . .

'Pull out, Bob!' he shouted across to me and his voice sounded tinny above the noise of crashing mortar bombs and banging fifties.

Jeeps slowly reversing . . . flaring streams of tracer curving into the bridge . . . mortar bombs exploding in the piazza . . . on roof-tops . . . slithering, falling, smacking tiles . . . splintering glass. . . . Brrrrrrt . . . brrrrrrt . . . brrrrrrt. . . . Wruuuumph . . . wruuuumph . . . wruuuuumph. . . .

The whistling bombs followed us out of town, landing in flower gardens, damaging houses, terrifying the hidden Caldaro-lians crouching under beds within doors.

We pulled up by the roadside out of range and tried not to laugh when a well-intentioned householder rushed from a nearby villa to warn us that the Germans were shelling the town and it wasn't safe to go in!

Popski reached for his map-board and beckoned. I walked over to his jeep.

'We can't do anything here, Bob,' he said. 'We'll go back to Sarnano and try to get over the range. I'm told there's a group of partisans in Bolognola.'

The map showed a splotch of high grey on the other side of the red line running through Sarnano. From Bolognola, on the top of the grey, a wiggly road ran downhill to the blue River Chiente. Along the north bank, following the line of the river, ran the lateral road which the Germans were using.

The remainder of the day was spent trying to find a jeep route over the 4000-foot-high mountain range between Sarnano and Bolognola. Time and again, straining, pinking jeeps thrust to within a hundred yards of the crest only to find progress barred by out-jutting rocks. We spread out and quartered the range and eventually Sergeant Saunders got his front wheels over the top of the escarpment, stalled his engine, but refused to admit defeat. He and his gunner unloaded their jeep, turned the lightened vehicle at a precarious angle and finished the climb in reverse. From the plateau, they looked down upon the roof-tops of Bolognola.

Later we found a better way, and the next morning ten jeeps crawled up a sheep-track in low booster gear, bumped across the grassy plateau like a file of well-disciplined ants and skidded down the opposite slopes into Bolognola, to the great delight of Major Ferri from Piza University and his eager band of partisans.

It was while crossing the range that Curtis' trouble came to light. As we emerged on to the plateau, a dark object moved across the skyline of a neighbouring hill-top.

'It's an armoured car,' said Curtis.

'It's a hay-cart, Bum,' I said, looking through binoculars.

'No, Skipper,' Curtis insisted. 'It's a German armoured car.'

'Nonsense, Bum. It's a hay-cart.'

Curtis became very agitated and kept insisting that it was an enemy armoured car. I looked at him, saw fear in his eyes, and the penny dropped. Curtis had contracted the fell P.P.A. disease. Good God, I thought, shocked by the realization, Curtis, of all people. How could this happen?

It happened very easily. On the way to Sarnano, before I linked up with him from Fermo, Popski had driven into an ambush. Popski's driver, Cameron, was killed and Lieutenant Rickwood badly wounded in the stomach. Curtis had watched Cameron

244

being buried—Cameron, Popski's hand-picked, intuitive driver—
and wasn't the same man afterwards.

So it happened to many of us during the war. Full of confidence, enjoying the fun, we were eager for adventure, sure it
couldn't happen to us and then one day we were wounded and
felt physical pain or saw a pal blown to bits or the strain of continuous action told upon us and we began to think, 'Can my
luck last?' From that moment, the rot set in.

What should I do about Curtis? He was a good man, one of the
very best, and I must do everything I could to help him. In his
present state of nerves he was useless as patrol sergeant. Was his
condition permanent or temporary? Would a period of rest at
base do the trick? I didn't think so. Curtis had just come from
base. If I sent him back he would just moon about and eat his
heart out, feeling he was a reject. What Curtis wanted, I thought,
was some interesting job in which he would feel he still counted,
but which kept him out of the danger zone until he recovered his
nerve.

I said nothing to him, but that evening when Popski and I
were planning to bring up supplies of arms and ammunition for
the partisans I saw how to handle his case.

As we fought our way through the Apennines a supply truck
would have to ply between base and the forward patrols. The
driver would have to be a reliable, resourceful man, able to find his
way to a map reference on a dark night. It was just the job for
Curtis.

I said to Popski:

'Put Curtis in charge of the supply truck. He needs a change.'

Popski looked at me.

'You mean the hay-cart?'

I nodded.

'Very well, Bob.'

So the problem was solved. When a supply truck from San
Gregorio arrived in Sarnano two days later Curtis transferred to
it and Riches took his place in the patrol.

Partisans. There were two kinds in Italy—the fighters and the
marauders. The fighters were the more difficult to find. They
were the serious-minded ones, ex-army types, professional men,
university students, professors, patriots who had the interests of
their country at heart and were not afraid to die. The marauders

were legion and appeared in every liberated village, flashily dressed bandits, armed to the teeth, who strutted and preened before the girls in the piazza, lived off the *contadini* and kept carefully hidden when Germans were about.

As we progressed through the Apennines, we found that there were also two Italys, the Italy south of Rome—indolent, untrustworthy, unreliable—and the Italy north of Rome—intelligent, resourceful, courageous.

The Bolognola group were fighters. From their guarded mountain fastness they had been harrying the German convoys using the supply routes to Foligno on the other side of the river and they sported quite a collection of trophies to prove their claims—a staff-car, two motor-cycle combinations and a selection of Schmeisers, Spandaus, Mausers and Lugers.

Their commander, Major Ferri, was alert, dynamic, sun-tanned, vigorous. Under close-cropped iron-grey hair his intelligent dark eyes darted hither and thither observing all that went on. He was a born leader of men and his ragged band of partisans, some eighty youths and men dressed in an odd assortment of bits and pieces of German and Italian army uniforms and armed mostly with captured weapons, was well-disciplined and completely under his control.

The supply truck from San Gregorio brought Tommy-guns, sten-guns, ammunition, grenades, road-mines and turds, Calabrian. We ferried them (what a ghastly pun!) over the mountain and got down to business.

Five miles from Bolognola the swift-flowing Chiente curved its path through a rugged valley of vivid blues and greens, the bright green of grass on the lower hill slopes, the darker green of pine-forest on the mountainside, the blue-green water hurrying down to the sea under an azure sky. The river's erratic passage was punctuated by townships—Muccia, up-river, Caldarola and Tolentino, down-river—and a tortuous mountain road hair-pinned from Bolognola down to the crossing where the bridge was blown. On the opposite hillside, six miles from the river, the walled city of Camerino, occupied by the Germans, basked in the morning sun.

From our mountain stronghold, 3000 feet up, we had a glorious view of the surrounding country, of the lateral road running along the north bank of the river towards Foligno, of the winding road from Muccia to Camerino, of Camerino itself, perched on its hill-top and flashing its windows in the sun; but the enemy had just as good a view from his observation posts on the opposite hills so that neither of us moved much by day.

At night we were both active.

Under cover of darkness the enemy sent escorted supply trucks to outposts along the north bank of the river. Because of the blown bridges, we couldn't drive our jeeps across to the German side, but found we could manœuvre them into positions on the south bank from where their guns commanded the lateral road. 'Popski Ambushing', as the game was called, became a popular after-dinner sport. Compèred by The Heavenly Twins, it attracted many enthusiasts from Ferri's eager band and it was quite surprising how quickly the partisans mastered the tricks of our specialized trade.

'Who's coming Popski Ambushing?' I asked one night when we'd eaten our fill of *pasta* in the big hall where we fed with the partisans. The Heavenly Twins stood up and there was a chorus of '*Io . . . Io . . . Io*,' from many partisan throats.

Gliding silently down the cork-screw road, we manhandled the jeeps into position along the river bank and two road-mining parties, carrying a large supply of turds, Calabrian, waded waist-high through the dark, swirling water. One party mined the road 300 yards up-stream and recrossed the river. The second party crouched in the bushes by the roadside 300 yards down-stream, waiting for a convoy to pass.

Time went by.

We stood behind our jeeps, turned broadside to the river, with fingers itching on the trigger-guards of the twin Browning guns. The range was between 200 and 300 yards. Small groups of partisans armed with sten-guns and grenades sat in the bushes beside us, waiting to cross the river after the first broadside was fired.

The summer night was warm and slumbrous and the song of the rushing water rose and fell in gurgling cadences, soothing to the nerves. Mosquitoes danced above the water and settled on our hands and cheeks. Somewhere across the river a farm-dog barked at the rising moon, orange and bloated, and the echo of its mournful cry was thrown back by the mountainside towering darkly behind us.

247

'Come on, Jerry,' Ben Owen breathed impatiently, longing to let go with his well-oiled fifty.

An hour dragged by and we became restless.

'Perhaps there won't be a convoy tonight, Ben,' I whispered.

I glanced at the luminous dial of my wrist-watch. It was ten past ten and the moon, shedding its orange for a silver coat, was climbing in the star-signposted sky.

Twenty minutes later we heard the sound of a vehicle changing gear.

'Pssssst!'

We listened, holding breath.

The throb of an exhaust vibrated faintly in the night air and grew louder and louder. . . .

Excitement gripped us, an exultant, breath-catching surge of mingled fear and joy.

'Not yet,' I breathed into the night, fearing the gunners would fire too soon and spoil the ambush. 'Wait for it . . . wait for it. . . .'

The German convoy moved slowly across our line of fire—the dark outlines of two supply trucks escorted by an armoured scout car fore and aft. I let them go past. . . .

There was a flash of light and an echoing explosion from the road as the leading armoured car hit the turds, Calabrian. A green Very light fizzed starwards, our signal for the second road-mining party to lay their turds and recross the river.

The convoy stopped.

A confusion of voices and grating gears disturbed the balmy night and the line of vehicles reversed into our gun-sights.

'Fire!'

Six pairs of quick-firing Brownings commenced a deafening clatter. Tracer, incendiary and armour-piercing bullets whammed across the river, zipping and thudding, plopping into the water, threshing the bushes, smacking into the moving vehicles. One of the trucks was carrying petrol. It suddenly erupted like Vesuvius. 'Got the bastard!' crowed O'Leary and fired another vicious burst into the flames. Brrrrrrrrrrrrrrrt. . . . There was a flash and another echoing explosion as the second scout car (now leading) ran into the mines laid after the convoy had passed. Caught in the 'Popski Ambush'—between two lots of mines—the convoy was trapped and we hammered it unmercifully, pouring a deadly fire

248

into the stationary vehicles. Tracer ricocheted off the armour-plating of the scout cars and sailed in beautiful scarlet parabolas through the velvet sky. The second truck took fire. Hoarse cries came from the other side of the river and little darting flames shot out as one of the scout cars fired back at us, making us duck as bullets whined past our heads.

'Get that scout car!' I shouted.

The guns swung on to it and the darting flames died. . . .

Brrrrrrt. . . . Brrrrrrrrrt. . . . Brrrrrrrrrrrrrrrrt. We raked the burning convoy from end to end.

'Cease fire!' I called.

A deathly silence ensued, pervaded by the sound of rushing water and the crackle of flames.

'O.K., Twins,' I said. 'Over you go.'

Followed by the partisans, The Heavenly Twins waded into the river holding their Tommy-guns above their heads. Before they were across, a self-starter rasped . . . an engine revved furiously . . . the leading scout car made a dash for freedom. By a miracle, its engine had escaped our bullets and was still functioning.

Fearful of killing our own men wading across the river, we could only stand idly by our guns and watch the gallant German driver escape. . . .

'He'll blow up on a mine,' Ben Owen exclaimed.

But he didn't.

By a chance in a million, his tearing wheels missed what remained of the unexploded turds and we cheered involuntarily as the dark shadow raced on down the road and out of sight. Courage deserves its reward in any nationality.

The night's bag was one wrecked armoured scout car, two burned-out supply trucks, three dead Germans. The others got away.

Reprisals came an hour later as we were wending a yawning way towards Bolognola and bed.

Seven up per jeep, we were growling round the steep corners in low booster gear when a shell exploded on the mountainside with a reverberating clatter. '*Mama mia*,' we cried in mock alarm, and laughed happily. . . . We changed the expression a minute later when a salvo crashed into the road and narrowly missed O'Leary's jeep. Heads ducked smartly, brakes squeaked

249

and an indignant duet echoed through the moonlit gorge: 'The mucking bastards . . . bastards.'

Three days later, because of pressure on the coastal flank, the German front line moved back another river and Camerino became a forward outpost. The news arrived at breakfast time, brought in by one of Ferri's night patrols which had been across the river as far as the city gates.

'*Tedeschi scapati*,' they announced jubilantly. (The Germans have gone.) Popski looked across the table at me.

'Get a bridge built, Bob.'

All that day we laboured. The pine-forest rang with the bite of woodmen's axes and revving jeeps plied up and down the twisting mountain road hauling logs to the river.

The bridge was built by nightfall and I took a patrol of jeeps across. The lateral road was dark and mysterious, peopled by the ghosts of the German drivers we had killed in ambush.

We crossed the Chiente the following morning.

Camerino squatted on its hill-top, like a giant mushroom, looking peaceful and serene in the morning sunlight. Within its medieval walls a nervous German commander listened to conflicting reports. Ferri's partisans had friends in the enemy camp and had caused rumours to circulate that a large British force was converging upon the marooned city.

Eyes upon Camerino, we drove cautiously along a dusty road between green fields agleam with dewy diamonds. A large building with a red-tiled roof drew my attention—one of its windows caught the rays of the sun and flashed like a signalling lamp.

In the leading jeep, Popski drove to the bottom of the steep hill which led upwards like a winding staircase to the city gates, and put up a hand. The jeeps drew up in staggered formation behind him and we examined the walled city through binoculars. Solidly built, impregnable, Camerino stood upon its rock bastion like an Edinburgh Castle.

There were only two roads into the city, both through guarded gates, one from the south which we were on and another from the north. A frontal attack was out of the question. We would merely spend our strength against unimpressionable stone walls. Camerino would have to be taken by subterfuge.

It didn't seem possible that the city was strongly garrisoned.

There was no visible evidence of German occupation, no sign of machine-gun nests, field-guns or mortars, no steel-helmeted soldiers manning the battlements. Washing hung from the line between buildings, and civilians appeared on their iron balconies. We grew careless, climbed from our jeeps and stood in the road looking at the city walls, chatting, smoking cigarettes, speculating upon the best means of attack. . . .

Wruuuuuuumph! A mortar bomb crashed alongside Popski's jeep, making him jump. The bomb was most unexpected. The wind was blowing towards Camerino and no one heard the whistling approach.

Wruuuuumph . . . wruuuuumph . . . wruuuuumph. A salvo of bombs crashed in the road before we had time to recover from the shock of the first one. Dust blew into our faces and stones and gravel smacked against the metal sides of the jeeps. 'Christ!' we muttered and leapt for our seats. . . .

There was a mêlée of turning, revving jeeps and exploding mortar bombs all jumbled together in the dust and for a moment, until the jeeps got under way, we were in grave danger of annihilation.

One by one the jeeps revved away, tearing at the gravelly surface with spinning wheels as the drivers fiercely let in the clutch. I hung back, waiting for Popski to pass me and take the lead so that I could fall into my customary place at the rear of the column.

Popski shouted something, but above the racket of the exploding bombs I couldn't hear what he said. I looked enquiringly at him and shouted, 'What?', cupping a hand to my ear. He mouthed the word 'smoke' and put two fingers to his lips as if smoking a cigarette.

In times of stress, a cigarette steadies the nerves and the thought flashed through my mind that Popski craved a cigarette at that particular moment and didn't have one. 'Bloody awkward time to ask for a cigarette,' I muttered to Sonley, but if my commanding officer wanted a cigarette so badly I thought I'd better give him one.

'Hold everything, George,' I called to Sonley, who was raring to go, pulled my cigarette-case from my pocket and ran across the road. . . . Wruuuuumph. . . .

'No, you fool!' Popski yelled in my face when I stood beside his throbbing jeep offering him a cigarette. 'Smoke,' and he jerked his thumb towards the rear.

'Oh, *smoke*!' I yelled, comprehending. . . .

Wruuuuumph . . . wruuuuumph. Bombs fell dangerously close, spattering us with earth. I ducked and ran to my jeep . . . leapt aboard as Sonley revved after the others. . . .

Remembering Jan Caneri's effort in Bari, I looked round to see how Popski's smoke-screen was working. It was the first time we'd used it in action. Smoke was pouring from the tail of his weaving jeep, mushrooming in a dense cloud, filling the road and drifting across the fields, hiding Camerino. Soon, even the sun was obscured. . . .

The bombing ceased abruptly.

I pulled up round the first bend and waited for Popski.

His jeep was still trailing a thinning coil of smoke which fizzled out like a damp squib as he drew up beside me.

'Bloody effective smoke-screen, Popski,' I congratulated him.

He laughed, pleased with the first results of his invention, and put two fingers to his lips and said:

'Please give me a cigarette, Bob.'

I made a face at him and extended my cigarette-case.

We drove back to the river, brewed-up in the shade of some bushes and sat by our jeeps cudgelling our brains for a plan to drive the Germans out of Camerino.

The Heavenly Twins were for scaling the walls at night, over-powering the guards and opening the gates to admit the jeeps, but Popski ruled this out as impracticable and eventually decided to simulate a large-scale infantry attack to mislead the enemy into giving up the city.

East of the road upon which we'd been mortared, the terrain was broken and wooded, full of hillocks and clumps of bushes. Creeping up under cover of these, we drove the jeeps to within a thousand yards of the city walls and opened a heavy machine-gun fire.

Tracer bounced off the roof-tops of Camerino, describing beautiful scarlet filigree against the blue sky. Some found its mark in balconies and windows, terrifying the householders, but mostly it ricocheted off the impregnable walls and was wasted.

As dusk fell, we moved the jeeps quickly from bush to bush,

from hillock to hillock, firing bursts from each stance and working round in a semicircle to give the impression of a battalion closing in for the kill. Popski and I wandered about with Very pistols and periodically sent coloured lights arching through the violet sky.

Under cover of darkness, The Heavenly Twins force-marched a patrol of partisans to the north gate, mined the road and lay in wait by the bushes. Maintaining a steadily advancing fire from the jeeps accompanied by strategically placed Very lights we staged a very realistic show and by one o'clock in the morning the German commander, convinced that he was being attacked by a superior force and would be completely surrounded by dawn, decided to withdraw while withdrawal was still possible. Slipping surreptitiously out of the back door in the moonlight his dispirited echelon drove into turds, Calabrian, and came under a devastating sten-gun fire directed by The Heavenly Twins.

Entering the city gates at dawn, we drove triumphantly through narrow, cobbled streets to the piazza and accepted the freedom of the city from an over-wrought and emotional *podestà*.

Popski installed Ferri as civil governor pending the arrival of Amgot (Allied Military Government in Occupied Territories) and dispensed summary justice in a crowded city hall. Quislings and collaborators were quickly rounded up and clapped into gaol without too much attention being paid to their protestations of innocence while Popski's Private Army, taking their social duties to heart, called upon the daughters of all the best families.

A banquet was held in our honour in the city hall.

Popski made a speech. *Viva Popski! Viva gli alleati! Viva!* Ferri made a speech. *Viva Ferri! Viva gli partigani! Viva!* Bob Yunnie made a speech. *Viva Capitano Bob! Viva gli Scotchesi! Viva!*

We all ate too much, drank too much, talked too much, and woke the following morning with throbbing heads. But it was worth it.

A squadron of Lancers drove in from Foligno. We handed over to them, said good-bye to Ferri and his gallant band and sped after the retreating Germans.

16

W E TARRIED a day at Castel Raimondo on the banks of the swollen Potenza. Heavy rain had fallen during the night and all the bridges were blown. In the warmth of the drying sun we thrust up and down the river bank testing for a way across.

The banks were high and the water raged. 'Careful, Skipper,' Ben Owen warned as I dropped my front wheels over a grassy bank. 'Watch you don't strand in mid-stream.' I eased the brake-pedal and the flat bonnet sank further into the brown turbulence. Water splashed over the radiator and I still hadn't touched bottom.

'No good, Ben,' I shouted. 'Too deep.'

I jammed on brakes, grated into reverse and let in the clutch. I felt the rear wheels spin in the grass. The bonnet remained under water.

'Quick, Ben!' I yelled, panicking. 'Pull me out.'

Ben Owen reversed his jeep up to mine, coupled up the tow-rope which each jeep carried wound round its front bumper, and yanked me out.

'Thanks, Ben.'

My engine was dead—water in the magneto.

'She's all yours, George,' I said to Sonley. 'Get cracking.'

'Mucking hell, Skipper,' he complained. 'I told you you wouldn't get through.'

While George dried the magneto I walked along the river bank searching for a crossing. The Germans had pulled right back and I wanted to catch up with them. Popski and I were separating as soon as we crossed the Potenza. He was going eastwards towards Cingoli, I was continuing north towards Fabriano. I was impatient to get over the river.

A *contadino* rambled past, leading an ox team. Oxen, I thought, that's the answer.

'Hey, Gino,' I yelled, startling the oxen.

Gino came running along the bank.

'Gino, tell that *contadino* to bring his oxen and pull the jeeps through the river.'

'*Si, Capitano.*'

Gino and the *contadino* quick-fired and gesticulated for ten minutes and then the oxen were brought—ponderous, grey-white, mild-eyed beasts with sweeping, sharp-pointed horns. One was hitched to the front of my jeep and I climbed into the driving-seat.

'Aw, Skipper, not again . . . Jesus!' from Sonley.

'It's all right, George,' I soothed. 'I won't use the engine. Waterproof the mag.'

Sonley tucked a rubber ground-sheet all round the engine and let the bonnet fall with a clang.

'Right, Gino,' I called. '*Avanti!*'

I steered along the river bank behind the plodding ox until we came to a disused ford. The *contadino* rolled up his trousers and waded into the rushing water, leading the dubious ox. The ox paused to sniff the water, was satisfied and plunged boldly in. The water rose almost to its belly.

The river bed was stony and the jeep jolted and jerked. Water cascaded over the bevel of the passenger aperture and swirled about my feet. I felt the jeep drag sideways with the force of the current and for a moment I was fearful of being swept downstream and swamped, but we were past the deepest part and almost across. Another bump . . . a lurch . . . a jolt . . . and we were free-wheeling up the far bank.

'Hurray!' came a chorus from the opposite bank.

I was unhitched and the *contadino* led the docile ox into the river again. Water dripped from every bolt-hole in the jeep chassis and made little runnels in the sand.

'Wrap up your engines well!' I shouted across the ford.

In an hour and a half ten jeeps stood dripping on the north bank and the *contadino* went happily on his way with a packet of American 'Camels' in his pocket.

We had difficulty in starting the engines, but eventually they all ran sweetly and we drove on to the road.

Popski was turning right. I was going to the left. We climbed from our jeeps and shook hands.

'I give you *carte blanche*, Bob,' Popski said. 'Harry the enemy. Keep advancing. Try to slip behind the lines if you can. Send in a daily sitrep.'

'O.K., Popski.'

'Good luck, Bob.'

'And you, Popski.'

Popski slid behind the wheel, adjusted his dust-goggles, glanced round to make sure his patrol were ready, and revved away with a backward wave of the hand. His four jeeps hurtled after him. The wind brought me 'Good hunting, Skipper,' from The Heavenly Twins as their jeep roared past.

I watched them go and turned to my patrol with a glad heart, rubbing my hands. I was my own master again. *Carte blanche*, Popski had said, a completely free hand to do as I liked within a hundred square miles of virgin territory. What a wonderful thought!

Sergeant Riches, a bow-legged cavalryman, waddled up, fingering his beard. He was clad in an Airborne jumping jacket three sizes too big for him, fastened between the legs and gripped at the waist by a web belting holding compass pouch and heavy Colt revolver. He cocked a quizzical eye at me, looking like Klondyke Pete.

'What's the form, Skipper?'

I slapped his five-foot-four on the back, making him cough.

'The form, Rich, me boy, is that we're on our own. *Carte blanche*. We're going to have fun. *Avanti!*'

Riches burst into song and the strains of 'Torno Sorrento' floated along the banks of the Potenza as the rest of the patrol joined in.

I climbed into my jeep with a light heart and cannot remember ever feeling so happy and carefree. The sun shone, the grass was green, adventure called, anything could happen. We had jeeps, petrol, rations, ammunition. We were in the pink of physical condition and there wasn't an allied soldier within a hundred square miles.

Gino settled himself comfortably on the load, gripping a Tommy-gun. George Sonley cocked the fifty and swung it into position. I revved the high-powered motor.

256

'Everybody O.K.?' I sang out.

'O.K., Skipper. Take 'er away,' Riches called.

'*Avanti!*'

I let in the clutch and we zoomed up the dusty Matelica road
—George Sonley, Gino and self; followed by Ben Owen and
J. C.; Danny O'Neil and Toddy Sloan; Mee and Williamson;
with Riches and Don Galloway bringing up the rear. We didn't
zoom far.

Rounding a bend, a German sniper took a pot-shot—and
missed. I felt the wind of the bullet, ducked and braked violently.

'Look out! Sniper!' I yelled to the jeeps piling up behind me.

Ben Owen's quick eye saw a uniformed figure running up the
hillside.

'There he is, Skipper!'

Brrrrrt . . . Brrrrrrrrt. We raked the green hillside with
machine-gun fire. The running figure vanished.

'The bastard!' exclaimed George Sonley indignantly, as if no
German sniper had the right to fire at us.

The incident sobered us and we drove cautiously towards
Matelica, keeping a wary eye on both sides of the road.

We were in a narrow valley between high green slopes. Beyond
the ridge on our right were the mountains of Cingoli where Popski
had gone. On the other side of the ridge on our left the main road
ran north from Foligno and beyond it were Perugia and Lago
Trasimeno where Eighth Army battled for control of the roads
to Florence. Ten miles north of Matelica a main lateral road
from Fabriano wound down the Esino Valley to Ancona and the
Adriatic coast.

A few miles south of Matelica we turned off the main road and
took to one of the Apennine sheep-tracks which from then on
became our private runways. The track followed the contours of
the ridge, dipped into gullies, curved behind hillocks, disappeared
into clumps of bushes, traversed scree slopes at a perilous angle
and linked farmstead with farmstead dotted over the fertile
mountainside.

Thrusting along the narrow, bumpy track, scraping the sides
of the jeeps against high gravelly banks, catching the under-
carriage on hummocky tufts, wobbling in muddied ruts, feeling
the sun hot on the backs of our necks, we stopped at every farmhouse to enquire news of the German whereabouts and drove at

midday into the little mountain village of Esanatoglia—a cluster of houses built round a cobbled piazza from which a few narrow streets ran off. We jolted down a steep gully, rattled over a rickety bridge spanning a frothing torrent and entered the village by the back door, through a cobbled alley where hens scratched and clucked and bright-eyed piglets squeaked after a grunting, mud-encrusted sow.

Gino slid off as we drew up in the centuries-old piazza.

A hush gripped Esanatoglia. Frightened eyes peered at us through the cracks of shuttered windows. Shopkeepers locked their doors, mothers held their bambinos close to their black skirts.

One *cóntadino*, more courageous than the rest, came to take a look at us.

'*Inglesi!*' he suddenly shouted.

Shutters banged open, heads popped out, door-locks rattled, men, women and children rushed from alleyways and doorways, yelling and shouting, and crowded round our jeeps.

'*Viva Inglesi! Viva Inglesi! Bravo! Bravo!*'

Flasks of wine appeared, glasses were thrust at us. '*Beve* . . . *beve*. . . .'

'*Grazia* . . . *grazia*. . . .'

'*Salute*, Skipper.' George Sonley raised a glassful of amber wine and quaffed it in one, like beer.

'Go easy, George,' I admonished, quaffing one myself.

'*Dove tedeschi?*' Gino enquired of the group milling round our jeep.

'*A Matelica*. . . . *A Fabriano*. . . . *Molti tedeschi*. . . .'

Exaggerated estimates of the German strength issued from the mouths of the excited crowd. I discounted the numbers and arrived at the approximate truth. There was a strong German garrison in Fabriano with a forward post at Matelica, machine-gun nests and observation posts in the hills.

An alert, pleasant-faced young man with an attractive personality pushed his way through the crowd. He wore civilian trousers tucked into grey woollen socks above black army boots, a faded Italian Army officer's tunic, and carried a rifle slung across his back. He stood expectantly in front of me and announced himself as Guardone, Guillelmo Guardone, a partisan from the mountains in search of the advancing Eighth Army.

Something about Guardone held my interest. I looked him

up and down, liked his rounded, sun-tanned, honest face, his firm chin and spaniel-brown eyes. I felt drawn to the man, so honest and trustworthy did he look, and a voice inside me said: 'Recruit this man. He'll be useful.'

Turning to Gino, I said:

'Ask Guardone if he'd like to join P.P.A.'

Gino put the question, explaining who and what we were.

Guardone's sensitive mouth opened in a wide grin, showing excellent teeth.

'*Si, si, Capitano*'—enthusiastically.

Guardone thereupon became a member of 'B' Patrol and remained with P.P.A. until the end of the war. Like Gino— fearless, intuitive, resourceful and loyal—he became invaluable to us on patrol. We nicknamed him Gigi—from his initials (G.G.)—gave him a Tommy-gun and he clambered on to the back of Riches' jeep. The crowd in the piazza cheered wildly.

'*Bravo! Viva gli partigani! Viva Italia! Viva Inglesi! Viva!*'

Engines revved. The crowd stood back and we rattled over the cobbles, under an echoing sandstone arch and on to a dusty white road which wound through the hills towards Fabriano.

It was the hour of siesta and the countryside dozed under the sweltering sun. I was obsessed by a desire to slip behind the German line and, as we drew ever nearer to Fabriano without encountering a sign of the enemy, hope began to rise. Matelica was far behind us on the flank. Could we do it? I wondered, feeling excitement play. What a feather in 'B' Patrol's cap if we managed to slip through!

We tip-tyred up to a white-walled cottage by the roadside near a wood. The cottage had a green door, green window-sills, a green wooden fence enclosing a flower garden and a vegetable patch and a green gate invitingly open. 'What a nice little cottage,' I thought, 'we'll stop here and enquire within.' Like many an attractive-looking flower, the cottage hid a vicious sting. I held up a hand and the patrol halted behind me. Gino slid off and made towards the half-open gate, but before he'd taken two strides, the cottage door opened and a man and a woman stepped out.

The man was nondescript, but the woman was stunning. A ripple of interest surged through the patrol.

'Hell, Skipper,' George Sonley muttered. 'Look at this!'

I watched the woman approach. Dressed in a white silk blouse

259

and red skirt, with shapely legs encased in sheer nylons and terminating in black court shoes, her upper structure was superb —firm, pear-shaped, pointed breasts pushing out her blouse above a slim waist, with the top button cleverly undone, peach-complexion, oval face, a vivid red mouth, aquiline nose with dark, sensuous nostrils, ice-blue eyes, smooth olive-skinned forehead crowned by a glory of rich, wavy, auburn hair. 'She's like a film star,' I thought. 'What a gorgeous figure!' And then I thought, 'What the hell's she doing here?'

The ravishing creature walked confidently up to my jeep, appraised my officer's insignia, the ribbons above my breast pocket, the Colt revolver at my belt. 'She's got poise,' I thought, and noticed that her eyes were hard.

'*Buona sera, Majore*,' she greeted me in honeyed tones, knowing perfectly well that I was only a captain.

'*Buona sera, Signorina*,' I flattered her, keeping my eyes on hers. '*Come sta?*'

'*Bene, grazia, Majore. E lei?*'

The conversation was unnatural, too polite and calculating for a first meeting under such circumstances. And those smiling eyes were hard! What game's this woman playing? I wondered, feeling suddenly suspicious.

Her companion hung back, saying nothing, and the woman began to ask questions—where had we come from and where were we going, how many were we and were we alone?—not at all the sort of questions your welcoming Italian asked when you entered an Apennine town. Be careful, an inner voice warned, this woman is a spy.

I bored my eyes into her soul. The hussy didn't even blink, but continued to probe in her honeyed voice. 'Right, my girl,' I thought, convinced now that I was dealing with a German spy, 'I'll play you at your own game and give you a run for your money.'

We were the advance patrol of a large allied force, I told her, through Gino. Tanks, guns, armoured cars, lorried infantry were pouring across the Potenza; a whole division was advancing from Foligno; more troops from Camerino; all converging upon Fabriano, which would be reached the following night. I laid it on thick, like Disraeli with his trowel, and watched her lap it up. 'Take that to your German masters,' I thought, 'and maybe they'll retreat.'

Feeling she'd made a scoop, the woman ceased asking questions and invited me in for a drink.

'No, *grazia, Signorina,*' I declined, fearing that if I once became entangled in her web I might never get free.

Realizing she couldn't entice me, she gave me a dazzling smile and re-entered the cottage with her companion, who had never uttered a word.

'Olga,' I thought, 'Olga the Beautiful Spy.'

'What do you think, Gino?' I asked when the cottage door closed behind the pair.

'*Spia, Capitano,*' said Gino decisively.

I nodded.

'I think so too.'

Apprehensively, hackles raised, I drove into the wood and followed the path through its resiny shade. It was cool under the trees and the jeeps rode softly over the carpet of leaves.

'Keep your eyes peeled, George,' I muttered to Sonley. 'This place is beginning to stink.'

'Spy, Skipper?'

'Definitely.'

'Pity, Skipper,' said George sadly. 'Marvellous pair of tits.'

'Never mind her tits, George. Keep your mind on the fifty.'

'Yes, Skipper.'

The trees thinned, showing rolling green hills beyond the wood. I braked under an out-rider and reached for binoculars. A stony sheep-track wound across a bare, tumbling hillside and disappeared over a green spur, beyond which the green shoulders of other hills bulged in a protective shield round Fabriano, hidden at their base.

'We'll go up to that spur,' I muttered to George.

Out of the trees, as if emerging from a tunnel, feeling exposed and unprotected, with the hot afternoon sun beating on our heads and glaring the track. . . . I had my eyes on the distant spur and saw something move. Braking, I grabbed the binoculars and focused them in time to see a German infantryman jump up and run over the shoulder.

'We're spotted, Gino,' I muttered. 'Tell Riches to reverse.'

From his seat in the back of the jeep Gino signalled to Sergeant Riches in the last jeep.

Five gear-levers snicked and five jeeps slowly reversed along

the bumpy track. . . . I kept glancing nervously at the spur. . . .
Wheeeeeeeeeeee. . . .

'Here she comes, Skipper,' warned George, getting ready to
duck. Wruuuuuumph. The mortar bomb exploded ten yards up
the track. We were close to the first trees and heard gravel spattering the leaves.

'That's that, George,' I said ruefully. 'No slipping behind the
lines tonight. Out we go—back to the road.'

Reversing the jeeps between the trees we drove hurriedly
along the cushioned pathway. A few hundred yards from the
road a little boy passed us, going towards Fabriano.

'Don't go that way, sonny,' I called to him. 'You'll get hurt.'
Gino translated, but the little fellow, small and dark, aged about
nine, with obstinate eyes, continued on his way, giving us a wide
berth. 'Ah, well,' I thought, 'if he wants to go that way, it's no
business of mine. He's been warned.' But when we bumped on
to the road and the cottage came in view the thought struck me
that there might be a connection between the little boy and Olga.
Was he carrying a message from Olga to the German commander
in Fabriano? What a mean thing, to use an innocent little boy as
go-between. I thought I'd have a word with Olga.

I drew up in front of the little green gate.

'Come, Gino,' I said. 'We'll call on Olga.'

'Can I come too, Skipper?' asked George with a lecherous
gleam in his eye.

'Certainly not, George,' I said severely. 'You keep your eye
on the wood.'

'Yes, Skipper.'

There was no reply to our knock on the closed front door.
We waited a minute and knocked again, louder. No reply. I tried
the door-handle. The door was locked.

'That's funny, Gino. Let's try the back door.'

The back door was also locked.

'The birds have flown, Gino,' I observed.

'*Entrare?*' Gino asked. (Shall we break in?)

I hodded.

Putting our shoulders to the panelled door we heaved . . .
stood away . . . heaved again. The lock gave a little.

'Again, Gino. Harder.'

We stood back and threw ourselves against the panels . . .

262

again . . . again . . . the door splintered and cracked . . . again . . . the lock burst its socket and we stumbled into a small kitchen, smelling strongly of garlic. Breathing heavily, we stood beside a kitchen table and listened. There wasn't a sound but the crashing of mortar bombs in the wood.

The cottage was empty.

We ransacked it from top to bottom, opening cupboards, pulling out drawers, rummaging amongst the contents of sheets and blankets, bed and table linen, looking behind cushions and below mattresses, under beds, but we found nothing to prove that Olga was a spy.

'We'll make enquiries about her in Esanatoglia, Gino,' I said. 'Come on, let's go.'

Jamming the broken door with a piece of wood, we returned to the jeeps.

'You've been a long time, Skipper,' Sonley remarked meaningly.

'Don't be rude, George. The birds have flown.'

'Oh, sorry, Skipper.'

In thoughtful mood, I drove slowly back to Esanatoglia where Gino and Gigi asked questions of the *contadini*. The cottage, it appeared, belonged to an old lady who hadn't been seen lately. Nobody knew anything about Olga.

I liked the atmosphere of Esanatoglia and decided to make it my headquarters, but first we must drive the Germans out of Matelica on our flank.

While Gino and Gigi gleaned information about enemy dispositions I took the patrol into a nearby vineyard and told Riches to brew-up. I would much rather have sat down to *pasta* in a house in Esanatoglia, but that meant wine, and I thought it wiser to keep my men away from temptation until the job was done.

I gave Toddy Sloan a sitrep and by the time he was finished transmitting the moon was rising and Gino and Gigi returned.

Matelica, four miles from Esanatoglia, wasn't strongly held, they informed me. There was a machine-gun post in a house near the road-junction, and the main road coming in from Castel Raimondo was mined. As they spoke, a simple plan of attack came to mind. We would drive towards Fabriano again, leave the road before we reached Olga's cottage, cut across country, strike the Matelica–Fabriano road a mile or two outside the village and attack it from the rear. It was a simple, straightforward plan and nothing could go wrong. The patrol gathered round my jeep and I explained what I had in mind.

'Matelica isn't strongly held,' I said. 'We'll attack from the rear. We go towards Fabriano for a mile or two, cut across country, strike the Matelica road, turn right and drive up the main street. The machine-gun post is at the road-junction, in the house on the left-hand corner. We shoot it up and turn *right* into the Esanatoglia road. The Castel Raimondo road is mined. Watch you don't over-shoot the road junction and hit a mine. O.K.? Any questions?'

'Where do we rendezvous if we get separated, Skipper?' asked the thoughtful Ben Owen.

'The piazza of Esanatoglia, Ben. We all know it.'

'What happens if we get chased by armoured cars, Skipper?' Riches asked facetiously.

'Put down smoke, Rich,' I joked. 'Come on, let's go.'

Slipping quietly out of the vineyard, we drove along the moonlit road towards Fabriano, covered a distance of three miles on the speedometer and branched off into a farm-track. Everything was softly mysterious under the great shining orb, ethereal, stirring up vague longings in the heart and I thought what a rare quality Italian moonlight had, like poetry spilling over from heaven. . . .

Ben Owen's shadowy jeep appeared and I drove on down the rutted track with four burbling shadows tailing me at ten-yard intervals . . . crossed a sleeping farmyard where geese cackled indignantly . . . paused at a gate which Gino opened and Gigi closed after the last jeep . . . bumped along the side of a wheat-field . . . turned into another track . . . jolted downhill to a ford and stopped.

'Can we cross, Gino?' I whispered over my shoulder.

Gino removed his boots and socks, slipped off the jeep and waded through the ford. The water came up to his calves.

'*Va bene, Capitano,*' he called softly. '*Avanti!*'

I snicked into low booster gear and crawled gently through the ford, lurching a little on the uneven, stony bed, drove up the opposite incline and waited for the other jeeps to cross. Then on again by the sides of wheat-fields and vineyards until we came to the Matelica road lying quiet and deserted under the moon.

Leaving the jeeps in the shadows of vine trellises, Gino, Ben Owen and I padded softly up to the road and stood in the moonlit dust looking towards Matelica from the German rear, feeling strong and very powerful with five jeeps, ten machine-guns and complete surprise.

I looked towards Fabriano, hidden behind its bulwark of silvered, shadowy hills, at the two high ridges touching the stars on either side of the valley and again towards sleeping Matelica, two miles down the road. I listened. The whole valley slept. There wasn't a sound, not a breath of wind.

'O.K., Ben?'

Ben Owen nodded and we tiptoed back to the waiting jeeps.

'Now remember.' I whispered last-minute instructions to the crews. 'Hold your fire until you hear me open up, then give it everything you've got. Turn *right*—remember, *right*—at the road-junction—and don't over-shoot. O.K.?'

There was a whispered chorus of 'O.K., Skipper.'

Hearts beating fast, butterflies playing in the pit of the stomach, we jolted out of the vineyard and on to the moonlit road. . . .

The crews were silent, tense, gripping steering-wheel or gun, minds wholly concentrated on the road. I glanced sideways at George Sonley. He was one with the black-barrelled fifty he grasped with both hands, ready to jab; and I felt Gino's comforting presence behind me. Gino never panicked and always did the right thing. . . .

Making very little exhaust in top gear, we sped noiselessly over the dust-cushioned road, five destructive shadows creeping up on an unsuspecting outpost. I visualized the German machine-gunners peering down the moonlit road towards Castel Raimondo and smiled grimly to myself. . . .

The first buildings of Matelica came in sight, a bungalow in its own garden . . . taller buildings . . . a row of cottages . . . a shop. . . .

We entered the main street.

I felt my hands sweating and slowed to a crawl . . . tall buildings on either side . . . dark shadows on the pavements . . . shining glass windows, reflecting the moon . . . single trees. . . .

The street was dead. Nothing moved. I felt my heart pounding.

Five hundred yards to the road-junction . . . 400 yards . . .

300 yards. . . . 'Left-hand side, George,' I whispered. . . . 'Not yet . . . hold it . . . hold it. . . .' And then I saw the armoured car standing close to the wall of the corner building and my stomach turned over.

An armoured car! I hadn't bargained for this. Thank God its guns would be trained in the opposite direction. I looked quickly at George Sonley. He felt my eyes on him and nodded without looking up. He had seen the armoured car, too, and had his gun trained on it.

Fear suddenly left me and my brain was icy cold. I lifted my foot from the accelerator and let the jeep slow almost to a stop . . . the dark bulk of the armoured car against the wall . . . the empty, moonlit road-junction beyond it . . . safety round the right-hand corner. . . . How bizarre to be sitting in a jeep in the middle of the main street of a moonlit Italian village with a German armoured car fifty yards in front . . . creeping up on it all unsuspecting . . . like coming up behind someone in the street and slapping him on the back. The situation seemed ridiculously funny and I started to titter. . . .

'O.K., George,' I heard a strange voice say.

Brrrrrrrrrt. The jeep shuddered and bounced. Tracer streaked into the armoured car and flashed off its armoured flanks in scarlet fireworks. Streamers of scarlet flashed past us as the following jeeps opened up. Brrrrrrrt . . . Brrrrrrrrt . . . Brrrrrrrrt. Smoke, the tang of cordite, assailed our nostrils and our ears buzzed with the deafening clatter which filled the street. . . .

Brrrrrt . . . Brrrrrrt . . . Brrrrrt. A steady stream of bullets smacked into the armoured car which didn't fire back, but suddenly jerked forward and disappeared round the corner of the building to the *left*.

'Charge!' I yelled when I saw it move, snicked into low gear and revved. . . .

We plastered the corner house with bursts from both guns, pouring a flood of stabbing, searing bullets through splintering windows and doors . . . swung sharply *right* . . . crashed into second gear and raced up the Esanatoglia road . . . braked and looked back. . . .

Tracer whammed into the corner building, ricocheted off the walls and sprayed across the moonlit road-junction. A minute later a dark object careened round the corner and raced towards us.

'Just the job, Skipper,' chortled Ben Owen as he drew up alongside.

We watched the corner.

Curving streamers of scarlet light darting across the road-junction, like blood-red water pouring from a hose . . . the screech of brakes . . . another dark object tearing towards us. . . .

More tracer pouring across the road-junction . . . another dark object racing up the Esanatoglia road. . . .

D-r-r-r-r-r-r-r-t . . . D-r-r-r-r-r-r-r-t. The staccato rattle of a different calibre gun came to our ears from the direction of the main street . . . gears crashed . . . a jeep engine revved in low gear . . . a jeep skidded round the corner . . . raced towards us spewing out smoke like a spiralling Messerschmitt wounded in combat.

'What the hell . . . ?' I muttered, and began to laugh, remembering Bari and thinking Riches had inadvertently pressed the button of his smoke-discharger. Riches drew level with me, filling the road with smoke.

'Quick, Skipper!' he gasped. 'There's an armoured car on our tail!'

'What?'

At first I thought he was joking, but soon realized he was serious.

'Crept up behind us in the main street' . . . gasp . . . 'Gigi saw it just in time.'

Above the swooshing sound of Riches' smoke-discharger we heard the steady D-r-r-r-r-r-t . . . D-r-r-r-r-r-r-r-t of a machine-gun firing in Matelica—a stationary armoured car firing blindly into the clouds of smoke which filled the main street. Instead of returning our fire the armoured car had appeared to run away, doubled up a side street, regained the main road *behind* us and crept on to our tail—a clever manœuvre which would have wiped out at least one jeep crew had it not been for Gigi's quick eye, Riches' presence of mind and Popski's novel invention.

Protected by Riches' smoke-screen, we listened to the noises in Matelica, the pointless D-r-r-r-r-r-r-t . . . D-r-r-r-r-r-r-t of the machine-gun firing at nothing . . . the grating of gears when the firing eventually stopped . . . the sound of an exhaust going towards Fabriano. . . .

Riches' smoke-discharger died out with a throaty hiss and the road began to clear.

I shook Gigi's hand.

'*Bravo*, Gigi. *Grazia.*'

Gigi was pleased, but modest as became a man of his character.

'*Niente, Capitano*,' he said, making little of it.

The patrol crowded round him, pumping his hand, slapping him on the back, congratulating him. Gigi had proved himself in his first action and became one of us.

A deathly silence enveloped Matelica. Eddies of smoke rose above the main street and drifted over the roof-tops towards the moon, like the wraiths of departed men.

Riches chuckled reminiscently and started to hum 'Torno Sorrento'.

'Home, boys,' I called.

Five jeeps raced up the moonlit ribbon of road towards Esanatoglia. . . . Esanatoglia slumbered. We snarled under the ancient sandstone arch and rattled over the cobbles, our exhausts echoing hollowly in the deserted piazza. At the witching hour, all good Esanatoglians were in bed. A shame to wake them, I thought, wheeled, circled the piazza and led out of the sleeping village.

We found a convenient vineyard on the hillside and leaguered for the night. As I wriggled into my sleeping-bag and drifted off to sleep, well pleased with the night's work, I heard Riches chortle from afar:

'Put down smoke!'

17

A SWITCHBACK road led upwards from Esanatoglia to a ruined monastery on the top of a hill.

'That's the place for H.Q., Rich.'

From our leaguer in the vineyard I examined the tumbled buildings in the penetrating light of the morning sun.

'Come on,' I said, lowering the glasses, 'let's go and have a shufty.'

We snaked up the tortuous road and emerged upon a green plateau 2000 feet above sea-level. The whole valley was exposed to us like a colour photograph, the white ribbon of road coming in from Castel Raimondo disappearing between the red-tiled roof-tops of Matelica, reappearing beyond the village and running on towards Fabriano hidden behind the rounded green hills enclosing the top of the valley; the dark green patches of forest on the mountainside, the lighter green vineyards on the lower slopes, the squares of yellow grain in the valley, the white- and pink-walled farmsteads dotted about, the ragged line of the escarpment abruptly severing the azure sky.

I entered the crumbling monastery and walked through pillared cloisters hoary with age and creepered by encroaching Nature. Following closely behind me in their iron-heeled boots the patrolmen rang hollow echoes from the damp, moss-grown flagstones worn smooth by the daily tread of habited monks telling their rosaries. One wing of the building was in good repair, the roof intact and the floor dry. A door opened on to a pergola-ed terrace overlooking the valley and ten yards from the terrace a spring of purest water bubbled up through a faucet of vivid green moss.

'Ideal, Rich,' I said. 'Move in.'

The patrolmen selected their sleeping places, dispersed their jeeps and brought in their kits. They set primus stoves roaring on the terrace and soon the mouth-watering aroma of frying bacon and eggs wafted through the monastery, disturbing the guardian spirits of vegetarian monks. Toddy Sloan slung his aerial to the cross-bars of the pergola, opened the deceptive suitcase and tapped out his call-sign to the Back-room Boys in distant San Gregorio. With black headphones framing his sun-burned, boyish face and a V of twisted flex dangling from his ears like a doctor's stethoscope, he looked strangely out of place in those cloistered surroundings.

While breakfast was cooking I studied the map and roughed-out a plan of campaign. The valley was ours. The enclosing hills at the Fabriano end were dominated by mortar and machine-gun fire. Fabriano itself was occupied by a strong German garrison. From Fabriano the German front line followed the Esino Valley eastwards to the Adriatic and westwards through the hills north of Perugia to Leghorn on the Tyrrhenian. As allied pressure increased on the flank, the enemy divisions would fall back to prepared positions in the mountains north of Florence. I was pessimistic now about our chances of slipping behind the lines—the hills were too well guarded—and for the time being I thought the best thing was to simulate the story I had told Olga and lead the German commander in Fabriano to think he was opposed by a much stronger force than was actually the case.

Sitting in the warm sunshine on the terrace I pictured Olga in a villa near Fabriano reclining seductively on a cushioned settee, smoking a cigarette in a long ivory holder, appraising a monocled, jack-booted Prussian officer with her calculating, ice-blue eyes. Her bright red skirt revealed just enough knee to be disturbing and the top button of her blouse was invitingly undone. A clever girl, Olga, I thought, and hoped she'd come to a sticky end.

Enjoying a leisurely breakfast, we washed and shaved, those of us who didn't grow beards, and set forth to deceive the Hun.

With nothing in our jeeps but machine-guns, belts of ammunition, hand-grenades and small arms we back-fired down the switchback and roared towards Fabriano, raising as much dust as possible. Farm tracks wide enough for jeeps criss-crossed the valley and we spent the day dust-raising on a five-mile stretch beginning at Matelica and terminating half-way to Fabriano. To the enemy observer in the hills, it must have appeared that a whole Allied division was advancing up the valley, preparing to attack.

We drove through bullet-holed Matelica, apologized to its worried *podesta* for making so much mess, de-mined the Castel Raimondo road and returned to Esanatoglia in time for evening *pasta* thoughtfully arranged by Gino.

After *pasta* and wine, replete and mellow, an hour of faultless, heart-lifting pianoforte music played by a Polish jewess refugee (from the neck up, the ugliest I ever saw) put us in excellent fettle for manœuvres and at ten o'clock, instead of going to bed like good Esanatoglians, we drove towards Fabriano in our jeeps and tore up and down the lateral tracks from one vantage point to another flaying the moonlit enemy slopes with whistling scarlet darts. At intervals, Very flares tumbled through the sky, spilling starlets of coloured light, 'Just like bloody Guy Fawkes,' as J. C. aptly remarked.

We played at the exhausting game until dawn, then soft-pedalling, yawning, up the hill to our cloistered eyrie, wirelessed a sitrep to Jan and lay down thankfully on our sleeping-bags. . .

The piazza was packed. Standing on the flat bonnets of our jeeps, looking over the heads of an excited crowd, we had a ring-side *première* of partisan justice. In the centre of a circle formed by the watching populace two terrified girls were bound to chairs on a platform made of planks. Trussed hand and foot, unable to move, the girls sat stiffly upright with their long, glossy black tresses hanging down the backs of the chairs, almost touching the platform. The local barber stood behind them, brandishing the tools of his trade—a pair of sharp scissors and a pair of close-clippers.

'What have they done?' I asked of Gino, who was talking to a man in the crowd.

'*Collaboratori, Capitano.* They slept with German officers.'

'One costly night of love,' I thought, and watched the developing drama.

The barber, a broad-shouldered, bull-necked man with a florid face and black hair showing at his open shirt front, grasped the tresses of one of the girls and held them aloft in a podgy hand. A roar of applause burst from the throats of the watching crowd. A shudder ran through the bodies of the imprisoned girls. The

271

barber brandished his scissors and jerked the gleaming black tresses, hurting the poor girl's scalp and causing her to bite her lip in pain. Opening his scissors the barber paused dramatically and waited for the jury's final decision before enacting sentence.

'*Si!*' the jury yelled unequivocally. '*Si . . . si . . . si . . . si.*'

The sibilated 'Yes' rose from the ringed piazza like the hiss of escaping steam.

The barber's scissors flashed in the sun and clicked viciously. He cut close to the nape of the neck . . . held up a fistful of hair like a Red Indian waving a scalp. Tears coursed down the shorn girl's cheeks.

'*Bravo!*' roared the jury. '*Bravo . . . bravo . . . bravo.*'

The barber seized the other girl's locks, tugging roughly, and cut. . . .

'*Bravo . . . bravo . . . bravo.*'

The girls hung their heads and sobbed. The barber took up clippers, paused once again for the jury's decision. It came unfalteringly as before, in a loud hissing.

'*Si . . . si . . . si . . . si.*'

The barber bent to his awful task . . . from the nape of the neck . . . clip . . . clip . . . clip . . . over the crown to the forehead . . . clip . . . clip . . . clip. Black hair fell to the platform like autumn leaves . . . clip . . . clip . . . clip . . . until both heads were shorn as bald as coots.

'*Bravo! . . . bravo! . . . bravo!*' The jury bawled its approval.

Their agony over, branded like convicts for all to see, the heartbroken girls were released. They stood for a moment wild-eyed, like cornered animals searching the unrelenting multitude, plucked up courage, jumped from the platform and dashed across the cobbles. The throng opened to let them through, pushing and jeering at them as they ran, sobbing, to their homes. . . .

The crowd dispersed, rumbling comments, like the sound of approaching rain. The barber returned to his shop. Four stalwart *contadini* dismantled and removed the platform. The piazza reverted to normal and Esanatoglia sat down to lunch.

Too many for one table, we repaired to different households in parties of two or three and reassembled later at the jeeps.

Gino, George Sonley and I sat down to *pasta* in the house where the refugee musician lived and the meal was served. A woman with a well-developed bust and a bandanna tied round her head sat next to me, saying little. Her eyes were red-rimmed from crying and there emanated from her personality a desperate unhappiness. A refugee bottling up some private misery, I thought, and turned to speak to her, thinking to divert her thoughts.

'How awful,' I remarked, 'to be a woman and have your hair cut off. It must take years to grow.'

With a quick movement of the hand she whipped off the bandanna. Her head was close-cropped, bald as a coot.

We drove towards Fabriano in the afternoon, turned into our private runway to begin another dust-raising campaign and surprised a German patrol come to test our strength. The patrol heard us coming and lay in wait round a bend, but they weren't quick enough.

I felt my hackles rise as I approached the bend. 'Careful,' my sixth sense warned, 'there's danger ahead.'

Sniffing the air like a jungle animal I crawled gingerly round the bend—to glimpse a helmeted head pull quickly back behind a clump of bushes.

'Look out,' I shouted and braked violently, 'those bushes, George!'

An angry stream of tracer threshed into the bushes, eliciting a sharp yelp of pain and the noise of running feet. Bullets whined past my ear as Gino fired his Tommy-gun. Brrrrrrrrt . . . brrrrrrrrrrrt . . . brrrrrrrrt. George Sonley poured a devastating fire into the clump of bushes, swinging his gun from side to side, spraying tracer in a wide area. . . .

Wheeeeeeeeee . . . wruuuuuuuuuuumph! A mortar bomb exploded on the track, narrowly missing Ben Owen's jeep.

'Back,' I yelled frantically, 'ambush. Pull out. Quick!'

Brrrrrrrt . . . brrrrrrrt . . . brrrrrrrrt. Firing blindly, spraying to protect our flank, we reversed out of the trap. Wheeeeeeeeeeee . . . wruuuuuuuuuumph . . . wruuuuuuuuuumph . . . wruuuuuuumph. A barrage of mortar bombs pursued our wake. . . .

'That was a narrow squeak, George,' I observed when we were out of danger. 'The old sixth sense saved us that time.'

It saved us again the very next day.

Returning from patrol the following morning I was thinking about Olga—not of her sexual charms, but of her mental processes. Where was Olga and what was she doing? Her cottage remained empty. I was uneasy and cursed myself for being a fool. Instead of playing Olga's game I should have clapped both her and her companion into gaol. It was too late now, and the enemy had called my bluff.

Approaching Esanatoglia, I had a premonition of impending danger, a strong urge to pack up and leave the valley. I drew up before the mellowed sandstone arch and tried to persuade myself I was just being 'windy', but the feeling persisted. I'd had premonitions before, but never so emphatic, so impelling as this. It was insistent, like an all-wise, trusted friend tugging at my elbow, imploring me to go.

Experience had taught me to heed premonition. I signalled for Riches to come alongside.

'Up to the monastery, Rich,' I said. 'Pack up. We're leaving.'

He looked at me incredulously.

'What? . . . Why, Skipper?'

'I've got a hunch.'

'But *pasta* will be ready, Skipper. Can't we———?'

I cut him short.

'Don't argue, Rich. We're leaving. Up to the monastery, quick.'

Riches shrugged and passed on the order.

We wheeled about and raced up the switchback to the monastery. Impatient to be off, I strode up and down the terrace, pulling at cigarettes, urging the men to hurry. 'Ready, Rich?' I kept asking.

The patrolmen thought I'd gone round the bend. 'What's got into the Skipper?' I heard J. C. ask. . . .

'Ready, Skipper,' Riches reported at last.

Self-starters rasped and engines revved, echoing through the creepered ruins. Five jeeps hurtled downhill to Esanatoglia. . . .

I drew up in the piazza and went into a house to speak to Gino. He had developed a raging malarial fever the previous evening and wasn't in a fit condition to travel. I would have to leave him behind.

He was lying in bed, propped upon pillows, being competently nursed by a pretty signorina. The fever had broken, leaving him limp, but he would be all right in a day or two. I signed to the girl to leave the room.

'We're leaving, Gino,' I told him when we were alone. 'I've a feeling something's going to happen. Lie here quietly until you're

274

better and join us over the ridge. We're only going to Gualdo. Rich has got your kit.'

'*Va bene, Capitano.*'

Gino was quite unperturbed and I wasn't worried about leaving him. He was already on the mend, he would be well looked after and would find his own way to Gualdo in a day or two.

Why Gualdo? Every time I looked at the map, at least ten times a day, the curious name 'Gualdo Tadino' caught my eye. It was a black dot near a red line connecting Foligno with Fabriano. The name intrigued me and I knew I'd go there one day. Gualdo was on the other side of the high western ridge and no road led to it from Esanatoglia, but by following sheep-tracks over the mountain I thought we'd be able to reach it.

We left Esanatoglia by the back door, ostensibly on patrol, telling no one our destination. For an hour the going was easy. We struck a well-defined sheep-track which led in the right direction, but beyond a tree-girt farmhouse at the top of a valley the track narrowed and became very precipitous.

Engaging lowest booster gear I drove carefully up the hazardous pathway, hugging the inside of the track where it sloped outwards and canted the jeep at a fearsome angle. There was a sheer drop on one side, a steep grassy slope tumbling down to a rushing torrent. I crawled up the worst section of the track with George Sonley and Gigi leaning inwards like side-car passengers cornering in a motor-cycle race, halted on the top of the rise and waved to the others to come up.

Ben Owen came up safely and passed me, and I was standing by the side of the stony track warning Danny O'Neil not to drive so close to the edge when I saw the accident happen. O'Neil's offside rear wheel hit a loose stone and bounced off, causing the tail of his jeep to swing. One wheel slipped over the edge, Danny tried desperately to correct the fault, but before I could even cry out the jeep toppled over and fell down the slope, turning over and over. Sloan was thrown clear and escaped injury, but O'Neil was badly hurt. The jeep landed on top of him, pinning him down and crushing his kidneys.

We rushed to his aid, pulled the jeep off him and righted it. Danny's face was ashen and he groaned pitifully, catching his breath and muttering incoherently, 'Sorry . . . Skipper. . . . Sorry . . . Skipper. . . . Sorry, Skipper.'

275

His injuries were internal and there was no first-aid we could administer. If he were to live we must get him to hospital.

'Will the jeep run?' I asked Riches.

While I sat with my fingers on O'Neil's pulse and told him not to worry, the others man-handled his jeep on to the lower part of the track and drove it a little way.

'The steering's a bit wobbly, Skipper, but ,it runs,' Riches reported.

'Right!' I decided. 'Mee and Williamson will transfer to Danny's jeep and drive him to the nearest military hospital.'

Lancers were in Camerino and would have access to a field ambulance. There had been no rain for days and crossing the Potenza should present no difficulty. After delivering their patient, Mee and Williamson would drive to San Gregorio and return with a replacement jeep.

Gigi hurried to the farmhouse at the top of the valley and returned with an obliging *contadino* carrying a couple of wooden planks. We gave O'Neil an injection of morphia, laid him on the planks and strapped him to the jeep, and Mee and Williamson set off on their errand of mercy. (They reached Camerino that evening, transferred O'Neil to a field ambulance, and were in San Gregorio the following night. O'Neil recovered and served with P.P.A. until the end of the war.)

I rearranged the crews and continued with four jeeps—Sonley and self; Ben Owen and J. C.; Don Galloway and Sloan; Riches and Gigi. Sloan was none the worse for the harrowing experience and his nerve was unimpaired.

All afternoon we laboured uphill in the sweltering sun, widening the track, cutting sandstone banks with machetes, digging out boulders, pulling and pushing and heaving. Agonizingly slowly we ascended the mountainside . . . and reached the final rise, a bottle-neck of scree between the harsh lips of a gully which cleaved the black rocks of the escarpment . . . loose gravel spun under our wheels . . . we hung precariously between heaven and earth . . . clawing desperately at the treacherous surface with screaming tyres . . . bonnet almost perpendicular . . . engine pinking . . . all but stalling . . . a final skid . . . a jolt . . . a jerk . . . a sideways lurch . . . and we were up and over the escarpment . . . driving bumpily on the roof-top of Italy in the glow of the setting sun with a cool, clean wind blowing in our hot faces.

276

The plateau was freshly green. Mild-eyed sheep grazed the succulent grass and baaa-ed at our approach. In a saucer of brighter green, like a mirror carelessly flung down, a silver tarn reflected the flaming banners of the evening sky and . . . We couldn't believe our eyes. No, it couldn't be, not handed to us on a plate! But it was.

'Do you see what I see, George?' I burbled to Sonley.

'I do, Skipper,' happily.

George cocked the swaying fifty and I turned to catch Ben Owen's eye, pointing excitedly towards the lake. Ben Owen had seen them, and grinned.

Nude bodies bathed by the lake-side, male bodies, German bodies.

Brrrrrrrrt . . . brrrrrrrt . . . brrrrrrrrt. Scarlet tracer leapt ahead of our jolting passage and curved into the rippling water. Hoarse cries rose from German throats . . . naked bodies splashed wildly out of the lake . . . bent to retrieve bundles of clothing . . . dashed helter-skelter across the greensward without pausing to dress. . . .

Never did German infantry run so fast. Roaring with laughter —which upset our aim—we watched the nudist colony skip, hop and jump across the plateau, tall ones and short ones, fat ones and thin ones, red ones and white ones, all jostling, bumping and tripping, stubbing toes, straining desperately to get out of the path of our searing bullets.

George Sonley's nose was close to the breech of his bouncing fifty and his tracer fell wide of the target.

'Slow down, Skipper,' he pleaded. 'Let me get a bead on the bastards.'

I lifted my foot from the accelerator, but the jeep continued to bucket on the uneven grass and the range was extreme.

'No use, George. Let me get closer.'

I snicked into lower gear and revved. The jeep stotted over the springy turf and the guns clattered and banged in their sockets. Thirty yards to my right Ben Owen ran into stones and had to slow down.

'This way, Ben,' I shouted.

I swerved in a wide left-hand sweep to avoid the stony patch. The other jeeps followed and we reached the lakeside a few minutes later shaking with mirth. The nudist colony had gained an outcrop of rocks and its members were darting and skipping amongst them like a herd of nimble goats.

We jumped from our seats, swung the guns and fired from the stationary jeeps. Brrrrrrrt . . . brrrrrrrrt . . . brrrrrrrrt. The nudist colony hopped and jumped behind the rocks. . . . 'Bloody fat arse' . . . brrrrrrrrt . . . 'winged the bastard, I think' . . . brrrr-rrrrt. . . .

Our tracer flashed amongst the rocks and we watched the bodies disappear over the edge of the escarpment. I doubt if we hit any. But it didn't matter. We'd caught the enemy on the hop, literally with his trousers down, and given him the fright of his life. That was what pleased us most, not killing or maiming the enemy, but twisting his tail, taking him by surprise and throwing him into a panic.

I pictured an unimaginative *feldwebel* marching his platoon to the lake on bathing parade . . . undressing them by numbers . . . goose-stepping them into the water . . . thinking of the Black Forest at home . . . looking up in amazement to see our jeeps bearing down. Armed jeeps on a mountain top at sunset. It was against all the rules and regulations!

Riches spotted a steel helmet left behind in the rush and stuck it on his jeep as a souvenir. Don Galloway found a leather belt. The sun was sinking, spreading red streamers in the sky. The wind died and shadows crept out from their hiding-places in the rocks. A great hush settled over the plateau.

'We want to be off the hill before dark,' I said. 'Let's get jeeping.'

Bumping round the shore of the lake, we picked up the sheep-track and jogged happily downhill in the red glare of the sinking sun, chortling over the German discomfiture. Gigi sat next to Riches, holding the swinging fifty, a blissful smile illumining his cheerful face. His cup was full. Riches said something to him. Two heads went back, two throats opened wide and the strains of 'Torno Sorrento' burst upon the unsuspecting mountainside.

Dusk fell as we reached the outskirts of Gualdo Tadino and drove into a crowded piazza, heralded by a group of partisans.

'*Inglesi! Inglesi! Viva! Viva!*'

'*Dove tedeschi?*' we asked.

'*Niente tedeschi . . . tedeschi scapati . . . va via . . .*' came from a hundred throats.

In their rapid retreat from Foligno the Germans had by-passed Gualdo, blowing only the bridge on the main road south of the town. Partially uniformed figures moved about in the crowd, men and youths carrying rifles with *bomba-manos* (Italian grenades) slung at their belts. One of the men, a tall, square-shouldered, handsome fellow, approached my jeep and introduced himself as *capo partigani*, leader of the partisans. 'This,' I thought, 'is where I get organized.'

'Gigi.'

'*Capitano?*'

Gigi stood beside my jeep.

'Tell the *capo* I command all troops in the area,' I said. 'He is to place himself and his men at my disposal. He will immediately put a strong guard round the town to give warning of enemy approach. I will inspect the guard sometime during the night and any sentry found asleep at his post will be shot at dawn. Translate.'

Gigi, an ex-Italian army officer, rose to the occasion and translated what I had said into flamboyant, awe-inspiring, Italian military language. The *capo* sprang to attention, sibilated '*Si, Commandante*' after every sentence and waited expectantly when Gigi had finished. . . .

'I want the pick of accommodation for my men,' I continued. 'Tell him to requisition the best hotel and see that we get the best food and wine. Tell him we are the Armata Privata di Popski and expect nothing less than perfection.'

Gigi translated in flowery language . . . the *capo* stiffened at attention. . . . '*Si, Commandante*' . . . '*Si, Commandante.*' . . . Gigi issued my final command with a dramatic gesture towards the jeeps. The *capo* drew himself up to his full height (towering above the medium-sized Gigi), saluted dramatically, barked an order to his men and strode importantly through the crowd.

Wine was brought and gurgled musically into clinking glasses. '*Salute . . . salute.*'

A thought occurred to me.

'Gigi.'

'*Capitano?*'

'Ask if any other allied troops have been seen in the area.'

279

Gigi put the question. A dozen voices quick-fired the reply.

'*Niente, Capitano.*'

I breathed a sigh of relief. We were still in virgin territory.

The *capo* was efficient and took his duties seriously as behove one wishing to impress. Within the hour we were all comfortably installed in the local pub with everything laid on, including a private, walled-in, cobbled courtyard for the jeeps, with a sentry at the gate.

Baths . . . drinks on the house . . . an enormous dinner of *pasta* . . . music . . . songs . . . yawns . . . bed.

I dreamt of Olga. She had found where we'd gone and was sitting in the German commander's villa, telling him. The monocled Prussian rang a bell and an aide appeared. Orders were given and the aide withdrew with upraised hand '*Heil Hitler*'. The Nazi commander crossed the room and stood by Olga, fondling her pretty neck. 'Jewels and pretty clothes for Olga when the English patrol are caught,' he flattered. Olga looked up and her calculating, ice-blue eyes fell before eyes harder and more calculating than her own. . . . Gualdo was surrounded . . . a Spandau fired close at hand . . . rat-a-tat-tat. . . .

I woke up sweating and leapt out of bed. Someone was knocking on my bedroom door. I opened. It was the *capo* come to escort me on a tour of guard inspection! I cursed him inaudibly and went.

The days we spent in Gualdo were our happiest of the war. The German front line—a lateral extension of the Fabriano front —was five miles up the main road. South of Gualdo, all the bridges were blown between Nocera and Foligno so that we were completely isolated in a green and fertile valley, miles from our nearest troops.

Like the *condottieri* of old we sallied forth at dawn to do battle with the enemy and withdrew within the safety of our city walls at dusk—to hot baths, *pasta*, wine, good music, good company and comfortable beds.

Our day began at crack of dawn when tea was brought to our rooms. We gulped it and rose immediately, pulled on clothes and thumped downstairs to the waiting jeeps, crouched on the damp cobbles like greyhounds straining at the leash.

' 'Morning, Skipper.'

' 'Morning, Rich. Bowels moved?'

'Morning, Skipper.'

' 'Morning, George. Sleep well?'

' 'Morning, Skipper.'

' 'Morning, Ben. Everything under control?'

I went from jeep to jeep checking that all was well. Gun covers were whipped off, self-starters whined and we sat in the crisp light of the welling dawn waiting for engines to warm.

'O.K., Rich?'

'O.K., Skipper. Take 'er away.'

Engines revved noisily, reverberating round the walls. The partisan guard flung open the heavy wooden gates and stood stiffly to attention as the four jeeps clattered over the uneven cobbles and thundered into the street. . . .

Accelerating hard in second gear we hurtled through the narrow lanes rudely awakening the sleeping town with the hammer of our exhausts, turned sharply right at the city gate and zoomed up the tarmac to the front. The cold dawn wind swept over us like a shower-bath, plucking at tousled hair and sleep-encrusted eyelids, snatching from the rear jeep the swelling notes of Riches' 'Torno Sorrento'.

Having driven the enemy out of Fossato-on-the-hill (our nudist colony came from there) we now kept hammering at the line of mortar and machine-gun posts dug-in on the forward slopes of the hills rolling westwards from Fabriano.

Leaving Fossato on our eastern flank, we zigzagged up to the top of a rise bathed in the morning sun, past vineyards hung with gleaming pearls and grass ablaze with shining light, heavy with the humus smell of dew-soaked, drying earth.

On the hill-top, set back a little from the road, a red-tiled campanile belled its welcome to the day—ding . . . dong . . . ding . . . dong . . . ding . . . dong—sweet, trilling cadences which rippled through the golden air like wavelets on the surface of a mountain tarn.

'Whose turn is it, Rich?'

'Gal and Toddy, Skipper.'

We took it in turns to confirm, daily, that the enemy was still there, for nothing is more stupid than to continue firing into positions which the enemy has vacated during the night. 'Matins', the game was called, and consisted of driving into full view of the enemy, drawing his fire (if a man fires at you, you can confidently report that he is actually there) and withdrawing without getting hit. The top scorer was the jeep crew which remained longest under fire.

Don Galloway grimaced and swallowed hard, simulating a terror he didn't feel. A quiet smile played round Toddy's mouth.

'*Avanti*, Gal,' I called.

Their jeep swung out and revved over the rise. . . . We cupped hands to ears and listened. . . .

Wheeeeeeeeeeee . . . wruuuuuuuuumph . . . wruuuuuuuu-umph . . . wruuuuuuuuuph.

A laugh went up when three mortar bombs crashed on the hillside and the tail of a jeep reversed quickly over the rise. . . .

'Windy!' we cried derisively when the jeep came alongside.

'Windy be damned, Skipper,' said a breathless Galloway. 'That was bloody close!'

More laughter and derisive remarks from all except the thoughtful Ben Owen who had been sitting quietly, listening to the bells, adding two and two together and making five.

'Skipper.'

'Yes, Ben?'

'That bloody bell rings every time we leave Gualdo and every time we show ourselves on the hill down comes the stonk.'

There are *campanili* on hill-tops all over Italy and bells were constantly ringing so that I hadn't connected the two, but I caught Ben's meaning.

'O.K., Ben. We'll go up and investigate.'

Wheeling hard about, we drove to the little chapel on the top of the hill. The bells stopped ringing as we drew nigh. A black-frocked priest walked out of a side-door, piously crossed himself, and made to hurry away.

'*Momento*,' I called and signed to him to come back.

Reluctantly, the priest turned and walked hesitantly towards the jeeps.

'Hang on to him, Rich,' I said. 'Ben and I'll take a look at the tower.'

Riches waggled a Colt forty-five and said rudely, 'Sit down, cock.'

The priest crossed himself fervently and sat, pulling at his skirt like a woman.

Ben and I climbed to the top of the bell-tower, which com-manded an uninterrupted view of the country on both sides of the ridge. Looking north, our eyes rested upon the forward slopes occupied by the enemy. To the south we had a clear view of the road issuing from Gualdo Tadino. Anyone standing on the bell-tower would see the jeeps as soon as they turned into the main road.

I looked at Ben Owen.

'What do you think, Ben?'

'Too easy, Skipper.'

I nodded. 'Let's talk to the priest, Ben.'

We rattled down the stairs and returned to the jeeps.

The priest was sitting on the grass, telling his beads. I looked hard at him and didn't like the way he avoided my eyes. I suggested there might be a connection between mortar-bombing and bell-ringing, but the idea seemed to shock the holy man. He appeared nervous, however, and didn't sound very convincing. 'We'll put it to the test,' I thought.

'Take him aboard, Rich,' I said. 'We'll take this bird back to Gualdo.'

We bundled the fat, well-fed priest on to the back of Riches' jeep where he sat uncomfortably on the load, his black habit whipped by the wind, revealing flabby white calves which contrasted oddly with his brick-red face. His lips moved soundlessly as in prayer.

'You may well pray,' I thought, as we took the road to Gualdo.

Arrived in the piazza, I sent for the *capo* and gave the priest into his charge.

'Lock him up and guard him well,' I said through Gigi. 'Put him on bread and water.'

'*Si, Commandante.*'

Eager hands grabbed the priest and unceremoniously clapped him into gaol.

A satisfactory day was spent firing into the German positions from vantage points along a five-mile lateral stretch of ridge and we returned to our comfortable hotel in the evening like country gentlemen returning from a pheasant-shoot.

'Good life this, eh, George?' I remarked as we drove past a saluting sentry into the cobbled courtyard.

'Skipper,' said George fervently, 'I could live like this for ever.'

Next morning when we drove towards the front no bells rang from the campanile and no mortar bombs greeted us when we showed ourselves over the rise. It may have been coincidence, but only his cloth saved that priest's life.

Two days later, Gino joined us. He told me a staggering tale. At one o'clock in the morning, a bare twelve hours after we'd left, a strong German infantry force came over the hills from Fabriano and surrounded the monastery. Enraged to find us gone they descended upon innocent Esanatoglia and vented their spleen upon it. Gino escaped by the skin of his teeth, disguised as a village idiot.

My blood ran hot and cold as I listened to Gino's tale. What a disgrace if I'd been caught napping in the monastery with half the patrol down in the village, drinking wine! At best, we couldn't have escaped without heavy casualties and even if I, personally, had come out alive the disgrace would have well-nigh killed me; to be caught napping by the Hun was the unforgivable sin in P.P.A. Olga, my love, I promised myself as I listened to Gino recounting how he'd been wakened by the sound of rifle-fire in the piazza, if ever we meet again I'll wring your pretty neck; for there wasn't the slightest doubt in my mind that Olga was at the back of it. Emblazoned by Gino, the story of our narrow escape served only to increase my men's faith in their patrol commander. Knowing how nearly both men and faith had been destroyed, their patrol commander was humble.

What is this sixth sense, this mysterious telepathic communication which warns men of impending danger? Animal instinct, subconscious activity, Universal God-mind? Whatever it is, it saved our lives on so many occasions that we came to rely implicitly upon it, as a fog-bound ship relies upon its radar, for it is a form of radar, a human form of radar, more sensitive than any radionic instrument devised by man.

It was a faculty we found we could develop and the more we consciously developed it, the more powerful and reliable it became until literally we could all 'smell' danger a mile away and knew, long before we bumped into them on patrol, where German mines and mortars and machine-guns were. 'Sixth Sensing' eventually took precedence over all other forms of patrol training—our very lives depended on it—and some members of the patrol, Ben Owen and Don Galloway particularly, developed the faculty to a very high degree.

A sixth-sense awareness became the intangible but essential qualification I looked for in patrolmen, and my stubborn refusal to accept the otherwise first-class recruits Popski sent me from time to time used to infuriate him. 'But what's wrong with him, Bob?' Popski would ask irascibly when I'd rejected a new patrolman after watching his (negative) reactions on 'Matins'. 'Nothing, Popski,' I'd reply, 'except that he can't sense danger. He's a liability to me, not an asset,' which invariably drew from an exasperated Popski, 'You're impossible, Bob.'

Maybe I was impossible, but it paid me. I came right through the war without a scratch and the recorded fact remains (P.P.A. War Diary) that although 'B' Patrol was more continuously engaged than any of the others, we had the smallest number of casualties; and as we came safely through action after action a legend grew up around us; 'Lucky "B" Patrol' we were called, and had a long waiting list. Luck had little to do with it. It was our highly developed sixth sense which kept us alive and only Jan Caneri, I think, really understood how our minds worked.

Jan Caneri and I were in constant telepathic communication during the war—people in mental harmony always are—and it saved us a deal of signals and correspondence. Sitting in a vineyard or on a mountain top in the Apennines, I would find myself in need of some patrol requisite, a new tyre, a new tube or some spare part for a jeep. I would 'wish the thought' to Jan Caneri 300 miles away and sure enough, on the next supply truck from base, there would be the very thing I wanted. From time to time, when we met, we held post mortems. 'How did you know I wanted so and so, Jan?' I'd ask. 'Don't know, Bob. I just felt you wanted it,' and checking up on times we invariably found that Jan had had the feeling round the time I'd sent him the thought-form.

Don't ask me to explain this strange phenomena. I can't—unless it be that all minds in the universe are but the different expressions of one Universal Mind and the human brain a delicately tuned receiving and transmitting station able to communicate directly with other human wireless stations tuned in to the same wave-length. This explains telepathy, but it doesn't altogether explain premonition. I can't explain the sixth sense. I only know it works.

The happy days at Gualdo passed all too quickly. Toddy Sloan handed me a cypher one morning. It was from Popski and read. 'Joining you Gualdo seventeen hundred hours.' Groans all round. Not that Popski was unpopular. It was just that we preferred to be on our own.

285

18

Popski and his men rode over the hills from Cingoli, and a squadron of Lancers, forcing a devious way round the blown bridges between Foligno and Nocera, debouched into the valley. We joined forces and closed in on Fabriano from the flank.

The main road into the town wound over a steep hill and the German sappers had dynamited the steepest mile, collapsing a part of the hillside, but there was a railway tunnel under the hill blocked by the twisted remains of a dozen blown-up goods trucks.

'We'll soon shift that, Popski,' said 'S' Patrol's Lieutenant Reeve-Walker confidently. 'Give me an oxy-acetylene welding plant and I'll clear the tunnel in no time.'

South African mining-engineer Reeve-Walker tooth-combed the valley for a welding set and found one in a garage in Nocera. He came haring back brandishing his prize. 'Got one, Popski,' he exclaimed jubilantly. 'Now we shan't be long.'

Donning welder's goggles which rendered him grotesque in the glare of his jeep headlamps, Reeve-Walker started work immediately, flame-sawing the mangled trucks into pieces small enough for his jeeps to drag out of the tunnel. Ably assisted by The Heavenly Twins—who had distinguished themselves in an action near Cingoli—he worked all through the night and by dawn a major portion of the debris had been cleared. Working in shifts, 'S' Patrol went hard at it all through the next day and twenty-four hours later the tunnel was sufficiently cleared for jeeps to drive through. In the meantime, we staged diversionary tactics on the other side of the hill and the Lancers, O.P.d by our jeeps, pumped artillery shells into the town.

The Germans, thinking the blocked tunnel was impassable, didn't trouble to guard it. We drove through it during the night,

crawling bumpity-bump along the railway line in pitch darkness
hoping to God the roof wouldn't fall in and bury us all alive.

As dawn broke, we roared into Fabriano firing our guns and
yelling at the top of our voices—to find a bomb-happy rearguard
on the point of pulling out. We hastened their retreat and by ten
o'clock Fabriano was ours.

Nerve-racked, shell-shocked and jeep-ridden, the hysterical
population flowed into the cratered piazza to welcome us.

'*Viva Inglesi! Viva valorosi liberatori! Viva Churchill! Viva
Stalin! Viva!*'

I searched high and low for my darling Olga, but couldn't find a
trace of her.

'Did you know you were famous, Skipper?' Riches asked the
following morning.

'No, Rich. I didn't. How d'you mean, famous?'

'Come and I'll show you, Skipper.'

Wondering what it was all about, I followed Riches to the outskirts of Gualdo where he braked his jeep and pointed to the
gable wall of a building. 'Look, Skipper,' he guffawed. I looked and
guffawed also. I was sharing seats with the mighty. Written in
bold letters—with coloured chalk—beneath an obliterated Fascist
slogan were the words:

VIVA CHURCHILL VIVA STALIN VIVA CAPITANO BOB

And then I remembered the priest.

'Good God, Rich. The bloody priest's still in clink.'

We revved into Gualdo and shouted for the *capo*. He came,
running.

'*Si, Commandante,*' he informed me, the priest was still in
prison under a strong guard. The illustrious *commandante* had
given no orders for his release and so, naturally, he had kept him
in prison. Had he done wrong?

'Still on bread and water?' I hardly dared ask.

But of course. Weren't those the *commandante's* express orders?

'Take me to him. Quick!' I commanded.

I followed the *capo* to the gaol in some trepidation, expecting
to find an emaciated, dying priest. I was amazed to find a chastened, healthy young man.

The week's fast had worked wonders. The priest's eyes were bright, the red puffiness was gone from his cheeks and he had lost his paunch. He looked ascetic and celibate, as a good priest should.

I hoped he'd learned his lesson, and told the *capo* to release him.

Popski hadn't been feeling well of late. He went to hospital in Rome for a check-up and Jan Caneri drove up from San Gregorio to take command of 'R' Patrol, bringing with him more men and more jeeps.

I made myself up to strength and went off on my own again, probing.

The Germans had pulled back behind another river, behind another range of hills, and blown a few more bridges. We bumped into their rearguard on the outskirts of Scheggia and sat uncomfortably on the reverse slope of a rise trying to induce a fanatical Nazi commander to surrender the town. The commander appeared to have unlimited supplies of ammunition and every time we poked our noses round a bend in the road on the forward slope we got unmercifully stonked. We dubbed the bend 'P.P.A. Corner'.

During after-lunch siesta one day a *contadino* wandered over the rise and nonchalantly informed us that the Germans had evacuated Scheggia. We sat up and looked at him. He was a nondescript fellow, weather-beaten, roughly dressed, and didn't look too intelligent. He regarded us bovinely, gestured towards Scheggia and pronounced tonelessly:

'*Tedeschi scapati.*'

I didn't believe him and neither did Ben Owen. We'd been duly stonked on 'Matins' that morning, but the Germans had a very annoying habit of suddenly withdrawing from a town without giving us notice and it was just possible that they'd withdrawn from Scheggia during the forenoon.

There was only one way to find out.

'Come on, Ben,' I said. 'We'll go and see. Just the one jeep—you and Gino and I.'

Ben Owen settled himself behind the fifty—he always looked at peace behind a gun—Gino cocked the rear thirty and I drove cautiously over the rise. . . .

Very, very gingerly, sniffing the air like bloodhounds, we picked our way through the mess of bomb-holes in the road and

288

showed ourselves round P.P.A. Corner. I braked and we sat in full view of Scheggia with our sixth-sense antennae waving invisibly ahead, picking up danger signals.

Beyond P.P.A. Corner the road dipped gently for about a mile, went past a white-walled house set amongst trees, made a bend, ran straight for another mile, took another bend and then ran into Scheggia past a walled cemetery.

We sat in the jeep for a full five minutes, watching the grey walls and red roofs of Scheggia. How peaceful the town looked in the softening light of the afternoon sun, a typical Apennine market town enjoying the hour of siesta. We listened for the familiar wheeeeeeeeee of approaching mortar bombs, but none came.

'That's funny, Ben,' I remarked.

'It's a trap, Skipper,' Ben Owen muttered grimly. 'They're waiting for us.'

I let in the clutch and we crawled on down the road, hugging the verge. . . . We approached the white house. There wasn't a breath of wind and the trees drooped their leaves. No birds sang, no dogs moved about, the valley was gripped in a tense, brooding silence. We lost all sense of time. Our world was bounded by the blue-grey ribbon of road and Scheggia at the end of it. We drew level with the house, searching its upper windows for signs of a sniper, and felt uncomfortable when the building was behind us, expecting a shot in the back. . . . Nothing happened and we rounded the bend into the straight. . . .

The straight was bordered by a single line of trees which ticked past our slowly moving jeep like the sands of Time running out. Each tree was a cherished extension of Life, a precious breathing space before a burst of Spandau-fire tore into us. Life seemed doubly dear and we were acutely conscious of the light and warmth of the sun. . . .

The jeep crawled slowly on. Ben Owen crouched behind the fifty, both hands, knuckle-white, on the grips, thumbs ready to jab the firing-button. He was looking at Scheggia, at the wheat-fields and vineyards on either side of the road, at a pink stucco house in the foreground, glimpsed between the trees, looking all ways at once, alert, pent-up, ready for whatever came. . . . I felt Gino's intense presence at my back. . . .

We passed the last protective tree surprised to find ourselves alive and turned the bend in a dragging eternity of hovering death. We were on tenterhooks, taut as hell, knowing what was coming, free to turn back if we wished, but irresistibly drawn onwards like a criminal to his crime. . . .

'What do you smell, Ben?' I muttered, sniffing the atmosphere.

'Ambush, Skipper. They're waiting for us. Any minute now.' Ben's voice was grim and he didn't take his eyes from the road.

A thousand yards down the last straight which led into the town the grey stone walls of the cemetery loomed, with the heads and shoulders of the tombstones leering ominously. Across the fields to our left at another thousand yards' range the pink stucco house squatted menacingly with an upstairs window open like a watching eye. There was a gateway into a field on our right a little way ahead, and a clutch of haystacks on the hillside. The sun blazed down upon the silent valley and even Nature seemed expectant waiting to see what would happen.

The jeep was barely moving now and my heart was pounding. Inside my brain a gramophone record played continuously: 'Any minute now. . . . Any minute now. . . . Any minute now' . . . until I could have screamed with the suspense. Nine hundred yards from the cemetery gate . . . 800 yards . . .

As we drew level with the gateway into the field on our right I heard the alarm bell ring—a silent inner voice which said: 'No further. Turn here.' I braked.

'We'll turn here, Ben,' I croaked. My throat was dry and rasping.

'The cemetery's handy anyway,' Ben wisecracked in a mirthless undertone.

I reversed into the gateway. . . .

D-r-r-r-r-r-r-r-t. A vicious burst of Spandau-fire cut the air an inch above our heads. We ducked and felt the sweat break out.

'The pink house and the cemetery gate!' I shouted, wrenching desperately at the steering wheel.

Ben Owen's fifty clattered and I saw his tracer plunging into the pink stucco, tearing pieces off the walls. A stream of bullets whistled past my head from Gino's barking thirty.

I crashed into first gear and badly jerked the clutch. I felt the rear wheels spin and for an awful moment I thought I'd bellied the jeep . . . then the rear wheels caught on a hard patch and the jeep shot into the road. D-r-r-r-r-r-r-r-t. Another burst of Spandau-fire cut across our front and spattered on the grass verge. I ducked and swung the wheel wildly, upsetting Ben Owen's aim. I was about to accelerate madly when something held me back, a momentary hesitation. . . .

Wheeeeeeeeeeee. . . . Wruuuuuuumph. . . . Wruuuuuumph. . . . Wruuuuuumph. Mortar bombs crashed in the road ten yards in front—just where the jeep would have been if I hadn't hesitated. What made me hesitate?

Then we were off . . . zigzagging from side to side. I pressed hard on the accelerator, urging the screaming engine with my mind, crouching my body as small a target as possible. Ben Owen swung the fifty and sat precariously on the swaying bonnet firing his scarlet bursts in front of my face, pouring defiance into the open upper window of the pink house. . . . Squatting behind me, a leg on either side of the gun-mount, Gino plastered the cemetery gate with the rear thirty. . . .

D-r-r-r-r-r-r-r-r-r-t. . . . D-r-r-r-r-r-r-r-r-r-t. Spandau bullets whistled over and past our bent heads, ricocheted off the hard road surface, smacked into the trunks of the trees, tore through the vine-leaves and the wheat. Wruuuuumph . . . wruuuuuumph . . . wruuuuumph. Mortar bombs pursued our weaving passage . . . crashed behind us . . . accelerate . . . exploded in front of us . . . brake. . . . Wruuuuumph . . . on the grass verge . . . swerve . . . wruuumph . . . zigzag. . . . D-r-r-r-r-r-r-t. . . . 'Christ' . . . duck . . . zigzag. . . . Wruuuuuuumph . . . wruuuuumph . . . wruuuu-umph.

We roared round the second bend, taking the corner straight. My foot was hard against the floorboards with the speedo needle flickering about the fifty mark. Ben and Gino were still firing. . . . Brrrrrrt. . . . Brrrrrt. . . . Brrrrrrrrrrrrt . . . but their bursts weren't aimed and fell wide of the mark. . . . Wruuuuumph . . . a bomb fell on the roof of the white-walled house as we roared past it, making a loud bang and a gaping hole in the tiles. . . . Wruuuumph . . . wruuuuumph . . . wruuuumph. A cluster of bombs fell in the road, making me brake violently and swerve so that Ben Owen nearly fell off the bonnet. . . . 'Christ, Skipper,' he gasped and hung on grimly . . . accelerate . . . zigzag . . . wruuuuumph. . . .

Touching fifty miles an hour, flat out in second gear, we screamed towards P.P.A. Corner, fleeing the outstretched hand of

Death. The bend was sharp and the surface rough, pot-holed with many mortarings. . . .

'Hold tight, Ben!' I yelled.

Wruuuumph . . . wruuuumph . . . wruuuumph. A salvo fell right on the corner. I braked desperately and swung the wheel. . . . Ben Owen clenched his teeth, ducked and hung on . . . swerve. . . . I sawed at the wheel, spitting dust from my mouth . . . accelerating . . . zigzagging . . . foot hard down again . . . going like the wind. . . .

The jeep leapt forward . . . slewed dangerously . . . thud-ud-udded over the pot-holes . . . stotted on the verge . . . raised two wheels off the tarmac and careened round the corner . . . to the accompaniment of cat-calls, whoops and a derisive 'Windy, eh?' from the patrolmen who, hearing the firing, had gathered on the rise to watch the fun.

'Mucking close shave, Skipper,' panted Ben Owen, grinning, as he slid off the bonnet in the safety of our leaguer.

'*Cristo!*' breathed Gino, wiping sweat from a mud-spattered brow.

'Scheggia evacuated, my foot!' I declaimed hoarsely. 'Where's that bloody *contadino*?'

But when we went to look for him he was nowhere to be found.

So the days passed, in imminent danger of sudden death or comfortably in some well-found villa or *albergo*, and it was the balanced interchange of action and inaction, the balancing of nervous tension with complete relaxation, interspersed with hilarious fun, which kept us free from neurosis. Boredom was out of our ken, for no moment was dull. If we weren't pitting our wits against a cunning enemy and enjoying the excitement of the chase, we were relishing creature comfort in novel surroundings with the immediate prospect of more thrills to balance indulgence.

Health was assured by the open-air life we led and the whole-some food we ate. Following the sound advice my father gave me as a boy—'Eat natural food, put your faith in God and keep your bowels open'—I kept my patrol free from the ills and chills which normally beset troops on the march; our only trouble was the occasional bout of recurrent malarial fever contracted in North Africa.

Our tinned army rations we gave to the *contadini* in exchange for home-made *pasta*, wine, eggs, cheese, poultry, fresh fruit and vegetables and, curiously, the *contadini* were pleased with the bargain, preferring our *scatoli* (tinned goods) to their own plain but much healthier food.

The days merged into weeks and became jumbled memories of fierce, high-tension action with death very close, of green sunny days sitting on hillsides watching and waiting, of dark shadowy night patrols and yawning at dawn, of blistering hours man-handling jeeps up mountainsides, of wet miserable days soaked to the skin; of bowls of steaming *pastà*, *minestrà*, *ràvioli*, of rose-red Chianti and ruby lips, soft feminine bodies. Things happened quickly, situations changed rapidly, we were constantly on the move, seeing new places, new faces.

Summer imperceptibly faded into autumn and rain fell more frequently, swelling the rivers. Slowly, deliberately, blowing every bridge, contesting every inch of the way, the disciplined German divisions retreated through the lovely central mountains to the prepared positions of their Gothic Line from Rimini to Pisa.

Pressure was on the coastal flanks and P.P.A. roamed far and wide through the mountain gorges of the central sector, skirmish-ing miles ahead of the heavy divisional transport halted by the German demolitions. We lived on the roof-top of Italy, scaling the mountain ranges like sure-footed chamois and switching by sheep-track from valley to valley as whim—or premonition—and the movement of battle dictated.

Popski came out of hospital rested, but no whit the better; even then he was troubled by the brain tumour which killed him after the war.

Jan Caneri moved our base from distant San Gregorio to a medieval castle near Perugia, brought up a fleet of replacement jeeps and carried out a rapid three-day refit in the cobbled court-yard which had known Mussolini's heavy tread.

Lieutenant John Campbell (Argyll and Sutherland High-landers), a promising new recruit, took over 'S' Patrol from Reeve-Walker, recalled to the South African Forces, and Lieutenant Steve Wallbridge, another new officer, understudied Popski in 'R' Patrol.

With base in Umbria, close at hand, our supply position was considerably improved and we stepped up the pace of our probing activities.

Led by the will-o'-the-wisp idea that I might yet slip behind the German defences, I took my patrol of six jeeps on an extended mountaineering expedition which finally convinced me that the only way to get behind the lines was by parachute or by landing from the sea.

We went by Citta di Costello and San Sepulchro, crossed a river during a thunderstorm and couldn't get back, spent the night in a dream mansion caretakered by two beautiful, unattached Italian girls and went on (regretfully) the next day when the torrent subsided.

Across bleak, windswept, mountainous country running with water we thrust uphill to Sestino, a place of mist and squat grey houses peopled by shrill querulous voices clothed in black, crossed a deserted mountain road, 'sniffing', slithered into a valley, struggled through a raging stream and crawled damply uphill to the village of Carpegna perched like a cap on its mountain top.

It was the palazzo which caught my eye, a long white frontage punctured by many windows, standing aloof from its satellite village. I regarded it hopefully through the pouring rain which fell upon our water-logged jeeps in straight steel rods.

'That's the place for us, George,' I remarked, blowing rain-drops off my nose.

'Decent-sized casa, that, Skipper.' George Sonley took his hands from the grips of the dripping fifty and outlined the shape of the female form divine.

Skidding, wheel-spinning, side-slipping on the greasy surface of the precipitous rain-washed sheep-track we clawed our way up to the mountain top and drove through the dismal village to the locked and barricaded manor-house. It was a huge pile, complete with a drawbridge-and-moat entrance from the rear. In its dust-sheeted, hundred-roomed solitude a frail old countess lived like a caretaker in one scantily furnished suite on the second floor surrounded by the decaying remains of her feudal glory. Faith-fully served by an ancient family retainer and his ageing spouse, the countess, bordering upon eighty, dressed in sombre throat-high black and wearing a lace cap on her snow-white hair, heard our bangings on the portcullis and philosophically awaited the worst. The Germans had emptied her wine-cellar and looted most of her silver; there wasn't much left for the British to take.

The rusty portcullis creaked up in response to our insistent demands and we drove thunderously across the narrow, weed-grown moat into the bowels of the mansion. There was no cobbled courtyard. We drove directly into a vast hall between marble pillars, our muddied wheels leaving wet ochre stains upon the priceless mosaic. Six jeep exhausts made a deafening racket in the enclosed space and the atmosphere rapidly became carbon-monoxide plus.

'Christ, Skipper,' George Sonley tittered. 'What a bloody lark!'

'First time you've driven a jeep in a drawing-room, eh, George?' I laughed.

Sergeant Riches stepped from his jeep and gazed about him in wonderment. The guardian spirits of long-departed Lords of Carpegna took one horrified look at his dripping, rain-bedraggled five-foot-four in its ill-fitting green and khaki jumping jacket and shrieked through the twelve-foot walls.

'I dreamt that I dw-elt i-in m-a-arble halls . . .' Riches sang raucously and broke off to guffaw loudly at the echoes of his own voice.

'Just the job, Skipper.' Ben Owen's comment was accompanied by the tinny rattle of a primus stove as he proceeded to brew-up on the tiled figure of the Madonna and Child.

I became aware of the feudal retainer regarding our outlandish presence with rheumy, fear-filled eyes.

'Tell the old boy not to worry, Gino,' I said. 'We're only sheltering from the storm.'

Gino allayed the old man's fears and he tottered away, muttering to himself. He was back again within a short space of time. 'Would the *Signor Commandante* please step upstairs to speak to the Contessa?'

Accompanied by meaningful coughs from certain patrolmen I followed the old man up musty, squeaking stairs to the second floor and was bowed into the presence. 'Queen Victoria,' I thought. 'The living spit.'

The countess was a spry old thing, not a bit crotchety, and chatted amiably about the course of the war. She insisted upon my having dinner with her and apologized for the paucity of her condition, yanking a bell-pull with surprising vigour until the ancient retainer appeared. The bent old worthy conducted me to a bedroom where a towel and soap were laid out beside a basin of steaming water. I washed and spruced-up as best I could in the dim light and returned to the *salon*.

We dined romantically by candlelight, facing each other across a gate-legged table faultlessly laid, with the old man waiting upon us and standing respectfully behind the countess' chair. 'What a pity,' I thought as I drank her health, 'you aren't fifty years younger.'

Soup was followed by *pasta*—no terrors for me now—then fresh green salad, cheese, fruit. A frugal-enough meal but so impeccably served as to seem regal.

There we sat, the old countess and I, shadowed by the flickering candles, like characters out of a story book, with the wind howling outside, lashing the rain across the dark mountain. 'Wuthering Heights,' I thought.

Downstairs on the ground floor six mud-encrusted jeeps, prickly with machine-guns, were ranged grotesquely round the pillared Great Hall with the glow from six blaring primus stoves casting rings of light on the rich mosaic and showing brobdingnagian figures moving between the pillars.

I slept like a top on a soft feather bed in a dark room and woke early next morning to a clear day and blazing sky.

The view from my bedroom window was breathtaking. Square in the foreground, back-dropped by the limitless blue Adriatic, the fantastic Republic of San Marino sat like a flashing tiara on its head of massive black rock—an independent state the size of a postage stamp. Left of it, the solid crag of S. Leo basked in the risen sun with fold upon fold of purple mountains tumbling against the sky. Nearer at hand green hillsides fell steeply, cut by foaming torrents, patched by vineyards and criss-crossed by ochre runways. A high wind blew, calling me to go out and fill my lungs with its pure mountainy breath. 'What it must have been in olden days,' I thought as I went outside, 'to be Lord of Carpegna, lord of all one surveyed from this impregnable eagle's eyrie.'

I filled my lungs with God's fresh air, thanked God I was alive, and entered the Great Hall.

Bright sunlight poured in all-revealing streams through the high cathedral-like windows, emphasizing the Alice-in-Wonderland quality of the scene—the gleaming marble pillars, the priceless mosaic floor upon which titled ladies and gentlemen in eyemasks and powdered wigs should have been treading a stately measure in place of the sleeping-bagged, snoring patrolmen curled by the sides of their armed, blunt-nosed jeeps.

'Wakey, Wakeey!' I bawled at the top of my voice.

The recumbent figures twitched and the echo of my voice boomeranged about my ears.

'Up, you lazy bastards. Show a leg!' I went from sleeping-bag to sleeping-bag, pummelling its contents.

'Jesus, Skipper. . . . Lay off.'

' 'Morning, Skipper.'

'Go easy, Skipper.'

'O.K., Skipper, O.K.'

One by one the bodies came to life, sat up, yawned, rubbed eyes and wriggled out.

'Sleep well, Skipper?' George Sonley enquired meaningly. 'How's the Contessa?'

'She's eighty, George. Be reasonable.'

'Oh, sorry, Skipper,' apologetically.

The cloying smell of methylated spirits pervaded the air and primus stoves spluttered, blared and settled down to a steady roar. . . . Eggs plopped satisfyingly into sizzling bacon fat. . . . Tea was brewed.

We breakfasted.

As I munched, leaning against a marble pillar, I thought of the countess ekeing out a penurious existence in her vast domain.

'Any spare rations, Rich?'

'There's some tins of M and V, Skipper.'

I nodded.

'Give them to me.'

Riches reached into the back of a jeep and handed me half a dozen tins of meat and veg. I took them upstairs to the countess' suite and pressed them upon the old retainer, bad with a wheezy asthma at that early hour. 'My respects to the Contessa,' I said 'and give her these with my love.' The old man's rheumy eyes gleamed and he clutched at the tins as though they were nuggets of gold. Changed days, I thought. What a present to give a countess!

Pandemonium reigned in the Great Hall as six jeep engines burst into vibrant life. I clapped my hands to my ears and revved.

'O.K., Skipper,' Riches yelled above the din.

Describing a figure of eight round the marble pillars, we drove out of the hall and on to the wooden drawbridge, leaving wispy blue smoke-rings dangling in the air and the smell of burned oil

. . . under the rusty portcullis . . . sharp turn to the right. . . .
Good-bye, Carpegna.

We slid towards Pennabilli, down a perilous mountain track
with the wind whipping the sun into our faces and drying the damp
jeep loads. A broad river flowed through the valley and high on the
opposite bank the village of S. Agata, clinging to its rocky founda-
tion like a limpet, glared at us with evil intent.

'Bet there's an O.P. up there, Skipper,' said George.

'I bet there is, George. Keep your eye on it.'

The bridges were blown and we drove up and down the river
bank looking for a way across. Brown flood-water swirled past,
sucking ominously at the grassy banks.

'In you go, Gino.'

Gino peeled off boots and socks, rolled up his trousers and
waded in. The water rose to the level of his knees.

'Hell, Skipper. It's deep,' Ben Owen exclaimed.

The water pulled at Gino's sunburned legs and wet the bottoms
of his turned-up trousers but didn't reach higher than his knee-
cap. He crossed to the other bank, turned and waded back.

'*Cosi, Capitano*,' he said, putting a hand at knee height to indicate the water's depth.

'What's it like underneath, Gino?' I asked. 'Hard or soft?'

'*Buono.*'

'O.K., Rich,' I shouted. 'Fan-belts.'

Experience had taught us that the main cause of trouble
crossing rivers was the cooling fan which picked up water and
sprayed it over the engine, wetting the plugs and magneto. We
solved the problem by uncoupling fan-belts for the crossing and
recoupling them as soon as we were across. The only snag about
this procedure was that you had to keep the engine revving
otherwise the submerged exhaust pipe sucked in water and stalled
the engine, and if the crossing was a long one, the radiator
boiled.

Six jeep bonnets were raised and six heads bent over six
radiators. Six spanners clicked furiously, loosening six clamping
nuts. One spanner slipped and banged against the hot engine,
scraping the skin off a knuckle. The spanner fell with a clatter
and a head shot up.

'You mucking bastard,' cried Fitter Stewart, dancing on one
leg and gripping an oil-stained, bleeding knuckle.

298

'Tut, tut, langwidge,' clucked J. C. mockingly, putting fingers to his ears.

Six jeep bonnets clanged.

'O.K., Skipper,' Riches called.

Bumpity-bump . . . splash . . . gurgle . . . jolt . . . phurr. The jeeps nosed into the water like a string of pack-mules, feeling the current tugging at their wheels. The exhaust pipes gurgled throatily as they sank, steaming, beneath the surface and water poured over the floorboards, inducing the gunners to draw up their feet and sit on the back of the passenger seat, high up, like roosters perched on a bar, while the drivers sat ankle-deep in frothy, brown pools.

We were forging ahead nicely when George Sonley, eyeing lofty S. Agata, bent from his high estate and whispered in my ear in his 'don't-look-now-Skipper-but-there's-an-armoured-car-on-our-tail' sort of voice:

'Skipper, we're going to be mortared.'

The gentle warning sounded in my ear like a death-knell.

Wheeeeeeeee. . . . Wruuuumph. A ranging shot whistled overhead and exploded up-stream in a fountain of muddy water.

'Oh, God,' I thought, 'what do I do now?' Carry on or try to turn back? Could we possibly turn the jeeps in mid-stream, could we reverse with our exhaust pipes under water without stalling the engines? I'd never tried it and didn't know. 'What a bloody awkward place to get mortared,' I muttered. Grimly, I saw the humorous side. Time and again we'd caught the enemy with his trousers down; now, he'd caught us—with our fan-belts off!

Wheeeeeeeeeeee . . . wruuuuuumph . . . wruuuuuuumph . . . wruuuuuumph. A salvo exploded close to the jeeps, spraying us with water.

We ducked, crossing our fingers. 'Carry on,' the silent inner voice commanded.

I glanced quickly round. The five jeeps were following in line astern. The faces of the crews were serious, but I saw no sign of panic.

'*Avanti!*' I yelled, and pointed ahead.

'Here goes,' I thought, and put my foot down. The jeep plunged forward, breaking water like a motor-boat at sea. . . .

Wheeeeeeeeeee . . . wruuuuuuuumph . . . wruuuuuuuumph . . .

wruuuuuumph. Mortar bombs fell close, splashing and wetting us. 'Don't stall. . . . Don't stall. . . . Don't stall,' I prayed inwardly. . . .

Suddenly remembering the uncoupled fan-belts, I broke out in a cold sweat. We couldn't race for cover when we gained the opposite bank. We'd have to stop to recouple fan-belts, otherwise we'd ruin the engines. The engines were boiling now. 'You've done it this time,' I chided myself. But the inner voice still directed, 'Carry on.'

Twenty yards to go . . . ten yards. . . . Another thought frightened me. Suppose we get chased by armoured cars and have to run for it? We'll have to stop at the river bank and uncouple fan-belts again. I visualized the jeeps at the water's edge, crews fiddling with fan-belts, cursing while armoured cars closed . . . jeeps stalling in mid-stream . . . sitting targets for the enemy guns . . . saw tracer leaping across the flood-water. . . . 'Don't be silly, Yunnie.' I pulled myself up. 'How can they use armoured cars on a mountainside?' End of panic.

Wheeeeeeeeeee . . . wruuuuumph . . . wruuuuuumph . . . wruuuuuumph. Acclaimed by splashing mortar bombs, we emerged from the water one by one and charged, dripping, up the bank.

'Disperse and couple fan-belts,' I yelled.

Steaming jeeps drove in all directions and halted. Crews jumped out, bonnets flew up, emitting more steam, and fan-belts were coupled up in record time.

'O.K., Skipper.' George Sonley clanged the bonnet, fixed the clips and jumped behind the fifty.

A hundred yards away, the bonnet of Stewart's jeep banged and a thumb stuck up.

Riches signalled 'O.K.,' then Ben Owen. . . .

Wheeeeeeeeeee . . . wruuuuuumph . . . wruuuuuumph . . . wruuuuuumph. Mortar bombs crashed on the hillside, falling harmlessly between our widely dispersed jeeps. We ducked, fingered our noses towards S. Agata and jeered 'Missed.'

I led up a winding sheep-track and S. Agata disappeared from view. A few more bombs fell, desultorily, and the mortaring stopped. Temporarily we were safe, tucked into a fold of the hillside where the O.P. couldn't see us.

What was the enemy strength in S. Agata? I wondered as we crawled up the steep track in low booster gear. An O.P. with mortar and machine-guns and a platoon of infantry? I didn't think there was more. . . .

Our runway linked the isolated homesteads which clung to the mountainside within their hard-won patches of vineyard and we thrust upwards to the nearest one, wheel-spinning in the drying mud. A *contadino* ran out as we approached.

'*Tedeschi . . . tedeschi*,' he warned in a frightened conspiratorial whisper, pointing up the hill.

'*Dove?*' Gino asked him. (Where?)

'*A Sant Agata.*'

'We know,' I said scathingly, but my sarcasm was lost on him.

'*Quanti tedeschi?*' Gino asked. (How many Germans?)

The *contadino* hesitated and scratched his head.

'*Molto? Poco?*' Gino prompted.

'*Poco*,' the *contadino* conceded at length, overcoming the desire to exaggerate and sound impressive.

'Just what I thought,' I muttered to Sonley. 'O.P. Mortar post and platoon.'

Should we rush S. Agata in the jeeps and drive the Germans out of it or make a preliminary reconnaissance to confirm the German strength? Rush it, said Bravado. Recce, said Caution. Bravado won. We'll rush it, I decided.

The *contadino* returned to his vineyard and we crawled on towards S. Agata, sweating in the hot sun. . . .

Another cottage appeared, with S. Agata still out of sight over the brow of the hill.

'Check up, Gino,' I said.

Gino slid off the jeep and I held up a hand. The patrol halted behind me. The cottage door was opened by a wrinkled old crone who leaned heavily on a stick, cupped a gnarled, leathery hand to her ear and monotoned '*Chi e?*' to every question Gino asked.

'She's stone deaf, Skipper,' Sonley laughed.

I nodded and grinned, observing Gino's efforts to make the old dame understand.

'Never mind, Gino,' I called.

A footstep sounded on the path and I looked up to see a *contadino* standing on the brow of the hill. He hesitated for a moment when he saw the jeeps and then came running towards us.

'*Tedeschi scapati*,' he cried excitedly, pointing over his shoulder in the direction of S. Agata. 'The Germans have gone.'

'No bloody fear,' I grunted, remembering Scheggia. 'Once bitten, twice shy. You don't catch me a second time. Grab 'im, George.'

Sonley leapt out and half-Nelsoned the surprised *contadino*. '*Per che?*' he asked in an injured tone. (Why?)

'Sling 'im aboard, George. We'll take him with us.'

George hustled the indignant *contadino* on to the jeep load and Gino jumped on beside him.

The deaf crone '*Chi e?*'-ed from the cottage door, banged irascibly with her stick and went inside.

I drove cautiously uphill . . . over the rise . . . the roof-tops of S. Agata rose from the ground. I glanced round at our hostage expecting to see him cringing with fear. He wasn't. He was grinning from ear to ear, thoroughly enjoying the ride. '*Avanti, avanti,*' he urged confidently, like a mother encouraging her shy child. 'Good God,' I thought, 'he's telling the truth. The Germans *have* gone.'

I turned a bend in the track and found myself looking up the cobbled main street of S. Agata. A few inquisitive heads popped out of windows and doors and popped in again . . . suddenly the street was filling with people. Our hostage waved a hand and shouted '*Inglesi!*'

Answering waves and shouts came back . . . the population poured down upon us like pent-up water released from a dam.

'*Inglesi! Inglesi! Bravo! Bravo!*'

The excited *contadini* milled about our jeeps, yelling and gesticulating, clapping our backs, kissing our cheeks. . . .

Wheeeeeeeeeeee. . . .

George Sonley heard the mortar bomb coming, grinned, ducked and put his fingers in his ears. . . .

Wruuuuuuuuumph. The bomb smacked into the village, making a jagged hole in a roof and raising a cloud of dust.

The *contadini* held their breath, put hands to hearts and scattered wildly. Hoarse cries of terror took the place of the jubilant words of welcome. I looked round to see how our hostage was taking it. He'd gone.

Wheeeeeeeeeeee . . . wruuuuuumph . . . wruuuuuumph . . . wruuuuuumph. A barrage descended upon innocent S. Agata. Dust and smoke mushroomed above the roof-tops, broken tiles clattered into the street and the tinkling sounds of breaking glass

302

mingled with the banging explosions. Bombs fell intermittently for a good hour, injuring no one but doing considerable property damage.

When the mortaring ceased, the *contadini* rose shakily to their feet and went furtively to inspect their homes.

'Bloody good stonk, Skipper,' George Sonley observed professionally. 'What about a brew?'

'Good idea, George.'

I turned and shouted to Riches in the last jeep.

'Brew up, Rich.'

While tea was brewing, I studied the map.

A mile or two beyond S. Agata a lateral road wound through the mountains, linking Cesena on the Rimini–Bologna auto-strada with Bibbiena and Florence through Mercato, Sarsina and Bagno.

There was empty, mountainy country on either side of the road between Bagno and Sarsina. If we could cross the road without being seen, I thought. . . . We hung about S. Agata till dusk, with the good S. Agatians bringing us peace offerings of wine, cheese and eggs and hoping fervently we'd go away before our presence brought another deluge of mortar bombs.

Our presence in many a front-line Apennine village proved both a blessing and a curse for its neutral inhabitants, for whilst we brought liberation from German occupation with one hand we invariably brought property damage with the other.

The sun sank gloriously behind the purple mountains, flooding the sky with flashing streamers of red and gold, and S. Agata went uneasily indoors for the night, indifferent to Nature's colour magic.

A deep hush crept over the mountain as darkness spread her inky cloak.

'Everybody ready?'

'All set, Skipper.'

Six jeeps moved darkly over the skyline and creaked towards the road. . . . The runway was steep and ill-defined. We lurched precipitously downhill, bumping from terrace to terrace, feeling our way over the rough ground in the engine-brake of lowest booster gear, grinding past shadowed vineyards and the dark shapes of shuttered homesteads where barking dogs announced our passing. Downstairs in the valley the creamy head-waters of the Savio gleamed in the light of the stars, posing for us the

303

problem of another river crossing. . . . Thump . . . creak . . . lurch . . . bump. The jeeps dropped down the inky mountainside, scraping their rear spare-wheel brackets on the tufty contour strips, held in traction only by the brake of the powerful engine. Driver and gunner peered down an almost perpendicular bonnet, pressing hard with feet to prevent their bodies falling forward. No one spoke. Thump . . . creak . . . lurch . . . bump. . . .

Time passed and we stood in shadow by the river, testing its murmuring depth, with the dark mountain rearing steeply behind us, a solid black wedge which blotted out a section of the star-spangled sky. 'Good heavens,' I thought, looking up, 'did we bring jeeps down that?' It seemed an impossible feat. Gino waded barefoot out of the ford and stood beside me.

'O.K., Gino?'

'*Buono, Capitano.*' Gino touched his calf half-way between ankle and knee. The river was fordable.

'Rich,' I called softly.

Riches came to my jeep.

'Wait here, Rich,' I whispered. 'I'll take a foot-party across and recce the road.'

'O.K., Skipper.'

Gino, Gigi, Ben Owen and I waded through the ford and walked gingerly up to the road.

It was silent and deserted, with no beginning and no ending, just a lonely section of enemy road mysterious under the stars. We stood in its central dust, holding breath, listening, sixth-sensing the atmosphere. Guns boomed in the distance, from the directions of Florence and Rimini. The wheel-tracks at our feet were those of a German armoured car.

If we crossed the road would we be able to get back? Was there just the chance that we might be able to slip behind the lines? Excitement surged intoxicatingly. . . .

'Should we cross, Ben?'

'I think so, Skipper.'

'What do you think, Gino?'

'*Si, Capitano. Avanti.*'

That settled it.

'Wait here and keep an eye on the road, Gigi.'

Gigi crouched by the verge and Gino, Ben Owen and I returned to the jeeps.

'O.K., Rich. We'll go across.'

'Fan-belts, Skipper?'

I thought of the finicky job of uncoupling and recoupling fan-belts in the dark and decided against it. The water wasn't very deep.

'No, Rich. We'll risk it. The water isn't deep.'

'Start up one at a time,' I added. 'Don't make a noise.'

I went across first, with Gino wading in front, guiding me over the stones. The dark water tugged at my wheels and swished under the chassis, lapping the floorboards. The engine ran evenly and I lurched up the opposite bank.

The remaining jeeps came across without difficulty.

'Wait here, Rich,' I whispered.

I tip-toed the few hundred yards to the road.

'O.K., Gigi?' I breathed.

'*Bene, Capitano.*'

Gigi rose from his bush and we walked along the verge looking for a track leading into the mountains on the other side. We found one about half a mile from the ford.

'Stay here, Gigi,' I whispered. 'Guide the jeeps in as they come.'

'*Si, Capitano.*'

Gigi stood at the cross-roads of no man's land and I padded back to the ford, feeling like I once did as a child when I slipped out of the house at dead of night just for the fun of playing in the moonlit garden when everyone else was asleep. (My father caught me coming in and tanned the hide off me!) The jeeps were dark shadows crouched like boulders by the river bank, barely distinguishable from the road.

'Rich,' I called softly. 'Rich.'

A shadow moved. 'Here, Skipper.'

'The track's about half a mile down the road, Rich. Gigi's there. Turn in when you see him. All set?'

'O.K., Skipper.'

'Quietly, remember,' I emphasized.

Self-starters rasped terrifyingly, broadcasting our presence. I mouthed and gestured quietening motions in the darkness, nervous of being heard from the road. . . . I ground up a steep bank . . . bumped on to the road . . . sped towards Gigi. . . .

His sentinel-like figure appeared on the verge and I turned

under his indicating arm, drove a few hundred yards along the track and waited for the other jeeps to catch up. Gino counted five dark shadows . . . *uno* . . . *due* . . . *tres* . . . *quatro* . . . *cinque*. . . . '*Va bene, Capitano.*'

'Walk in front, Gino,' I whispered.

Gino gripped a Tommy-gun, slid easily off the load and walked into the night. Six creaking jeeps followed his loping shadow. . . .

What was my objective and where was I going? I didn't really know. Guided by an intuition which had never let me down, I was simply going forward until I was stopped, hoping to slip behind the German lines. (Intuition is a better guide than reason, I have found. Reason knows all the things which can't be done. Intuition knows what can.)

Somewhere in the surrounding darkness German infantry were crouched behind machine-guns, peering into the night waiting, watching and listening. The invisible electro-magnetic vibrations emanating from the living cells of their physical presence were 'picked-up' by our human-radar sixth sense as we approached their hidden positions. Gino came to a fork in the track, paused to 'sniff' the atmosphere . . . chose the left-hand fork in preference to the right—for no reason other than that his sixth sense told him to go that way—and loped confidently on. The jeeps followed confidently after him.

How else can I describe the working of the strange phenomena that guided us? We advanced stealthily towards the Gothic Line.

I never took my eyes from Gino's shadowy back. George Sonley sat darkly beside me, both hands on the grips of the fifty, searching both sides of the track with penetrating eyes, 'sniffing' the air continuously. In the last jeep Gigi sat with his back to the driver, ensuring that nothing surprised us from the rear.

The dark miles slipped beneath our scrunching wheels. . . .

Curving obliquely downhill, I heard the rush of water and presently the dark outline of a homestead took shape in the murk. Gino motioned me to stop. I braked and watched his protective figure disappear, prepared for the shattering burst of Spandau-fire which never came.

Gino reappeared soundlessly, gliding like a shadow, and stood at my elbow. '*Venite, Capitano,*' he whispered. (Please come.)

Telling Sonley to stay put, I picked up an American carbine automatic, tucked it comfortably under my arm at the ready and followed Gino past the gable of a silent house and down an incline to a river bank where a twenty-foot breadth of foaming water surged past my feet like a mill-race.

'It looks bloody deep, Gino,' I breathed.

Gino sibilated '*Si*' and proceeded to test the depth. . . . In one stride the water was up to his thighs, threatening to sweep him away.

'Come back, Gino,' I commanded.

Gino held out a balancing hand and I steadied him to the bank.

'We'll never get jeeps through that, Gino.'

We stood for a moment, thinking. . . .

'Sssssssst!' Gino put a finger to his lips.

I held my breath and listened intently. Above the roar of the water I heard the faint note of a motor exhaust from the other side of the river.

Gino and I sat on our heels on the damp river bank and peered across the water, straining our ears . . . the exhaust note grew stronger . . . closer . . . closer. . . . I touched Gino's arm as the dark shape of a German armoured scout car appeared, like a truck on a railway embankment, patrolling along a road which ran parallel with the torrent. . . .

Gino and I exchanged glances in the darkness and watched the black outline of the scout car curve away from the river bank and disappear. . . . A few minutes later we heard brakes squeak . . . engine revs . . . the scout car reappeared, returning the way it had come. . . . We watched it melt into the darkness.

I visualized the map and knew where we were. We had reached the banks of the Ronco. The scout car had come from S. Sofia.

I glanced at the time. Just on 3 a.m. What should I do? Take my patrol back to S. Agata and try again in another direction or stay where I was and see what developed? I decided to stay.

Gino and I walked back to the jeeps, making a cursory inspection of the homestead on our way. It conformed to type—four stout walls, a good roof, a strong door, two shuttered windows, tumbledown outbuildings surrounded by a vineyard from which the *contadino* wrestled a bare living in a world of rising costs.

The patrol had heard the scout car go past.

'Was that an armoured car, Skipper?' Riches enquired.

'It was, Rich. Jerry's patrolling the north bank. We're on the

Ronco. Santa Sofia's just across the river. We'll wait here and see what cooks.'

Dispersing the jeeps between the high vine trellises we helped ourselves to a service of fruit and patiently waited for dawn to break. . . .

As soon as it was light enough to see, Gino and Gigi paid a social call on our host. The door was opened a crack in response to their urgent knocks and a suspicious voice asked '*Chi e?*'

'*Inglesi,*' Gino announced.

'*Oprire,*' commanded Gigi. (Open the door.)

A red-faced, white-haired old man with podgy hands and a scaly skin opened the door and Gino and Gigi went in.

'Brew up, Rich,' I called.

Hidden by the trailing vines, we were sucking at mugs of hot tea when Gino and Gigi returned.

'*Dove tedeschi?*' I asked with a smile.

The Germans were in Santa Sofia and the bridges were blown, they told me. The old man didn't think there were any Germans on this side of the river. There had been a footbridge but the Germans had taken it away. The armoured car patrolled the north bank every night.

As I listened to their report, a plan of action formed in my mind —remain hidden in the vineyard all day, road watch, ambush the armoured car at night.

'Road watch, Rich,' I ordered. 'We'll Popski ambush at night.'

'O.K., Skipper.'

The day passed pleasantly enough, sharing turns of road watch and dozing in the shade of the vines. At midday the *contadino's* spouse, a breathless, shapeless, humourless, sterile creature in flapping black skirts brought us *pasta* in exchange for a generous assortment of compo rations which failed to produce the slightest change in her glumly bovine expression when Riches crowded them into her flour-flecked arms. 'What a depressing female,' I thought, as I watched her sack-like body flap out of the vineyard, and marvelled that any man could live with her. Could she ever have been young and amorous? I wondered.

When night fell we manhandled two of the jeeps into a position in a corner of the vineyard from which their guns could rake the north bank. Riches manned the guns and Ben Owen and

I took road-mining parties across the river. With haversacks containing turds, Calabrian, slung on our backs we waded waist-deep through the frothy turbulence holding Tommy-guns high above our heads. The raging water coursed over loose boulders and we slipped and staggered, feeling for each foothold, pushing hard against the dragging current which threatened to bowl us over.

Ben Owen took his party down-stream to crouch in the bushes by the verge. I took mine up-stream, laid turds artistically over a section of the road and recrossed the river.

Hours passed and there was no sign of the armoured car. Nine o'clock . . . ten o'clock . . . eleven o'clock. . . . It was past midnight before we heard the exhaust note. . . .

'Here she goes, Rich,' I whispered. 'Get ready. Hold it till I tell you to fire.'

Through powerful night-glasses (a recent acquisition of Jan's) I watched the armoured car moving along the north bank, a steel box on four wheels with a machine-gun sticking out. It crawled past the place where Ben Owen hid and rumbled slowly round the bend, a lovely target at 600 yards' range. I let it go on, watching it curve away from the river towards the section of the road where my turds were lying like mule spoor in the dust, and waited for the flash. . . .

It came, a bright leaping flame in the darkness, accompanied by a series of muffled explosions which echoed along the hillside in rumbling cadences. I pulled the trigger of the Very pistol and a green rocket swooshed towards the stars.

The sound of questioning voices, the grating of gears, engine revs, floated across the river and a dark shape moved into focus, limping badly. . . .

'There she goes, Skipper,' said Riches in a tense undertone.

I waited until the armoured car was opposite . . . whispering 'Hold it. . . . Hold it' . . . until its dark bulk showed clearly between two clumps of bushes by the roadside. . . .

'Fire!'

Brrrrrrrrrrrrrrrrrrt. Tracer leapt across the river, searing a scarlet path through the darkness.

'You've hit it, Rich.'

I saw the scout car reel under the impact of Riches' first burst, swerve across the road out of control, smack into a bush, topple down the bank and burst into flames.

'Nice work, Rich.' I clapped him on the back.

Lusting to kill, Riches swung his gun and poured another vicious burst into the crackling flames which rose like a funeral pyre from the other side of the river.

'Steady, Rich,' I cautioned, 'Ben Owen's somewhere down there.'

Riches put up his gun. We watched the flames leap up, die away and leap up again like a camp-fire and waited for Ben Owen's party to return.

'Bloody good shot, Rich.'

'Got the bastard first shot.'

'Right in the mucking kisser.'

'That shook 'im.'

Excited whispers floated about Riches' jeep as patrolmen came up to congratulate him and shake his hand.

Presently Ben Owen and his party appeared, breathless and wet to the hips.

'Got 'im first shot, Ben,' Riches boasted, proud of his marksmanship.

He and Ben Owen vied for first place as the best shots in the patrol.

Riches wanted to inspect his prize.

'Wait a bit, Rich,' I cautioned, 'Jerry must have seen the flames. They may send a patrol to investigate.'

The funeral pyre burned itself out. An hour passed and there was no sign of a German patrol.

'Come on, Rich,' I said, 'we'll go across.'

Riches, Don Galloway, J. C., Gino, Gigi and I waded through the river. The acrid stench of scorched metal and roasted flesh led us to the burned-out scout car, an up-ended, charred, steel coffin lying on top of a broken, blackened bush. Wisps of smoke still coiled from the hot steel plates. 'Reminds you of the strafing we got in Blitz wadi——' I broke off, realizing with a shock that not one of the men standing on the river bank had been with me in Tunisia when the Messerschmitts strafed us. Heavens, how time passed, I thought, how much took place, what changes in men and equipment! Memory flashed back to the old days in Cairo. . . . Shepheard's Hotel . . . Groppi's . . . Abbassia Barracks . . . the wogs crying their sandwich wares at the gate, 'Eggs ee bread' . . . Popski's flat . . . the first jeeps I drew from the vehicle park at

Tel el Kebir. . . . Four little jeeps and two overloaded 3-tonners struggling through the sands of the Gilf. . . . It all seemed ages and ages ago, like another life in another world. . . .

'*Capitano.*' . . .

Gigi's urgent voice brought me from the burning sands of the Gilf Kebir to the rushing waters of the Ronco.

'Patrol coming, Skipper,' Riches warned.

Unsure which way to go, we stood for a moment by the wrecked scout car, gripping Tommy-guns, listening intently. . . . The faint note of an exhaust came to our ears and grew louder . . . louder . . . lights flashed between the dark blobs of bushes by the roadside . . . the noise of explosions rumbled along the hillside . . . confused shouting broke out a few hundred yards away.

'They've hit Ben's turds,' I muttered. 'Come on!'

Ducking along the dark river bank under cover of the bushes we closed in on a halted armoured car, a black silhouette upon the raised embankment . . . shadowy figures moving beside it. . . . My mouth was dry, my heart thumped sickeningly. . . . I made for the road, panting, with Riches and J. C. behind me, the others following . . . our footsteps rang harshly on the hard road surface as we fanned out and raced towards the stranded armoured car, spraying from the hip as we ran. . . . Brrrrrrrrrrrrt . . . brrrrrrrrrt . . . brrrrrrrrrrrt. . . .

Shouts of alarm, sharp cries of pain rose above the rattle of our Tommy-gun fire and some of the shadowy figures fell in the road. . . . Brrrrrrrrrrrrrrrrrrt. A roaring, shattering, flame-spurting explosion burst in our faces, stopping us in our tracks and by some miracle leaving us unhurt. . . .

'Back,' I yelled, 'down to the river.'

Brrrrrrrt. . . . Brrrrrrrrrrrrrrrrrrrt. . . . The German gunner fired viciously but wildly as we threw ourselves over the embankment and we felt his bullets clawing the air immediately above our heads . . . gears crashed . . . an engine raced . . . the armoured car reversed down the road, firing blindly. . . . Brrrrrrrrrt . . . brrrrrrrrrrrrrrt . . . brrrrrrrrrrrrrrt. . . .

The ice-cold water acted like a sedative on our taut nerves as we plunged through the river. I felt its cold grip creeping through my body, drawing the blood from my brain, slowing my heart-action. . . .

The crossing calmed us. Separated by running water from the

sudden onrush of terror, we could look back and see the action in its proper perspective. Death in the form of a tearing, ripping destruction had breathed clammily in our faces and passed us by. It was only by a miracle that any of us were alive. If the German gunner had pointed his gun an inch lower, I thought, and shuddered, visualizing our riddled bodies bleeding on the road. . . .

'Christ, Skipper, that wis a near yin,' J. C. breathed in a fervent whisper.

'*Ayeee*,' whistled Gino, cracking his fingers. '*Scapare io.*'

'*Paura*,' admitted Gigi. (I was frightened.)

'Whew, Skipper. That was touch and go!' Riches sucked in his breath and started to hum 'Torno Sorrento' to relieve his pent-up feelings.

I breathed a heartfelt sigh of relief and looked up at the stars, feeling the presence of an invisible Power and believing more than ever in my theory of a charmed existence.

'Anybody wounded, Skipper?' Ben Owen asked solicitously when we panted into the vineyard.

'No casualties, Ben,' I assured him, separating thumb and fore-finger a fraction to indicate how nearly we'd been killed.

'Close shave, Skipper?' George Sonley enquired.

'Very close, George. Close enough to deserve a drink.'

I reached into the back of my jeep and drew out my medicinal whisky bottle, took a deep pull and handed the bottle round. . . . Ben Owen made a strong brew of tea and we settled down for the night.

Somewhere in the no man's land between sleeping and waking I heard the whistle of an approaching shell and turned in my sleeping-bag, glad it was only a dream. . . .

Wruuuuuuuuuuumph! The vineyard rocked and I sat up, wide awake.

'What the hell was that?' I asked hoarsely.

Ben Owen was on sentry-go.

'Shell, Skipper,' he announced quietly, 'we'd better move the jeeps.'

Wheeeeeeeeeeeeeeee. . . .

'Look out. Here's another.'

I lay flat.

Wruuuuuuuuuuuumph. A bright flash lit the sky, showing the

trailing vines, and the hillside trembled. A piece of shrapnel whined dangerously and smacked into a trellis.

Everybody was awake now, hurriedly piling kit on to the jeeps.

'We'll pull back out of range, Rich,' I called. 'Listen for the shells and dodge 'em.'

Shell-dodging was a thrilling game. The art of it was timing, based upon ballistic principles. You listened for the whistle of the shell's trajectory and the moment you heard it you *stopped*, knowing that that shell would land somewhere in *front* of you. You waited for it to explode and immediately raced *forward*. Seven seconds later you heard the bang the shell made when it left the gun and you strained your ears for the whistle of the next shell, braked and sat tight when you heard it and raced on again after it had exploded in front of you. When you were out of range you breathed freely, patted yourself on the back, chortled derisively and drove on.

Choosing our own time, we dashed singly from the vineyard between the exploding shells and stuttered along the dark track alternately braking and accelerating, listening and counting, until we were safely out of range, leaving the hapless *contadino* and his shapeless spouse to quiver under the bed in their shaking cottage.

We brewed-up a mile from the river and sat by our jeeps in the darkness sipping tea and swapping jokes until dawn broke, when we crept back to the cratered vineyard to make sure no German infantry crossed the Ronco.

There was no sign of the *contadino*, but at midday, much to our surprise, his mirthless spouse appeared bearing a large bowl of *pasta* which she dumped wordlessly upon the bonnet of Riches' jeep and stood cow-like with unchanging expression while he piled tins of meat and veg. against her flabby, shapeless bosom.

When darkness fell, the little devil which made Ben Owen tick whispered temptingly in his nether ear, 'Let's take a foot-patrol into S. Sofia and see what Jerry's up to.'

I was tempted too.

Leaving Riches in charge of the jeeps with instructions to report to base if we didn't come back ('You're crazy, Skipper'), Ben Owen, Don Galloway, J. C., Gino, Gigi and I waded through the plunging current and double-filed along the road towards S. Sofia.

There wasn't a soul abroad in the dark, starry night. 'Leap-frogging' along the dew-wet, silent verges, crouching every few yards to look and listen, we drew level with a farmhouse set back from the road. I hand-signalled to Ben Owen and we crept towards it. . . . Geese cackled and a dog barked sharply . . . we 'froze' . . . went on again under the shadows of trees, advancing a feeling foot at a time to avoid stepping upon give-away, cracking branches. . . .

The dog arose from its bed by the farmhouse door as we entered the yard, growled threateningly and loped towards us. I hesitated, afraid of the snarling brute, and was put to shame by Gigi who advanced fearlessly, whispering soothing Italian doggy words so that the wolf-like animal became lamb-like, wagged a welcoming tail and proceeded to lick his hand

Accompanied by its docile guardian, we tip-toed through the sleeping farm and followed a track between the fields towards a grove of trees in whose dark security we stood for a time listening to the song of the rushing Ronco and the distant orchestration of the guns at Rimini. The wolf-turned-into-a-lamb sat on its tawny haunches with hanging pink tongue and gazed into Gigi's eyes.

'The dog's taken to you, Gigi,' I whispered.

'*Si, Capitano,*' he smiled.

Gigi bent to pat the dog's head and the delighted animal fawned and raised a paw. Gigi shook it and laughed.

S. Sofia was a mile away, shadowy and mysterious through the night-glasses. Along the track by the edge of a ploughed field breathing its earthy, manure-laden air . . . through another grove of trees with the dog trotting ahead like a well-trained scout and returning periodically to Gigi's side to report . . . on to a footpath which led us downhill to the road . . . along the grassy verge towards the first silent houses of S. Sofia. . . .

We stood in the deserted, star-lit piazza under the shadow of the village spire with the dog lolling a dripping tongue above Gigi's dusty boots.

'Want to go further, Ben?'

Ben Owen shook his head. His sixth sense told him that somewhere in the dark shadows at the bottom of the main street where it curved towards Galeata a German machine-gunner crouched behind a well-oiled Spandau, itching to pull the trigger. I looked askance at the shuttered windows of the houses, the tightly closed doors, the tall brooding village spire and 'sniffed'. Invisible fear vibrations pervaded S. Sofia. I twirled the knobs of my mental radar and picked up weak signals from the piazza, very strong ones from the shadowy main street running towards Galeata.

'Spandau at the bottom of the main street, Ben?'

Ben Owen nodded.

'*Andiamo,*' I mouthed. (Let us go.)

Down to the singing Ronco to inspect the blown bridge . . . back to the piazza . . . up and down a number of alleyways gripping Tommy-guns and peering between the cracks of shuttered windows . . . along the main street out of the village with apprehensive backward glances in the direction of Galeata . . . up the path towards the farm, breathing freely . . . through the trees . . . past the strong-smelling ploughed field . . . into the quiet farmyard where the dog suddenly sat down on its haunches, grinned toothily and said good-bye to Gigi with an upraised paw.

'Can you beat that, Ben?' I laughed. 'Like a circus turn.'

Gigi shook the dangling paw and patted the dog's head affectionately.

'*Grazia molto, bel cane. 'Rividerci,*' he said. (Thank you, lovely dog. Good-bye.)

Ducks slept under a tree with their flexible white necks twisted under their wings.

'*Piace, Capitano?*' Gino asked meaningly. (You like duck?)

I nodded and watched Gino tip-toe up to the unwary birds . . . bend over them and with a lightning motion of the hands hold two flapping birds aloft. Expertly wringing their necks, Gino tucked one downy bird under each arm and we strolled out of the farmyard with a last backward glance at the guardian-dog who remained motionless in the starlight, head cocked to one side, wholly approving our action.

We came to the river warm from our walk and the ice-cold water shocked our sweating bodies like an early morning shower-bath. Holding ducks and Tommy-guns above our heads we plunged into the strong current, feeling our way between the wobbly, hidden boulders. Almost across, I slipped, stumbled, tried to save myself, lost my balance and fell with a splash. The point of my chin connected with a jagged rock and I rose, dripping water and blood, cursing volubly.

315

'Listen to the Skipper,' said George Sonley standing with Riches in the nearby vineyard. 'What bloody shocking langwidge.'

I'd split the tight chin-skin to the bone and poured blood all over my chest. I must have looked a dreadful sight, like a filleted fish, when I stumped into the vineyard in the starlight, dripping blood at every step.

'Christ, Skipper,' Riches exclaimed in alarm, 'have you been wounded?'

'No,' I growled, 'I fell in the mucking river and split my mucking chin.'

Riches, patrol first-aid man, inspected the gaping wound and dabbed at it tentatively with a field dressing.

'This'll have to be stitched, Skipper,' he pronounced, 'we'd better get you to hospital.'

My jaw was stiffening and I felt sure I was disfigured for life. 'O.K., Rich,' I grunted painfully, 'let's get jeeping.'

Riches bound up my chin till I looked like a man with the mumps. George Sonley took the wheel and I sat beside him holding the fifty, feeling very sorry for myself. (It was the only wound of any kind I received during the whole of the war and I am reminded of it every morning when I shave.)

Miles back, at daybreak, we struck a winding road and were nearly destroyed by our advancing troops, a squadron of Lancers probing forward from Bagno. George Sonley waved just in time.

'Who the hell are you?' asked a pop-eyed, red-faced major, looking incredulously from my blood-stained chest to the grinning bearded men sitting in their muddy jeeps behind me.

'Popski's Private Army.'

The major recoiled as though he'd seen a ghost and his mouth fell open.

'Good God,' he muttered, 'I've heard of you. I thought it was a myth.'

My chin was throbbing unbearably.

'Where's the nearest field hospital?' I mouthed agonizingly.

'Bibbiena.'

I groaned. Bibbiena was miles away.

'Where've you come from?' the major asked in an awed voice.

George Sonley couldn't resist the temptation.

'Venice,' he said convincingly.

The major looked at me for confirmation.

'Santa Sofia,' I sibilated truthfully. I might just as well have said 'Venice'.

'But the Germans are in Santa Sofia,' declared the major authoritatively.

I shook my head, momentarily forgetting my split chin, and bit my lip with the pain.

'We were in the piazza six hours ago. We had a dog with us.'

The major regarded me doubtfully. Clearly I was telling a tale; but by this time I had a blinding headache and the sun was hurting my eyeballs.

'Bibbiena, George,' I grunted.

The jeeps hurtled down the road, leaving the puzzled major standing by his command car like a double-headed 'That's Shell —that was' advertisement.

In a requisitioned civilian hospital in Bibbiena a roughhanded Polish Army surgeon jabbed at my aching chin with a hypodermic needle, clipped the shy edges of my wound together and inserted half a dozen stitches. A few hours later, when the effects of the local anaesthetic wore off, my face felt as though it would burst.

Convinced that we couldn't slip through the German lines (I couldn't have cared less at the moment) I sent a sitrep to Popski. An immediate reply came back:

POPSKI TO BOB   RETURN TO BASE

Thankfully, I went, obsessed with only one idea—a soft pillow to ease my aching face.

19

Across Italy, from coast to coast, the allied armies were pushing hard against the Gothic Line and the battle for Rimini was developing.

Rimini was important and if you look at the map of Italy you will see why. At Rimini the mountains come down to the sea; beyond Rimini lies the flat open plain of Lombardy with the great auto-strada to Milan running through it, hugging the side of the Apennine spine. Rimini was the key which unlocked the side-door of the Gothic Line and Kesselring, like Francesca before him, hung grimly on to it. And no wonder, for who held Rimini held the gateway to the Po Valley and the industrial north.

The battle for Rimini waged fast and furious and there was a Staff theory current that as soon as Rimini fell the German divisions would run helter-skelter across the plain and entrench themselves in the foothills of the Alps, behind the security of the wide River Po. In anticipation of a rapid German retreat, Popski's Private Army was held in readiness in a farmyard south of Rimini, poised with full tanks for a lightning dash across the plain. Popski would much rather have landed his private army behind the Po, but the Planning Staff wouldn't play ball. So we sat in our jeeps in our farmyard, hoping and waiting for the great dash— and the only thing that was dashed was our hope.

Rimini fell, but instead of making a wild dash for the Po bridges as per theory Kesselring (the German commander in Italy) stepped back his weary divisions canal by canal and river by river, blowing bridges and canal banks as he went, ensuring dry standings for himself and leaving his opposition to wallow in the mud and the flood of his widespread demolitions.

Day after day I sat in my jeep alongside my patrol waiting, waiting, waiting, thinking about Bum Curtis. Poor old Bum. On

318

our way across the Apennines he met a tragic death. His nerve fully recovered, he was with us again, the same old Bum, breezy and full of life, invigorating our spirits with his spontaneous, horsy laugh.

We took a short cut (as we thought) over a mountain pass and found our way blocked by a demolished bridge over a ravine. To go round it meant hours of extra travel and we were eager to reach our destination. 'Build a bridge, Skipper,' Curtis suggested. 'Rope in the conta-mucking-dini' (horse-laugh). I was all in favour and told Curtis to get organized.

The Germans had a filthy habit of planting S-mines in the rubble of their blown bridges and Curtis stood on one when he was directing bridge-building operations, urging the sweating *contadini* to greater effort in his amusing half-army-slang-Italian. '*Prendere* the mucking thing *cosi*, Vincento,' he was instructing a panting *contadino* pulling at a heavy log. '*Buono . . . benissimo. . . .* Hold it, cock. . . . No, muck it, not like that . . . *cosi*. . . . *Si*. . . . *Bene*. . . .' His horse-laugh rang out and he stepped back . . . there was a loud explosion. . . . Curtis was lying on the rubble, screaming: 'My legs. . . . Oh, God, my legs. . . .'

We rushed to his aid . . . and were shocked by the sight. Both legs were severed between knee and ankle. The white, jagged bone ends protruded from the torn and bleeding flesh and his boots lay grotesquely apart from his body, the bloody feet still in them.

Applying a tourniquet above each knee to stop the awful bleeding, we carried his broken body up the bank and laid it gently on the verge while sympathetic, understanding *contadini* improvised a stretcher from a cottage door and brought vinegar to pour over his aching stumps—to prevent gangrene, they said. We lifted Curtis on to a jeep, strapped him firmly and drove him to the nearest village where an Italian medico did what little he could to save his life. Game to the last, Curtis looked up at me and joked—joked, in that condition!—'My dancing days are over, Skipper' (weak, brave little horse-laugh). . . . A lump swelled in my throat and I couldn't speak. Two jeeps raced through the night to the nearest field hospital and brought an ambulance. Bum died on the way to hospital. Mercifully, he died. Poor old Bum. Another of the P.P.A. originals had gone.

Death hit us hard in P.P.A. The unit was small and we were all intimate friends, a welded comradeship. Casualties were few and when they occurred we felt them keenly. In a division, the loss of a man is a daily occurrence. Divisionally speaking, he is only a number, a name, one amongst many. His death is a matter of small importance and he is barely missed. But in our intimate group of picked specialists every man was a personality and his death broke up a team.

We sat in our jeeps and waited. The days passed. Popski drove daily to Army Headquarters to keep in touch with the situation and daily returned to the farmyard with a long face. Hope gradually died and a day came when we knew there would be no exciting rush across the plain in the wake of a fleeing enemy.

The patrolmen grew restive.

'We can't keep the men sitting here indefinitely, Popski,' I said despairingly. 'Is there nothing we can do, no way we can land jeeps up the coast ourselves? What about amphibians?'

'I've been thinking about it, Bob. There's a new thing out from America called a duck—D.U.K.W. I understand the R.E.s have some at Ancona. We'll go down tomorrow and take a look at them.'

This sounded promising and I perked up a bit.

Breakfasting early the following morning, Popski and I drove south to Ancona, weaving an erratic way through the long convoys moving up the coast road to Rimini.

'DUKWs? Never heard of 'em,' said the R.E. officer at Ancona.

We drove down to the harbour.

'DUKWs?' The N.O.I.C. shook his head. 'DUKWs? No, not here.'

'Are you *sure*, Popski?' I asked as we drove out of the crowded docks. Popski gave me a withering look.

'Perhaps they aren't in Ancona, Popski,' I ventured a few minutes later. We drove to Senigallia.

'DUKWs?' said the R.E. officer dubiously, and shook his head.

'American amphibian craft,' Popski explained.

The R.E. officer brightened.

'Oh, you mean D.U.K.W., the new American amphibian. They're up at San Vito.'

We could have kissed him.

'DUKWs?' said the R.E. officer at S. Vito. 'Over there.'

But I'd spotted the outlandish vehicles and was already on my way to them. 'The very thing, Popski,' I declared when he joined me a moment later.

The DUKWs were grey, boat-shaped bodies mounted on a truck chassis with four big rubber-tyred road wheels and a water-screw at the rear. There was a windscreen, a commodious driving-seat, an ordinary steering-wheel and the usual four gears—three forward and reverse—with an extra lever for changing from land-drive to water-drive. Behind the driving-seat there was an empty compartment just big enough to hold a P.P.A. jeep. The only snag was how to get the jeep into the DUKW.

'How are we going to get the jeeps into them, Popski?'

Popski thought for a moment, then snapped thumb and second finger with a loud crack.

'Crane, Bob,' he said decisively.

We went in search of the R.E. officer and asked about the crane position. He bowled us over completely by quietly announcing that there were DUKWs available with crane already fitted, and he had one brought up for our inspection.

'May we try it?' I asked.

'Certainly,' replied the obliging R.E. officer, a soft-voiced quantity surveyor from Norwich.

I drove the jeep close to the DUKW. Two sappers drove the crane-DUKW alongside, fitted lifting chains to the jeep, swung it off the ground and deposited it neatly inside the DUKW.

'Perfect,' I exclaimed delightedly.

The jeep fitted snugly and there was a clear field of fire for the guns. I visualized a patrol of DUKWs chugging through the surf of an enemy beach . . . snicking into road-wheel drive and going inland in the moonlight. . . .

'It's the answer, Popski,' I enthused. 'Let's get organized.'

'Right, Bob,' said Popski. 'Back to the patrols.'

Before leaving S. Vito, Popski spoke to the R.E. officer, thanked him for his help, told him we'd be back the following day and asked him to reserve the DUKWs for us.

'Don't worry,' the R.E. officer smiled, 'nobody else will want them.'

'Seven DUKWs to a patrol, Bob,' said Popski as we roared past a long line of clanging tank-transporters outside Fano. 'Six jeep-DUKWs and one crane-DUKW.'

'The crane-DUKW can carry supplies,' I suggested as Popski swerved and narrowly missed a racing despatch rider on a popping motor-cycle. 'Extra petrol, ammo and rations.'

By the time we reached Coriano, where the patrols were biting their finger-nails, we had the DUKW patrol organization clear in our minds.

Popski drove to Army H.Q. to obtain authority to draw DUKWs.

I moved the patrols to S. Vito.

Whether it was due to the fact that we were all thinking and talking about DUKWs or just plain coincidence I cannot say, but coming round a bend on the hill road to S. Vito, Ben Owen realized a long-cherished ambition.

Ever since we'd gone jeeping in the Apennines Ben had tried to catch a goose by the neck without stopping or getting out of his jeep. We'd all tried, unsuccessfully, and given up trying. But not Ben Owen. Ben was made of sterner staff. Once he'd made up his mind to do a thing, he persevered until he succeeded. 'I'll get one yet, Skipper,' he said confidently every time he failed, and kept on trying.

Geese were plentiful in the Apennines. Every farmyard had its complement of cackling geese and we came upon them every day —waddling in line by the side of the road or crossing it as we shot round a bend. Often we'd run over a goose, try as we did to avoid them they *would* run under the wheels ('Liar!'), and there would be an exciting race between the jeep driver madly reversing to pick up a blood-stained, flapping goose from the middle of the road and the goose-owner running from his farmyard with the same object in view. Needless to say, the jeep driver invariably won. But not one of us had ever succeeded in catching a goose by the neck as we zoomed past.

Ben Owen did.

As we rounded a sharp bend on the road to S. Vito there, waddling haughtily along the sunlit grass verge, was a line of long-necked, yellow-beaked geese. Ben Owen's eyes shone when he saw them and he called to his driver who immediately swerved and Ben, leaning far out with ready, outstretched arm . . . grabbed . . . gave a shout of triumph and held aloft a squawking, flapping goose. . . .

'*Ladrone!*' shrieked the livid owner, running from his farmyard to shake an impotent fist at the laughing Ben. (Thief!)

'*Grazia*,' shouted Ben Owen, waving the goose. (Many thanks.)

322

Ben Owen pulled his prize aboard and expertly wrung its neck. The patrol roared past.

P.P.A. took to DUKWs as ducks take to water.

We spent a number of days at S. Vito familiarizing ourselves with the ins and outs of the strange-looking craft, reduced the art of craning to split-second timing, and then took to the water.

Driving the DUKWs to Ancona Harbour with the jeeps perched on their backs, we boarded an L.C.T. and put to sea, hove-to three miles off-shore and lowered the ramp with a splash.

'Right, Rob,' said Popski. 'Out you go.'

I squared the clumsy DUKW to the bouncing ramp and revved. . . .

'Hold tight!' I yelled to Gino and George sitting high up in the jeep behind me.

Splaaaaaaaaasssssssssssh! The DUKW hit the choppy sea with a resounding smack, shuddered and rocked perilously.

'Too fast, Bob,' Popski shouted from the top of the ramp.

I waved an acknowledging hand, snicked into water-drive and chugged away from the mother-ship. George Sonley clambered over the jeep and sat beside me in the DUKW driving-seat.

'Bit of all right, eh, Skipper?'

'Bloody good things, these, George. Watch this.'

I pressed hard on the accelerator and sawed at the steering-wheel. The DUKW bucketed violently and shipped water.

'Steady on, Skipper,' George said, shaking sea-water from his soaking battledress.

'O.K., Gino?' I called over my shoulder.

'*Benissimo, Capitano*. O.K.'

'Come back, Bob,' Popski megaphoned from Mother Duck. He wanted to be sure I could climb on board again before he let the other DUKWlings down the ramp.

I swung the steering-wheel hard round, as I did a jeep on the road. An oncoming wave hit the side of the blunt-nosed bow and all but capsized the DUKW.

'Christ, Skipper. Go easy,' George complained, holding tightly to the low gun'l. 'You'll have us all in the briny.'

I took my foot from the pedal, straightened the steering-wheel and chugged in a wide circle.

'Got to learn how to handle these things, George,' I soothed.

323

I steered for the swaying, plunging ramp . . . felt my front
wheels touch . . . accelerated . . . came to a stop with the rear
wheels rubbing against the ramp and the screw threshing the
water. . . .

'Change to wheel-drive,' Riches shouted from the L.C.T.

'Oh, blast!' I'd forgotten that.

I changed the drive and accelerated. The rear wheels burred
against the edge of the ramp, but wouldn't grip.

'Go back and try again, Bob,' Popski advised. 'Rush it this
time.'

I eased the clutch, let the DUKW slide back into the water,
engaged screw-drive again and went astern a good thirty yards.
The art of getting on board, I could see, was not to lose speed and
to change quickly from screw- to wheel-drive the moment the front
wheels touched the ramp.

I manœuvred the DUKW square to the ramp and revved. . . .

'Hold on, chaps!' I sang out.

The DUKW surged through the slapping waves at six knots
and hit the ramp with a wallop. I crashed into wheel-drive the
moment the nose lifted and we shot on board like a guided missile,
scattering the watchers at the top of the ramp.

'The art of coming on board, Popski,' I declaimed when order
had been restored, 'is to get square-on to the ramp, get up speed
and snick into wheel-drive the moment you feel the front wheels
touch.'

'Right, Bob,' said Popski. 'Down you go again—and don't
splash this time.'

I drove down the ramp again, braked at the bottom and eased
the craft gently into the water.

'How's that, George?' I enquired as we chugged away.

'Very nice, Skipper.' George put forefinger and thumb together and raised the other three fingers in a delicate, pansy
gesture.

'*Buono, Capitano*,' Gino commented from upstairs.

We chugged away from the ramp and the other DUKWs
followed us down one by one until a whole brood of little
DUKWlings were circling happily round Mother Duck.

'Right, Bob,' said Popski when we were all aboard again and
sailing back to harbour. 'Now we'll do a night exercise. We'll leave

harbour at dusk, anchor three miles out and you'll go ashore in the DUKWs, turn round on the beach and come back to the L.C.T.'

'Yes, Popski.'

'Without lights, Bob,' he added.

'Yes, Popski.'

Leaving Ancona Harbour in the sunset hush of the following evening, we sailed up-coast clear of the dock area, anchored about three miles offshore and waited until it was dark. Popski believed in making training exercises as difficult as possible.

I noticed that a wind was rising.

When you could barely see your hand in front of your face Popski said to me:

'Right, Bob. Off you go—and remember, *no lights.*'

I nodded in the pitch darkness and heard the ramp go down with a mighty slap.

'Everybody ready?' I called.

'O.K., Skipper,' in chorus from the crews.

I revved and moved towards the dark mouth of the ramp. . . .

One by one we wheeled down the creaking boards and flopped into the sea, like ducklings waddling down a river bank and plopping into the water.

Mother Duck immediately vanished astern and we bobbed like corks upon the dark surface of the heaving Adriatic, an abandoned brood of ugly DUKWlings swimming for the distant shore.

'It's bloody dark, Skipper,' George Sonley complained, cupping a hand over the luminous dial of the army-issue compass he held on his knee and checking our course by the lights of Ancona twinkling comfortingly on the starboard bow.

'Starboard a bit, Skipper.'

I sawed at the steering-wheel. . . .

'On course. Hold it, Skipper.'

We steered due west on a compass-bearing of 270°.

I peered through the spray-wet windscreen at the corrugated black line which marked the coast, at the rippling, surging, dipping water which slapped the DUKW a bare foot below the level of my elbow, at the churning wakes which marked the passage of the other DUKWs rising and falling on either flank.

Assisted by a following wind, we chugged steadily shorewards at six knots an hour, slewing a bit when an oily wave sucked at the sunken road wheels and pulled the craft sideways. The DUKWs were remarkably seaworthy but they dragged badly (because of the four road wheels) and you had constantly to be sawing at the steering-wheel to keep the blunt bow square to the waves.

'Port a bit, Skipper.'

I pulled at the wheel. . . .

'On course. Hold it, Skipper.'

Perched upon the jeep crow's-nest behind us Gino surveyed the surrounding darkness through night-glasses.

'No submarines, Gino?' I called up to him.

'*Niente, Capitano,*' he called down.

'Port a bit, Skipper,' George intoned.

I tugged at the dragging wheel. . . .

'On course. Hold it, Skipper.'

We chugged steadily towards the shore. . . .

The dark outline of the hills grew bolder and the headlamps of convoys moving along the coast road flashed intermittently like swinging lanterns guiding us to the landing-beach. A tiny red eye shone from the centre of the DUKW instrument panel, a friendly thing amidst the all-enveloping gloom of the inimical sea, and the electrically operated windscreen wipers maintained a benevolent chatter as they rubbed perpetually against the glass of their circumscribed arc . . . click, click . . . click, click . . . click, click. . . .

Imperceptibly we gained upon the shore and a strip of creaming surf became visible through the semi-circle of cleared glass.

'Breakers ahead, George.'

George Sonley nodded and intoned:

'Starboard a bit, Skipper.'

I steered into the correct bearing, eye-marked a dark blob of hillside and kept the bouncing, slapping DUKW in line with it. . . .

The sound of the foaming breakers swelled to a thunderous roar and the DUKW began to bucket and plunge.

'Keep her nose-on, Skipper, for Christ's sake,' George Sonley muttered.

The DUKW wallowed momentarily in a deep trough and a mountainous wave, creeping upon us from behind, lifted the shuddering craft high upon its rushing crest and we shot forward like a surf-boat, smothered in spray. . . .

'Keep her straight, Skipper. . . . For muck's sake keep her straight,' George Sonley shouted in a panicky voice.

I gripped the steering-wheel and tried to keep the bow square to the shore, but the DUKW was at the mercy of the leaping, pouncing breakers . . . we sank down . . . down . . . down . . . into a deep trough with the waves leering high above our heads . . . then up . . . up . . . up on the crest of a great forward surge of water, blinded by soaking, salt-tasting spray . . . tossed like a cork in a welter of seething froth. . . .

I felt the road wheels touch bottom and I snicked into land-drive . . . accelerated . . . heard the wheels scrunch on pebbles . . . saw foaming white surf running past the side of the DUKW . . . then we were bowling up firm sand like a racing yacht coming in on its beaching cradle. . . .

I drove up to the dunes, turned and braked.

A shoal of porpoises dived through the surf and advanced up the beach. I counted them . . . one . . . two . . . three . . . four . . . five . . . six.

The DUKWs were all present.

'O.K., Rich? How d'you like DUKWing?'

'*Molto bene*, Skipper.' Riches grinned as he drew up alongside. His pointed van Dyck beard was beaded with salt-spray and his right arm was soaking.

'Get wet, Ben?' I asked Ben Owen as he drove up.

'A little bit, not much. Just the job, these things, Skipper.'

The remaining DUKWs scrunched alongside and I became aware of J. C. standing beside me with his hands behind his back and a quiet smile playing amongst the curls of his Christ-like beard.

'Present for you, Skipper.'

J. C. brought a hand from behind his back and dangled a two-pound silver fish in my face. I drew back, startled.

A roar of laughter went up from the patrolmen.

'Where the hell did you get that, J. C.?' I asked.

'Caught it, of course,' he replied indignantly.

J. C. had been trailing a fishing line!

Smoking, talking and joking, imagining ourselves to have made a landing behind the lines, we rested for half an hour and then commenced the difficult return journey.

It was a relatively simple matter to come from the mother-ship to the shore with the lights of Ancona to guide us. We could hardly go wrong. But it was like looking for a needle in a haystack to find our own way back to a blacked-out ship on a pitch-black ocean.

'Keep each other in sight,' I called as we drove down to the surf.

Driving on road wheels until the DUKWs were afloat, keeping the nose square to the pounding breakers, we were flung about, tossed, bounced, slapped, side-swept, pitched, wetted and smothered in spray, all but capsized before the water-screw gave us headway and we picked up speed clear of the surf. . . .

'Bearing ninety degrees, George,' I said. 'Due east.'

George Sonley steadied the little compass on his knee and waited for the luminous arrow to stop flickering. . . .

'Port a bit, Skipper.'

I steered as George directed. . . .

'. . . bit more, Skipper . . . too much . . . starboard a little . . . that's better. . . . Hold it. . . . Hold it. . . . Dead on.'

On course, I put my foot down, and we surged ahead.

A fresh wind blew and the sea was rising. Every few minutes the bow lifted clear of the water, plunged through an advancing breaker, slapped sickeningly into a trough and pitched with the impact of the following wave. All I could see through the running windscreen was a dark mass of moving water with feathery spumes chasing each other past the prancing bow. Dark objects bobbed on either side of us ahead of white wakes and the red pin-points of light on the instrument panels shone in the darkness like the blood-shot eyes of sea-monsters. . . .

'Keep counting the DUKWs,' I called up to Gino. 'Tell me if anyone's missing.'

'*Si, Capit——*' Gino's reply was clipped by a gust of wind.

'Getting a bit rough, Skipper,' George observed as the DUKW reared frighteningly on a mountainous wave and another gust of wind blew spray into our faces. . . 'Bloody storm blowing up.'

The wind increased in intensity, whistling ominously past the edge of the windscreen and making the wipers falter in their dripping arc. Spray salted our lips and the DUKW slithered sideways with a horrible oily, crab-like motion . . . reared obliquely . . . slapped jarringly. . . .

328

'Port, Skipper. . . . Port . . . bit more . . . more . . . hold it . . . too far . . . starboard a bit . . . starboard . . . hold it . . . hold it . . . on course. . . .'

No sooner was I on course than the DUKW slewed again on a galloping wave and we rose at a threatening angle . . . poised like a bottle on the crest . . . plunged down . . . down . . . down. . . .

'Starboard. . . . Starboard, Skipper,' George shouted above the howling wind. . . .

I hauled at the dragging, dead-weighed wheel . . . a dark wall of water surged menacingly past my elbow . . . the DUKW righted itself and we chugged on like a prancing sea-horse. . . .

'Starboard a little, Skipper.'

The turbulent sea miles fell behind us. . . .

From his crow's-nest on the jeep, buffeted by the wind, Gino searched the surrounding darkness for signs of Mother Duck. When an hour had gone by I called up to him.

'See anything, Gino?'

'*Niente, Capitano*,' came the thin, windswept reply.

I began to get worried. There was a heavy sea running and the wind blew unabated. According to my calculation we had covered the three miles and Mother Duck should be somewhere close at hand. If only she would show a light. . . .

'Land up in bloody Yugoslavia——' George muttered into the wind.

I pranced on for another fifteen minutes and then, fearing I'd overshot the mark, I took my foot from the accelerator and said to George:

'We'll have to box it, George. Ten minutes on each bearing. Begin with north.'

'O.K., Skipper.'

Following George's directing voice, I changed course and swung due north with the brood trailing behind me. The blind following the blind, I thought grimly. . . .

Side-on to the waves, the DUKWs slewed and slithered, rose up . . . up . . . up, poised on the crest and plunged down . . . down . . . down, frighteningly, with great walls of water surging past our heads. It seemed impossible that we could ever rise again, that the wall of dark water must fall on top of us . . . but it never did. After a sucking, terrifying moment at the nadir of the trough the clumsy bi-sexual craft began its upward rise until we sat momentarily high and dry on the crest of a breaking wave. . . .

'Ten minutes up, Skipper.'

I lifted my foot from the pedal and the DUKW wallowed in a dark hiatus.

'See anything, Gino?' I shouted.

'*Niente, Capitano.*'

'Due east, George. Ten minutes.'

'O.K., Skipper.'

We changed course again, nose into the waves, prancing, slapping, slewing, plunging, pitching, smacking, jarring . . . held aloft on the crests with the screw racing free of the water . . . nose-diving into the onrushing threatening waves. . . .

Presently:

'Ten minutes up, Skipper.'

I decelerated and the DUKW hung in mid air, clawing at the swell. . . .

'See anything, Gino?'

'*Niente, Capitano.*'

I felt panic rise with the rising storm.

'Due south, George,' I said desperately. 'Ten minutes.'

'O.K., Skipper,' resignedly.

Running parallel with the waves again . . . sliding and slipping . . . canting at a fearsome angle . . . hovering . . . plunging obliquely . . . treading water . . . swinging up . . . up . . . up . . . poising for the plunge . . . a sickening, stomach-turning lurch . . . down . . . down . . . down . . . masses of water careening past, head-high . . . spray smothering . . . an awful moment of water-logged despair . . . then up . . . up . . . up. . . .

'Ten minutes up, Skipper.'

'See anything, Gino?'

'*Niente, Capitano.*'

There was only one side of the compass-box to complete.

'West, George. Ten minutes.' I spoke like a man at a gaming table staking his last chip.

Smacking, slapping, jarring, plunging and rearing again with the twinkling lights of Ancona mocking us from starboard, seemingly much further away than they should have been. . . .

'Ten minutes up, Skipper.'

'See anything, Gino?' I called hopelessly, knowing what the answer would be. Back it came, wind-lashed, depressing:

'*Niente, Capitano.*'

My heart sank and I admitted defeat.

Lost in the Adriatic . . . caught in a sudden storm . . . swamped by heavy seas . . . bodies washed up on shore. My imagination ran riot. I saw the DUKWs floundering one by one . . . filling with water . . men clawing despairingly at the great walls of water, calling desperately for help: 'Skipper. . . . Skipper. . . . Skipper' . . . engulfing waves . . . bodies sinking . . . capsized, empty DUKWs tossing on the surface of the cruel sea. . . .

'Lights, George. Muck it,' I heard myself say.

I reached forward to the instrument panel and switched on the headlamps. Two powerful beams danced a bright pathway on the surface of the mountainous sea, revealing its awful, leaping strength. . . .

An answering flash . . . a swinging beam of white light on the starboard bow far, far away.

'There she is, Skipper!'

'Quick, George,' I cried. 'Take a bearing.'

George fiddled with the compass on his knee and presently announced:

'Almost due south, Skipper. A hundred and seventy degrees.'

'O.K., George. Keep me on that bearing.'

I revved and plunged forward, uncaring now, with the other DUKWs prancing excitedly in my wake. . . .

Spray poured over us in cascades as we cut obliquely through the waves, feet hard on the accelerator, hearts, minds and eyes wholly concentrated on the distant searching, swinging beam of light. . . .

Slowly, agonizingly slowly, our homing beam drew closer. From time to time I glanced round to make sure the other DUKWs were following and saw their dark shapes plunging on either flank, blinking their bloodshot eyes. . . .

Of a sudden, Mother Duck was high above us, big and comforting, flashing her great light into our wet faces.

We ducked under her protective beam . . . squared up to the heaving ramp . . . rushed it . . . bumped on board—a brood of tired and frightened DUKWlings nestling thankfully into the warm security of Mother Duck's extended wing.

Hauling up ramp and anchor in a howling gale, we ran to port before the storm. I stood with Popski in the draughty, tilting hold, post-morteming the exercise.

'Yes, Bob, I know,' Popski admonished, 'but in a sea like this you should have used lights. You might all have been drowned.'

I laughed hysterically and tried to light a cigarette.

20

WHILST Popski's Private Army was perfecting the art of DUKWing, Eighth Army was splashing through the flooded Plain of Lombardy in the muddy wake of the slowly retreating German divisions, and forward troops had reached the gaping banks of the Savio River.

Crossing the Rubicon at the exact spot where Julius Caesar crossed it nineteen hundred and ninety-three years previously—and understanding my Latin history twenty years too late!—I took my patrol of DUKWs to the spreading Savio and gazed upon the dismal scene.

Rain fell upon a shell-shocked village awash to its window-sills in swirling, brown flood-water and upon a road recognizable as main only by the upper half of its submerged telephone poles and the drunken wires sagging between them. Water and dampness were everywhere and the only happy things were the ducks.

'This,' I grinned to Riches, 'is where we go DUKWing.'

Just like ducks, we chugged down the main street between forlorn little groups of marooned *contadini* who waved sadly to us from their upper balconies, past bedraggled hens perched on floating barns and haystacks until we came to the actual river, which we crossed in style.

Executing a snappy change from screw- to wheel-drive we revved up the visible tarmac on the far bank and were welcomed by an eager reception committee of mortar bombs which shook us vociferously by the hand and slapped us on the back. . . .

'Down this track,' I yelled. 'Quick!'

A track led off by the river bank to the famed Pineta di Classe. We drove haltingly along it, dodging the German shells as they whistled over. . . .

333

Approaching the pine wood, I saw a uniformed figure move behind a tree.

'Quick, George. A sniper. Over there.'

George swung the fifty and was about to fire when Gino shouted from behind us:

'No, *Capitano. Partigani.*'

'Hold it, George,' I called.

Sonley held his fire and I pulled up and waited. . . . More figures moved amongst the trees . . . a group of armed partisans surrounded us and welcomed us into their camp.

'*Inglesi! Inglesi! . . . Oh, Armata Privata di Popski. Bravo! Avanti!*'

Cut off in the *pineta* by the German retreat, the partisans were a detachment of the Brigata Garibaldi which, from its watery headquarters in the Comacchio marshes, had been harrying the German troops stationed in and around Ravenna. They were somewhat weary and dispirited and our arrival put new life into them.

I was introduced to Ateo, the detachment commander, a big, bluff, hearty man with a mighty laugh which rippled his rolls of flesh and reminded me of Friar Tuck in Robin Hood's merry band; to the thoughtful Rafuzzi, his meticulous quartermaster, a schoolteacher from Ravenna; to Ida and Isabella and the flashing, black-eyed Maria with the scar on her cheek—three cheery partisan girls, dressed like the men and armed to the teeth, who cooked and ran errands for the detachment and were under Ateo's watchful eye; to many others whose names I have forgotten, a group of about fifty colourful personalities.

Ateo held out a big hand. '*Va Bene, Capitano,*' he said jovially. 'Let us join forces and fight the Germans together.'

'You'll need better arms and more ammunition, Ateo,' I said practically. 'Give Riches a party of men and he'll bring up supplies in the DUKWs.'

We craned the jeeps from their mother DUKWs. Half a dozen delighted partisans clambered aboard an amphibian and Riches recrossed the Savio.

'Look out for the stonk, Rich,' I cautioned him as he left.

'Don't worry, Skipper, I'll duck it in the mucking DUKW.' he punned, grinning.

The *pineta* was dense and damp and partly flooded. It extended for a couple of miles towards the sea and about five towards Ravenna. Lateral canals flowed through its dank silence and it was criss-crossed by bridle-paths along which we drove our jeeps. On the left flank, parallel with the *pineta*, the coast road and railway ran north to Ravenna, which was occupied by a strong enemy garrison.

Riches returned with a large supply of rifles, Tommy-guns, sten-guns, hand-grenades and ammunition, and whilst he and the rest of the patrol were dishing them out to the excited partisans, George, Gino and I drove through the *pineta* on a tour of inspection.

Approaching the first canal in the footsteps of Byron and Boccaccio, we glimpsed a white-walled cottage through the trees. I braked at a bend in the path and 'sniffed'.

'Wait here, George,' I said. 'Gino and I'll walk up.'

George stood by the jeep fondling the fifty, and Gino and I picked our way through the trees towards the canal bank. . . .

The cottage was empty and we stood on the moss-grown canal bank a little apart, looking at the demolished bridge, calculating how long it would take to build a new one. I heard a rustle in the undergrowth on the other side of the water and 'froze'. . . .

D-r-r-r-r-r-r-t. A burst of Spandau-fire cut the air and whistled viciously past my head. I ducked. D-r-r-r-r-r-r-r-t. I felt the wind of another burst go past my thigh and stood rooted to the spot. I don't know why, but it saved my life, for if I'd run I would surely have been hit.

I saw something move behind bushes on the other side of the eighteen-foot-wide canal and leapt behind the nearest tree. . . . D-r-r-r-r-r-r-t . . . not a moment too soon. Another terrifying burst knifed past. . . . D-r-r-r-r-r-r-t . . . another . . . D-r-r-r-r-r-r-r-t . . . and another . . . D-r-r-r-r-r-r-r-t. . . . Then . . . D-r-r-r-r-r-r-r-r-r-t. An angry, sustained burst sprayed the canal bank (where I'd been standing) and smacked into the trees. . . . I looked round for Gino. He was standing behind a tree ten yards from me, grinning.

D-r-r-r-r-r-r-t. Another burst whistled through the trees. . . . D-r-r-r-r-r-r-r-r-t . . . another . . . D-r-r-r-r-r-r-t . . . and another. . . .

We pressed ourselves against our trees, making our bodies as small as possible.

D-r-r-r-r-r-r-t. The German gunners moved their position and fired at us from a different angle. Gino and I edged round our respective trees, comforting each other with sickly grins. Then a sniper cross-fired at us . . . phut . . . phut . . . and removed the grin from our faces. . . .

For a moment Life hung in the balance and Death was very close. As we sidled round our trees to avoid the Spandau-fire . . . D-r-r-r-r-r-r-t . . . D-r-r-r-r-r-r-r-r-r-r-t . . . the sniper fired at us round the other side . . . phut . . . phut . . . and I cannot understand why neither of us was hit. . . . D-r-r-r-r-r-r-r-t. . . . D-r-r-r-r-r-r-t . . . phut . . . phut. . . . The world stood still. There was nothing in the universe but our beating hearts and the killers on the opposite canal bank. . . .

If only George would drive up and fire the fifty across the canal to distract their attention, I wished, and yelled 'George . . . George . . . George' like a frightened little boy calling to his big brother for help. . . . 'George . . . George . . George.' . . . But we'd left the jeep a good way back and the intervening trees deadened the sound of my voice. George heard only the muffled sounds of firing and stood resolutely by his gun.

The German machine-gunners were determined to kill us, but Gino and I were just as determined to live and the action developed into a desperate game. The German gunners kept moving position to get a bead on us and every time Gino and I sidled round our trees to avoid their line of fire, the hidden sniper shot at us from a different angle so that we had to 'sniff' both ways at once and keep our bottoms pulled well in. . . . D-r-r-r-r-r-r-t. . . . D-r-r-r-r-r-r-r-t. . . . Gino and I sidling round our trees, pressing hard against their protective boles . . . phut . . . phut. . . . Gino and I jerking our bottoms in, feeling the wind of a bullet missing us by a hair's breadth . . . sweat breaking out . . . hearts pounding . . . breath catching. . . . D-r-r-r-r-r-r-r-t. . . . D-r-r-r-r-r-r-t. . . . 'George . . . George' . . . phut . . .phut . . . .

There came a momentary lull in the firing as the Germans changed position. Gino and I took a chance and hopped back a tree . . . Waited for the enemy to fire. . . . D-r-r-r-r-t. . . . D-r-r-r-r-r-r-t . . . phut . . . phut . . . hopped back another tree . . . waited again, breathlessly. . . . D-r-r-r-r-r-r-t. . . . D-r-r-r-r-r-r-t . . . phut . . . phut . . . hopped back another tree . . . phut . . . phut . . . hopped again . . . phut. . . .

Eventually we hopped out of range and ran to the jeep. . . .

'What's the matter, Skipper?' George asked innocently. 'Were you fired at?'

'Yes, George,' I replied shakily. 'We were fired at.'

Riches had acquired a field-mortar and a supply of ammunition. He set the weapon up in a clearing and we spent the afternoon lobbing mortar bombs over the canal. When dusk fell, we drove the jeeps up, staged an attack with the partisans and cleared the north bank.

We had one casualty—an obese partisan who couldn't find a big-enough tree and was furrowed in the bottom by a sniper's bullet.

When the battle was over, we withdrew to the Garibaldi encampment where the girl-cooks had prepared a royal feast in honour of the *Armata Privata di Popski*. Ateo liked his food and saw to it that there was plenty. The girls had roasted an ox on a spit and there were lashings of red wind to go with it.

We stood round a roaring log fire in the clearing in the *pineta*, helping ourselves to meat from the carcase and washing it down with wine. Secured by a guard of alert partisans patrolling the canal bank, we let our hair down in the clearing and burst into ribald song. Occasionally, a German shell exploded in the depths of the wood and Riches broke off to lob a few mortar bombs in reply, coming back to help himself to more meat and wine as if mortaring during dinner were the accepted thing.

Inevitably there were voices and as the evening wore on we were enchanted by arias from the operas and folk songs from the Romagna and, anti-climactically, 'B' Patrol's rendering of 'Torno Sorrento' (in Italian), which set Ateo's adipose tissue aquiver and brought the partisan house down.

I can see it now, that scene in the clearing—the leaping flames, the fire-lit circle of faces eager with life, the dark shadowy trees of the silent *pineta*, the wooden shed where we slept, the sparks flying upwards as a log crackled and fell sending up spiralling blue smoke, the hacked-at half-eaten carcase tied to the spit by its blackened hooves, the broached barrel of wine standing beside it, the bearded faces of the patrolmen alternating with the beardless partisans, Don Galloway's bushy black masterpiece, Riches' pointed van Dyck, J. C.'s russet replica, Maria's flashing black eyes and the livid scar on her flushed cheek, Ateo's towering bulk searching the group with his ever-watchful eye, making sure that none of his henchmen went nut-gathering with the vigorous Ida . . . and Death stalking us in the background. . . . Wheeeeeeeeee. . . . Wruuuuuumph! Ah, those colourful days in the Pineta di Classe. Nostalgic.

With the Canadians maintaining a machine-gun sweep across the flooded fields on our left flank and 'R' and 'S' Patrols snooping up and down the seaward marshes in DUKWs on our right, we probed forward daily and pushed the Germans out of the *pineta*.

There were amusing incidents.

There was a signalman's box on the railway line which ran between the *pineta* and the coast road to Ravenna. It was close to the German positions and made an excellent observation post. To approach it by day drew irate enemy machine-gun fire so that we could visit it only after dark. I put George Sonley and J. C. into it one night armed with a pair of powerful binoculars and told them to stay there ('Mucking hell, Skipper').

In glorious isolation, they were alone all day keeping a watchful eye on enemy movements across the canal and each night we walked along the raised railway embankment to see them and take them rations and water. We used a wheel-barrow to carry the load, pushing it in front of us, bump . . . scrunch . . . bumpity-bump . . . scrunch . . . bump over the sleepers of the single-line track. The sound was distorted by the dank mist which blew in from the sea every night and by the time the sound reached the Canadian lines on the other side of the coast road it was not unlike the clip . . . clop . . . clip . . . clop of a horse's hooves. A rumour began to circulate that a phantom apocalypsian horse roamed the front line at nights!

There was no horse, but there was a cat, a big, black, in-scrutable tom which scared the wits out of me one night. I was standing in the bushes by the side of the embankment in the small hours, peering across the canal in the mist and seeing a crouching German in every shadow when something foreign touched my leg. I smothered a shriek, missed a heart-beat and lived an hour in a second, afraid to look, sure that a German night-patrol had crept up on me and had me by the ankles. . . . I heard a purring sound, my heart beat again and I plucked up the courage to look down—the great black thing was rubbing itself against my legs, purring happily.

Night-prowling was a weakness of mine, I liked to know what was going on, and I strolled about the front for an hour or two, 'sniffing' and looking and listening. The cat came with me, all round the front line, and when I returned to camp at first light it trotted contentedly at my heels like a dog.

I have never been very fond of cats, finding them, like women, liable to scratch, but this cat attached itself to me. Being black, I took it as an omen of good luck and indulged its fancy, feeding it with the choicest morsels and letting it ride on my jeep. George Sonley christened it 'Popski' and it rode about with us for days, showing a marked contempt for clattering fifties and crashing mortar bombs.

Then, one day, it left us and we never saw it again.

'Where's Popski?' I asked, noticing that the cat wasn't in its usual place on top of the jeep load.

George Sonley blanched—was this an omen of bad luck?—and ran round and round the encampment frantically calling 'Popski . . . Popski . . . Popski.' . . .

Fortunately, O.C. Popski's Private Army was out of earshot at his headquarters on the other side of the Savio!

We cleared the Germans from the *pineta*, but a determined rearguard clung obstinately to a cluster of houses on the north bank of a canal near the coast road. Protected by flooded fields and a blown bridge the rearguard sat tight and machine-gunned everything that ventured closer than a thousand yards.

'Mortar them out, Skipper,' Riches suggested, keen to demonstrate his skill with the new weapon.

'Good idea, Rich,' I replied, equally keen to see what he could do.

Gino slung a pair of binoculars round his neck and climbed to the top of an old watch-tower on the edge of the *pineta* from where he obtained a good view of the enemy position; Riches set up his mortar a thousand yards back and started lobbing them over; in the absence of a field telephone, we organized a chain of partisan runners to bring Gino's messages to the mortar-post.

For a time, all went well. The first bomb whistled satisfyingly overhead and Gino's terse message came back:

339

'*Buono*. Up 300'—meaning that the direction was good, but the range 300 yards short.

Riches adjusted his angle of flight and lobbed another one over.

A runner brought Gino's message:

'*Buono*. Up 100.'

The bombs were still falling short of the target. Riches adjusted again and lobbed another one.

Back came the message:

'*Buono*. Down 100.'

Riches had overshot the mark. He adjusted again and his next bomb exploded amongst the houses.

'*Benissimo*,' the message came back.

Riches got down to it in earnest and lobbed them over in quick succession, every one a winner. . . .

But the ground was soggy and the backlash of continuous firing sank the heavy base-plate, raising the angle of flight. The mortar tube suddenly canted upwards. Horrified, I watched a bomb describe its trajectory and fall down . . . down . . . down . . . crash! . . . inside Gino's watch-tower.

'Christ, we've killed Gino,' I muttered through dry lips and hurried towards the tower. . . . I was intercepted by a runner who thrust a crumpled note into my trembling hand.

'*Grazia molto*,' it read. 'Thanks very much. Up 1000.'

It took a lot to upset Gino.

Riches re-set his mortar on harder ground and continued the barrage until dusk when we waded through the flooded fields, encircled the shattered outpost and closed in with a rush.

The Germans had had enough and surrendered without a fight, but they were truculent Nazis and wouldn't talk so we had to persuade them by a method of our own.

I sat at a table in the dimly lit shed in the clearing with the elated partisans milling about the crackling fire outside and the scar-faced Maria with the heavy bust flashing her passionate black eyes, itching to draw her gleaming butcher's knife across the prisoners' throats.

Sergeant Riches marched-in the first prisoner. He wouldn't talk.

'Away with him, Rich,' I said impatiently.

Ben Owen, J. C. and Don Galloway brandished Tommy-guns, hauled the prisoner outside and marched him before the eyes of his brother prisoners round to the back of the shed. A minute later a burst of Tommy-gun fire shattered the air, an exultant cry rose from the partisans gathered about the fire, and the escort reappeared minus their prisoner.

The next prisoner was marched-in. He wouldn't talk either, but he wavered.

'Away with him, Rich.'

Ben Owen and Company marched the prisoner outside . . . another burst of Tommy-gun fire echoed through the wood . . . another cry of exultation issued from partisan throats.

The remaining prisoners talked, freely and volubly. . . . And you can imagine their chagrin when they were marched behind the shed to find their companions alive and well, sitting on the grass smoking cigarettes under the watchful eyes of a partisan guard.

To Maria's intense disappointment the prisoners were spared, put aboard a DUKW and taken to P.P.A. headquarters behind the Savio.

A party of war correspondents visited the Ravenna front one day and expressed a desire to see actual fighting conditions in the front line. Popski provided them with transport and sent them up to me.

There was very little activity at the time. We were watching the German positions across the flooded fields and the Germans were watching our *pineta*. An occasional vagrant shell whistled lugubriously overhead and exploded dully amongst the wet trees, but apart from that, nothing. I think the war correspondents expected flashing and crashing shells, hoarse cries, blood and mangled bodies, heroics, brave stretcher-parties running the gauntlet of withering machine-gun fire. All they found was mud and flood and an eerie, misty silence.

Not wishing to disappoint them when they had come so far and risked so many dangers, I sent them down to the mortar-post and asked Riches to stage a demonstration of war-like activity for their benefit.

A field-mortar is merely an open-ended steel tube fixed to a solid steel base-plate. The mortarman inserts the bomb into the tube fins first and bangs it to the bottom where a firing pin sets off the expulsion charge. The bomb comes out with a swoosh and makes an ear-splitting crack as it leaves the tube, and if you have any respect for your eardrums you keep your head well down.

Riches failed to explain this when, to their manifest delight, he invited the correspondents to 'lob a few over' into the German positions. . . .

The last we saw of our visitors was a staggering posse shaking heads and poking fingers into ears as they hurried away from the angry stonk their efforts had drawn from the German artillery.

Riches chortled about their discomfiture for days. He had a thing about war correspondents.

Tailpiece.

Ben Owen and I were sitting in a ditch near a bend in the coast road one misty morning. We had an American bazooka with us, trying (unsuccessfully) to fire its high-powered projectiles into a German position round the corner. Our eyebrows were singed and our cheeks scarred from the white-hot phosphorus emission which followed the expulsion of each electrically discharged bomb. A face-guard was provided to protect the firer but it interfered with sighting and we discarded it.

The sound of a motor-cycle exhaust fell upon our ears as we struggled to fit another bomb into the breech and we looked round, puzzled. . . .

A despatch rider came into view, driving at speed.

'Stop him, Ben,' I cried when I saw him. 'He's on the wrong road.'

Ben Owen placed the primed bomb on the verge and backed down the ditch . . . waved frantically to the Canadian rider to stop. . . .

The Canadian took not the slightest notice. Goggled head bent over the handlebars, going like the wind, he roared past us and cornered in classic style.

We watched his khaki-clad bottom disappear round the bend as he raced towards Ravenna, and put our fingers in our ears. . . .

D-r-r-r-r-r-r-r-t. . . . D-r-r-r-r-r-r-r-r-r-r-r-r-r-r-r-r-t . . . crash! . . . silence.

During a night, the Germans hopped back another canal and demolished a few more bridges, blew holes in another canal bank.

Next morning the allied front line advanced another muddy mile.

21

Fʀᴏᴍ the last trees of the misty *pineta* we looked towards the grey church spires of Ravenna. The ancient city was still in German hands; the defence line ran before it along the north bank of the River Montone and Fiumi Uniti Canal.

Between us and the barely visible canal a vast expanse of motionless flood-water gleamed dully, like burnished gunmetal, under a cloud-filled, wintry sky. A mile and a half in front of us, a thousand yards from the canal, a farmyard stood clear of the water like a stranded Noah's Ark—a red-roofed white-walled house, a barn, haystacks, a line of trees, and animals moving about. Distant left, isolated by the flood, another farmstead seemed to hang from the sagging telephone wires which marked the wholly submerged coast road. Distant right, a long line of yellow sand-dunes bordered the sea and close up to the seaward end of the canal, connected to it by a causeway, a squat tower stood sentinel-like sweeping the flooded littoral with a baleful eye. In the tower and in both the farmsteads German machine-gunners watched and waited.

'How the hell are we going to get in there without getting shot?' I asked Ben Owen, lowering my glasses from the Noah's Ark in the foreground. 'Take a look, Ben.'

I passed him my glasses.

'DUKWs, Skipper?' Ben suggested after a moment.

I shook my head.

'They'll hear the engines and sink us with machine-gun fire.'

Ben returned my binoculars and I looked at the farmstead, at the white oxen moving about, at the rutted track emerging from the flood-water close to the farmhouse. . . .

An idea struck me and I slapped Ben on the back, making him jump.

'Oxen, Ben,' I cried. 'How deep's the water?'

Ben picked up a stone and threw it far out. It splashed into the submerged track with a dull plop.

'A foot, eighteen inches, Skipper,' he guessed.

'Come on, Ben. Let's go and talk to Ateo.'

We clambered into our parked jeep and drove through the dripping *pineta* to the Garibaldi camp.

Ateo's bull shoulders shook with mirth when I painted for him in my army-slang Italian a word picture of surprised German soldiers waking up in the morning to find their island home stocked by armed jeeps instead of horned cattle. '*Benissimo, Capitano,*' he chortled obesely. '*Si . . . si . . . bene . . . bene. . . . Ho . . . ho . . . ho. . . .*' They had a friend in the enemy camp, Ateo said, Alfonso, the farm manager. They would contact him and enlist his help. . . . '*Benissimo. . . . Ho . . . ho . . . ho.*' . . .

The short winter's afternoon was swallowed by a dank mist which crawled over the grey flood-water and filtered, ghost-like, through the *pineta*. We jeep-lifted two of Ateo's picked men as far as the edge of the flood and watched them wade into the inky dampness.

We waited. . . .

Three hours later we brought them back, complete with Alfonso, a burly, stocky, phlegmatic Romagnola type.

'*Ho, Alfonso, amico, come sta?*' Ateo boomed, slapping him on the back and thrusting a glass of wine and a hunk of roast towards him. (Alfonso, my good friend, how are you?)

'Eh,' jerked Alfonso, smiling, putting his head to one side and opening his palms, Romagnola fashion.

As Alfonso ate and drank, he told Ateo the situation on the farm. The Germans weren't in the house, but in the hay-stacks, he said. They'd hollowed-out the largest stack and lived inside it as in a dug-out. There were two machine-guns, one on either side of the stacks, manned day and night. The Germans, of which there were nine, a sergeant and eight men, seldom visited the house and he, Alfonso, took them a can of fresh milk every morning. Yes, oxen was a good idea. He would provide them. There were mines to be avoided at the end of the track. He would meet us on arrival and give us the latest report. When were we coming?

I planned the attack for the following night and Alfonso

returned to his Noah's Ark, jeep-lifted by Gino to the end of the *pineta*.

In the clammy murk of the following evening we sat in our jeeps on the fringe of the mist-bound *pineta*, waiting for the oxen. . . .

I peered into the blanketing gloom through night-glasses and saw nothing but amorphous flood-water and writhing serpents of mist.

'They're taking their time about it, blast them,' I muttered impatiently.

'*E difficile, Capitano*,' Gino chided. 'It isn't an easy matter to catch oxen in the dark with German machine-gunners watching and listening.'

I had momentarily forgotten about the enemy machine-gunners and mentally apologized to the intrepid Garibaldi men who were risking their lives to fetch the oxen.

Eventually the oxen came, led by a rope round their wide-swept, pointed horns—six grey-white, docile, ponderous, well-fed beasts. The partisans hitched one to the front of each jeep and we set off on our dangerous lark. . . .

It was a strange sensation to sit at the steering-wheel in the misty darkness and feel yourself moving forward without an engine answering to the pressure of your toe. You felt powerless without the engine, at the mercy of the plodding ox, for you could neither stop nor start of your own volition but just sit helplessly, half submerged, keeping the jeep on an even keel by steering into the swaying rump in front. Visibility was limited to a few yards and a cold dampness rose from the stagnant flood-water, chilling both bone-marrow and spirit. Somewhere ahead, hidden in the mist, was the German front line. Somewhere behind, similarly obscured, was the protective security of our own forward troops. We moved in the damp hiatus between the two, seeing nothing, hoping for the best. It was eerie, too, when we reached the island-farm rising ghost-like from the blowing mist. Alfonso waited at the end of the track, beside the gate of the house. His shadowy form glided noiselessly up to my jeep.

'*Va bene, Capitano*,' he breathed conspiratorially.

The partisans halted and held the oxen while I went with Alfonso to recce the ground. Wraith-like, we flitted past a garden fence, a black, smelly manure-heap, a dark barn and other vague, mist-hung buildings. Alfonso touched my arm and I crouched with him beside the dung-heap. The haystacks were down there, he whispered, pointing into the swirling mist, about a hundred yards away. I nodded in the darkness, knowing instinctively what we must do. The house was on the right, fifty yards from the manure-heap and level with it. The big barn was on the left about another fifty yards from the manure-heap and practically level with it. Park the jeeps behind house and barn so that they wouldn't be seen at dawn, get into position behind the dung-heap and rush the haystacks when the Germans were off-guard, having breakfast. That was the plan. Simple, straightforward, foolproof. Alfonso would tip us the wink when he returned from delivering the morning milk.

'*Buono*, Alfonso,' I breathed.

We glided back to the waiting jeeps. . . .

The partisans unhitched the patient oxen and we pushed the jeeps into position behind house and barn. There was little fear of our being seen in the mist and the oxen, wandering about the farmyard, covered up our movements.

By 3 a.m. Alfonso was asleep in the house and Riches, Gino, Rogers, Galloway, J. C., Ben Owen, George Sonley and I were crouched behind the stinking manure-heap with the partisans and the remaining patrolmen standing by the hidden jeeps.

Half-kneeling, cramped, damp and chilled, we waited for daylight, feeling the presence of the German machine-gunners lying beside the haystacks wrapped in mist a hundred yards in front. Guns boomed on the flank towards Forli where Eighth Army battled for possession of the Rimini–Bologna road and immediately behind us, making us jump every time they moved, the invisible oxen splashed on the edge of the flood-water. . . .

Time dragged. Shivering with the clammy coldness, longing for a cigarette, we breathed the acrid stench of organic decay and changed from knee to knee to ease cramped leg muscles . . . four o'clock . . . five o'clock . . . six o'clock. . . . It was daylight now with the mist hanging close and blanketing. . . . The door of the homestead creaked open and Alfonso appeared . . . walked past us towards the cowshed without acknowledging our presence . . . walked past us again half an hour later carrying a large can of milk . . . disappeared in the direction of the haystacks . . . reappeared a few minutes later minus the milk can and gave me the

O.K. signal as he turned to go into the house—a pre-arranged movement of the right hand.

'Ready?' I whispered to my crouching men.

Seven heads nodded.

We rose stiffly, bending low, stretched our cramped muscles . . . and raced for the mist-enshrouded haystacks—Riches, Galloway, Rogers and J. C. down one side and Ben Owen, Gino, Sonley and I down the other, each team with a definite, clear-cut plan of action in mind. . . .

It was the fastest hundred yards I ever raced and it seemed never-ending . . . eighty yards to go . . . breath catching . . . fifty yards . . . pain in the chest . . . forty yards . . . leg muscles aching . . . thirty yards . . . heart going to burst . . . twenty yards . . . haystacks becoming visible . . . ten yards. . . .

The German machine-gunners were off-guard, guzzling warm cow's milk like pigs at a trough and we were on top of them before they recovered from their surprise. The gunner on our side heard pounding feet and looked up from the trough, stunned, to see figures bearing down upon him. He tried to fire but Gino and Ben Owen, detailed for the job, kicked his gun aside and threw themselves bodily on top of him, hurting and half smothering the poor devil; on the other side Rogers, seeing the gunner about to fire, sprayed from the hip as he ran and one of his bullets shot the German's nose away. The wounded man reeled back, screaming. . . . Riches, J. C., George Sonley and I met round the back of the big haystack, at the entrance to the dug-out, gasping for breath. . . . I pulled the pin and tossed a hand-grenade into the dark hole. . . . Riches, J. C. and Sonley fired Tommy-gun bursts after it . . . muffled shouts and cries of pain issued from the depths of the dug-out . . . smoke coiled from the opening, mingling with the mist . . . the haystack caught fire . . . five terrified Germans sidled through the smoke with their hands held high . . . two others didn't come out—killed or badly wounded—and their cosy dug-out became their funeral pyre. . . .

The German front line on the canal, mercifully obscured by the morning mist, was a bare 800 yards away and we didn't linger by the burning haystacks.

'Quick,' Rich,' I gasped, still badly winded, 'get these bastards up to the house.'

Prodding them with Tommy-guns, we hustled our frightened

347

prisoners through the smoking stackyard and up to the house, where they gave the grinning Alfonso a very dirty look as we pushed them unceremoniously into an empty room.

The wounded machine-gunner was a shocking sight—two wide-open, terror-stricken eyes staring from a bloody, noseless face. 'For God's sake, Rich,' I exclaimed when I saw him, 'give the poor bugger a field dressing.'

Riches complied and the result was even worse—two terrified eyes staring above an open mouth with a blood-stained, khaki pad between.

I hurriedly closed and locked the door.

Down in the stackyard the haystacks were properly ablaze and dense clouds of smoke billowed up, weaving into the upper layers of mist.

'Jerry'll send out a patrol, Skipper,' Ben Owen said.

I nodded.

'Stand by your jeeps, everybody.'

We took up position and waited for the reprisal which was sure to come. Whatever came we would have to take for we couldn't leave the island until nightfall.

An hour passed and smoke still rose from the blackened ruins of the haystacks. . . .

'Here they come, Skipper,' Ben Owen announced quietly.

Through the lazily drifting smoke helmeted, uniformed figures advanced hesitantly, gripping bayoneted rifles. . . .

'Fire!' I shouted.

Two jeeps shot out from behind house and barn and their guns raked the stackyard. . . . Brrrrrrrrrrt. . . . Brrrrrrrrrrrrt. . . . A number of helmeted figures fell . . . the remainder vanished behind the smoke-screen. . . . Brrrrrrt. . . . Brrrrrrrrrrrt. . . . Brrrrrrrrrrr-rrrrt. . . .

'O.K., Rich.'

The firing ceased and the two jeeps were pulled back behind house and barn.

'Now for it,' I thought.

'Get ready for the stonk, Rich,' I warned.

It was twenty minutes before the first ranging shot whistled over and landed with a wruuuuuumph close to the manure-heap, flinging dung into the air. . . . Then they came, thick and fast . . . wruuuuumph . . . in the hen-run, scattering the squawking hens

348

and killing a number . . . wruuuuumph . . . on the manure-heap again, making a big hole and throwing back smelly dung in all directions . . . wruuuuumph . . . in Alfonso's garden, ruining his onion patch . . . wruuuumph . . . on the roof of the house, leaving a gaping hole, bringing Alfonso out with a rush and terrifying the German inmates . . . wruuuuumph . . . between house and barn, doing no damage . . . wruuuumph . . . close to J. C.'s jeep, drawing from a ducking J. C. 'Ye cheeky wee bastard' . . . wruuuumph . . . through the roof of the house again, making another big hole, clattering the tiles and causing panic in the locked room . . . wruuuuumph . . . on the manure-heap again, scattering dung. . . .

The barrage continued for an hour and suddenly died away.

So far so good. No casualties—apart from poultry. No damage to the jeeps.

Would a strong infantry force now attack?

We waited, on tenterhooks, hour after hour, expecting to be overwhelmed. . . . No infantry attack came in.

The sun won his daily battle with the mist, passed his meridian and sank towards the Apennine spine, transforming the surrounding flood-water into a sheet of molten gold.

As dusk fell and the mist rolled in from the sea Ben Owen's sharp eyes distinguished an enemy patrol snooping along the line of trees on the far side of the stackyard.

'Patrol coming, Skipper,' he whispered.

'We'll paste this lot good and proper,' I thought, 'and put an end to it.'

'Charge them in the jeeps,' I called to Riches.

Self-starters rasped and engines revved. . . .

'Charge!'

Six jeeps hurtled into the open, fanned out and charged across the blackened stackyard. . . . Brrrrrrrrrrt. . . . Brrrrrrrrrrrt. . . . Brrrrrrrt. . . . A flail of galloping tracer beat into the trees . . . the enemy turned and fled across the canal, leaving dead and wounded to wallow in the mud. . . . We reversed the jeeps behind house and barn and waited for the next move. . . .

It wasn't long in coming.

Wheeeeeeeeeeeeee. . . .

'Here she goes,' grinned Rogers, getting ready to duck. 'Moaning Minnie.'

349

Wruuuuuumph . . . on the manure-heap . . . wruuuuuumph . . . in the hen-run . . . wruuuuuuumph . . . in the stackyard . . . wruuuuuumph . . . on the house, clattering tiles . . . wruuuuuumph . . . stackyard again . . . wruuuuuuumph . . . barn . . . wruuuuumph . . . manure-heap . . . dung spattering down in horrible wet, stinking lumps . . . wruuuuuuuumph . . . on the house again . . . wruuuu- uuumph . . . wruuuuuumph . . . wruuuuuumph. . . . It was pitch dark now.

'Tell Alfonso we want the oxen, Gino.'

'*Si, Capitano.*'

Wheeeeeeeeee. . . .

Gino waited by the jeep until the bomb exploded wruuuuu- uuumph behind the barn and dashed across the open space to the house. . . .

Frightened by the explosions, the oxen had left the ark and were standing knee-deep in flood-water at a safe distance. The partisans waded in for them, slipped halters over their unresisting horns and pulled the unwilling beasts towards the jeeps. . . .

Then the fun began.

Wruuuuumph. . . . 'Muck it. . . . Catch the mucker, Roberto,' J. C. shrieked as an ox, almost hitched to his jeep, reared away from the explosion, slipped its halter and plunged away.

Wruuuuumph. . . . 'Hold the bastard, Vincento.' . . . Rogers and a partisan struggled with a terrified ox whose plunging hooves banged against the jeep bumper. The ox was too strong for them and got away. . . . 'Oh, muck it,' groaned Rogers despairingly.

Pandemonium reigned for a time as plunging, rearing oxen and sweating, cursing men milled about the jeeps under a down-pour of whistling, crashing mortar bombs and then, as always in a crisis, the man of the moment appeared—Don Galloway, un-expectedly shining forth, a bright star-turn at calming the stampeding oxen.

Indifferent to the mortar bombs falling all round him, Don stood immobile at the heads of the great beasts, crooning soothing, magical words and they stood quietly for him, quivering slightly when a bomb exploded, swinging their wide horns hypnotically while Don scratched the tufted hairs at their roots. . . .

The barrage died away about nine o'clock, enabling us to hitch the oxen in peace, and we commenced the wet, silent journey to the *pineto*.

Alfonso, a bachelor, waved good-bye to his Fascist master's ruined farm and came joyfully with us, riding on the back of a jeep. Our bomb-happy prisoners marched ahead through the flood, prodded by a strong partisan guard; and J. C.'s jeep, adding a touch of gaiety to our sombre journey, was festooned with dead poultry—five cockerels, six ducks, two long-necked geese—stonk casualties. . . .

D-r-r-r-r-r-r-t. . . . D-r-r-r-r-r-r-r-t. Fierce bursts of Spandau-fire sounded from the ark when we were half-way to the *pineta*. We pursued our marine course and J. C. chortled derisively into the muggy darkness: 'Too late, chum. We've gone,' keeping his eyes glued to the swinging rump six feet in front of him. . . .

It was nearly midnight when we reached the Garibaldi encampment, dog-tired but elated.

Ateo was there with his military hareem. They had a heartwarming fire roaring and roast meat and wine waiting.

'*Bravo, Capitano* Bob,' Ateo welcomed me, crushing my hand till I winced. He thrust a glass of wine at me and I raised it to him, saying: '*Bravo*, Brigata Garibaldi. We couldn't have done it without you,' meaning every word I said. '*Bravo*, Alfonso,' I added, remembering the leading part he had played at the farm.

A roar of applause went up from the circle gathering about the fire.

'*Bravo*, Alfonso! *Bravo*, Brigata Garibaldi! *Bravo*, "B" Patrol!'

'*Bravo*, Ida,' J. C. muttered in his russet beard, regarding that vigorous piece with his slumbrous, hypnotic eyes. He smothered the laughing Ida with his collection of poultry, dangling the two long-necked geese in front of her like bait. I saw Ateo looking at him, and hid a smile, watching Ateo observe the blatant approach. . . .

Maria was there, her scar livid in the firelight, brandishing her gleaming butcher's knife and our prisoners kept close to us, especially the noseless one. Maria walked up to him, merely to get a better look at such an unusual wound, and he drew back petrified, sure his last moment had come. I never saw such terror in a man's eyes. Not that I despised the poor wretch. Maria was muscular and uninhibited. She wouldn't have thought twice about slitting a German throat. If I hadn't been present I hesitate to think what might have happened to those German prisoners. I was too tired to interrogate them and told Riches to put them on a DUKW and take them across the Savio. It had been an eventful twenty-four hours.

I stood by the fire, comforted by its warmth and by the warmth of the comradeship around me. I wasn't hungry and didn't eat. Ateo kept filling my wine glass and I kept emptying it, feeling the strong red wine relaxing my strung-up nerves. I wasn't drunk, just delightfully sleepy and relaxed, at peace with the world.

A great desire for sleep swept over my tired brain. . . . I felt myself swaying . . . the voices about me faded . . . grew louder . . . faded again . . . my eyelids felt heavy as lead.

George Sonley was standing next to me. 'Shorge,' I slurred sleepily, clapping him on the shoulder, 'I'm off to bed . . . can't keep my eyes open . . . g'night, ole man. . . .' I swayed away from the fire, bumped into somebody, apologized, and made for the wooden shed, imagining myself already inside the comfort of my warm sleeping-bag. The last thing I heard was J. C.'s surprised voice, wafted to me from the fireside:

'What's the matter with the Skipper, George? Is he pissed?'

While I slept, my opposite number in 'S' Patrol, Lieutenant Jock Campbell, led his patrol of DUKWs along the beach a couple of miles below the sentinel watch-tower on the coast.

'We'll leave the DUKWs here,' he said to The Heavenly Twins, self-appointed masters of ceremony, and drove between high dunes.

Leaving his spare men to man the jeep guns and keep out of sight, Jock Campbell led his patrol on foot along the edge of the shadowy dunes, bent double and making little noise in the soft sand.

The watch-tower loomed in front of them, silent and eerie, swathed in creeping mist. They veered away from it and tip-toed into a damp, rank-smelling ditch along which they crawled on their bellies until they were within eighty yards of the heavy wooden door of the tower. There they lay until dawn, absorbing moisture from the ditch and listening to the euphony of the waves. . . .

About six o'clock, the door of the watch-tower opened and a *feldwebel* stepped outside, yawned, stretched his arms and walked towards the ditch . . . halted and undid his trouser buttons. . . .

The Heavenly Twins suppressed a titter, waited until the yawning *feldwebel* turned and walked towards the tower . . . rose from their ditch and swept him through the door, followed by Jock Campbell and the rest of the patrol.

In the single room of the tower, eight German soldiers sat up when they heard the commotion at the door and found themselves looking into the unwavering barrels of 'S' Patrol's Tommy-guns.

'One cheep from any of you bastards,' said Big Bill O'Leary, swinging his Tommy-gun menacingly, 'and I'll blow your mucking guts out.'

The bewildered, up-handed Germans kept their hands high and didn't cheep.

The watch-tower was connected by causeway to the German front line on the canal bank a thousand yards away and 'S' Patrol was marooned for the day. They spent it happily, teasing their prisoners and eating their rations—having none of their own—taking it in turns to watch the canal.

About 11 a.m. Sammy Taylor, who was keeping a vigilant eye on the causeway from a small window-slit, announced unemotionally:

'Three mucking Jerries coming along the causeway.'

Warning the suddenly hopeful Germans in the tower to remember their perishable guts, The Heavenly Twins stood by the door . . . and Tommy-gun welcomed-in three more prisoners.

There are days when everything runs in your favour, when the Gods are with you and no matter what you do, you cannot put a foot wrong. It was such a day for 'S' Patrol. At dusk, when they were preparing to leave, Sammy Taylor again announced:

'Patrol of mucking Jerries coming up the causeway.'

The Heavenly Twins again issued their grim warning to the expectant German soldiers in the tower and stood by the door, grinning . . . Tommy-gun invited-in the German relief patrol—nine more prisoners.

At seven o'clock, when all was quiet on the Ravenna front, Jock Campbell and his merry men hustled twenty-one dazed German prisoners out of the tower and marched them down the misty beach, piled their precious cargo into the DUKWs, plunged through the surf, chugged out to sea, swung in a wide arc and were having breakfast on the banks of the Savio at eight o'clock the following morning without having fired a shot—'Twenty-one bleeding Jerries and not a mucking shot fired,' as Hodgson crudely put it.

Big Bill O'Leary collected a Military Medal, Hodgson was mentioned in despatches and Jock Campbell received a well-deserved M.C.

Two of the enemy outposts had been liquidated; the third one still remained—the second Noah's Ark, distant left, hanging from the sagging telephone wires of the coast road.

Try as we did, we couldn't get into it. DUKWs were too noisy and the flood-water surrounding it was too deep for jeeps pulled by oxen. We made a couple of half-hearted attempts on foot, up to the navel in water, got machine-gunned from a thousand yards, swam back, gave it up as a suicide job and retired behind the Savio for a rest.

Sitting in the P.P.A. Mess at breakfast one morning, Popski suddenly had an idea.

'Get your jeep, Bob,' he said, rising from the table and striding from the room. 'Follow me.'

When Popski spoke like that it usually meant he had a job for me, pleasant or otherwise, and wondering what it could be I gobbled up my bacon and three eggs, took a few quick gulps of scalding tea, crammed a piece of buttered toast into my mouth and hurried after him.

His jeep was leaving the yard as I came out of the villa. I leapt into my own and revved after him. . . .

I followed Popski's stotting tail along the muddy coast road towards Rimini, weaving in and out of the Canadian Divisional convoys lumbering north. Popski turned off near Cervia and I followed him down a rutted, tree-girt track to an air-strip where lilliputian Auster spotter-planes were parked.

'Oh, Lord,' I thought, when I saw them. 'Not parachuting, please!' Popski drew up beside a black-and-white sign-board arrowed 'H.Q.' and entered a cottage. I sat in my jeep waiting for him to come out, regarding the toy-like Austers with a jaundiced eye and seeing myself dangling from a parachute above the flooded fields, being machine-gunned from the haystacks. . . .

But I'd got the wrong idea. I wasn't going parachuting. Popski's fertile brain had conceived a more ingenious plan.

'Go back to H.Q., Bob,' he said, coming out to speak to me.

'Fill up your jeep with grenades and incendiaries, bring a few Piat mortar bombs as well. I'll wait for you here. Hurry.'

I raced back to the Savio with my imagination working overtime. Low-level hand-bombing from artillery spotter-planes. My God, what next! . . .

'Quick, Harry,' I said to S.Q.M.S. Moss at stores. 'Grenades, incendiaries and Piat mortar bombs. Fill up the jeep.'

While Moss loaded, I dashed into the Mess to speak to Jan Caneri, who was finishing a leisurely breakfast.

' 'Ullo, Bob,' he greeted me, smiling. 'What's Popski up to?'

'You'll never guess, old boy,' I said, pouring myself a cup of lukewarm tea. 'Low-level hand-bombing from Auster spotter-planes. You'll be lucky if you see us again.'

I gulped the tea, clattered the cup in the saucer and hurried out.

'Christ . . .' I heard Jan mutter as I ran into the yard.

Back on the air-strip two little Austers were warming up. Popski and an R.A.F. officer were standing beside them, laughing heartily. 'Ha,' I thought, 'Popski's been turning on the charm.'

Popski waved to me as I crossed the strip and I drove up to the planes.

'This is Bob Yunnie,' he introduced me to the C.O.

'How d'you do,' we said, and shook hands.

'Right, Bob,' Popski said briskly. 'Load up and let's go.

'The idea,' he added, 'is that we fly over the farm and drop a few eggs on the heads of our German friends.' He said it matter-of-factly, as though his crazy idea were the accepted method of reducing flood-isolated enemy outposts.

'Yes, Popski,' I breathed.

Popski climbed ponderously into the passenger seat of the nearest Auster and the sturdy, frail-looking craft sagged beneath his weight. I put a Piat mortar bomb gently into his lap and followed it with a selection of primed hand-grenades and incendiaries. He nodded, waggled a hand at me and his Auster burped to the runway.

Similarly arming myself, I clambered aboard the second plane and clicked the little side-door.

355

'What d'you think of this racket?' I grinned into the sun-burned neck of the boyish, handle-bar-moustached one-ringer pilot as we jerked forward.

'Jolly good show, sir, what? . . . Ha . . . ha,' he enthused and burp . . . burp . . . burped his toy plane over the grass. . . .

The planes took off one after the other, Popski's leading.

We banked seawards, flew across the dunes and skimmed along the surf like sea-gulls, flying so low under the ceiling of mist that I felt I could lean out and touch the waves.

Up-coast, we picked up our landmark—Jock Campbell's watch-tower—and banked inland, flying about 300 feet with our shadows pacing us on the motionless gun-metal surface of the flood-water . . . by-passed the blackened remains of Alfonso's stackyard . . . circled above the third outpost. . . .

I looked down and saw the red-tiled farmhouse, the barn, the scratching hens, oxen, haystacks, but no Germans. I didn't expect to see any Germans. This was where Popski was clever.

Experience had taught the German front-line soldier that he had nothing to fear from the artillery spotter-plane which hovered above his head. It carried no armament and didn't drop bombs, but merely stooged about the sky taking photographs and looking for the tell-tale flash of gun-fire; and if he, the front-line soldier, sat absolutely still, didn't fire and didn't give his position away, no harm would come to him and no artillery stonk would later come his way.

Popski's Auster dived at the haystacks. . . . I saw Popski lean over the side and drop his Piat mortar bomb . . . saw the black, pear-shaped object fall obliquely . . . hit one of the haystacks . . . bounce off and roll on the ground without exploding. . . . 'Bad luck, Popski,' I thought . . . a dark bird-like shadow appeared on the haystacks as Popski's plane pulled out of its first dive. . . .

'Going down,' intoned my pilot. I leant from the fuselage . . . aimed my Piat mortar bomb at the haystacks and let go. . . . I watched it hit the sloping stack . . . slide off and roll on the ground just as Popski's had done. . . . 'Blast,' I muttered, 'something wrong with these Piats' . . . our bird-like shadow darkened the haystacks as the pilot pulled out of his dive. . . .

Popski dived again, dropping incendiaries . . . smoke rose from the haystacks . . . then flames, bright and leaping. . . . I saw uniformed figures emerge from the stacks and run wildly about the

356

stackyard. . . . My Auster dived. . . . I pulled the pins from grenades, knocking my elbow against the fuselage . . . leant over . . . dropped the grenades on the heads of the scattering, up-looking Germans . . . drew my Colt revolver and fired . . . phut . . . phut . . . phut. . . .

We circled round and dived a third time . . . blinded by the rising smoke. . . . Something tore through the wing and I became aware of little red darts streaming past the fuselage.

'Hoy,' I shouted to the pilot. 'We're being shot at.'

The pilot nodded, looked grim, roared his engine, banked steeply and wheeled away. . . . I looked back and saw Popski's Auster diving again, half hidden by smoke patterned with scarlet tracer curving up from the German front line . . . saw the plane pull out of the dive unharmed . . . bank and follow us. . . .

Climbing steeply, waving good-bye to the chasing, clawing tracer we burped across the silent flood-water towards the open sea . . . crossed the yellow sand-dunes . . . skimmed along the surface of the restless waves . . . turned inland . . . bumped upon the air-strip. . . .

'Well, Bob,' Popski laughed as we alighted. 'How did you enjoy that?'

'Bloody good fun,' I grinned, 'until the tracer started coming up!'

'Jolly good show, sir, what? . . . Ha . . . ha,' chortled my pilot, stepping down. . . . Then, 'I say, sir,' chortle, 'look at this'—pointing to the ripped wing. 'Haw . . . haw . . . haw,' twirling handle-bar moustache. 'Jolly good show, what? . . . Haw . . . haw . . . haw. . . .'

The C.O. came striding across the grass.

'Well, Popski, how did you get on?' . . . His eye fell upon the damaged wing and his smile vanished. . . .

22

I LIKE to think that it was our unorthodox methods of warfare
which induced the enemy to relinquish Ravenna, but I have a
strong suspicion that it was more likely due to Eighth Army
pressure on the flank. Whatever the reason for the German
withdrawal, a partisan walked through the floods from Ravenna
one night shortly after our Auster effort and informed us that the
Germans were pulling out. Wriggling from our comfortable
sleeping-bags at 0300 hours we were DUKWing across the
Montone River by first light, feeling our way cautiously through
mine-fields and avoiding booby-traps. . . .

Ravenna was ours.

It was also Ateo's home town, where he was a big noise in
local communist politics, and he organized a tremendous party in
honour of the occasion. Bulow, the valiant commander of the
Brigata Garibaldi and Ateo's immediate chief, crossed the German
lines and came down from his watery headquarters in the Comacchio to join us.

In a large hall made gay by paper streamers and coloured
lights we sat down at a long table to *minestrone . . . pasta . . .*
wine . . . roast duck . . . wine . . . roast ox . . . wine . . . cheese
. . . wine . . . coffee . . . wine . . . wine . . . wine. . . .

Popski was there and Jan Caneri, Jock Campbell, The Heavenly Twins, all the P.P.A. patrolmen; Ateo, Rafuzzi, Alfonso, all
the partisans from the *pineta*, Isabella, the hefty Maria with her
flashing black eyes and the scar on her cheek, Ida the vigorous one
(watched by Ateo), a noisy, clamorous, warm-hearted, impulsive,
courageous, vital crowd with sten-guns over their shoulders and
little black and red *bomba-manos* slung at their belts, some in
Italian, some in German Army uniform, many in civilian clothes
with Garibaldi arm-bands, all reaching out for food and wine, all

358

chattering and gesticulating at once. Some of them were monarchists, most of them were communists, their country and their currency was in ruins, the future was obscure; neither they nor anyone else knew exactly what they were fighting for.

There was much speechifying—by Popski . . . by Ateo . . . by Bulow . . . by Ateo . . . by Capitano Bob . . . by Ateo . . . by J. C. . . . by Ateo—much wine-bibbing, much *viva*-ing and *bravo*-ing, much ogling of Ida the vigorous one (with Ateo looking on), far too much to eat and drink and many splitting headaches the following morning, but we worked hard at our business of war, took our military duties seriously and didn't indulge in wild parties except very occasionally and reckoned that a splitting headache which gradually wore off as the day advanced wasn't too high a price to pay for a memorable evening.

Between Ravenna and the mouths of the Po, Bulow's Brigata Garibaldi played military hide and seek with the Germans amongst the misty, reed-grown islands of the Valli di Comacchio, a large marshy inland lake separated from the sea by a narrow strip of land cut by navigable channels, a place of dampness where wild geese flew and sea-birds echoed their plaintive cries, an eerie waste of swirling mist and lapping water, swaying clumps of water-weeds.

Bulow's men lived upon its myriad reedy islands in squelching mud, moving about its rippling surface in punts, emerging at night to harry the German infantry strung out along the winding Po and withdrawing to the safety of their fog-bound reeds at dawn—a wet, depressing, miserable, heroic, fish-like existence, I thought, and marvelled that men could live for months in such conditions without contracting pneumonia.

Supplies were his main difficulty, Bulow told us. Could we possibly help him? We could and did.

Loading our DUKWs with the supplies he wanted, we chugged down the Montone after dark and pranced up-coast to the marshy neck which enclosed the Comacchio from the sea, running the gauntlet of floating mines and landing our cargoes under the noses of the German coastal patrols.

'See anything, George?' I enquired of Sonley as we drifted in-shore one pitch-black, mist-ridden night, looking for the landing-point. The DUKW engine was just ticking over, the exhaust

359

burble hardly audible above the slapping of the surf on the invisible shore.

'Not a mucking thing, Skipper.'

I pressed the accelerator a little, fearful of being heard by an enemy patrol. . . .

'See anything, George?' I whispered a few minutes later.

'Not a muck—— Wait a bit. . . . Hold it, Skipper.'

'What is it, George?' I breathed urgently. 'What do you see?'

George stood up in the swaying DUKW and peered over the windscreen. He saw a vague, penguin-like figure waving a flipper.

'Somebody waving, Skipper.'

'Give me the glasses, George. Hold the wheel.'

George grabbed the steering-wheel and the DUKW rocked frighteningly as we changed places. I focused the night-glasses and barely distinguished the figure of a man standing on a marshy canal bank waving an arm backwards and forwards in the mist.

'It's the partisan guide, George,' I whispered. 'We're at the right place.'

George accelerated gently and nosed the DUKW through the surging water of a muddy canal . . . close up to a bank where the shadowy figure bent, grasped the gun'l, whispered the pass-word 'Popski' and clambered aboard.

'*Avanti*,' I whispered to George. . . .

Up-stream a little way, more shadowy figures loomed and George steered into the bank where eager hands held the DUKW stationary while our cargo of sten-guns, ammunition, grenades, rations and warm clothing was quickly transported to waiting punts. . . .

'*Grazia. Arivederci*,' hoarse voices whispered when the last load was carried, and the shadowy figures vanished like dissolving steam.

'O.K., George,' I breathed, and pushed hard against the bank.

Half turned in the driving-seat, George steered the DUKW into the muddy current and went astern. . . .

Fearful of a burst of Spandau-fire from the patrolled isthmus, we plunged across the bar and made for the open sea. . . .

Another night-delivery to Bulow had been safely made.

A wholly unexpected German counter-attack upset our plans for a full-scale DUKWing party on the Comacchio.

I was at P.P.A. headquarters in Ravenna when a message came over the blower warning us that German infantry were advancing through the woods towards the canal which marked the furthest point of our advance.

Popski called for his jeep and he, his driver-gunner, Burrows, and Gigi (on loan) went up to the front to see what was happening.

'Stand-by with your patrol, Bob,' he called to me as he drove off.

'Rich!' I yelled across the yard to my waiting jeeps. 'Stand-by. Something's cooking,' and went into the Mess to speak to Jan Caneri.

The next development was an urgent message from Porter Force (to whom we were then attached) advising that

1. Popski had been wounded and taken to hospital.
2. Jan Caneri was to take command of P.P.A.
3. 'B' Patrol was to go up to the front immediately.

'Good God!' I exclaimed, stunned. 'Popski wounded?'

'Off you go, Bob,' ordered Jan, gently assuming the mantle of command.

The front looked like this: There was a dark green pine forest lining the north bank of the canal with a road running through it from a hump-backed (unblown) stone bridge. South of the canal, the road ran up to the bridge on a raised causeway, like a railway embankment, with deep ditches and flooded fields on either side. To the left of the bridge, abutting the south bank of the canal a hundred yards from the road, there was a double-storeyed house in which a squadron of Lancers were marooned. A battalion of fresh German infantry lined the north bank of the canal and two snipers were hidden on the reverse slope of the south bank near the bridge.

When Popski drove up the causeway the German infantry were advancing through the wood and had not yet reached the canal. Halting his jeep fifty yards from the bridge and leaving Burrows to man the guns, he and Gigi walked along the south bank to have a look-see—and what they saw was German infantry, a horde of them, moving from tree to tree.

Popski and Gigi ran back to their jeep and reached it just as the leading Germans poured across the bridge.

'Fire, Burrows!' Popski shouted from the ditch and Burrows promptly sprayed the narrow infantry-filled bridge with the fifty, killing many outright, wounding others and forcing the remainder to beat a hurried retreat. . . .

Things happened rather quickly thereafter.

A Lancer bren-gunner opened-up from the house, a German infantryman fired a rifle-grenade which sailed across the canal and exploded beside the jeep, shattering Popski's left hand, a bullet entered Gigi's right upper arm causing him to stagger across the road, slide down the left-hand ditch and lie still. . . .

On the causeway, Popski felt pain, glanced down at his mangled left hand, put a tourniquet on the wrist with the fingers of his right hand and directed the fire of his guns so effectively that the German advance was halted on the north bank of the canal. Then, feeling the effects of loss of blood and appalled at the idea of becoming a stretcher-case, he turned and said politely:

'Please take me to hospital, Burrows.'

From his bed of pain in the ditch, Gigi dimly heard the jeep drive off, realized he was alone, summoned his reserves of strength and crawled into the house where, propped against a wall, he nursed his wounded arm and bolstered up the disintegrating morale of the occupants by repeatedly assuring them: 'The jeeps will come. . . . Don't worry. . . . The jeeps will come.' . . .

When 'B' Patrol arrived on the causeway a troop of light tanks was moving up.

'Fine,' I said to George. 'We'll follow the tanks,' and pulled to the side of the road to let them pass. . . . To my horror, I saw them lumber off the road and squat hull-down in the ditch a thousand yards from the bridge, leaving our six jeeps high and dry on the raised causeway, like sitting pheasants waiting to be shot. . . .

'This is no good,' I thought, 'we can't sit here, we'll get all the stonk'; but having been ordered up to the front I couldn't very well retreat. There was only one thing to do.

'*Avanti!*' I yelled. 'Charge!' And put down my foot. . . .

The most extraordinary thing happened.

I braked ten yards from the mouth of the bridge with the other jeeps braking in staggered formation behind me and sat for a full minute looking into the faces of the German infantry on the other side of the canal. It was the strangest sensation I have ever experienced. Everything was hushed and quiet, vibrant like an auditorium when the lights go out and the curtain begins to rise

362

for the first act of a drama. Time seemed to stand still, the water in the canal seemed not to flow, a tense, brooding, breathless expectancy gripped the *pineta*. . . .

Eternity was broken by the silent inner voice which prompted 'Fire!'

Brrrrrrrrrrrrrrrrrrrt. Tracer poured across the canal in a searing, terrifying, death-dealing scarlet curtain against which no human flesh and blood could stand. Brrrrrrrrrrrrrrrrrrrrrt. Jeeps vibrating violently. . . . German infantry lying face down, hugging the earth . . . a deafening, ear-splitting, nerve-shattering racket. . . . Brrrrrrrrrrrrrrt. . . . Smoke rising from blue-hot gun barrels. . . . Brrrrrrrrrrrrrrrrrrrt. . . . Spiteful, vicious, pricking, stinging, blood-red darts filling the air above the canal like a swarm of angry hornets . . . plopping into the water . . . thudding into earth . . . tearing into quivering human flesh . . . smacking against the trees. . . .

'Run for it!' I yelled to the marooned Lancers. 'Get out, quick!' Out of the tail of my eye, I saw a helmeted head rise above the level of the south canal bank, close to the bridge, ten yards from the barrel-mouth of my smoking fifty. I swung the gun and jabbed. Brrrrrrrrrt. . . . The helmeted head disappeared. . . .

I waved to the Lancers now furtively making their escape from the house and continued to fire across the canal. Brrrrrrrrrrrrt. . . . Brrrrrrrrt. . . . Brrrrrrrrt . . . in spraying, telling bursts. . . .

A minute or two later, I saw the helmeted head rise hesitantly above the verge of the south bank. I swung the gun and waited. . . . Brrrrrrrt . . . head popping quickly from sight. . . . Another helmeted head rising a couple of yards to the left. . . . Brrrrrrrrt . . . head popping down. I had a bead on the two German snipers dug-in on the south bank and an unfriendly game of 'See-who-can-shoot-first' developed, like this:

First helmeted head popping up. . . . Brrrrrrrt . . . head popping down. Pause. Second helmeted head popping up. . . . Brrrrrrrrt . . . head popping down. Pause. First helmeted sniper jumping up and pointing a rifle . . . phut . . . phut . . . me ducking smartly and jabbing. . . . Brrrrrrrrt . . . sniper vanishing. Interval. Second sniper jumping up and firing . . . phut . . . phut . . . me ducking and jabbing. . . . Brrrrrrrrt. Interval. Rifle coming up. . . . Brrrrrrt . . . rifle vanishing . . . another rifle coming up, hesitantly. . . . Brrrr-rrrrt . . . rifle quickly lowered. Interval. Two helmeted heads popping up simultaneously. . . . Brrrrrrrrrrt. . . Two helmeted heads vanishing. Interval. Two helmeted heads rising very cautiously, rifles coming up. . . . Inner voice whispering silently, 'Hold your fire, Yunnie.' . . . Two rifles being levelled. . . . 'Hold it. . . . Hold it.' . . . Two snipers in full view. . . . 'Now fire.' . . . Brrrrrrrrrrrrrrrrrrrrrrrrrrt. . . . Two snipers falling backwards . . . one helmet falling from a square, close-cropped head . . . a double splaaaash. . . . Two field-grey bodies disappearing under the bridge . . . bloodstains on the water. . . .

Wheeeeeeeeeeeeee. . . .

'Look out, Skipper! Stonk coming.' . . .

Wruuuuuumph. The shell whined harmlessly overhead and exploded on the causeway near the hull-down tanks which had been lobbing 2-pounders across the canal.

'We're safe, George,' I chuckled gleefully.

We were indeed safe from the German artillery, being too close to the front line for the gunners to risk shortening the range.

Wheeeeeeeeeeeee. . . . Wruuuuuumph . . . wruuuuuumph . . . wruuuuuumph. All exploding far behind us, but forcing the tanks to retreat! Brrrrrrrrrrrrrrrrrrt. . . . Brrrrrrrrrrt. . . . Brrrrrrrrrt. We maintained a devastating fire, rattling belt after belt through the guns until they became hot to the touch. . . .

'Come on!' I yelled to the escaping Lancers. 'Run for it. Hurry!'

A trooper ran along the canal bank, was hit by a German sniper, staggered and fell into the water. Don Galloway saw him fall and without a moment's hesitation leapt from his jeep, ran up the canal bank in the face of enemy fire, dived into the canal, rescued the wounded trooper, fireman's-lifted him on his shoulder, plunged down the canal bank and ran to his jeep where he dumped the Lancer, groaning, into the back, settled behind his gun and took up the firing where he had left off—until he himself fainted from loss of blood from a bullet wound in the thigh.

'Gall's hit, Skipper,' Ben Owen shouted.

I glanced round and saw Don Galloway lolling behind a silent fifty.

'Quick, Ben,' I yelled. 'Reverse out!'

Ben Owen leapt into the driving-seat, crashed into reverse gear and backed the jeep to the end of the column where he attended to Galloway's wound. J. C. drove his jeep up to take Don's place.

Brrrrrrrrrrrrrrt. . . . Brrrrrrrrrrrrrrrrrt. . . . Brrrrrrrrrrrrrrt. The clatter was deafening. My ears sang and my head buzzed, as if bumble bees were inside it. My whole nervous system was jagged and on edge with the soul-searing, penetrating vibration. . . .

But the house was empty now and a long line of straggling, ducking, back-glancing troopers filed down the protective ditch by the side of the raised causeway. A familiar figure waved and I was surprised to recognize Gigi, not knowing he'd been in the house. . . .

Our guns began to jam from the heat of the incessant firing and our fire became erratic.

'Pull out, Rich,' I shouted above the din.

One at a time, we ceased fire and backed away from the carnage . . . dodged the whining shells . . . turned round when we were out of range.

We stopped to give a lift to the stragglers—and to Gigi.

'Gigi, *amico, come sta?*' I greeted him.

'*Bene, grazia, Capitano,*' he smiled painfully, gripping his wounded arm as he clambered aboard.

'Strong smell of petrol, Skipper,' George Sonley observed, sniffing.

I looked down.

'No wonder, George. Look!'

George looked—and saw my feet awash to the ankles in ethyl-coloured petrol.

I stepped hurriedly on to the road and shook the petrol from my soaking feet while George examined the petrol tank. . . .

'Whew! Jesus, Skipper,' I heard him exclaim. 'Look at this.'

I looked—and exclaimed also.

The petrol tank was riddled like a colander an inch below the level of the seat.

'Seen the Skipper's jeep, Rich?' George Sonley held up a thumb and forefinger separated by a hair's breadth. 'Missed his arse by that.'

I went to see Popski in hospital.

He was lying in bed with an arm swathed in bandages. His normally tanned face looked a bit yellow against the white pillow, but apart from that he was fine, quite unconcerned about the loss of his hand, in fact he seemed rather proud of it.

'How are you, Popski?' I asked solicitously.

'Very comfortable, Bob.'

'Not sore?'

He shook his head.

I asked him what happened. He told me.

He asked what I'd done. I told him.

And then we both felt tongue-tied and embarrassed and a Canadian nurse came bustling in and I left.

I went to see Don Galloway in hospital.

Don was in a bad state, very depressed, and his pale face looked vaguely unfamiliar. I tried to cheer him up.

'Cheer up, Don,' I said. 'It's only a flesh wound. You won't lose your leg,' and then, when I saw this didn't have much effect, I bullied him. 'Get a grip of yourself, man. . . .'

But I'd sadly misjudged my man. It wasn't the wound in the thigh that was troubling Don Galloway, but the loss of his beard.

'The bastards shaved it off, Skipper,' he groaned, ruefully fingering his naked chin.

I sat back and laughed, relieved that that was all that was troubling him. 'Don't worry, Don,' I soothed. 'It'll grow again.'

But Don refused to be comforted. His big, bushy, black beard had been the pride of the patrol. It would take months to grow again and even as he lay in bed Don could hear the jeers of his patrol mates when he reappeared without it.

I went to see Gigi in hospital.

He was depressed too, but for a different reason.

'*Come sta*, Gigi?' I greeted him.

'*Male, Capitano*,' he groaned.

'*Per che?*' I asked. (What's the matter?)

Gigi had heard that all hospital casualties were discharged to base depot and he was obsessed by the terrible fear that he would be caught up in the coils of British Army red tape and never see P.P.A. again. When I assured him that all P.P.A. personnel were returned to P.P.A. by special arrangement he brightened up.

'*Come sta*, Gigi?' I asked when I rose to go.

'*Bene, grazia, Capitano*,' he smiled.

.   .   .   .   .

366

The German counter-attack marked the end of the allied offensive for 1944 and both armies settled down to a long winter of waiting and watching in the snow.

Popski's Private Army had been continuously in action since the middle of June and was now pulled out of the line for a well-deserved rest. Knowing that the patrolmen would only get into trouble if he kept them hanging about at base, Jan Caneri very wisely requisitioned accommodation at Terminillo in the Abruzzi, engaged a team of the best Alpini instructors and our wild and woolly patrolmen spent the winter healthily and happily learning how to ski.

I had been abroad for five years and went home, apprehensively, on leave.

23

THE troop-ship was slow, overcrowded and dry. We wearied through Christmas in the Med. and dopped anchor in the Clyde on a grey and miserable January day.

Tenders and naval boats came and went. No one was allowed to leave the ship. We leant against the rail watching dockers entering and leaving a public-house on the quay, undergoing an acute form of Chinese torture, since none of us had had a drink for a month and most of us had forgotten the taste of real beer. When we did eventually go ashore the self-advertised pub did a roaring trade until well after closing time ('Time, Gentlemen, *please*').

I had left Britain in December 1939 when Britain was still Britain and the pound sterling was still worth a pound sterling. I was shocked by the changes the war years had wrought. Not the bomb damage nor the black-out nor the food rationing nor the high cost of living, but the change in the people themselves. They seemed to me to have lost their pride. Was it just war weariness, the natural and inevitable result of the years of danger and nerve strain, of malnutrition? Or did it go deeper than that, had some fundamental change taken place in the British character? The people I met seemed apathetic, careless of what happened and an alien atmosphere prevailed. I felt strange, out of place in my own country. Was it I who had changed?

I dined in the Royal Hotel in Glasgow and a joke I cracked with the tired-looking waitress fell flat. 'God help us,' I thought, 'if they've lost their sense of humour.' But perhaps it was I who was out of touch.

I caught the night train for Aberdeen, and couldn't get a sleeper. Sleepers were available, but they were all reserved for civilian V.I.P.s and I was only an Eighth Army captain who had been abroad for five years. I could hardly expect such privilege and counted myself lucky to procure a corner seat.

Hunched in my cheerless corner, chilled to the bone and wishing I'd spent my leave in sunny Capri, I rubbed the condensation from the carriage window and looked out upon familiar scenes as the train drew out of Stonehaven Station in the cold light of the breaking dawn. . . . I was back again in the days of my ill-spent youth . . . diving into the Stonehaven Swimming Pool to the strains of 'Blue Moon' . . . roaring along the coast road at eighty in Gordon Bisset's sports M.G. . . . stroking the winning Eight under the suspension bridge on the River Dee . . . the crossed oars and A.B.C. of the Aberdeen Boat Club smiled wanly from the weather-beaten roof of the clubhouse as the train rattled over the bridge . . . into Aberdeen Station where my wife and son awaited me on the platform. I barely recognized them.

My wife had remained the same. I had changed. We found ourselves out of harmony. We were no different from thousands of other married couples whom the war had separated and shown to be basically incompatible, but that didn't make it any easier. Conversation was the main difficulty. We spoke different languages and couldn't find anything to say to one another. It was awful. 'You poor man,' kind relatives commiserated, 'you've had an awful time,' and were shocked to realize that I enjoyed the war. 'But you don't understand,' I tried to explain, 'it isn't like that at all. I haven't had an awful time. I've had a wonderful time. It's fun in P.P.A.' Shocked looks all round. Clearly, I was past redemption.

In the side bar of the Caledonian Hotel the silver tankard bearing my initials still hung from its hook.

'Pint, sir?' asked the barmaid, taking it down and wiping it.

I nodded.

But it wasn't the same. The old faces had gone and I didn't like the new ones.

I wandered disconsolately about Town, visiting my old haunts, feeling like a fish out of water. Three months of this, I thought, hell, no! I stuck it for a month and could stick it no longer. Popski was in England having an artificial hand fitted. I arranged to meet him and took train to London Town. . . .

We met in Claridge's. He was standing in the crowded foyer

jostled by many uniforms (mostly American), dangling a stiff, gloved hand and smoking a cigarette.

'Popski, how are you?' I greeted him joyfully.

'Bob,' he beamed, pleased to see me.

In the crowded lounge we grabbed at a table when some people rose, and ordered sherry.

'Enjoying your leave, Bob?'

'No. It's awful. Can you get me back to Italy?'

Popski laughed.

'Do you remember, Bob, asking for leave in North Africa and I wouldn't grant it?'

I remembered it well—in Philippeville at the end of the Libyan campaign.

'Yes,' I replied, looking into his inscrutable, green-flecked eyes.

'Now you know why.'

The waiter brought our sherry.

'You were right, Popski,' I said, raising my glass.

'Cheers.'

'Cheers.'

We drank up our sherry and went in to dinner. . . .

'Did you hear the joke about Tindall?' Popski asked, breaking a piece of roll and taking a spoonful of soup.

Tindall was one of the first of our men to go home on leave.

'No. What about him?'

'He was walking down the Strand and a brigadier pulled him up for not saluting.'

Popski took another spoonful of soup.

'And?' I prompted.

'The brigadier asked him to what unit he belonged'—Popski broke off to laugh heartily—'and when Tindall replied "Popski's Private Army, sir!" the brigadier put him on a charge for insolence.'

'Aaaagh,' I spluttered, putting down my spoon and shaking with laughter. 'Good God, Popski. What a scream! . . . What happened?' I asked, wiping my eyes.

'He got off, of course.'

The waiter removed our empty soup plates and brought the next course.

370

I noticed Popski's awkwardness with knife and fork but hesitated, not wishing to hurt his feelings, for he was sensitive about matters of this kind. . . .

'May I?' 'Would you?' we asked at the same moment, and laughed, removing the embarrassment.

'I haven't quite got the hang of it, Bob,' Popski explained a trifle self-consciously as I cut up his meat. . . .

'Thank you, Bob.'

We ate in silence for a while.

'You really want to cut short your leave, Bob?'

'Yes, Popski.'

'Sure?'

'Definitely.'

'All right, I'll arrange it, Bob.'

Popski had friends in high places. Doors opened and signals were sent. A fortnight later I was on my way back to Italy.

At crack of dawn one chilly morn I walked across the soaking grass from a manor-house 'somewhere in England' and boarded a York transport plane with other bodies more correctly uniformed than I—a chic little Wren officer, a severe-looking hospital matron, a lot of sam-browned brass clutching important-looking despatch-cases. . . .

The York rose blindly through tumbling grey clouds and emerged above them into a dazzling fairyland of white and blue and gold. We flew high above the invisible Channel, then along the line of the Pyrenees and I looked down upon an enchanted world of snowy peaks rising from a foaming ocean of pink-encrusted breakers. How vast are the airman's horizons compared to his earth-bound brother's, what glorious freedom of spirit he enjoys in the limitless reaches of the upper air! I sat close to my little window on the inside, looking out, and remembered the rare words of a poem which was found pasted inside the cockpit of a crashed Spitfire:

> Oh, I have slipped the surly bonds of earth,
> And danced the skies on laughter-silvered wings;
> Sunward I've climbed, and done a hundred things
> You have not dreamed of: wheeled and soared and swung
> High in the sunlit silence. Hovering there
> I've chased the shouting wind along, and flung
> My eager craft through footless halls of air.

Up, up the long, delirious burning blue,
I've topped the windswept heights with airy grace,
Where never lark or even eagle flew—
And so with silent lifting mind I've trod
The high untrespassed sanctity of space,
Put out my hand, and touched the face of God.

John Gillespie Magee, R.C.A.F.

A lovely, sincere expression of feeling by a man who obviously knew.

We droned across the Med., the bluest sea on Earth, over Corsica and Sardinia, rocky, surf-washed jewels flung spendthrift upon the surface of a shining mirror . . . across a wide expanse of glinting water blemished at intervals by little toy ships . . . towards a straggling coastline . . . a green island . . . tiny fishing smacks . . . mountains . . . a winding river . . . a spreading city . . . vineyards . . . dusty white roads . . . houses . . . roof-tops . . . giant birds crouched on the grass . . . a runway . . . burp . . . bump . . . burp . . . burp . . . bump-ump-ump-rumble . . . Rome Airport.

Sonley was waiting for me with a jeep.

'George, you old bastard,' I greeted him boisterously, feeling a wave of nostalgia when my eyes fell upon the familiar *ensemble*— the worn desert-boots, the faded battledress blouse with the blue and white parachute wings, the Eighth Army ribbon and star, the P.P.A. flash, the silk neckerchief, the black beret with the gun-metal astrolabe badge, the American Army trousers, the eager, grinning, weather-beaten face by the low-slung, racy jeep with its long black-barrelled Brownings and welded array of petrol-can brackets.

'How's Blighty, Skipper?'

'Bloody awful.'

'What?'

'Terrible place, George,' I said, sliding happily behind the wheel. 'Queues and black-outs, rules and regulations, Yanks everywhere, spit and polish—Tindall was put on a charge.'

'What for, Skipper?'

'Insolence—he told a brig what P.P.A. stood for.'

I told George the story. He collapsed over the fifty. . . .

'No, Skipper,' thinking I was pulling his leg.

'It's a fact, George,' I assured him, 'Popski told me. I met him in London.'

'How's the old man?'

'Fine. Got an artificial hand.'

I pressed the self-starter and the engine purred sweetly. I revved. What a heavenly sound!

'Where's everybody?'

'The Patrols are at Terminillo, ski-ing. H.Q.'s at Florence.'

'Florence!' I exclaimed. 'When did it move there?'

'About a month ago.'

'How's Jan?'

'R.T.U-ing the faces that don't fit.'

'Good old Jan,' I laughed and let in the clutch, eager to see my best friend again. . . .

I found him in a luxurious villa set amongst the Florentine hills. I walked along a cool terrace, entered a sun-blinded room, stood to attention before a glass-topped mahogany desk, banged my right heel and saluted extravagantly.

'O.C. "B" Patrol reporting for duty, sir.'

'Bob!'

'Jan!'

We danced a jig round the elegant, shaded room and collapsed into leather armchairs, breathless and laughing.

'Hell, Jan, it's good to be back,' I panted.

'Did you see Popski, Bob?' Jan hawed on his spectacles and wiped them with a handkerchief.

'We'd dinner in London one night. He's fine. Got an artificial hand.'

'I was surprised when I got the signal saying you were coming back. Didn't you enjoy your leave, Bob?'

I shook my head.

'Bored to tears, Jan. God knows how we're going to settle down after the war. The peace'll be deadly dull after this.'

We were thoughtful for a moment, thinking of the aftermath to come, for the war was nearing its end.

'What's cooking?' I asked, changing the subject.

'A landing behind the Po as soon as the spring offensive starts.'

'Nice work, Jan. Did you arrange it?'

'Of course, Bob. I've been busy,' mock-indignantly.

'How are the patrols?'

'Fit, Bob. They're at Terminillo. Ski-ing. We'll run up there tomorrow.'

We had dinner together in the villa, an Italian dinner cooked and served by an Italian woman—*pasta*, scalloped veal, green salad, cheese, fruit, red wine—and sat on the terrace afterwards sipping coffee, smoking cigarettes, talking and looking into the star-lit bowl of Florence.

'You're a born organizer, Jan,' I congratulated him. 'This villa's terrific.'

'Look, Bob,' Jan leant forward and poured himself another cup of coffee. 'Any bloody fool can be uncomfortable. Discomfort's all very well in the front line when you've no option, but why live like a pig at base when you can be comfortable by using your nut?'

'Absolutely. I couldn't agree with you more.'

The guns boomed distantly from the hills above Bologna where the Americans were uncomfortably crouched in the snow.

'What are you going to do after the war, Jan?' I threw at him.

He didn't reply immediately, but sat pulling at his cigarette, causing it to glow redly in the darkness.

'Don't know, Bob,' he replied at length. 'Some sort of business, I suppose. Something to make money. Going to have a holiday first, though.'

'It'll be easy for you, Jan. You're a batchelor, no wife and family to consider. You can do as you like.' I envied him his freedom.

'What about you, Bob?'

I shrugged.

'Have to go home, I suppose. Back to the old insurance grind. I'm not looking forward to it.'

'Cheer up, Bob. It mightn't be so bad. You'll get used to it.'

I shook my head gloomily.

'Not after P.P.A., Jan. It's going to be hell trying to settle down.'

Jan stubbed his cigarette, stood up and put a friendly hand on my shoulder.

'Bed, Bob. Don't worry about the peace. The war isn't over yet.'

'It would be funny, wouldn't it,' I said, 'if I got bumped off at the last moment after coming through it all scot-free?'

374

I went to bed with this idea playing in my subconscious mind.

Terminillo is a winter sports resort fifty miles from Rome.

Housed in comfortable chalets behind one of the hotels, bereft of transport (there were no flies on Jan), the patrols had spent the winter ski-ing on the sun-lit snow-slopes which fell steeply from their door, breathing a glorious health into their bodies instead of abusing them in wine-shops and causing trouble with the military police.

'You did a very wise thing, Jan,' I remarked as we clanked round a bend in the snow-bound track with the rear-wheel chains slapping the chassis.

'Couldn't have coped otherwise, Bob,' Jan breathed smokily into the crisp air. 'The blokes would never have been out of trouble. You know what they're like.'

I nodded.

Jan skidded round another corner of the twisting mountain road and the chalets and hotel came into view.

'Almost there, Bob.'

'Just like St. Moritz, Jan,' I exclaimed. 'The blokes don't know how lucky they are.'

I turned to George Sonley, sitting in the back of the jeep. Thoughtfully, knowing how it would please me to find my own driver-gunner waiting at the airport, Jan had brought George all the way from Terminillo to drive my jeep to Rome Airport.

'Can you ski, George?'

'Yes, Skipper.'

'Are you good?'

'Not too bad, Skipper,' said George modestly. In fact he was very good.

'You can teach me.'

'Right, Skipper.' A gleam shone in George's eyes. He looked forward to some fun until I found my ski-ing legs.

Sergeant Riches appeared round the gable of the first chalet as Jan drew up beside it. Piercing blue eyes, pointed van Dyck beard, loose-fitting Airborne jumping jacket, he hadn't changed, and, balancing a pair of skis on his shoulder, his diminutive five-foot-four looked more bow-legged than ever. He stopped short when he saw me and his eyes popped.

'Skipper!' he shouted, ran forward a few steps, changed his

mind, turned and disappeared behind the chalet in a scamper of snow.

'What's got into Rich?' I muttered.

A minute later I heard his parade-ground voice bawl:

'Paaaa . . . trol 'shun. . . . Ri . . . turn. . . . Qu . . . ick march. . . . Lef. . . . Ri. . . . Lef. . . . Ri. . . . Lef. . . . Ri. . . .'

'B' Patrol goose-stepped round the gable, chests out, heads up, right arms swinging, left hands holding skis rigidly on left shoulder. . . .

'Paaaaa . . . trol. . . . Halt. . . . Ri . . . turn.'

The patrol halted in front of the chalet with a slickly dug-in right heel and a smartly straightened right arm . . . right-turned (Rogers turned left and his ski became entangled with J. C.'s causing a loud 'Mucking hell, Rogers' to vibrate in the still air) . . . stood stiffly to attention . . . threw back their heads and shattered the mountainside with their raucous rendering of 'Torno Sorrento' . . . broke off half-way through the song and rushed upon me, roaring a welcome. . . .

'Skipper! How are you?'

'*Come sta*, Skipper?'

'Welcome home, Skipper.'

'*Viva Capitano Bob.*'

My men looked fit and well, bursting with health and vitality. It did me good to look at them.

'You're all looking damned fit,' I said. 'Congratulations.'

'*Niente signorini. Poco vino*,' Riches explained.

'Ah,' I said knowingly. 'That explains it.'

'Can you ski, Skipper?'

I shook my head.

'Wooooohu! We'll teach you, Skipper,' in chorus.

'Gather round,' I said, 'and I'll tell you a funny story.'

The patrol made a semi-circle, leaning on their ski-ing sticks.

'Once upon a time,' I began, 'there was a patrolman called Tindall'—George Sonley hid a smile—'he was walking down the Strand one day and met a brigadier . . .'

'The art of ski-ing, sir,' said my English-speaking Alpini instructor, 'is to keep control of the skis.'

'How do you do that?' I asked, subsiding on my bottom for the umpteenth time.

376

'Like this, sir.'

The instructor put his weight on his skis and moved each foot separately in a sawing motion so that the skis glided backwards and forwards in parallel lines, then he drew the points together in the shape of a V.

'Oh, like that,' I said.

I tried to do what the instructor had done . . . and promptly sat down on my bottom again. . . .

'In trouble, Skipper?' Riches shouted as he flashed past, bent double, executing masterly Cristiania turns in flurries of powdery snow.

'No, Skipper. On your *feet*!' George Sonley yelled as he swished past, going like the wind.

'Keep trying, Skipper,' Ben Owen encouraged, pushing hard with his sticks.

'How long have they been at it?' I asked the instructor as I watched my patrol zoom downhill.

'Two months, sir.'

'Then there's hope for me?' I suggested, struggling awkwardly to my feet.

'Of course, sir. You'll soon get your balance. Try again.'

I tried . . . away they slid again . . . and down I went. . . .

'I've laid on a Mosquito for you, Bob,' Jan informed me. 'The pilot will fly you over the Po delta and come down as low as he can. Take a good look at the roads. I want to know if they're mined or road-blocked.'

'O.K., Jan.'

We were back again in the Plain of Lombardy, preparing for the spring offensive.

'Which strip is the Mosquito on?'

'Carpinello, south of Forli. Morley will drive you in my jeep. He knows where it is.'

'Fine.'

'Good luck, eh?'

'Thanks, Jan.'

We shook hands and I went out to the waiting jeep.

'Know where the air-strip is, Morley?' I asked Jan's driver.

'Yes, sir.'

I slid into the passenger seat and we drove off. . . .

A Mosquito was warming up on the strip.

'Good morning,' I said affably to the experienced-looking flying-officer who sat at the controls pulling, pushing and twisting at an imposing array of knobs, switches and dials. He looked up, nodded and smiled, and continued to push and pull with thoughtful concentration, listening to the beat of his engines.

'Nice morning for a flip.'

'Isn't it?'

I climbed into the empty co-pilot seat. The F.O. adjusted my parachute.

'Know how to use it?'

I nodded, indicating my parachute wings.

'Put this on,' he said, unhooking a flying helmet with mouthpiece, oxygen attachment and headphones. 'Your oxygen's there,' he added, pointing to a knob at my side.

'Thank you.'

'What d'you particularly want to see?' pulling at a knob on the crowded panel.

'The roads mostly—for mines, road-blocks, machine-gun posts.'

The F.O. nodded understandingly and closed the cockpit. Efficient, I thought, and felt safe with him.

The Mosquito was then one of the fastest planes in the sky and I was looking forward to a few thrills. I wasn't disappointed.

'Comfortable?' the F.O. asked as we burped gently to the runway.

'Fine,' I replied, feeling happy.

The powerful engines clattered deafeningly, vibrating the fuselage, momentarily died away and clamoured again at pitch as we roared down the runway and rose like a bird . . . up . . . up . . . up into the empty sky. . . .

From 10,000 feet, the highest I'd ever been, I looked down upon the Po delta, upon Bulow's watery Comacchio, upon distant Venice. Blue was everywhere, blue sky, blue sea, blue water, dazzling white snow peaks against a blue horizon. 'Hell,' I thought, 'this is something.' . . .

'Going down,' a voice crackled in my headphones.

The Mosquito seemed to fall out of the sky as we plummeted down . . . down . . . down . . . at 400 miles an hour. . . .

I gripped the seat, pressed hard with my feet and felt my

378

stomach coming up. Blood rushed to my head. There was a loud singing in my ears, pin-points of light jangled in front of my eyes ... down ... down ... down ... faster ... faster ... faster ... with the wind screaming past the cockpit and the Po delta rushing towards the nose. ...

The delta was laid out like a model—white roads, blue rivers and canals, green fields, yellow sand-dunes, white walls, red roofs ... coming closer ... closer. ... I saw a horse and cart on a road near a canal bank ... saw the *contadino* look up ... a road stretched from the nose of the plane. ... I looked along it for mine-spots. ...

The Mosquito was down to 500 feet and it seemed that we must crash into the road. ... I felt my body rigid, straining away from the instrument panel ... the pressure suddenly eased ... blue sky took the place of the ribbon of road ... my stomach returned to its normal position ... up ... up ... up into empty sky again. ...

'That what you wanted?' the voice crackled.

'Wonderful!' I crackled back, fighting nausea.

'Want to go down again?'

'Yes, please.'

I felt my body fall sideways as the plane tumbled out of the sky again ... down ... down ... down ... stomach coming up ... ears buzzing ... lights flashing ... hands sweating ... back straining ... blue water, fields, canals, roads rushing towards the screaming nose ... little red darts flashing past the wings, clawing at the fuselage ... little red darts ... little red darts. I saw them detachedly as in a dream and suddenly realized what they were.

'Tracer!' I panicked into the mouthpiece and saw a *contadino* wave from a roadside. The road flattened out. ... I searched the surface for mines. ... Tracer tore past the wings, frighteningly close ... the pressure eased ... the road fell away and I was looking into blue sky again ... stomach subsiding, body muscles relaxing. ...

'Bit of stuff coming up,' the voice crackled unemotionally.

'Did they hit us?' I enquired, breathlessly.

'Don't think so.'

The Mosquito banked steeply and we flew out to sea, came round in a wide turn and bumped gently on the air-strip. ... I removed my helmet, shook my head and opened and closed my mouth.

379

The pilot cut his engines and opened the cockpit. There was a smell of burned oil and the silence was impressive.

'Got what you wanted?'

'Yes. Thanks very much. I enjoyed that.'

'Pleasure. Any time you like.'

I climbed out and felt my legs shaking when I stood on the grass.

'Bad news for you, Bob,' Jan greeted me when I returned to H.Q. He handed me a telegram from home. I read its clipped message and was stunned. My son was dead.

Three nights previously I had had a horrible dream from which I awoke in the small hours, sweating. I was in a black gorge somewhere, digging . . . digging . . . digging, digging a long line of graves, and I kept seeing my son's face.

'Have I time to fly home for the funeral, Jan?'

Jan put an understanding hand on my shoulder.

'I'll go up to Army and ask. Come with me?'

Sorry, they said at Army, can't be done. Yunnie's just been home.

We drove back to our villa and I threw myself into the all-absorbing task of preparing the patrols for the landing behind the Po, refusing to let myself think of anything else.

The days passed. . . .

Jan Caneri and I stood on a green hillside above Forli watching the opening round of the allied spring offensive. The patrols were at Cervia on the coast, keyed-up, ready to board the craft which would land them in their jeeps behind the Po.

Along the banks of the River Senio, smoke serpents writhed skywards from dischargers placed to indicate to the pilots of the American Flying Fortresses thundering overhead were the allied army ceased and the German one began. The spiralling serpents uncoiled into the still morning air like smoke from Indian wigwams and high above them, glinting in the azure sky, wave after wave of ponderous, four-engined aircraft opened their bomb hatches, dropped their lethal eggs (mostly) beyond the Senio, wheeled and returned to base. Down in the plain, orange gun-flashes marked the position of Eighth Army artillery, clattering and banging, hour after hour. All along the south bank of the

Senio River, from the Apennine spine to the sea, men sat tensely gripping their guns, waiting for the order to advance. . . .

Man proposes and God disposes, runs the proverb. A man's destiny is not entirely within his own hands and he is wise when he listens to the small voice which sometimes speaks within his heart. I didn't apply for it. Jan Caneri didn't apply for it. Popski didn't apply for it. My wife didn't apply for it. It just happened, right out of the blue—a home posting.

'I'm not going, Jan,' I said impulsively when the signal was thrust into my hand. 'Cancel it. I don't have to go, do I?'

'Don't do anything rash, Bob,' Jan advised. 'Think it over for a day.'

I watched the bomb clusters falling from the silver bellies of the Flying Fortresses and a battle raged within my breast.

'Go home,' said Wisdom. 'You've done your bit. The war's as good as over. You won't be running away.'

'Stay and get killed,' said Folly. 'Go out in a blaze of glory. The peace will be awful. You'll never settle down.'

'Don't be a fool,' urged Wisdom. 'Life is a precious thing. Somehow you'll find a way.'

'Don't go, don't go,' pleaded Folly. . . .

Concurrently with the allied battle for the Po, my private battle waxed and waned and was suddenly decided for me.

Two days passed and a signal came from Army cancelling our seaborne landing.

'It's Fate, Bob,' Jan said philosophically, putting a hand on my arm. 'Go home, old boy. You've done your bit. You won't be running away. The war's as good as over.'

I hesitated still, afraid to go home to the peace.

'You can't go against your Fate, Bob,' Jan urged. 'It's meant. Go home.'

In the end, I took his advice.

I said a tearful good-bye to my patrol in the pine woods near Cervia.

'Good-bye, chaps,' I tried to say. 'Remember the name we've made. You've got tradition behind you now . . .' but the words wouldn't come. I felt hot tears behind my eyes and I turned away with a broken heart. . . .

Tears? Amongst fighting men? But tears are women's things.

. . . In war, there is a love of comrade for comrade which far sur-
passes the love of a man for a woman and it is a love which women
do not understand. Having no connection with sex, it is an emotion
entirely of the heart, a deep, enduring bond forged from risks taken
together, hardships and dangers equally shared, death looked in
the face time and time again. There wasn't a man in that patrol
but would willingly have given his life for all or any of the other
patrolmen, aye, been proud to give it, and would never have
counted the cost. . . . Tears? Why not?

I gripped Jan's trusty hand, gave him a letter for Popski, and
slumped into the jeep which was to take me to Naples. . . .

I turned back at Florence, unable to break the bond, thinking I
could force the hand of Fate.

'It's no use, Bob,' Wisdom whispered in a voice I could barely
hear. 'Turn round again. You know you've got to go home.'

I turned the jeep at Pontassieve and drove brutally towards
Rome. . . .

'Don't go, don't go,' cried Folly in my ear, and I revved through
the streets of Arezzo.

I turned back once more.

'You're going the wrong way, Bob,' Wisdom chided. 'Turn
round. You know you've got to go home.'

'This bloke gone nuts?' wondered Driver Yates.

I swallowed a lump in my throat, reversed the jeep in a gateway
and drove towards Naples like a bat out of hell. . . .

24

I REMEMBER very little of the journey home.

I hung about the Naples transit camp awaiting passage, morose, unsociable, boorish. In a long line of other officers I submitted to the indignity of routine V.D. inspection and went on board a troop-ship overloaded with cheering men glad to be going home. I didn't share their enthusiasm and stood dejectedly by the rail watching the sad sea waves roll past, falling behind me for ever like the good old days in P.P.A., I thought bitterly. . . .

We anchored in the Clyde again.

I was in no hurry to go ashore and stood on the upper deck cynically watching 4000 hilarious men shoulder their kit-bags and tramp down the swaying gangway thinking: 'You poor muts. You don't know what you're going home to,' and finally went myself, the last to disembark.

I sat in a pub until closing time and then took taxi to a Glasgow hotel where I lay in bed for three days—thinking.

Folly and Wisdom still wrangled.

'Apply for a posting to the Far East,' Folly tempted.

'Go home and take what comes,' urged Wisdom *sotto voce*.

'Think of it,' cackled Folly. 'Office at 9 a.m. Yes, Mr. Jones. Certainly, Mr. Smith. Don't be a fool. You'll never stick that.'

'Go home, Bob,' Wisdom insisted, 'you'll find a way. There's a reason for this.'

Eventually, I got up and went home. . . .

When I reached Aberdeen for the second time in four months the war in Europe was over and an airmail letter from Jan Caneri awaited me. It was brief and to the point:

Austria,
May 1945.

Dear Bob,

    It was Fate. You were meant to go home.

    We crossed the Po a few days after you left. The officer who took your place—McCallum—his jeep and driver were blown to bits by a *panzerfaust*.

    The war is over and you are still alive.

Good luck,

Jan.

Epilogue
The Life of Robert Park Yunnie After the War

At the close of World War Two, my father was unable to settle down in post-war England with all its food rationing. He refers to his 'fear of going home to the peace' in his book whilst still in Italy. Still keen for adventure, he got involved in the rescue of a Czech family just prior to the communist take-over in Czechoslovakia.

He brought his family out to South Africa in 1949, landing at Cape Town—a period I, as no more than a toddler, can barely recall. Homesick for his P.P.A. jeep, Bob bought one with which to drive to the Transvaal (now Mpumalanga). He farmed for a while near Amersfoort before moving to Natal (now Kwa Zulu Natal), where he managed a farm in the Karkloof district. He was innovative in his application of crop rotation and hay making and had several articles on his successes published in the *Farmers Weekly* magazine and the *Natal Witness* newspaper.

He later moved to Howick in order to practise as a Doctor of Naturopathy. He became well known in the field, and provided relief for sufferers from arthritis and other complaints where conventional medicine had failed. He published a book on the subject entitled *The Cause and Cure of Disease*.

Following this publishing success, Bob made the decision to re-write his war memoirs and have them published. (His first attempt, 'Jeep Fever, had failed to find a publisher.) To fulfil this endeavour, Bob moved again and set about his task with characteristic zeal. I recall him travelling to his office in Durban on a bus so that he could write and wouldn't waste the time driving! He was a very good organiser, and once he had things arranged and working to his satisfaction he would again seek new challenges and want to move on. In late 1958 he left on a trip through Africa to Europe and London, where his manuscript was to be published. *Warriors on Wheels*, by 'Park Yunnie of Popski's Private Army', appeared in print the following year.

In 1961, still restless for adventure, he joined the so-called 'white mercenaries' fighting communism in the new Congo Republic. Here a civil war had developed between provinces, leading to the secession of the Katanga region. Bob was a member of the Kalondjust Army in South Kasai, employed to form a group whose key function was to patrol intensively. In late March 1961, he went out on a peace-keeping mission to a village called Kamponde, to visit two chiefs of the Kanioukas tribe in the Territoire de Dibaya. The purpose was to avert a clash between the two parties. On the return journey to Bakwanga his patrol was ambushed. He escaped from the ambushers and made his way on foot to Tshiculudumba by Poygna. He was again caught, and executed two days later by the Administrator of the Territory. One year passed before we, his family, were notified of Bob's death. To this day, I have no idea where he is buried.

DON YUNNIE
Hilton, South Africa, 2002